ARTHUR VANDENBERG

Arthur

Vandenberg

The Man in the Middle of the American Century

. . . .

HENDRIK MEIJER

. . . .

THE UNIVERSITY OF CHICAGO PRESS

Chicago and London

The University of Chicago Press, Chicago 60637
The University of Chicago Press, Ltd., London

Published 2017
Paperback edition 2019

Printed in the United States of America

28 27 26 25 24 23 22 21 20 19   1 2 3 4 5

ISBN-13: 978-0-226-43348-6 (cloth)
ISBN-13: 978-0-226-68203-7 (paper)
ISBN-13: 978-0-226-43351-6 (e-book)
DOI: https://doi.org/10.7208/chicago/9780226433516.001.0001

Library of Congress Cataloging-in-Publication Data

Names: Meijer, Hendrik G., 1952– author.
Title: Arthur Vandenberg: the man in the middle of the American century /
Hendrik Meijer.
Description: Chicago; London: The University of Chicago Press, 2017. | Includes
bibliographical references and index.
Identifiers: LCCN 2017015718| ISBN 9780226433486 (cloth: alk. paper) |
ISBN 9780226433516 (e-book)
Subjects: LCSH : Vandenberg, Arthur H. (Arthur Hendrick), 1884–1951. |
Legislators—Michigan—Biography. | United States—Biography.
Classification: LCC E 748. V 18 M45 2017 | DDC 328.73/092 [B]—dc23
LC record available at https://lccn.loc.gov/2017015718

♾ This paper meets the requirements of
ANSI/NISO Z39.48- 1992 (Permanence of Paper).

For Liesel

The sense of danger must not disappear:
The way is certainly both sharp and steep,
However gradual it looks from here;
Look if you like, but you will have to leap.
W. H. Auden,
from "Leap Before You Look," 1941

"What a pity he is so dreadfully senatorial!"
said Mrs. Lee; "otherwise I rather admire him."
Henry Adams, *Democracy*

CONTENTS

CONTENTS

Photographs follow page 244.

PROLOGUE

Arthur Vandenberg's stature owed something to his size and swagger as well as his political authority. Gore Vidal, drawing on childhood memories, described him somewhat sardonically as "The Great Van." Whether briefing reporters or holding forth at a diplomatic reception, he could command the room.

It was not always so. "The American Senator drank a little more than he could conveniently manage," wrote his hostess, the wife of the Argentine ambassador, in her diary in 1934. He had emerged from the embassy library, pale and unsteady after brandy and cigars. He stumbled over the Aubusson carpet, knocked against a slender French chair, but "managed to right himself in order to walk out . . . in proper senatorial dignity." Why is it, she mused, that "the American man has never been able to drink? Or is it that he has never learned to drink?"[1] Arthur Vandenberg was nothing if not dignified, but she might have asked what else the imposing senator with the bright, dark eyes had to learn, for the answer would have foretold momentous lessons for the American people, too.

Vandenberg knew how to oppose things, certainly. But that was easy. One could just say no. He had said no to FDR and much of the New Deal. He had opposed as well any compromise of American independence in foreign policy. He pounced on any hint of a treaty or alliance, any foreign entanglement, in a world growing ever more dangerous.

Within five years the ambassador's wife noted in the margin of her diary, alongside the earlier entry, "How this particular Senator has changed! He has become little by little a man of the world." Never again had she seen him tipsy. Indeed, his prospects were bright: "He is, at the moment," she wrote, "the leading aspirant for the Republican nomination in 1940."[2] She wrote this late in 1939. Hitler had invaded Poland only weeks before, triggering a second world war. As leader of the Senate's isolationist bloc, Vandenberg had fought unsuccessfully to keep the United States out of war. His opposition brought him notoriety and stature, but he had sacrificed his electability. Wendell Willkie swept to the nomination instead.

Yet Vandenberg's odyssey had only begun. Five years later, in 1945, as the war neared its end, his speech "heard round the world" changed his life—and the American political landscape. He had proposed a postwar treaty among the victorious allies, the very foreign entanglement that he, like George Washington and so many who came after him, had been so wary of. The isolationist had turned world statesman—and the capital's darling.

In quick succession came his appointment as delegate to the United Nations organizing conference, his role in postwar peace talks, his success in steering through Congress the Marshall Plan and the resolution to create the North Atlantic Treaty Organization. With George Marshall, Vandenberg helped save a continent. *The Economist* urged Europeans "to consider the christening of a Rue Vandenberg or a Vandenbergplatz."[3] Harry Truman was in trouble without him.

All too soon, peace gave way to the Cold War, with the Soviet Union and its satellites ranged behind the infamous Iron Curtain—a coinage Vandenberg employed before Winston Churchill made it famous. The Kremlin decried the sinister influence of the senior senator from Michigan. He was a bogeyman, the devil on Truman's shoulder, an exemplar of American imperialism. For the Western world, however, Vandenberg became the voice of an American people groping for new answers, for a shared voice in foreign policy, for a politics that stopped "at the water's edge."[4]

When Truman addressed a joint session of Congress to urge passage of the Marshall Plan, Vandenberg, as president pro tempore of the Senate, occupied the vice president's seat above him on the dais. The president's speech fell flat. "This was a setting for a roaring lion, high in spirits . . . , bursting with determination," wrote a reporter for *Time*. In contrast to Truman, "A Vandenberg, a Roosevelt or a Churchill would have played Congress like a harp, and spoken in tones of thunder, defiance, confidence."[5] Today's reader might find that sequence of statesmen somewhat jarring. Roosevelt, Churchill—their eminence is understood. But Vandenberg?

Not only did the senior senator from Michigan reflect and express the anxieties of the American people; he worked with politicians across the aisle in a search for national security. He was trusted by colleagues and presidents and no small portion of the press. He had come by the sort of gravitas that led some to think him the steadiest leader in a time of crisis. A young Democratic senator named William Fulbright had the temerity to suggest that the untested President Truman, thrust into office with so little preparation, appoint the Republican Vandenberg as his secretary of state—and then resign. In the absence of a vice president, Vandenberg would succeed him. (Truman, not amused by the suggestion, dismissed the idea's proponent as "Senator Halfbright.")

One pundit proposed Arthur Vandenberg for "president of the world." Edward R. Murrow called him "the central pivot of the era." With the advent of the Cold War, Americans turned to him for guidance and wisdom—for the very security that had been his lifelong obsession.[6]

Decades later, the qualities that defined him are again in demand. But who was he?

PART ONE

The Cause of Ruin

We hunt the cause of ruin, add,
Subtract, and put ourselves in pawn;
For all our scratching on the pad,
We cannot trace the error down.
Theodore Roethke,
from *The Reckoning*,
1940

· · · · · · · · · · · ·

CLASS OF 1900

· · · · · · · · · · · ·

The Panic of 1893 ruined the brisk harness trade of Aaron Vandenberg. His son, Arthur, nine years old, was profoundly affected. "I had no youth," he insisted decades later, with typical hyperbole. "I had one passion—to be certain that when I grew up I would not be in the position my father was."[1]

Aaron was a native of the Genesee Valley in upstate New York— "Mohawk River Dutch," he called it, a tribe with "gumption enough to get out of New York and hew its way in the wilderness." He had been postmaster of tiny Clyde, New York, during the administration of Ulysses S. Grant. A young widower with two small children, he married Alpha Hendrick, whose family's Republican fervor was at least the equal of his own. Alpha's physician father had served as a Lincoln delegate to the 1860 Republican National Convention and had provided a stop on the Underground Railroad.

Ready for a fresh start, the newlyweds ventured west. Michigan had been the near frontier for New Yorkers since the opening of the Erie Canal. In the lumber-rich west of the state, Aaron found a burgeoning metropolis where his surname blended in with those of recent immigrants from The Netherlands. There, in Grand Rapids, he opened a harness shop. And there, in 1884, in an upstairs room of their ample Victorian home, Alpha gave birth to her only child, Arthur Hendrick. He was eleven years younger than his half-sister; his half-brother was already eighteen.[2]

Grand Rapids was no isolated outpost. Forty trains a day passed through, bound for Chicago, Detroit, or the Straits of Mackinac. Around the Union Depot ranged the freight yards, markets, and warehouses of a trading center. By the 1880s, as immigrants from Germany and Poland as well as Holland joined descendants of French traders and Yankees, the population had swelled to fifty thousand. City hall and the county building were Romanesque temples, flush with civic pride. Tolling church bells, factory whistles, the clatter of trains—all echoed across the valley.

Spiked boots of flannel-shirted lumberjacks scarred the plank sidewalks. Millions of logs from the great pine forests floated down the Grand River. Sprawling factories shaped and tooled the timber. By the end of the century, Grand Rapids was America's "Furniture City."

This was a place, said one reporter, "big enough to have the conveniences of a city, but small enough to enable everybody to know everybody else." Everybody knew the amiable Aaron Vandenberg. His shop was just up Division Avenue from the Cody Hotel, with its enormous bison heads supplied by the proprietor's uncle, Buffalo Bill, whose visits gave the town a tenuous link to a wilder West.[3] As "Vandenberg the Harness Man," Aaron developed a thriving mail-order trade. The family enjoyed middle-class comforts, the luxury of freshly starched collars, the social rewards of the Shriners and Masons. On the Fourth of July, father and son watched veterans of the Grand Army of the Republic march up Fulton Street—a vivid reminder of how Republicans had rescued the nation in the Civil War.

Then came the Panic of 1893. Exactly what happened to the harness business is not clear, but large orders, perhaps government contracts, were canceled. Aaron Vandenberg could not meet his payroll. Later claims of insolvency seem exaggerated, but Alpha took in boarders. The stigma of failure clung to the Vandenberg household.[4]

The collapse of Aaron's business was the seminal event of Arthur Vandenberg's early life. At the age of nine, as he recounted it, he left boyhood behind to help support his family. In a world of rising expectations, the trauma of so sudden a reversal "made a permanent notch" in his character, he said later. In his mind, at least, he was on his own: "And ever since I've held to the conviction that if you really want to go somewhere in life, you can." This reaction to failure feels akin to an adult's sense of taking charge. The loss of security, the shock to a comfortable existence, seems to have kindled in the boy an entrepreneurial impulse that knew few bounds.

Arthur devised one scheme after another. He started a delivery service, using pushcarts from his father's shop to haul crates of shoes from a downtown factory to the Union Depot. He sold vegetables, flowers, lemonade. He ushered in a theater and peddled newspapers. He set up a trading business for stamp collectors under the name Comet Stamp Company.[5]

The precocious teen entered Central High School a year earlier than most of his classmates. He was slender, with pursed lips and a small mouth, his dark eyes peering from beneath wide brows, black hair parted in the center, jug ears jutting out. He was enamored of a classmate twenty months older, Eslizabeth Watson, whose father owned a hardware store on the West Side. (She was, their yearbook noted, "To all, most attractive / by all, most admired," a shy brunette, "blushing and sweet.")

Arthur received better marks in science and mathematics than in literature, yet it was in English class, as well as rhetoric, where his passion for speeches and stories was on display. "A is for Arthur, the man with a voice," the yearbook said. In his junior year, classmates wrote, "When will Vandenberg stop talking?" At fifteen he addressed his fraternity banquet with the speech "Our Progress." His subtitle: "Not What We Have Done Avails Us, But What We Do and Are." In another speech, "Success," Arthur told his audience that "the world's given a reward to him who makes an honest effort."[6]

The youngest member of the class of 1900 also boasted the second-longest entry in the yearbook—which, perhaps not coincidentally, he edited. He also edited the *Daily Whoop*, sang in the chorus, and managed the baseball team. And he endured the jibes of classmates, not only for his preening zeal but also for riding to school "on his pneumatic-tired ear." That year Arthur won second prize in a speech contest with his address "The Peace Conference at The Hague: Cause and Effect." In 1899 delegates from the Great Powers had convened, he said, to do "something tangible toward the promotion of a better understanding between the nations, and to lay the foundation of a durable peace."[7] The silver medal, engraved with his initials, became his talisman.

He was going places, his class prophecy predicted: "Then Vandenberg a diplomat / will grow quite corpulent and fat." In mock elections he won a seat in the U.S. Senate. He was also named secretary of the Treasury, an apt choice for a teenager whose idol was Alexander Hamilton. He took government seriously, later claiming that he began reading the *Congressional Record* at the age of fifteen.

Arthur graduated with two goals: to make a fortune and to become a senator.[8] First, however, he needed a job. He soon found full-time work as a billing clerk in a biscuit factory. That lasted until September 1900, when the campaign train of Theodore Roosevelt, President William McKinley's running mate, arrived in Grand Rapids. The energetic hero of San Juan Hill, now governor of New York, was to parade uptown from the railway depot in early evening, passing within a block of the biscuit works. For a teenager with a penchant for hero-worship, Roosevelt was irresistible. The streets were filled with "Teddy" fans and curiosity seekers, and Vandenberg was both.

The siren song of a band "playing lively airs" drew him from his desk. "Not so fast, sonny," said his supervisor. Defying orders, he slipped out. He cheered as a squad of Rough Riders, rakish in khakis and slouch hats, reined in their horses to stay abreast of the carriage from which the mustachioed candidate flashed his toothy smile. The biscuit clerk was swept up in the tide of pomp. "I marched behind that Roosevelt parade," Arthur recalled, behind men who would later be his bosses and boosters, his rivals and heroes, "but when I got back to my desk, I was fired."[9]

In search of work, he walked the next day to the offices of the city's morning newspaper, the *Herald*. Editor E. D. Conger, who knew young Vandenberg's stories from the *Daily Whoop*, put him to work rewriting news gleaned from other Michigan papers and from "flimsy," the thin sheets of telegraph copy. He was given scissors, a glue pot, and $6 per week.[10] He had been on the job for eight weeks when William McKinley was reelected, with Roosevelt as his vice president. When the Sunday *Herald* ran a full-page history of the Electoral College, the byline belonged to its youngest staffer. Assigned to the police beat, Vandenberg explored the dark side of his city, its miscreants and its secrets. He reveled in the stories and could wring drama from a loose dog's raid on a hen house. He was frugal, too. In August 1901 he combined his savings with a check from his half-brother and boarded the Michigan Central Railroad for the University of Michigan, where he enrolled in the law department.[11] Autumn was a heady time in Ann Arbor. Under new football coach Fielding Yost, the Wolverines were on their way to the inaugural Rose Bowl.

Vandenberg was chairman of the freshman banquet, to which he escorted a Delta Gamma girl, Hazel Whitaker. "Look out," a mutual friend warned her, "Arthur's engaged." That was not quite so, but he made no secret of his attachment to a girl back home. Still, he and Hazel became close, and when Elizabeth Watson came to visit, Hazel, in a big-sisterly way, entertained her.[12] Vandenberg's college life lasted barely a year, however, before he ran out of money. He dropped out after his second semester.

Returning to Grand Rapids, he returned as well to the *Herald*, where Conger assigned him to cover city hall for $15 per week. The young reporter quickly impressed colleagues with his ingratiating manner and considerable energy. "He got the news in a wonderfully pleasant way," an older staffer recalled, always with "the right slant on things. . . . He seemed to understand every situation and treat it with sincerity rather than any belittling spirit." Vandenberg became the *Herald*'s most prolific writer. No one was better at bulking up a story with five-dollar words. Reporters tacked their copy to a newsroom wall. At the end of each day, his was always the longest string.[13]

He also began to write short stories. In one he described a reporter's routine: "It was the manner of his task to make the daily rounds of the municipal offices in the great City Hall, dropping in for a friendly word with the Treasurer, a passing pleasantry with the Clerk, a story here, a joke there, but always with a cheery smile and a hearty hand-grasp."

His stories blended wide-eyed ambition of the Horatio Alger variety with the cynical edge of a city-hall reporter torn between righteous muckraking and the urge to make a buck. He collected rejections by the dozen. There were letters from legendary editors S. S. McClure and Frank Munsey, from *Cosmopolitan* and *Smart Set*. The editor of *Everybody's* wrote, "We like the way this story is told, though the story itself seems to us too slight."

While publishing his fiction presented an uncertain prospect, Vandenberg thrived on the allure and immediacy of politics. The *Herald* was hotly partisan. Its eighteen-year-old ace reporter was elected secretary of the Young Men's Republican Club of Kent County. The owner of the paper, Republican congressman William Alden Smith, took a special interest in the "bright-appearing lad."[14]

If Vandenberg belonged in Grand Rapids, it could not contain his ambition. In the fall of 1903, he managed somehow to secure a job in the art department of *Collier's* magazine in New York. The position was a mismatch for his skills, and the teeming metropolis was an alien place. "Have you ever known the loneliness of a great city?" he wrote later. "There is no misery like it." The haunts of his hero, Alexander Hamilton, were in the grip of corrupt Tammany Hall. Elections back home were tame compared to "real ones" in New York. He closed a letter to Elizabeth with a plea for news, adding, in French, "Je vous aime."[15]

By the spring of 1904, he had returned again to the *Herald* newsroom. While college had come to naught, and New York as well, Vandenberg believed he had only to work harder. Nowhere more than in Michigan were men of humble origins prospering beyond all expectation. Henry Ford, the Dodge brothers, and Ransom Olds were creating a new industry for automobiles. The Kelloggs and C. W. Post in Battle Creek became nutrition tycoons with their breakfast cereals. In a profile of Marshall Field, from nearby Chicago, Vandenberg called the merchant's story "another tale of the rise of a barefoot country urchin to a proud position among America's noblemen." He was becoming a student of self-help. "Field succeeded because he was thorough," he wrote, "because he was conscientious, because he was self-controlled, because he was abstemious, because he was economical yet progressive, . . . because he was keen, because he was careful."[16]

As for the careful young reporter, Vandenberg saved enough from his pay to buy a little stock in the *Herald*. As the paper's fortunes fluctuated, he rode out one change in ownership, then benefited in a startling way from another.

William Alden Smith had been elected to Congress in 1896 as a defender of Michigan interests in tariff debates. Popular with his colleagues, he was mentioned as a vice presidential possibility for Theodore Roosevelt in 1904. Smith had peddled newspapers as a boy, but he knew little of publishing in early 1906 when he acquired controlling interest in western Michigan's leading Republican journal.[17]

Then editor E. D. Conger died. There was no obvious successor. Smith strolled into the city room on March 17, 1906, days shy of Arthur Vandenberg's twenty-second birthday. The congressman's gaze fell upon the "dark-eyed lad" with the long strings of copy and a grasp of politics from city hall to the Electoral College. "You are now editor-in-chief and general manager," Smith informed him. He nodded toward the editor's office. "Go over and kick your feet under the mahogany."[18]

Vandenberg was stunned, or so he said afterward: "There was just no sense to it. It was one of the most amazing incidents. One of those fortuitous circumstances that changes a whole life."[19]

A year later, when the owner of the *Herald* was elected to the U.S. Senate, a *Herald* reporter told his young editor that someday he hoped to vote for Vandenberg for senator. The self-conscious retort? "You're crazy."[20]

THE SHREWDNESS
OF VANDENBERG

. . . .

Theodore Roosevelt defined the Republican Party for Arthur Vandenberg. He had invented the bully pulpit and inspired a generation. He understood the rise of American power. Even as he approached the self-imposed end of his presidency in 1908, he cast a giant's shadow across the political landscape.[1]

Herald editorials reflected Roosevelt's blend of progressivism and traditional Republican virtues. Twenty-five years before Senator Vandenberg brought to pass federal bank-deposit insurance, editor Vandenberg proposed a similar state initiative. He attacked John D. Rockefeller and called for vigorous enforcement of new antitrust laws. "A few stiff sentences," he wrote, "will have a greater salutary effect on Big Business . . . than all the fines . . . which ever were or ever will be meted out to corporate offenders."[2] He supported the right of socialists to assemble, urged suffrage for women, and favored direct election of senators. He proposed a national agency to administer public welfare funds. He had known what it was to make a living as a child, and he took a keen interest in child labor.[3]

Vandenberg's understanding of politics found expression in his stories, too. He was twenty-two when "Revolt of the Puppets" appeared in *Popular Magazine*. Here, an idealistic county chairman challenges the boss of the state party machine. With the sudden death of its Supreme Court nominee, the contentious majority party decides to put the selection of his replacement before a smoke-filled caucus of county chairmen. The "coming man," in the eyes of party boss Samuel T. Rich, is Watson Kairns, who resembles a young Abe Lincoln. Kairns discovers that the machine has already settled on a nominee—a crooked lawyer. Rich dismisses Kairns's concerns: "This ain't a college oratorical contest, my young friend." Kairns's colleagues seem prepared to go along with the machine, hiding behind a call for party harmony. "When the slave-driver used to curl his whip about his Negro's leg he usually secured harmony," the hero declares.[4]

Rich laughs at Kairns's pretensions; the younger man's idealism poses little threat. But Kairns springs a legal maneuver that forces the boss to back down. Cowed colleagues, taken by surprise, awake to the discovery that the caucus is out of bondage. Here was the *Herald* editor's image of himself—eloquent, of course, but also savvy about the way things really worked.

That sense of self was evident again in "The Shrewdness of Hawkins," which appeared in *Lippincott's* in 1905. Hawkins, a city-hall reporter, plays off the greed of rival gas companies and a corrupt assessor to line his own pockets. In the shadow of an actual Grand Rapids water scandal, Vandenberg observes of his hero: "He had run to earth more than one political highwayman—with the result that the schemers feared him. He knew the charter and the ordinances and the Council procedure by heart—with the result that his advice was of exceptional value. . . . Hawkins was a power—and Hawkins knew it." The reformers' world is turned upside down, and the muckraker gets rich.

Roosevelt, the progressive hero, stayed true to his rash pledge not to seek reelection in 1908. Instead, he anointed as his successor his able friend, Secretary of War William Howard Taft. Smith recruited Taft to address the Kent County Republicans' Lincoln Day dinner. The *Herald* described the banquet as "the greatest day in the political history of Grand Rapids." The rotund Taft shook hands with thousands, "a big man in every sense." And then, before Vandenberg and a hall of stalwarts, he announced his candidacy for president. It is hard to imagine a young man in the hinterlands feeling more intimately connected with the ruling forces of the republic.[5]

In the summer of 1908, Vandenberg covered his first Republican national convention. In Chicago's cavernous Coliseum, delegates gathered under steel girders "looped with bunting and ablaze with electrical devices, while on every side the national colors were woven into sunbursts, shields and patriotic symbols."[6]

As the gavel dropped on the first day, the Ohio delegation swung down the center aisle, bearing aloft a blue banner with a portrait of its native son. "Taft, Taft!"—the cheers echoed from the floor to the gallery and back. Wisconsin delegates touted progressive senator Robert La Follette. The galleries were filled with fans of Roosevelt, cheering their hero despite his determination to depart the presidency.[7]

Support for Taft was tepid, and Vandenberg claimed a scoop in revealing plans for Roosevelt backers to stampede the convention. Chairman Henry Cabot Lodge sparked pandemonium when he declared Roosevelt the most abused—and most beloved—man in America. In the galleries, spectators leapt onto their chairs, waving coats, tossing hats in the air. As the chairman pounded the gavel, someone produced a giant "Teddy" bear. Again the crowd roared. The conductor sliced the air with his baton, but the band was drowned out. Finally, Lodge gaveled the assembly to order and announced that his friend Theodore's decision was irrevocable.

The young editor savored this convergence of pomp and power and hustle. When Taft secured the nomination, Vandenberg pronounced the country's future secure.[8] Not even a thin veneer covered the *Herald*'s Republican bias. Vandenberg rarely resisted a jibe at the "Peerless One," perennial Democratic candidate William Jennings Bryan. He attacked the Nebraskan's "fancy cure for ailments which never existed." He recoiled at the fervor of the populists, recalling in a rather personal way that in the Panic of 1893, "Bryanism" was "injurious to retail trade," its policies leading to "nearly five years of the hardest times back in the '90s."[9]

On election night a stereopticon projected images onto a canvas draped across the *Herald* building's facade. "Every scrap of information" would be thrown up on the screen, the paper promised, whether from its staff, from a dedicated telegraph wire, or from Associated Press reports. Fulton Street was impassable for two blocks. Streetcars nudged through a crowd of thousands. After two hours of bulletins came the news many had been waiting for: the victory of Taft and his running mate, Congressman James "Sunny Jim" Sherman. One reader recalled Vandenberg at his second-story window shouting out the recent World Series play-by-play of Ty Cobb and the Detroit Tigers. The *Herald* "gave us baseball scores," he said. "Now they give us election returns."[10]

The Republican triumph proved short-lived, however, and with it went Vandenberg's happy blend of reformer and party man. Four years later, at twenty-eight the youngest member of the GOP state central committee, he was to face a very different world. Roosevelt would come to rue his choice of successors and yearn to get back in the White House. The governing party would splinter, and the editor in Grand Rapids would find himself straddling ever more divergent tracks.

The *Herald* labored in the shadow of its afternoon rival, the *Grand Rapids Press*. Luckily, Vandenberg proved adroit at wooing advertising from some of the town's leading merchants. He loved contests and gimmicks to boost circulation. He created a Christmas charity, the "Santa Claus Girls," and enlisted reader support. Before long, the *Herald* was turning a profit. Its editor was becoming a civic leader, a bank director, a joiner. In the wider world, he was elected president of the North American Press Syndicate, which supplied artwork to member newspapers. Smith increased Vandenberg's salary by $1,000 per year. After five years, the twenty-seven-year-old editor-manager was making a generous $7,500 (nearly $200,000 today). By then, said Smith, "I was getting tired of these annual raises." He told his protégé to fix his own salary.[11]

By his mid-twenties Vandenberg found himself in demand for his catchy comments and florid oratory. In 1910 he was toastmaster when famed tenor Enrico Caruso entertained a gathering of advertising clubs with songs from *Faust*. On another occasion he introduced homespun philosopher Elbert Hubbard as the "greatest epigrammatical bunkshooter." His brashness and swagger amused his fellows at the Peninsular Club and the Chamber of Commerce.[12]

His hairline was receding, but a dark forelock swept toward his brow. He had a habit of waving a long forefinger when making a point, and a reputation, as reported in a tongue-in-cheek *Herald* account of his speech to an advertising group, for "great modesty, which is a by-word among the admen."

Yet Vandenberg was still a young man in search of himself. His reforming impulse led to a campaign for a new city charter, and, in 1910, his first bid for public office. He won a seat on a commission to draft the charter and promoted reforms he had argued for in the *Herald*, including a council-manager city government. In the spirit of the Progressive Era, the mayor and city commissioners would be elected on a nonpartisan basis. When love of party collided with his idea of good government, Vandenberg had little hesitation in choosing the latter. Partisan politics at the local level led to corrupt machines. Though the charter was constitution writing in microcosm, where sewer financing, not national defense, was at issue, it roused the passions of this demi-Hamilton eager to write the rules.[13]

Perhaps smaller stakes made consensus more attainable. If municipal reform was a nonpartisan enterprise, such collaboration was not the case at the national level.

To Roosevelt's supporters, President Taft was a reactionary placeholder. He lacked Roosevelt's charisma and reformist zeal, to be sure, yet his chief crime in the eyes of a generation of younger Republicans seems to have been that he simply was not Roosevelt. Eager to reassert himself, Roosevelt attacked Taft for replacing progressives in the cabinet. The next election was two years away, but Roosevelt's disaffection presaged an unprecedented opportunity for Democrats. Meanwhile, Taft's popularity plummeted.

Vandenberg had come of age in a Republican Party infused with the vigor and passion of Roosevelt. Now the vocal ex-president was moving outside the fold. Nowhere more than in Michigan was this rift raising havoc for the GOP. Publisher Frank Knox, a former Rough Rider and Vandenberg's friend from his cub reporter days in the *Herald* newsroom, became vice-chairman—and organizing spirit—of the national Roosevelt campaign. Local congressman Gerrit Diekema, whose election Vandenberg had engineered, led the Taft delegates. Vandenberg stayed on the fence, yearning for compromise.

His instinct was to cling to the security of the party structure. He was also a pragmatist. Solidarity won elections. He had no patience with rumors that Roosevelt would come "back from Elba": "We cannot see where precedent or possibility prophesy another term of Roosevelt in the White House—wonderful though he is in works and popularity." Hero-worship met prudence, and prudence prevailed. Vandenberg saw his duty in defending his president.[14]

When Smith snared Roosevelt for Kent County's Lincoln Day dinner in 1911, Vandenberg joined the ex-president's train to escort him into Grand Rapids. Although the editor had lately criticized his hero, he was not without awe. Roosevelt gripped the younger man's hand, thundering, "By George, it does me good to meet a good Dutchman." That night Roosevelt launched into a tirade against the status quo—and, by implication, the incumbent in the White House. "Those who shudder are Whigs," he declared, suggesting that Taft backers represented entrenched interests, fearful of change. But many of those who shuddered were GOP regulars like Vandenberg, who caught a whiff of populism and feared for the future of the party.

Indeed, when Michigan Republicans convened in 1912, they offered up a foretaste of their party's future. Dueling delegations arrived at the armory in Bay City. Dueling speakers tried to shout over each other from opposite sides of the building—Knox for the Roosevelt contingent, Diekema for Taft. A brawl erupted. Police were summoned. Roosevelt's boisterous followers were ejected. When a majority of the remaining delegates backed Taft, Knox and the Roosevelt group cried foul. Vandenberg saw the future, and it scared him.[15]

In Chicago again for the 1912 convention, he witnessed the "hottest and most sensational, bitterest and most problematical fight in the history of the party." Outside the hall, an anxious crowd of twelve thousand awaited the outcome, watched by firefighters ready to wield their hoses. Vandenberg, perhaps wishfully, reported "an undercurrent of desire" for compromise, not immolation. He suggested Michigan governor Chase Osborn for vice president—a Roosevelt man on a Taft ticket.[16]

As in Bay City, Taft forces held the upper hand. Roosevelt arrived to rally his supporters, but his "sway and magnetism" ultimately counted for little. The Rough Rider's delegates bolted across town to the orchestra hall, where the Progressive Party was born, with the "Bull Moose," Theodore Roosevelt, as its candidate for president.[17]

Vandenberg tried to put the best face on a party in shambles. "We must choose between the lesser of two evils," he lamented. That was to say, *he* had to choose. Day after day, pro-Taft stories appeared on the front page of the *Herald*. Week after week, Vandenberg stumped for the ticket. When a visitor asked him why Roosevelt's picture still hung behind his desk, he jumped up and swung it to face the wall.

He spoke in Lake Odessa and Howard City, Holland and Hastings. He fell back on what he called Republican principles—chiefly the protective tariff. He attacked the *Chicago Tribune*, a zealous Roosevelt backer, for seeking the "defeat of the Republican Party and the political assassination of President Taft." "Damnation," he wrote, "is not argument."[18]

With the election only days away, seventy-four-year-old Aaron Vandenberg suffered a fatal heart attack. At his bedside, the editor leaned close to hear his father's last words: "Son, promise me you'll always be a Republican." If Aaron's admonition were not so perfectly suited to the temper of the time and his son's situation, one would have to consider it apocryphal.

Vandenberg was true to his father. "Don't throw your vote away," he cautioned *Herald* readers, lest a GOP schism deliver the presidency to Woodrow Wilson and the Democrats. But his worst fears were realized. Taft finished third. Roosevelt carried Michigan. Democrat Woodrow Wilson carried the country. The notorious Bryan was installed as secretary of state—although the Nebraskan's aversion to foreign adventure was something Vandenberg could applaud.

Republicans licked their wounds. Vandenberg was eager to welcome his progressive friends back to the fold. He had held the middle ground, and the party, at least temporarily and superficially, was reunited.[19] The portrait of Roosevelt, framed with an old note expressing thanks for the *Herald*'s support, faced outward once again.

....

HOME FIRES

....

Arthur Vandenberg married Elizabeth Watson at the home of the bride's parents on a warm May evening in 1906. Elizabeth's piano teacher played the "Wedding March" as the bride, preceded by the groom's young nephews, Hoyt and Shedd, stepped through a foyer fragrant with white lilacs.

Within two years, the couple had a son of their own, Arthur Junior. The editor built his young family a Tudor Revival home on Morris Avenue, just blocks from his birthplace. Two daughters followed, Barbara in 1911 and Elizabeth (Betsy) in 1913.[1]

Vandenberg had become a familiar figure in his hometown, but there was something distant in his manner. He had a habit, as he walked to work, of ignoring other pedestrians. Some mistook it for aloofness, and there may have been an element of that, but he also identified himself with his hero, Hamilton, who was said to walk the streets of New York "muttering his lessons, to the concern of the passer-by."[2]

The editor gathered his thoughts. He memorized poems. He suffered few fools, though he talked to many of them. "The people who waste your time," he wrote in an editorial, "shall someday be cast into a pit from which there will be no escape." A neighbor girl, amused by his incessant talk, called him "Mr. Blab-in-Your-Noodle." Friends could torment him by keeping up such a continuous chatter that he himself could not get a word in.

His closest and most patient adviser was Frank Sparks, a feisty *Herald* reporter from Sault Ste. Marie. Before giving a speech, Vandenberg would try out his lines on Sparks, then commit the speech to memory and summon the reporter to hear it. Later, Sparks would sit in the audience and gauge its reaction.

Vandenberg was also quick to exploit the columns of the *Herald* to build more distant relationships. Prominent Republicans received copies of editorials praising something they said or did, and warm correspondence often ensued. A favorite editorial gambit was to imagine the reactions of the Founding Fathers to issues of the day. Regarding tariffs, for example, the editor enlisted not only Washington and his beloved Hamilton in the cause of protection, but also Madison and even Jefferson.[3] Closer to home, the little orbit of Grand Rapids plutocracy generally applauded the *Herald*'s editorial stands. A furniture maker or flypaper producer was grateful for unstinting attacks on imported goods.

Homilies of self-advancement were his oxygen. Reporting that 163 of 170 Pennsylvania Railroad executives had started out at the bottom, Vandenberg admonished his readers, "It pays to stick!" Great notions were one thing, but "the world pays its rewards to finishers." The point of freedom was opportunity. "The first personal liberty there is in the world," he wrote, "is where a man takes every opportunity to make himself a clean, diligent and purposeful man, arranging his actions on the side of his true aspirations." The self-made man was central to his own self-image. He spoke from experience in an editorial entitled "Thrift and Destiny": "Men who have climbed the ladder to success have only done so after persistent struggle and acts of self-denial."[4] He supported a stiff inheritance tax—so long as "it doesn't sap the incentive to provide for one's family after death." He collected these thoughts and phrases, hackneyed and clichéd, yet true in the way truisms often are, intent on putting them to a larger purpose.

He wrote a column he hoped to syndicate, called "What Makes a Man." The first essay, "Industry," was his ode to work—his tonic and security. A middling mind struggled to harness Emerson to Edison to an Algeresque creed soon to be known as Babbittry. "You cannot depend on a lightning rod for your connection with the dynamic power of the universe," he wrote. "You must generate your own electricity."

{ 19 }

The clichés were buttressed by quotations, from Daniel Webster to Shakespeare to Schiller. Ensuing columns addressed morality, ambition, perseverance, honesty, "human kindliness," loyalty, patriotism. There is no record that "What Makes a Man" ever appeared beyond the pages of the *Herald*.

Still, the man Vandenberg would become was discernible as he struck themes he never abandoned. Common sense: "Most of us go sky-larking after higher, fancier philosophy—when we have but to buckle on the burnished armor of our common sense in order to be panoplied for any fray." Dependability: "The wilder the storm, the more stalwart is Gibraltar." Initiative: "Don't dawdle in the back-stair-by-ways of might-have-been and never-was."[5]

These not-too-deep thoughts found their mark. In anticipating the 1914 elections, more than a few Republican leaders saw promise in the young orator who also ran an influential newspaper. Would he challenge the Democratic governor, Woodbridge Ferris? Party officials urged Vandenberg to run. Not so Sparks. "A governor must necessarily make more enemies than friends," Sparks recalled counseling his boss, "and the Senate was his goal."[6]

In June 1914, the world of Arthur Vandenberg still revolved around Grand Rapids—even as the wider world was spinning out of control. When a Serbian student in Sarajevo drew a pistol from his coat and killed Archduke Franz Ferdinand, heir to the Austro-Hungarian throne, he triggered a war unlike any seen before. And it all happened so quickly. Austria declared war on Serbia, which was backed by Russia. Germany was allied with Austria, and France and Great Britain joined the Serbs. Massive armies mobilized.

Americans gaped in disbelief. But many felt that a distant war was none of their concern. Vandenberg disagreed, and tried to bring home its implications. For his countrymen to think themselves immune from the European conflict, he warned, was to exercise the "daily discretion of the ostrich . . . simply because an ocean separates us from the present scenes of mighty cataclysm." The shadow of war was lengthening even to the middle of America. Vandenberg strained for analogies that might help *Herald* readers comprehend it. Austrian aggression against little Serbia, he said, was like all the other American states picking on Indiana.

And yet he advocated neutrality, seeing the war as a family feud among kindred royals.[7] He called for "non-partisanism and non-interference . . . in the White House, in Congress, in the pulpit, in the journal. . . . This is no time to rock the boat."[8]

Neutrality was hard to maintain, however, especially as German U-boats challenged neutral shipping in the North Atlantic. "We can no longer rely upon our isolation in world affairs," Vandenberg wrote, "for that no longer exists."[9]

Theodore Roosevelt preached preparedness as the best American response to the European conflict, and preparedness became Vandenberg's mantra as well. To those who viewed an expanded military as the first step toward war, the editor asked, "Do our theoretical peace friends realize that the new athletic stadium at Yale could contain the entire regular army of the United States as now constituted, without crowding?" He paraphrased Washington's dictum: Work for peace, prepare for war.[10]

Preparedness seemed a wiser course than the naive idealism of the magnates, Henry Ford and Andrew Carnegie, with their extravagant subsidies for peace initiatives: "We again submit that sane, legitimate 'preparedness' is a *peace movement*." He viewed skeptically the vague calls, even from Roosevelt, for a "world peace league."[11]

Trying to sort out the causes of war, Vandenberg lit upon a factor that would loom ever larger in his thinking: greed. "No Wonder He Wants War!" declared a *Herald* editorial that reported the king of Italy's substantial interest in Krupp, the German arms giant. U.S. Steel also owned shares. And American brokers advertised in the *Herald* and throughout the land to sell French bonds. The United States became, almost overnight, the world's chief creditor.

There was a terrible irony, Vandenberg wrote, in Americans "hoping and praying for peace, yet working day and night . . . to produce the munitions and means for continuing the war. . . . The greater our war business the greater the war. The greater and longer the war, the larger and more profitable our own war business." With intertwined financial interests came the risk of "Croesus-like profit-pinching for the benefit of the few at the expense of the many."[12]

When, in May 1915, a U-boat torpedoed the British liner *Lusitania*, American sentiment tilted further against Germany and its submarine "piracy." Preparedness took on greater urgency. The *Herald* presented a sensational series of stories called "The Invasion of America." "Boston Doomed" ran one headline. The editor stressed that the fictional articles were a plea for vigilance, not militarism.[13]

Vandenberg applauded President Wilson's firm warning to Germany. "The United States will not—cannot—yield one jot or tittle of the new 'Declaration of Independence' which has just been announced," he wrote. "Self-respect, without which man is an invertebrate animal, requires that we should be prepared to protect that which we cherish, which not only includes our material possessions, but that intangible something which makes us a distinctive nation in the eyes of the world."[14] When Wilson's antiwar secretary of state William Jennings Bryan resigned, Vandenberg cheered and noted that "just now the President is stronger than his party."[15]

Cataclysm in Europe portended great hazard, yet it also affirmed America's emergence as a world power. "The old era is passing," Vandenberg wrote. "While the warring nations will have been robbed of the most virile and desirable of their male populations, and those that survive will be so physically and mentally affected that future generations will be influenced, the current will flow undisturbed in the United States. . . . We do not wish to be entangled in alliances or the European political imbroglio."

War in Europe did nothing to dampen prosperity at home. Grand Rapids boomed. Horses drawing wagons were no longer startled by the rackety onrush of an automobile. The *Herald* urged restrictions on street vendors: they created a "peanut skyline," a "village scenery . . . out of place in a grown-up city." Young Pablo Casals visited, performing in the Central High School auditorium. At the Powers Theater, Anna Pavlova appeared in scenes from *Pagliacci*. Of course, neither drew a crowd like the twenty thousand who watched a "human fly" climb the wall of a department store.[16]

Vandenberg's boosterism knew few bounds. After a lake-effect snow, he observed, "No city in the country is more fortunately situated for providing coasting pleasures for boys and girls than Grand Rapids." A photo layout showed children from Lafayette School romping in the snow—among them the publisher's daughter Barbara, a cherubic brunette. An awareness of children informed his editorials. When police collared a boy for roller-skating on a sidewalk, the *Herald* declared, "We're for the 'kids on skates.' And we're selfish about it, too, because our 'kids' skate—and it makes their cheeks rosy and their eyes bright and their hearts light."[17]

When Vandenberg arrived at the office at 9 a.m. a copyboy would have returned from the depot with the big-city papers: the *News, Free Press,* and *Times* from Detroit, the *Tribune* from Chicago. At a creaky typewriter flanked by an unabridged dictionary, a thesaurus, and a massive concordance to the Bible, Vandenberg pecked out single-spaced editorials while tossing cigar butts behind the radiator. How that office must have reeked of smoke when, at noon, he emerged sporting a fresh cigar and a homburg—or boater, depending on the season—and strode three blocks to lunch at the Peninsular Club. In the afternoon he reviewed news and advertising layouts for the late-night press run. Later he might reappear in the office wearing a cutaway coat and striped trousers, en route to a banquet. Younger staffers trembled at the booming voice and imperious manner, but those who knew him better looked past the bluster.[18]

In May 1916 Vandenberg rode a Republican train to Detroit to hear Theodore Roosevelt preach preparedness. A woman in the auditorium balcony interrupted the former president to declare, "I have two sons who will respond." For a moment, silence hung over the audience. Then Roosevelt called out, "Madam, if every mother talked that way, there would be no need for any of our sons to fight, because the power of our national defense would save us from all trouble." "Like a clap of thunder," wrote Vandenberg, "the applause of the inspired multitude made the very rafters ring." Regarding the Wilsonian policy of "watchful waiting," hedged with warnings and caveats, Roosevelt observed, "When I intervened in Cuba, I intervened."[19]

Republicans built a campaign based on the "five Ps": protection, prosperity, patriotism, peace, and preparedness—in contrast to what they saw as Wilson's rudderless foreign policy. When the state GOP convened in Lansing in May, thirty-two-year-old Arthur Vandenberg addressed the subject in his keynote speech. "The ostrich," he observed, his deep voice booming as he thrust out his right forefinger for emphasis, "thinking he is safe because his head is buried in the sand, is Solomon in all his wisdom compared with Uncle Sham who carries a chip on each shoulder and both arms in a sling." Blasting Wilson ("a minority president") for his "foreign policies framed in cloister," the young editor brought delegates to their feet again and again. "We stand for protection—protection for American lives and property," he declared, "protection for American taxpayers who demand economy and efficiency in government—protection for American industries—protection for the American flag."[20]

Party regulars and Bull Moosers reunited at the 1916 GOP convention in Chicago to nominate the Supreme Court justice Charles Evans Hughes, a compromise candidate who, though lacking charisma, also lacked enemies. In the fall campaign, Democrats said of Wilson, "He kept us out of war." Yet the drift toward war seemed inexorable. Vandenberg picked at Wilson's cautious diplomacy. He fancied himself in the hardheaded tradition of Hamilton, against Wilson, the Jeffersonian schoolmarm.

The Vandenbergs decamped to Lake Michigan in July 1916 as record heat settled over the Great Lakes. For some months, Elizabeth had suffered persistent but mysterious headaches. At Ottawa Beach, Vandenberg contemplated the vast indifference of the lake, its ceaseless waves lapping the shore. In an editorial entitled "A Cure for Egotism," the egotistical editor urged his readers to "go out on a lake." There, he said, you realize "what an insignificant performer you are." Elizabeth's pain intensified. University of Michigan specialists diagnosed a brain tumor.

Vandenberg's editorials acquired a more reflective tone. "A daily paper is often a journal of unhappiness," he wrote. In "A Little Praise Goes Far," he asked, "Do you ever congratulate or praise the wife when she provides a good meal?" He was confronting the greatest uncertainty. "Men and women, not houses nor automobiles, make happiness," he wrote. He found a "homely and trite lesson" in domestic contentment from a Sunday stroll through his leafy neighborhood: "The man who can combine an optimistic view of life with a real interest in the things about him" was "happiest and most often successful."[21]

In Ann Arbor, surgeons performed a delicate procedure to remove Elizabeth's tumor. They were unsuccessful. It was only a matter of time, they said—months, no more.

In the days leading up to the election, while Elizabeth suffered and her sisters watched the children, Vandenberg stumped for Republican candidates. Hughes carried Michigan easily, and the *Herald* went to press predicting a GOP victory. But Wilson won California and four more years in the White House.

The staggering tragedy of trench warfare filled the world with horror. Vandenberg became obsessed with preparedness on every level: national, local, personal. Was America about to slip into the ghastly quagmire across the sea? "Nothing but gross national error (past, present and future) could bring us to such a calamity," he wrote on the eve of 1917. The war was a haunting backdrop to the drama at home. Elizabeth stayed with a sister to spare her children the sight of her. Doctors could do nothing except ease the pain. Vandenberg could do even less. Never had he felt so powerless—so *unprepared*. He tried to console his wife, but he could hardly console himself.[22]

The crisis that arose early in 1917 when Germany ignored Wilson's warnings and declared unrestricted submarine warfare pushed Vandenberg to make common cause with the administration. "The White House controls our destinies this morning," he wrote. This was the hour for "unpartisan action," for the nation to rouse itself in the "cause of righteousness." The day the Senate approved Wilson's call to break off diplomatic relations with Germany, Vandenberg addressed a banquet of furniture dealers. His topic was to have been "Honesty in Advertising." In light of the news, he changed it to "Honesty in American Citizenship." He recalled Benjamin Franklin's toast to George Washington. He raised a glass to Wilson, charging every American to stand by the president. "Business Feast Turns to Riot of Patriotism," the *Herald* boomed.[23]

Wilson had yet to ask Congress to declare war, but "armed neutrality" was not sustainable. The president knew more of foreign dangers than anyone, Vandenberg wrote: "Pray Heaven that this information is of a character to justify our lethargy." When Wilson called for a special session of Congress, however, Vandenberg, for all his zeal, had trouble envisioning American soldiers in Allied trenches. "Preparedness" sounded active, manly, yet the near-inevitable next step was harder to imagine.[24]

German submarines sank three unarmed American merchant ships. Dozens of sailors died, including one from western Michigan. "Unpreparedness," Vandenberg wrote, "has not saved us from being kicked into the anteroom to war." George Washington had warned against "entangling alliances," the *Herald* observed, but "we may safely trust to temporary alliances for extraordinary emergencies."[25]

The protégé of Senator Smith took a seat in the House gallery on April 2, 1917, when Wilson asked Congress for a declaration of war. The world, the president said, "must be made safe for democracy." Vandenberg agreed. He wrote of a "glorious and honorable crusade to spread even further into Europe the freedom which now dominates the governments of those countries, Russia, France and Great Britain, whose battle also is now ours." He lapsed with ease into jingoism, declaring this "the greatest revival . . . since Christ came upon the earth."[26] When Wisconsin senator Robert La Follette opposed granting Wilson greater authority, Vandenberg threw the *Herald* behind the president. "America First," he wrote, employing a Wilson campaign slogan that gained wider usage a generation later.

Jingoism simplified a complex state of affairs. "We of the west are far removed from the eastern harbors where Americans go down to the sea in ships," Vandenberg told a crowd of twenty thousand at a "loyalty" rally in Grand Rapids. "Any man who says this is a war for money, lies," he added, glossing over earlier doubts. "He slanders not only the president, but the country and the flag."[27] It was clear, he intoned in an editorial, that "we shall all stare DUTY in the face before there is an end to this affair." As part of his duty, Vandenberg helped organize the Michigan branch of a new veterans group, the American Legion, as a rallying point for preparedness. But with his wife dying and three small children to care for, he recognized that his own patriotic duty would never be performed in uniform.

"Gone to her reward," despite the efforts of "the best surgeons in the northwest," read the *Herald* headline of May 8, 1917. Elizabeth Vandenberg was "the sunbeam of the sickroom," her husband wrote. He sought solace at the typewriter, composing a booklet of eulogy: "So much do I owe my friends—her friends—that no fragmentary sentence on a card, no formal brief of thanks, can seem to satisfy my heart's desire to put into these few attempted words . . . some little measure of gratefulness." He struggled for a short sentence—and found one: "Heaven has gained new charms."[28]

Death at home and war abroad left Vandenberg contemplating the fragile bonds of human relationship. Theodore Roosevelt had said all men had a duty, but Vandenberg pondered his through a veil of loss. Yet war also inspired a thin-lipped and righteous hostility. Life was uncertain enough; in war, at least, one could suspend doubt. In June the *Herald* deployed a phrase that accompanied every related editorial until the shooting stopped: "Clear the Track." To obstruct the war effort in any way was deviant. The *Herald* reported blandly on the beating of a Traverse City socialist who remained seated when a band struck up "The Star-Spangled Banner." Those with German sympathies "must henceforth be considered guilty until proven innocent."[29]

In Grand Rapids an electric sign visible from Vandenberg's office urged residents, "Buy Liberty Bonds." Michigan led the nation in the proportion of men registered for the new draft. Eighteen *Herald* employees joined the service. But their boss, a thirty-three-year-old widower, could write only of "The Patriot at Home": "Mr. Stay-at-Home—the uneasy, dissatisfied fellow who wishes, with all his heart and soul, to be in the thick and fighting forefront of this war but who, for one honestly good reason or another, cannot—must not—follow his country's beloved flag down into the driving battle zone." He offered the very consolation he struggled to accept: "There's work for you. . . . It may be unromantic, unspectacular. There are no bands to play; no plaudits from the throng. . . . You can help maintain impenetrable unity throughout the Republic—so that Sammy can . . . confidently keep his face to the enemy without fear that his country shall be Russianized behind his back. . . . And the home shrines, where little children linger, must be preserved—or any victory is empty beyond words."[30]

But bands would play, as duty led him to the podium and the pulpit. His weapons were words—to be aimed at "traitors," to boost morale, and, with an election year ahead, to paper over partisanship in pursuit of the common cause.

In September 1917 he was invited to address the Commerce Club of Toledo, where the senatorial bête noire of intervention, Robert La Follette, was scheduled to defend a pacifist professor who had criticized American involvement in the war. Vandenberg was asked to tailor his talk to counter La Follette's.

The pompadoured Wisconsin senator was known for a ploy favored by evangelist Billy Sunday, who began his oration in a full suit, then, as he warmed up, dispensed in dramatic sequence with coat, vest, collar, tie, and even shirt. By his sweaty conclusion he stood before the audience in trousers and undershirt. In Toledo, Vandenberg was introduced to three hundred businessmen as a "second Patrick Henry." When he rose to speak, he said nothing. Instead, he bowed deeply and, with great deliberation, removed first his coat, then his vest, then tie, collar, and finally starched white shirt.[31]

"It seems necessary," he told his listeners at last, "to strip to this audience—why not get all that out of the way now, so that your attention need not be distracted from what I have to say." Although the crowd cheered, he confessed to a friend later, "What would I have done if they hadn't seen the joke? There I stood in my dirty undershirt!"[32]

But the crowd got it—and approved of Vandenberg's bombast. There could be no true neutrality, the publisher declared. Neutrality would result in a "weasel peace." As for Germans who claimed God for their side, "If there is a hell for blasphemers, its gates gape wide for the blood-hungry Hun who rapes and murders . . . with the name of the Supreme Father upon his lips." Again and again the speaker paused for the applause to subside. "Jail Neutrals, Says Publisher" was the headline in the *Toledo Blade*.[33]

In April 1918, Vandenberg's "Patriot at Home" accepted his duty to sell war bonds. He embarked by train with a thirty-six-piece "Jackie Band" of musicians from the Great Lakes Naval Training Center outside of Chicago for a journey "up one side of the Wolverine state and down the other." In seventeen days, he gave eighty-two speeches. Most stops began with a parade from the station. The band drew crowds in its wake as it marched to a band shell or the steps of a courthouse or the stage of a five-cent moving-picture palace, where Vandenberg would thrust one hand in his pocket and stab the air with the other, his sonorous voice doing patriot's work.[34]

He returned home to find a letter from a woman in Detroit, a volunteer with the Red Cross. She was seeking speaking engagements for a wounded veteran. A mutual friend had suggested she contact the editor of the local paper, whose name she would recall from the University of Michigan. Her name—and Arthur Vandenberg remembered it vividly—was Hazel Whitaker. "Your letter was horribly business-like," he replied immediately. "You said not a word about the Huron River or Grangers or Delta U. House parties or any of the other blessings of yesterday." He dug out an old college scrapbook. "Not unexpectedly," he wrote, "I found you featured in it more than once."[35]

She should visit soon, he urged. He asked for a photograph. She sent a letter, but no picture. ("The inference being, of course," she told friends later, "that there had to be some good reason why a woman of my age wasn't married.") "It is true, as you say, that I have drifted a long, long way from my old Ann Arbor friends," Vandenberg wrote. "But I would love to drift back again, and I am sure, when you come to Grand Rapids, we can reminisce . . . indefinitely."

Hazel offered a different sort of companionship than Elizabeth had. An only child, she had been raised to speak up. Her mother, an early suffragette, reared her with the expectation that she earn a living. She taught school in Fort Wayne and Saginaw, then moved to Chicago to do social work. She was hired by the *Tribune* to produce an advertising feature called "How to Earn Money at Home." And as the assistant to an advice columnist, she was soon offering sisterly counsel to hundreds of young women.[36] In 1915 she moved to Detroit to write advertising copy for the J. L. Hudson department store.

For Vandenberg, Hazel Whitaker was a kindred spirit, reentering his life at a moment when he hungered for company. The practical challenge of juggling career ambitions and the needs of small children added urgency to the prospect of remarriage. He insisted she visit Grand Rapids, and he charmed her with a little bombast about his work: "This is no slouch of a newspaper, if you please. It is the biggest morning newspaper—speaking in circulation terms—in any city of 150,000 people in the world!"

When Hazel's mother died, he sent her a copy of the booklet written for his late wife:

> Perhaps some of its philosophy—which is your philosophy, too— will help just a little in those moments when the "unhappiness" of which you speak crowds in. Sometimes I think we get some of our most exalted happiness (a strange word to use in such a connection) out of our sorrows and our "unhappiness." Is that an utterly impossible paradox? No: because I am gaining a *real* satisfaction out of reading *your* letter and in writing *this* one. I am sure you know what I mean. I feel that it is making us *better* friends—because the *best* friends are those who *understand*.

Enough of that, he added. ("I have always wanted to be a preacher, if I could be something else the other six days of the week.") It was time to switch "into the living now." She spoke of a visit at the end of

May. Certainly, he wrote, "I should be doubly proud on Memorial Day, marching at the head of my Company of Michigan State Troops in a sojer [*sic*] suit, if you were on the sidelines."

At thirty-five, Hazel was not an obvious beauty, and she seemed half-resigned to spinsterhood. A note of caution tempered her excitement. Vandenberg worried about pushing too fast. "Our friendship is to be renewed on the *right* basis," he declared.[37]

Within weeks of her visit, however, he proposed marriage. Hazel accepted. The children seemed won over by the arrival of this warm woman with a quick laugh. The house at 316 Morris, which Vandenberg had built ten years earlier in what felt to him like a different life, "seemed sort of all 'run down,'" he wrote his fiancée, "but I shall not touch a thing until *you* are general manager."

He pressed her for a wedding date. "Men talk to me each day about getting into the senatorial race," he wrote her. "It is all very nice—but what does it amount to compared with the everlasting love of a wonderful girl? I would rather *just once* hear *you* say 'I love you' than to hear the governor say to me 'you are Senator for life.'"[38]

They married in June 1918. Hazel's Presbyterian minister performed the brief ceremony, witnessed by the church janitor and his wife, in the minister's second-floor flat just off Detroit's Woodward Avenue. "It hardly seems fair," Vandenberg had written from Grand Rapids before his departure, "that I should have this great, good fortune just now when others are traveling the Valley of the Shadow. Yet, there is something absolutely *holy* about it all, to me, and I *know* I am going to be able to do more than I have ever before to help 'win the war' and to help make life easier for others. After all, that's about all there is worth living for."[39]

Vandenberg watched with mixed emotions in the fall of 1918 as the Michigan Senate campaign unfolded. His mentor, Senator Smith, had decided not to run. Reformers, including Vandenberg, hoped a primary would make the process more democratic, with a secret ballot replacing smoke-filled rooms in Lansing.

Instead, the election became a national scandal. Voters were asked to choose between wealthy Detroit Republican Truman Newberry, secretary of the navy in the Roosevelt administration, and auto pioneer Henry Ford, who ran in both the Republican and Democratic primaries, winning the latter. Ford's vast wealth, along with the lavishly financed Newberry campaign, raised spending to a level that would not be equaled for generations.

Vandenberg's indignation at Newberry's tactics was compounded by his own simmering ambition. "The world is not 'Safe for Democracy,' " he wrote, "when Senatorships go for $150,000 . . . because there are not twenty men in the state who can wield a sufficiently trenchant checkbook [Ford] or command a sufficiently generous coterie of rich friends [Newberry] to qualify in a game with such stakes." What a torment, then, to support Newberry! Yet Ford was now a Democrat. And he had dismissed American victims of the *Lusitania* sinking as "fools," observing churlishly, "They were warned." Ford loved peace, Vandenberg wrote, "more than he loved America's rights and reputation as we all now understand them. . . . All credit to him for the wonderful industrial works. . . . But the Senate is not an industrial institution. It makes laws—not lizzies."

In the space of a week in November 1918 came the election and the armistice. Newberry edged Ford. Republicans swept the state and were resurgent nationally. Germany accepted Wilson's terms. In Grand Rapids, church bells and factory whistles greeted the news of peace.[40]

Leaders of the Great Powers made plans to gather at Versailles. Vandenberg predicted that the peace conference would "bequeath a reign of justice to the world because the victors are democratic nations believing in world justice. That is probably as near as the world ever will come to internationalism." But the reign of justice proved elusive. The victors were bent on spoils. The peace they imposed dashed the *Herald* publisher's naïve hopes. The world was not a safer place for democracy.[41]

Even before the peacemakers convened, seeds of discontent were evident. Voters had returned a Republican majority to Congress, but the American delegation to the conference was, in the *Herald*'s words, "chiefly conspicuous for the strong men whom it might include but doesn't." Where were the Republican statesmen—Taft, Hughes, Henry Stimson, Elihu Root?

Senate Republicans, charged with ratifying any treaty, had the same question. Wilson's arrogant tactics had won him few friends at home, even as he was lionized abroad. He had ignored Senator Henry Cabot Lodge of Massachusetts, incoming chairman of the Foreign Relations Committee. The Senate needed to be "in continuous touch with the peace situation," Vandenberg argued. "This is essential not only as a matter of constitutional theory, but as a matter of elementary common sense." This was what "advise and consent" was all about. A strong foreign policy depended on it.[42]

Then there was the president's personal role. Should he lead the American delegation himself? When Wilson embarked for Paris, the best the *Herald* could say was that he was needed precisely because he had appointed such weak delegates. His message to Congress on the eve of his departure disclosed "the theory upon which the delegation was formed," Vandenberg wrote, "by its liberal use of the pronoun, first person singular."[43] He knew egotism when he saw it. Vandenberg had warned against Wilson's vision of the League of Nations even before the United States entered the war. He was more inclined to support Theodore Roosevelt's idea of a league of allies to contain the defeated aggressors. Yet Vandenberg was willing to take a middle road between "enthusiastic idealists who insist that an artificial agency of this type is the only reliance necessary to perpetuate the peace of the world" and those who insisted that U.S. participation was "fatal to America's independent rights." His mind was open: "The truth and the proprieties probably lie somewhere between these extreme views." No covenant could guarantee peace. Yet "to condemn the whole project through fear that its ultimate application would emasculate American independence" was also absurd.

By the end of January 1919, the diplomats meeting outside Paris in the great Hall of Mirrors were, as Vandenberg put it, "down to cards and spades" in their plans for a League of Nations. The most—and least—to be said for the whole enterprise was that "it will be an experiment."[44]

Before the war, Vandenberg had endorsed Theodore Roosevelt's conception of nationalism supported by military preparedness— "vigorous neutrality," in the words of Henry Cabot Lodge. Before the war, Vandenberg's "Americanism" reflected a wary, essentially defensive view of the world. He tied "independence" to unilateralism.[45] Before 1917, Wilson also had favored neutrality and resisted intervention, sharing with Vandenberg a belief in America's moral superiority, a vaunted notion of exceptionalism. Now Vandenberg opposed the League as designed, claiming it was easier for leagues and alliances to cause wars than to cure them. He worried that membership could leave the United States "a perpetual recruit to Mars." Only strict neutrality meant peace, and removed the United States from the "convulsions" of the Old World. He was a nationalist, not an internationalist, he wrote later, while stressing that his nationalism was not a chauvinist thing "of brags and boasts."[46]

Americans had clung as long as they could to conflicting wishes: maintain a firm line with Germany, yet do nothing that might mean war. After the United States joined the conflict, Wilson appealed to the same moralizing impulse: The war was fought to make the world safe for democracy, he declared. With the fighting over, the mission remained.

The United States was ripe for a wider role in the world. Its policy foundered as to what that role would be. Republican elders such as Taft and Root were inclined to back Wilson in some form of league. Lodge might have accepted League of Nations participation but so distrusted Wilson that his motives were mixed. He insisted that a raft of reservations be attached to approval of the League covenant. Wilson insisted there be none. Vandenberg searched for compromise. In doing so, he better reflected public opinion than either leader.

Late in June, Wilson returned to the United States and embarked on a speaking tour to build support for his vision of the League. The quest proved too much for a weary man. He collapsed in Colorado and was rushed back to Washington, where he suffered a stroke. Taft embarked on his own tour to pursue the same goal. One stop on his itinerary was Grand Rapids.[47]

Ahead of that visit, Vandenberg surveyed 250 veterans. His postcard poll offered three alternatives. "The first," he explained, "proposes sled-length ratification . . . exactly as President Wilson has brought it home." The second was rejection of the covenant. The third, outlined with a care that declared the editor's bias, was ratification "without textual amendment [per Taft], but *with* American reservations which shall clearly interpret questionable obligations in the covenant and which shall make forever clear that we do not intend to yield up any element of our sovereignty and which will specifically limit our obligation to participate in future foreign wars." The reservations included: "(1) proclamation that we shall never permit alien jurisdiction over our immigration and tariff laws; (2) proclamation that we shall never allow the 'League' covenant to be interpreted as limiting our 'Monroe Doctrine' authority in any respect; (3) proclamation that we shall always construe our right of withdrawal from the 'League' as being absolute and unhampered by 'League' veto."[48]

On the front page of the *Herald*, Vandenberg challenged Taft with a battery of questions, particularly regarding Article 10 of the covenant, which authorized the League to act against any nation making war for territorial conquest. The only reservations he could accept, Taft replied, were those that did not require concurrence of the other powers. The Senate had no interest in such constraints. So Taft, too, was caught in the middle as his train approached Grand Rapids. How sincere were Senate Republicans' reservations about the treaty? Was Vandenberg's fear of infringement on the prerogatives America enjoyed with the Monroe Doctrine justified or a partisan misreading?

Wilson's refusal to consider even mild changes galled the *Herald* editor. Four GOP senators who called on the ailing president were lectured on America's obligation. They had hoped that the president would "go along" with "reservations pioneered"—according to the *Herald*—by Vandenberg. This was not to be.[49]

"I do not know whether you were the first to propose a program of reservations or not, but certainly you have carried on a fine contest on that line," Lodge replied after receiving a Vandenberg editorial. "I read your articles with greatest interest, and . . . I shall unscrupulously steal . . . the part in which you say, 'There is menace in unshared idealism.' " So, while Wilson indirectly rejected Vandenberg's suggestions, Lodge employed his words to powerful effect in Senate debate, and Taft was moved by his arguments. From his second-floor desk overlooking the little square in downtown Grand Rapids, Arthur Vandenberg could fancy himself an influence on the biggest foreign policy question of the age.

"The great danger *now*," he wrote Taft in September, "is that persistent refusal on the part of President Wilson . . . to agree to *any* reservations is so irritating to popular opinion that the first thing we know the pendulum will swing to the other extreme and we shall confront a situation which will produce complete rejection of the entire undertaking."

And so it came to pass. Sadly, said Vandenberg, "Uncompromising extremists at both ends of the line have defeated a common-sense, middle-of-the-road composition which a majority of the country wanted."[50]

William Alden Smith's retirement signaled a generational shift in the state Republican Party. "I am almost ashamed to confidentially confess to you that I am giving serious consideration to entering into the 1920 governorship fight," Vandenberg wrote Frank Knox. "I *hope* that I shall be able to resist temptation, because I cannot convince myself that it is the root [*sic*] which leads to the *real* thing I ultimately want"—namely, a Senate seat.[51] The governor's chair was rather more coveted by the state's energetic attorney general from Detroit, Alex Groesbeck. Vandenberg had no stomach for the fight. "It is no more trouble or work to fight for a big nomination than for a little one," he wrote, "and, if I must 'fight,' it is not going to be over a handful of peanut shucks."[52]

As Vandenberg saw it, Newberry had bought the Senate seat to which he aspired. The contrast between Vandenberg's friend Smith and the conniving Newberry gang could not have been starker. Newberry's campaign paid small-town editors to endorse him and local officials to get out the vote. And indeed, late in 1919 a grand jury in Grand Rapids indicted Newberry and dozens of supporters for violating the Federal Corrupt Practices Act. In 1920 Newberry was convicted and sentenced to prison. In May came a *Herald* headline on the subject: "Resign!"[53]

If Newberry did resign, the pool of candidates to succeed him was not large. Vandenberg was likely on the short list. He chose to stay out of the gubernatorial race, instead determining to influence the debate in the center ring: the presidential election.

CHAPTER 4

THE BEST OF BABBITT

· · · · · · · · · · · ·

At first Arthur Vandenberg hardly gave a thought to Senator Warren Harding of Ohio. But then, neither did anyone else. Vandenberg's choice for president in 1920 was Judge Kenesaw Mountain Landis of Chicago, famous for his handling of the Chicago Black Sox baseball scandal. He was a Republican in the Teddy Roosevelt mold, as ready to wage war on Standard Oil as on the kaiser. Harding, a freshman senator, was a small-town editor of the sort Vandenberg swept along in his wake as he organized a trade association or fought an increase in the cost of newsprint—maybe a boon companion, hardly an inspiration.

Landis did not emerge as Vandenberg hoped. General Leonard Wood, a conservative and a Rough Rider, was an early favorite, with Frank Knox as his floor manager. Also in the running were Illinois governor Frank Lowden and California senator Hiram Johnson. Herbert Hoover, hero of wartime relief, was a fresh face. For Vandenberg the convention was reflected in the delegate with a Wood feather in his hat, a Lowden button on his coat, a Johnson teddy bear for a watch charm, "and an earnest inquiry on his tongue as to who would make the most available 'dark horse.' "[1]

Ohio's favorite son? Maybe a vice-presidential prospect. But the senators and financiers who met at the Blackstone Hotel in Chicago had other ideas. Harry Daugherty, Harding's adviser, emerged from their conclave predicting almost to the hour when his man would be chosen.

By the fourth ballot, Harding rose to fifth place. By the tenth, he was the nominee. "A tin-horn politician with the manner of a rural corn doctor and the mien of a ham actor," sniffed H. L. Mencken. Vandenberg's hope lay in promoting Harding as "the glory of 'normal'" as the Democrats nominated Governor James Cox of Ohio and a young New Yorker with a famous last name, Franklin D. Roosevelt.[2]

Early in September, Will Hays, running Harding's campaign, summoned Vandenberg back to Chicago. "Need your help," his telegram read, "very important matter." The help needed was a speech on the central issue of the campaign, Article 10 of the League covenant. "No American today," wrote Vandenberg, "can be simultaneously for Article X and for the Constitution of his Republic any more than an American in Lincoln's time could be simultaneously for Emancipation and for Slavery." Days later, Harding gave his major foreign policy address. It was Vandenberg's draft verbatim.

Often the editor's gift was less for original argument than for deft sloganeering. In 1920 it was "With Harding at the helm, we can sleep nights." Such influence made it easier to summon enthusiasm for a mediocre candidate. The *Herald* proved an eager cheerleader.[3]

Vandenberg returned a check from Hays for travel expenses. "For twenty years I have been campaigning for the Republican Party," he wrote. "During all this time I have yet to accept so much as one penny. . . . I am happier to leave the 'account' open. I prefer to let the 'obligation' draw 'compound interest.' I have yet to see the time or occasion when this sort of 'obligation' seemed to come 'due.' But I am an optimist and I rather anticipate that sooner or later final compensation may be forthcoming in some form worth more to me than cash (poor as I am)."

In November 1920 Americans elected Warren Harding and running mate Calvin Coolidge, voting overwhelmingly for a "return to normalcy." The awkward coinage, Vandenberg admitted a quarter century later, "sounds like something I might have said."[4]

The editor understood the anxieties of his countrymen. In speaking for himself, he spoke to the uncertainties of the age. War had led to the recriminations of Versailles and a bitter debate over the League of

Nations. Revolution in Russia and the triumph of the Bolsheviks led to a red scare at home. Prohibitionists were near victory in their long struggle to outlaw liquor. Farmers struggled while industry thrived. Immigrants jostled for jobs. It was an age of hurry-up, as automobiles and radios and electrical wonders were changing the very pace and pattern of life. Change was so swift it was overtaken only by a fear of it.

At a personal level, Arthur Vandenberg wondered what came next. He was remarried. The *Herald* was thriving. He had been editor for more than a dozen years and occupied the publisher's chair as well. In *Who's Who* for 1920 he declared himself, with no pretense to modesty, "widely known as a popular and political orator." He was writing most of the editorials for his newspaper—all of them on his "faithful, ancient vintage typewriter," an Underwood he would not trade "for the latest model of any other kind done in solid gold."[5]

His dreams of literary fame faded after publication of a handful of stories and a lone poem in *Collier's*. His "What Makes a Man" columns attracted little interest. But he was still bubbling with ideas. He wished to be noticed beyond the occasional editorial inserted in the *Congressional Record*.

At the dawn of the Harding years, he wrote, "Many of our public troubles—aye, most of them—are traceable to the efforts of 'second-class men' (and worse) to function in 'first-class' responsibilities." Wilson had employed soaring Jeffersonian rhetoric and Vandenberg found it wanting. Harding was the quintessential "second-class man," endowed at best with an aura of amiable dignity.[6]

Vandenberg found his model in Alexander Hamilton, the Federalist visionary who brought structure out of chaos. Hamilton's America emerged from the cauldron of revolution, Vandenberg's from the tempest of world war. Each experience gave its generation a sense of starting anew. Inspired by a magazine listing of "first-class" men that omitted his hero, Vandenberg set out to write a book. His idea was to solicit public notables regarding their candidates for "the greatest American," which he used as the title. "Nearly all of us," he wrote, "have built a shrine within our hearts and souls to some one favorite above all others."

A who's-who of political and academic figures replied to Vandenberg's survey, although Henry Cabot Lodge, a Hamilton biographer, declared the exercise simpleminded and declined to participate. Abraham Lincoln was the respondents' first choice, favored by such disparate figures as Winston Churchill and Upton Sinclair. William Borah was among those who refused to choose between Lincoln and the runner-up, George Washington. The president of Cuba picked Washington, as did Franklin Delano Roosevelt. Senator Albert Beveridge, a Lincoln biographer, noted that history revealed "distinct periods when leadership sinks appallingly; while at others . . . supereminent men appear among us."[7]

Vandenberg himself, of course, chose Hamilton. He was eager to see his hero's life reflected in his own. Hardly as precocious as Hamilton, Vandenberg nonetheless identified with the youth who supported himself as a clerk, inspired elders with his eloquence, and was devoted to his mother. (Even his signature, an elegant *AH* swept into the surname, vaguely resembled his hero's.)

Writing in one age, celebrating another, he cataloged Hamilton's "diversified" achievements in light of their implications for the present day. Hamilton had preached strict neutrality, preparedness, a government of checks and balances, a census that fully counted slaves, emancipation, sound public credit, the creation of a national bank, and certainly a protective tariff. How better, finally, to define the "Americanism" that Vandenberg frequently invoked than to cite Hamilton? "We need his immutable loyalty to the constitution," Vandenberg concluded, in a paroxysm of jingo, "his unhyphenated attachment to 'America First.'"[8]

The Greatest American, published in 1921 by G. P. Putnam, came with a letter of commendation from Warren Harding. (The president's prose resembled the author's—it would not be the first time Vandenberg supplied Harding's words.) The *American Historical Review* found it "an amateurish survey of Hamilton's life and qualities, couched in the language of a conventional eulogy," but Vandenberg was undaunted.[9] No sooner had he visited his publisher in New York and made a pilgrimage to Hamilton's tomb in the yard at

Trinity Church than a sequel was under way. In the summer of 1922 at a cottage on Lake Michigan he composed *If Hamilton Were Here Today*. Here, the emerging conservative tried to temper the roar of the 1920s. He found unnerving "the heresies of a radical and thoughtless age which boasts an independence, as dangerous as it is blind, of precedent and tradition and experience." Distinctions were drawn between liberty and license. He warned of the dangers of "speak-easy radicalism" and attacked populist opponents of the Supreme Court as "tools for Moscow." Via Hamilton he argued for tolerance and saw danger in faction—but not necessarily the tolerance of untrammeled free speech or the faction of party politics. "Faction takes the law into its own hands and lynches negroes," he wrote. "Americans are entitled to be intolerant only of un-Americanism."[10]

As America's immigrant population swelled, Vandenberg suggested that its assimilation was "one of the chief duties of American statesmanship." Hamilton himself had arrived as "a friendless foreigner on the docks of Boston." Yet now the melting pot was "running over," Vandenberg fretted, the country becoming "a polyglot boarding house." Americans had "an obligation to defend our immigration gates against an influx of alien races which . . . could overwhelm our white complexion." He joined that "obligation" with another: *not* "to trespass upon law and morals in our treatment of other races already here." Of the African American he observed, "His mass development . . . has been little short of marvelous, considering his environment and opportunities—in the short half-century since he was a slave. . . . No negro is half so black as the blemish lynch-law puts upon the white man's record."[11]

When *If Hamilton Were Here Today* was published in 1923, the *American Political Science Review* found that "what the author has really done in an interesting and ingenuous manner is to give us his own views on these various issues supported by frequent references to Hamilton's writings and public utterances." The *New York Times* concluded that "allowing for the defect of its style, which may be called flamboyant, from which many adjectives could be cut with advantage, this book will be found to be a stimulant for those who have lost sight of the teachings of Alexander Hamilton. . . . [I]t will be news to many a hardened reader of modern shallow political documents to discover what the real principles of the demigods who formed the Constitution were and are." This was music to Vandenberg.[12]

Perhaps the "real principle" that counted most for the author was the one he took as the theme of his third book: Hamilton's sense of nationalism, and his prescription of neutrality as a key to protecting the fledgling republic. *The Trail of a Tradition*, published in 1926, sketched the history of American foreign policy, with the aim of clarifying America's role in the world.[13] Vandenberg drew a distinction between "nationalism"—a policy of Hamiltonian reason and good sense—and "internationalism, in all its threats, dilution and impracticalities."[14] In a 1925 speech, he argued that the right kind of internationalism was "a mutually respected 'justice' between sovereign 'nationalities.'" That appealed to William Borah, the Senate's leading isolationist. "I hope you will preach this doctrine like Peter the Hermit, with a tongue of flame," the legendary "Lion of Idaho" exhorted him. Then Borah added, "Vandenberg, do you think you could get up a movement in this country, a real movement, with an organization behind it to rehabilitate these principles, to reinstate these beliefs?"[15]

Vandenberg had just such an organization in mind—the Republican Party—and a very specific pulpit from which to preach—the U.S. Senate. He was routinely caustic about the generally second-rate caliber of the men in that holy chamber. Charles Curtis, the majority leader, fit comfortably with the reigning "mediocrity in modern statesmanship," Vandenberg observed. "There are few great figures in the Senate any longer."

In 1922, as Vandenberg wrote his second book on Hamilton, a contemporary Midwesterner published to rather greater acclaim his second novel. *Babbitt*, by Sinclair Lewis, tapped a fund of intellectual contempt for the pieties of middle-class American life. In George Babbitt, the petit bourgeois striver in the Midwestern city of Zenith,

H. L. Mencken and other social critics found a shared reference and an easy target. *Babbitt* became a sensation, its protagonist trumpeted as the epitome of middlebrow mediocrity by the sort of gleeful East Coast know-it-alls who had rejected a younger Vandenberg's stories of junior achievers. *Babbitt*: the very name hung like a cloud over Midwestern pretensions.

George Babbitt was a troubling figure for Arthur Vandenberg, who might have looked in the mirror and seen him there: a progressive-enough Midwestern Republican possessing, as Lewis wrote, "some genius of authentic love for his neighborhood, his city, his clan." It took nerve, to Vandenberg's way of thinking, for Lewis to harpoon this cigar-smoking Rotarian, "given to oratory and high principles, [who] enjoyed the sound of his own vocabulary and the warmth of his own virtue." Vandenberg was master of his sufficient little world, with its perpetual cloud of cigar smoke, billiard-playing camaraderie, and windy after-dinner speeches.

Lewis had the gall to name Babbitt's supercilious son "Theodore Roosevelt Babbitt." This was near sacrilege in Vandenberg's office, with the bunting-draped portrait of Roosevelt behind his desk. And yet, just like the publisher, George Babbitt was "an organization Republican" who would not have bolted to the Bull Moose.

Vandenberg worried, as Babbitt did, that his life could never be anything but what it already was. He had had so much promise, but the real thing was somehow not yet in sight. Some days this was a sort of sanitized hell, as Lewis had put it, which he could not comfortably contemplate. Vandenberg, like Babbitt, believed in self-improvement, what the critic Reuben Maury in the *American Mercury* called the "conviction that it is humanly possible—nay, easily feasible—for a man to be somewhat other than he is. . . . Mr. Babbitt believed himself able to . . . add unto himself characteristics and talents which inherently he did not possess." Alas for earnest Arthur Vandenberg, walking to work with his eyes fixed straight ahead as he worked up a passage of verse in his memory.

Vandenberg's editorials promoted modestly progressive civic initiatives in Grand Rapids. So did the "Good Citizens' League" in Babbitt's

Zenith. *Grand* Rapids: the name itself was Zenith-like in its hyperbole. Vandenberg loved his own Zenith; he identified with it as deeply as any man could. His sort of boosterism was the target of Lewis's clandestine conservatism. Lewis despised any facile notion of human improvement, declaring, "To the question . . . 'What is the matter with America and how shall we do something about it?' there is one final answer: There are too many people who ask, 'What is the matter with America?' and then dash out and try to do something about it."[16]

Maury and the other Babbitt baiters laughed at the middlebrow's pretensions, which were fueled "by a concerted and continuous gas attack from press, pulpit, rostrum and blackboard." Concluded the critic, "He thought he became automatically a gentleman when he dressed like one, a scholar by reading the *Literary Digest*."[17]

The contempt was palpable, and Vandenberg could not abide it. "Let Us Save the Best of Babbitt" was the title of his editorial rejoinder. Despite his doubts about the course of his own life, he decried the way "a lot of intellectual snobs"—Mencken and Lewis among them—"have been preening their own rarefied wisdom at the expense of this poor yokel. . . . Babbitt has been buried beneath the scornful contempt of these metropolitan sophisticates who pity his confinement to the lesser realities of life." Vandenberg wrote of Rotarians in New York who spoke out for their maligned Midwestern brethren, of a former Michigan governor addressing Kiwanians on the virtues of the "noonday luncheon club movement . . . tying together the social structure of America with ideals of unity and justice." Did he realize that these very expressions of uplift—along with his cherished notions of "what makes a man"—were to Mencken and Lewis objects of ridicule?[18]

"Babbitt has a right to strike back," Vandenberg wrote. "Without him this would be a sodden land. . . . He is happy and satisfied to be a part of his own 'home town'—and to strive, with his neighbors, to make the old 'home town' a little better and a little cleaner and a little healthier. . . . Save us," he continued, "from a society that is all 'Mencken' and 'Sinclair Lewis.' Give us 'Babbitt' at his best—interested in his home—living with his own wife—striving to educate his children—

helping along his church—still believing in a just God—loving his country and his flag."

Vandenberg was desperate to see in George Babbitt more than a caricature—which should have been easy, for even with his knee-jerk reaction, the editor was himself a more complex figure, hardly representative of "the noonday luncheon club movement." This was the newspaperman whose morning shave had once been interrupted by a telephone call from a man who refused to identify himself before declaring, "I represent a one hundred per cent American organization and we don't like certain kinds of people. I discovered you have working for you in your news room a man who is of a religion we don't like."

"That's enough," Vandenberg growled into the mouthpiece. "If you don't have the guts to tell me your name I have only this to say: That fellow you mention has worked for us for a long time. I don't care what his race or religion is or the color of his skin as long as he continues to do a good job. Good day to you, sir, and please don't bother me again."[19]

Later that day a battered Model T pulled up to the curb as Vandenberg walked back to the office. Driver and passenger wore Ku Klux Klan robes, while their caps identified them as Lansing streetcar conductors. The Klan was holding its state "konklave" at a circus ground on the south side of the city. "Hey, buddy," one of the men called out, "we're from out of town and we want to know how to get to the fairgrounds." Vandenberg unhesitatingly described a route past the pumping station and the soldiers' home, over the bridge to the fairgrounds—not the circus grounds on the other end of town.[20]

Vandenberg's notions of civil liberty had recovered from the days of Great War jingoism, even when the liberty in question was that of Babbitt's chief antagonist, H. L. Mencken himself. In 1926 Mencken's *American Mercury* published the story of a small-town prostitute. A Boston censor appealed to the U.S. Post Office, which barred the magazine from the mails. The case became a national sensation. Yet only two newspapers responded to Mencken's appeal for more support, the *Lynchburg News* and the *Grand Rapids Herald*.

Vandenberg found himself at a cultural crossroads: full of frustrated creativity and unrealized political ambition, fighting a rearguard action in defense of his home and readers and presumptive constituents—in defense of his life so far—even as his thoughts ranged farther afield.

Could the defender of Babbitt also transcend him?

CHAPTER 5

. . . .

DESTINY

. . . .

Justice triumphed in 1922. The tainted senatorial election of 1920 was nullified; Truman Newberry bowed to pressure and resigned. Although Vandenberg was a leading prospect to fill the vacancy, he was no friend of Governor Alex Groesbeck. Instead, the governor appointed James Couzens, Detroit's reform mayor and the wealthy former partner of Henry Ford.[1]

Neither Couzens nor Groesbeck was a party stalwart. Their Republicanism was a little suspect, a little liberal. Couzens and Vandenberg overcame their differences, however, and Couzens encouraged Vandenberg's ambitions. But the editor and the governor never warmed to one another. In 1926 Arthur Vandenberg set out to end the reign of Alex Groesbeck—and install a governor ready to support his own candidacy for the Senate.

The *Herald* promoted furniture manufacturer Fred Green, longtime mayor of the town of Ionia. The day before the gubernatorial primary—where victory was tantamount to election in reliably Republican Michigan—Vandenberg organized and addressed a massive rally for Green in downtown Grand Rapids. Green swamped Groesbeck in the primary, won easily in November, and backed Vandenberg's candidate for state party chairman, former congressman Gerrit Diekema.[2]

Orchestrating the Green campaign only whetted Vandenberg's appetite. With the next senatorial election less than two years away, and with Couzens occupying the other seat, the time was coming for Vandenberg to commit to action. He was a natural choice to challenge the Democratic incumbent, seventy-five-year-old Woodbridge Ferris. Vandenberg had boosters across the state; most newspapers were in his corner. "I have at least come to this conclusion," he confided to

Couzens late in 1926: "If I am *ever* going to do this thing, it ought to be in 1928."[3] Family and business circumstances were also favorable. Two of his children were in college, the third in high school. Hazel was an astute companion in the political life. He would soon merge the *Herald* with newspapers in Battle Creek, Lansing, and Port Huron to create Federated Newspapers, an arrangement that would make him nearly a millionaire. He declined an offer from the Hearst chain to become a publisher in Boston or Chicago for a staggering $100,000 per year.

And yet, he was not the perfect candidate. Smith's ready charm eluded his protégé, who was never at home glad-handing on the campaign trail. Vandenberg had held no public office beyond city charter commissioner. His struggle with small talk and his unwillingness to suffer fools combined with a sober demeanor put few people at ease. And despite his party activism, other prospective candidates were better known. Newberry's friends resented the editor who hounded their man from office. Vandenberg expected Governor Green's support, but had earned it only by antagonizing the Groesbeck camp. Liberal Republicans in the Couzens mold thought him too conservative. Foes of Prohibition thought him too dry.

Nor was he terribly decisive. He could court Hazel or fire off an editorial with alacrity but was paralyzed in the face of this commitment. He possessed a blend of ego and insecurity that meant he hungered to be more sought-after than seeking. "The senatorship is not in any degree essential to my happiness," he declared unconvincingly in 1927. His only concern was "not to disappoint my friends or shirk what proves to be a duty (if it does)." But this was only one more step in a dance of barely masked ambition.

Frank Sparks, by then the *Herald*'s city editor, harbored none of his editor's doubts and was quick to take Vandenberg's political fate into his own hands.[4] For more than a decade, Sparks had been helping Vandenberg amass IOUs within the Republican Party. He moved to incite a grassroots clamor that would simultaneously push his boss off the fence and enhance his chances of winning the nomination.[5]

The bantamweight Sparks was Vandenberg's prod and sounding board, a pragmatist who admired his boss even when they disagreed.

Their frequent debates often ended in truces. Sparks recalled a landmark day when Vandenberg walked into his office, put his feet up on the city editor's desk, and proposed an idea with which Sparks promptly agreed. "Hooray!" Vandenberg yelled. Then he strode into the newsroom. Reaching as high as he could on one of its massive white columns, he started to write. Sparks was forced to climb onto a footstool to see what his boss had posted. First the date, then: "For the first time in twenty years, Frank and I agree on something. A.H.V."[6]

In September 1927, Sparks organized a rally in Grand Rapids that drew a crowd of five thousand. Diekema, the state GOP chairman, endorsed Vandenberg, as did a clutch of state and congressional officials. In February 1928, Vandenberg's Grand Rapids backers staged a banquet at which he received petitions bearing signatures of more than eleven thousand supporters. By March, when Vandenberg embarked on his first campaign tour, Sparks had set up fan clubs in more than twenty counties. He secured the endorsement of former governor Chase Osborn in return for a promise of support for Osborn's bid to be the 1928 vice presidential nominee.[7]

Although Sparks was convinced Vandenberg could win the nomination as well as the general election, Vandenberg himself was far less confident. Then lightning struck—twice. First, the popular incumbent, Democrat Woodbridge Ferris, announced in early March that he would retire on account of illness. Three weeks later, he died. The seat Vandenberg had coveted since he was a schoolboy suddenly stood vacant—and he had every reason to believe that the governor would appoint him to fill it.

Sparks assured Vandenberg that Green "would not dare appoint anyone else" and had said as much during the 1926 campaign. Art Ogle, state editor of the *Detroit News* and a hunting companion of the governor, thought the same.[8] But Vandenberg was not the only Republican who believed the seat should be his. Nor had he been the only key to Green's challenge of Groesbeck: former governors Osborn and Albert Sleeper had also been allies, and both were eager now for the appointment.

Green faced the unhappy prospect of picking one supporter over others. As a compromise, he proposed to appoint former congressman Joe Fordney of Saginaw. "Sugar Beet Joe," of Forney-McCumber tariff fame, would then serve as a placeholder for Vandenberg until November and spare Green an unhappy decision.

Green may have regarded the Fordney option as his safest course, but supporters of Vandenberg and the former governors disagreed. The governor went into hiding at his hunting cabin in northern Michigan to escape the deluge of calls and telegrams. He left word that he had made no decision and might be gone several days.

As Green dithered, Vandenberg fumed. Friends of the governor reported that a messenger had been dispatched to Saginaw to inform Fordney of his appointment, only to be intercepted en route by a state trooper on a motorcycle and sent back to Lansing. Finally, the phone rang in Vandenberg's office. Moments later, he threw open his door and emerged with a broad smile. He had been summoned to Lansing. For an hour and a half, as his Willys-Overland bounced over rough pavement between newly plowed cornfields, his anticipation grew. But when he arrived at the governor's suite, Green was not there. Instead, the governor's executive secretary assured a perplexed Vandenberg that Green would support him in the fall. In the meantime, it would be Fordney.

The editor was stunned—so apoplectic, a wave of nausea nearly overcame him. Back to Grand Rapids he drove, his fury mounting with every mile. At the *Herald*, where the staff expected exciting news, he marched up the stairs without saying a word and slammed his office door behind him.

Come the next day, a Saturday, Green sent word that he would make his decision known on Sunday. In the meantime, the wrath of the Vandenberg camp had already begun to rain down upon him. Green was "digging his own political grave," Sparks warned in a meeting with the governor in Ionia. State treasurer Frank McKay of Grand Rapids, a ruthless party kingmaker, had extended large loans to Green's furniture business. GOP chairman Diekema, another Vandenberg ally, told the governor that extending those loans depended on Vandenberg's appointment.[9]

In Detroit, Ogle of the *News* thought he had a scoop to protect: Vandenberg had been spotted arriving at the governor's suite. The *News* ran a banner headline announcing his appointment. A furious Green called Ogle and demanded a retraction, but he was cornered. "You can double-cross Arthur Vandenberg," Ogle told the governor, "but you can't double-cross the *Detroit News*." Green sputtered and groaned, but dispatched a note to Grand Rapids telling Vandenberg he would be appointed to the Senate.[10]

The suspense did not end there, however. When Vandenberg received Green's envelope, he assumed it confirmed the Fordney appointment. He tossed it, unopened, into his wastebasket and departed for a speaking engagement two hours away in Charlotte. That afternoon, a copyrighted report of Vandenberg's appointment appeared in the *Detroit Times*, so when he reached Charlotte, the wire services were trying to track him down. He called the *Herald*, where copyboys and printers rushed to the trash bins. Pawing through wastepaper, someone found the sealed envelope addressed in green ink and opened it to reveal news of Michigan's next senator.

Publicly, Governor Green was equable. With supreme understatement he announced that "newspapers are a good guide in matters of this kind, and I found that a very large majority of them had already declared their choice." Of Vandenberg, Green added, with a noticeable lack of passion, "he is a Republican and knows why."[11]

In the first week of April, accompanied by Hazel and the children, Arthur Vandenberg packed his bags for Washington. He drafted a letter placing a colleague in charge of the *Herald*'s editorial page. "I am—for the first time in nearly a quarter century—relinquishing immediate contact," he wrote. But his voice would not be confined entirely to quotations on the news pages. "I shall always be in telegraphic reach," he told Carl Saunders, his successor as editor. "My own wires to you will be signed 'Hamilton.'"[12]

His family watched from the gallery on April 5, 1928, as "Pops" entered the chamber at the elbow of Senator Couzens to be sworn in and claim a heavily varnished desk in the back row. There, double-breasted and pin-striped, with a polka-dot tie snug in a high starched collar, Vandenberg found himself encircled by new colleagues, his canary-eating grin broadening into a grateful smile.

The next day the chamber was nearly deserted when Vice President Charles G. Dawes handed the new senator his gavel and asked him to preside. The vice president wanted to pass a bill on which Vandenberg had yet to declare his position. On the dais the freshman asked Dawes how he should vote. When he returned to his seat and roll was called, a new Midwestern voice said, "Aye."

On Saturday came an audience with President Coolidge. The Vandenbergs watched children hunt for Easter eggs on the White House lawn. On Sunday the family attended services at New York Avenue Presbyterian Church. The preacher was a graduate of Hope College in Holland, Michigan. "This was Lincoln's and Roosevelt's church, also Dawes's," Hazel wrote in her diary. "Such four days can never be repeated."[13]

Hazel helped her husband present the proper appearance of a U.S. senator. ("I wouldn't get to first base in this job without Mama to guide me," Vandenberg confided to one of his daughters.)[14] She chose the dark suit and the bow ties; noticed the stain on his shirt; sent him out the door to Capitol Hill looking dapper. His round face, inquiring eyes, and eager, slightly bumptious manner soon led someone to dub him "Buster Brown." Even those who admired the newcomer's zeal and evident seriousness were sometimes put off by a "high hat" air. *Owlish* was an adjective reporters came to favor. Cartoonists had fun with his round black glasses. He combed his sparse hair vainly across a balding scalp, suggesting someone born middle-aged, an effect reinforced by the watch chain smiling from his vest, the spats, the pinkie ring, and the inevitable ash-laden cigar.

Shortly after his appointment, Vandenberg addressed a meeting of the American Society of Newspaper Editors: "I may be a senator only until next December. . . . But I shall be an editor until I die. I am incurably daubed . . . with printer's ink." He had no intention of returning to his old vocation soon, however. After two decades of flirting with elective office, he finally occupied, he said, "the only job I ever wanted and the only one I'd ever take" in public life, and he meant to keep it. With only six months to secure a full term, he set out to get noticed, both in Washington and at home.[15]

He asked Dawes, "What can I do to make the Republican leaders recognize me?" The vice president suggested he take a leaf from the book of Montana Democrat Burton K. Wheeler and "raise a little hell." Defying the veterans who expected a freshman to bide his time, he threw himself into the role and soon was telling a friend, "This is the busiest job I ever ran into."[16]

On the Senate floor, and in the corridors of the Capitol, he exercised his new duties with none of the freshman's traditional humility. With committee assignments to Commerce, District of Columbia, Printing, and Territorial Affairs, bills and ideas sprang forth from his little office. He pushed through a resolution for construction of the International Bridge between Detroit and Windsor, Ontario. He proposed that Detroit's Fort Wayne be designated a national park. He won funds for a hospital at the Selfridge army airfield just north of Michigan's largest city. On behalf of farm interests, he advocated tariff expansion. He secured a fourth judge for the Sixth Circuit, which brought congratulations from Chief Justice William Howard Taft of the Supreme Court. And he pressed (unsuccessfully) for an overdue reapportionment of the House of Representatives, a just cause that would boost Michigan's congressional delegation from thirteen to seventeen—a likely boon to Republicans. He even tried, without success, to have a submarine christened the *Grand Rapids*.[17]

Senior colleagues were bemused by his pretensions. "You could tell at a glance he is important," one wag later wrote. "Vandenberg rose in Grand Rapids, that serious city where they cane the chairs of the mighty. He can't even write his name in a hotel register without writing the word 'grand.' "[18] Worse, his cockiness seemed to get in the way of what he was there to do. One day he was flattered when President Coolidge summoned him to the White House and asked him to speak in a tariff debate. He had been training for this role as long as he could remember, ready to ape William Borah's tics and windy style. He was quite pleased with himself when Senator Daniel Hastings of Delaware stopped by. "Art, that was a great speech you made this afternoon," Hastings announced, and Vandenberg swelled with pride. "But did you notice that we lost six votes right after it?" The senator's ego was like a balloon, deflating with a sudden puncture.[19]

Still, most of his new colleagues were favorably disposed. "Not in my time," the cherubic and partisan Dawes observed later in the year, "have I seen a senator come to Washington who held as much promise as Arthur H. Vandenberg." Flattery came from all directions. "There is a feeling abroad that Michigan is sending to Washington not just one more average senator," wrote a political scientist at the University of Michigan, "but rather a man who will become one of the leaders of the nation."[20]

This sense was fueled by Vandenberg's eagerness to tackle far-reaching issues. Noting the depression devastating European economies, he called for a "prosperity reserve" program for the long-range planning of public works projects. If such work could be ready to proceed at the onset of a recession and financed through public funds diverted temporarily from debt payment, it might avert a more serious depression. "The time to study this problem and prepare for a rainy day," he said, "is when it isn't raining."[21]

He was quick to identify with the ascendancy of Herbert Hoover, the odds-on choice for the GOP presidential nomination in 1928. Hoover's progressivism troubled some Old Guard Republicans, but Vandenberg was comfortable with his calls for collective bargaining and government regulation of monopolies. At the *Herald*, Vandenberg had defined his model statesman as "progressive enough to meet our new emergencies with new methods, yet . . . conservative enough to remember and profit by American political and constitutional history." In Hoover, with his starched collar and zeal for efficiency, he saw such a man. By contrast, he saw in the Democratic nominee, New York's Governor Al Smith, a Wilsonian weakness for "entangling alliances" in foreign policy and a symbol of the corrupt Tammany Hall political machine. (Tammany's "first great genius," Vandenberg noted sardonically, was Aaron Burr, slayer of Alexander Hamilton.)[22]

In Michigan, Republicans swiftly affirmed Vandenberg's nomination, although Governor Green was hardly enthusiastic. Indeed, veterans at an American Legion convention in Detroit noticed that the two men, sitting side by side, shared not a word. Nor did either applaud the other. But Vandenberg's nomination went unchallenged. From the state convention he cabled his wife, "Three speeches, three ovations, unanimous endorsement . . . [former governors] Osborn and Sleeper joining."[23]

Sparks managed the campaign with help from Arthur Junior, who had just graduated from Dartmouth. Vandenberg, in a dazzling white suit, ran hard, crisscrossing the state while the Democratic candidate, Mayor John Bailey of Battle Creek, mounted a weak campaign. "You certainly carry around with you somewhere a golden horseshoe," wrote Frank Knox in October.[24]

On Election Day, voters approved of nearly a decade of GOP prosperity. Hoover won handily. Michigan Republicans swept the ballot. Vandenberg carried sixty-three of eighty-three counties, his margin of six hundred thousand votes the largest in the state's history.

He had arrived.

CHAPTER 6

· · · · · · · · · · · ·

YOUNG TURK

· · · · · · · · · · · ·

Back home, the new senator looked like an energetic freshman fighting for Michigan. But old Washington hands regarded Vandenberg
with more jaundiced eyes. He was earnest, a hard worker, but hardly
the humble public servant. A colleague called him "the only Senator
who can strut sitting down." Citing the classic caricature of a Southern
Senate blowhard, one reporter found him more "Claghornesque than
any Northerner in history." Another noted, "He is going to receive a
severe bump on the head by some brother senator some day."[1]

When the Senate convened in lame-duck session early in 1929, Vandenberg resumed his fight for reapportionment. According to the 1920
census, Michigan, with its booming auto plants, deserved four more
congressional seats. Worse, inaccurate distribution of House seats
meant an imbalance nationally in the Electoral College, with twenty-
three votes "misplaced." Yet House districts were still apportioned
according to the census of 1910.[2] Congressmen from the South, in no
mood to see their representation reduced, opposed any change. By
Vandenberg's own calculations, nine southern states would see their
combined House delegations shrink by more than half.[3]

On the Commerce Committee, Vandenberg threatened to hold
up funding for the impending 1930 census—bad news for politicians
eager to dispense patronage jobs for home-state census takers. He declared his readiness to filibuster. In January 1929 he made his case on
a Sunday-night radio hookup, his first exposure to a nationwide audience. Borah and California's Hiram Johnson joined him to reintroduce
the bill. This time it emerged from committee and was sent to the floor.

Outside the South, editorials showered praise on Vandenberg. The
apportionment issue was finally being addressed, wrote columnist

Mark Sullivan, "due to the energy—and the outraged indignation—of one man." Rare was the Senate newcomer who "managed so quickly to set his mark on proceedings."[4] Yet while his doggedness impressed his allies, he aroused resentment among Southern colleagues. His senatorial nemesis was Alabama's Hugo Black, who challenged the right of industrial states to count their large populations of alien immigrants. Vandenberg replied that if nonvoting aliens should not be counted, neither should disenfranchised blacks.[5]

Hazel was in the gallery the night her husband pressed for a vote. The lean and clever Black—decades later a champion of civil rights on the Supreme Court, but then still marked by his recent membership in the Ku Klux Klan—was absent. In his place, Pat Harrison of Mississippi ("suave and shifty," Vandenberg wrote in an unsigned editorial for the *Herald*) rushed to the floor in evening dress to threaten a filibuster of his own. Vandenberg was "dead tired and disgusted," Hazel reported, and his proposition was stymied. Yet the session ended with agreement that no action would be taken on a new census before reapportionment. Vandenberg was halfway there. But temporarily, at least, the status quo prevailed.[6]

In March 1929 Vandenberg began his first full term. New president Herbert Hoover cemented his affection by declaring an urgent need for reapportionment. Southern Democrats heckled Vandenberg, but soon the Senate approved his bill, 57–26. "Much celebration; Dad dead tired," Hazel wrote in her diary, referring to her husband. The House followed suit, and with the president's signature, Michigan gained four seats. Rarely had a politician found a happier combination of state interest and constitutional integrity. *Time* ran a photo of the "bookish man behind large spectacles" who "writes with more force than he speaks."[7]

He was beginning to find his way in Washington. His diary reflected intense thought on the workings of the Senate. He complained of colleagues who voted one way but hoped for the contrary result. He saw votes cast in ignorance. He faulted a system requiring senators to attend committee meetings while legislation was perfected in open session. Shrewder colleagues who got past the bombast found him diligent and likable, and with time he even toned down his stump speaker's boom. With Borah's backing, he was assigned to the coveted Committee on Foreign Relations.[8]

As early as 1929, Vandenberg had begun to immerse himself in matters of foreign policy, quietly engineering a compromise to aid passage of the Kellogg-Briand Pact to "outlaw" war. Kellogg-Briand was a patently utopian notion. Only the most naïve peace advocates believed jawboning would replace war. But the treaty's very harmlessness made it acceptable to senators willing to agree only on platitudes. Vandenberg conceded as much when he described it with backhanded hyperbole as "the greatest contribution ever made to peace psychology." Ratification coincided with a vote authorizing construction of fifteen new battle cruisers. "The world pays more attention to our peace proposals when it understands that we do not propose to disarm alone," Vandenberg wrote. "We confront"—and here he employed a phrase that would serve him in more dangerous times—"a condition and not a theory."[9] In the uncertain terrain between the two lay his future.

In 1929 the Vandenbergs moved into the Wardman Park Hotel, a fashionable apartment tower on Connecticut Avenue with leafy views of Rock Creek Park. It was one of the few deluxe residential buildings in the District. Neighbors included Secretary of State Henry Stimson, Secretary of the Navy Charles Francis Adams, the postmaster general, judges, and congressmen. Their apartment was modest—two bedrooms, a bath, and kitchenette. When they dined in, Hazel opened a gate-legged table in the living room. On those rare evenings, once the new senator was up to date on pasting clippings into his scrapbook, he might play a rubber of bridge.

But protocol imposed an ambitious social calendar on official Washingtonians. On Mondays the wives of Supreme Court justices were "at home" to receive visitors between 4 p.m. and 6 p.m. On Tuesdays wives of House members welcomed callers. On Wednesdays it was the wives of cabinet members and of the vice president. On Thursdays Hazel opened her home, as did other Senate wives. Hers was a popular stop, not only for her congeniality but also for her potato doughnuts. Friday she called on ambassadors' wives—an important duty once her husband joined the Foreign Relations Committee. Saturdays belonged to generals' and admirals' wives. Finally, on Sunday the governmental routine yielded to the society of old Washington, the "Cave Dwellers." Here, too, the Vandenbergs became popular fixtures.

Senator and Mrs. Couzens and Vice President Dawes befriended the new couple. The vice president was "a good old sport, devoted to Pops," Hazel reported. But all was not elegance. "Oh, such table manners," Hazel wrote after dinner at Dawes's houses with a pair of prominent senators. "Knife grabbers, both of them!"[10]

With Hoover in the White House, Vandenberg hoped for the sort of consensus government with which he was most at home. But in Congress the Republican majority was polarized. At the conservative end were fifteen senators, mostly easterners, styled in the press as the Old Guard. These included granite-jawed George Moses of New Hampshire and Majority Leader James Watson of Indiana, a blowhard relic of the Gilded Age. They had grown accustomed to running the show during the administrations of the figurehead Harding and austere Coolidge. To them Hoover, who had never held elective office, was suspiciously liberal.

Opposing the Old Guard was the great generation of Republican progressives, the Insurgents. Mostly westerners, they included Borah, as well as George Norris of Nebraska and Robert La Follette Jr. of Wisconsin, none of whom paid much heed to party allegiance. Some of these onetime Bull Moosers had been alienated by Coolidge and had voted with the Democratic minority when the White House resisted reform. To them as well Hoover was suspect, but at the other end of the spectrum: he was too much the businessman, too cozy with Wall Street.

That the party of the status quo could also be the party of reform was to Vandenberg no contradiction. His approach, as much from a desire for harmony and problem solving as from expediency, had been to blend the two attitudes. He was pulled in both directions but identified himself with a group of two dozen Republicans inclined to moderation. For him a close relationship with Hoover was the starting point for action.

His search for a middle path was tested quickly in debates over McNary-Haugen and other farm bills. McNary-Haugen was complex, but it proposed generally to support American farmers by restricting foreign trade through tariffs—and a tariff debate was an invitation to discord. In the 1928 campaign, Hoover had promised Borah he would call Congress into special session to pursue farm protection, although he did not want to do so via tariffs. He failed to recognize that a majority of senators salivated over the prospect of setting exchange rates that favored their constituents.

The tariff bill became a morass of special-interest logrolling, to which Vandenberg was not immune. He came to favor lower tariffs on chemicals imported for Michigan's printing and paper industries, and higher rates for Cuban sugar—a threat to Michigan's beet sugar producers—as well as for beans and chicory, cement and plywood. Imported flypaper competed with a Grand Rapids product. Opponents argued that Americans preferred the foreign variety, but Vandenberg won a small raise in flypaper duty. Was this the proper role of the noble solon? To substitute flypaper protection for the grand bargain that would befit a Senate leader?[11]

He fought to protect Grand Rapids makers of reproduction furniture from an influx of "fake" European antiques. "As everyone knows," H. L. Mencken wrote, "Dr. Vandenberg's home town, Grand Rapids, is the center of the American furniture industry, and so it was not unnatural for several senators to suspect that his high dudgeon against bogus antiques from abroad was inspired in some way, however innocently and unconsciously, by a tender solicitude for his constituents." Vandenberg admitted that faux antique furniture was made in the United States also, "but none of it cheats American labor, none of it cheats American capital, and none of it undertakes to defraud the treasury of the United States. That is a very big distinction." Said Mencken, "This reply plainly satisfied the Senate."[12]

This was American government at its most parochial. And even as they argued over specific tariffs, Republicans could not come together on a bill. In the cloakroom the Old Guard and the Insurgents—the "sons of wild jackasses," as George Moses called them—were miles apart. Between them stood the bloc dubbed by the Old Guard's Simeon Fess as the "Young Turks." Two freshmen, Vandenberg and Henry Allen of Kansas, were their leaders. But they lacked, according to the *New Republic*, "a sense of direction and a sense of humor." As one pundit noted, "Their day usually began with a footrace to the White House for the ear of the President and a sprint to Capitol Hill for the ear of the press." But when it came to compromise, Hoover had a tin ear.[13]

Vandenberg tried unsuccessfully to oust Moses, the Senate's president pro tempore, as chairman of the Republican Senate Campaign Committee. For his temerity he earned the nickname "Enver Bey"—in memory, a reporter said, "of that ambitious though slightly addled leader of the Young Turks of the Ottoman Empire. As for Enver Bey, he has his eye on the presidency: What boy orator in politics does not? Arthur, or Enver, feels the party needs new blood, new leadership and a new slogan of service. He brings to the Senate the best ideas of the Rotarians."[14]

The tariff debate assumed a graver aspect when the New York Stock Exchange suffered a record crash late in October 1929. Vandenberg was not alone in fearing that failure to agree on a tariff bill would send the wrong signal to Wall Street and exacerbate its collapse. He lined up pledges from his colleagues for continuous evening attendance until the work was done. Yet the White House was reluctant to pressure the Old Guard or to compromise with the Insurgents. The Turks had nowhere to turn. Vandenberg met with his Old Guard colleagues and tiptoed back from rebellion. "I've said enough," he told reporters when the meeting ended. "I've gotten in enough trouble already."[15]

But the insurgent Borah tutored him as well. After issuing a statement rebuffing the Turks, the Lion of Idaho told his pupil: "Don't get excited; read the statement carefully; it is purposely ambiguous; in a general way we shall accomplish results we both desire." The quote could have been Vandenberg's two decades later, when his sometimes "purposely ambiguous" statements reconciled the White House,

Capitol Hill, and public opinion in the interests of American foreign policy.[16]

Vandenberg's self-confident activism was being noticed as something more than freshman swagger. As one newspaper reported, "He not only talks up, but 'sasses' back. . . . The country is beginning to fancy there may be something to him." "If he isn't careful," the *San Francisco Chronicle* wryly observed, "some of his colleagues will begin to suspect that he is a bit queer." He had fought for reapportionment that was "overdue only a little matter of eight years," had urged a public works jobs bill—"by this unheard of insistence that the Senate act instead of talk Senator Vandenberg is striking an unusual note if he wants to be popular in the Senate."[17]

His allegiance to the president was tested in April 1930, when Hoover nominated Judge John J. Parker of North Carolina to the Supreme Court. Parker was a segregationist who in one opinion had written: "The participation of the Negro in politics is a source of evil and danger to both races." He had also upheld an anti-union labor law. African Americans and organized labor were quick to oppose the nomination. Both groups mattered to Vandenberg, who found Parker's position on voting rights loathsome. When Vandenberg and sixteen other Republicans petitioned Hoover to withdraw Parker's name, the president turned to Southern Democrats for support. Rocked by the Depression, Hoover was desperate for a legislative victory—and tone-deaf to the moral and political fallout.

The president downplayed Parker's decade-old quote, but a civil rights activist who had interviewed the judge informed Vandenberg that Parker's views were unchanged. The National Association for the Advancement of Colored People organized a campaign; Vandenberg was barraged with letters opposed to the nomination. The fight took on a symbolism beyond the question of Parker's qualifications. "The Republican Party, least of any party, has no right to shut its eyes to the outraged sensibilities of 18 million colored citizens," he said. "Our party was practically born with the 14th and 15th amendments."[18]

After meetings with the NAACP and labor groups, Vandenberg wrote, in a vein that made Borah proud: "We are on the threshold of awakened liberalism in the United States. That does not mean bolshevism. American labor is our surest bulwark against bolshevism. The Republican Party cannot afford, ostrich-like, to be blind to the wave of liberal thought that is sweeping the country."[19]

A representative of a manufacturing state, Vandenberg was sensitive to labor issues, and he supported collective bargaining. But it was Parker's insistence upon black inferiority that most rankled him. More than any issue in his first years in Washington, the nomination of Judge Parker forced him back to fundamental principles—even if that meant defeat for his president. "The course of least resistance was to go along with the GOP majority," he wrote later. "If it were properly a 'party' matter, I should have done so. But I decline to see (or play) any 'politics' where the Supreme Court is involved."[20]

Led by progressives, the Senate rejected the nomination, 41–39. Vandenberg's vote was decisive. The Old Guard accused the Young Turk of desertion. His own newspaper criticized him. In public, Vandenberg declined comment. In his scrapbook he was less guarded. "This experience (with my violent critics) impresses me with what a slim chance the 'underdog' has in this 'democracy of equal rights,' " he wrote. "These critics do not chasten me. They drive me toward liberalism. I think the 'underdog' deserves a few more friends."

The president later claimed that Vandenberg pandered to labor, and he charged in his memoirs that Vandenberg and colleagues "ran like white mice" over the Parker vote. But right after the vote, Hoover invited him to the White House. The lonely man in the Oval Office, fretting over a presidency coming undone, urged the senator not to let this disagreement come between them. Hoover at least gave lip service to forgiveness. "It was a very beautiful, thoughtful thing for him to do," Vandenberg wrote. "I repeated that the hardest job of my life was voting against his nominee."[21]

Not all Republicans were in the mood for reconciliation. Vandenberg was vexed by the growing rift between Hoover and Borah, who told his protégé that the president had "become a dictator." One evening, Vandenberg talked with Hoover at the White House for three hours, chiefly about Senate Republicans. The president was anguished by the breach with Borah, recounting their break over the farm bill, the tariff, and Borah's backing for diplomatic recognition of Soviet Russia. Hoover lamented, "I want him to be close to me. But everything seems to have failed. My heart is still in the right place. If you get a chance, you might tell him so."[22]

Vandenberg did, to no avail. Yet there were rare occasions when he found consensus among the party's dominant figures. In June 1930, Hoover sought ratification of the London Naval Treaty, which proposed to fix a ratio of warships among the fleets of Great Britain, Japan, France, Italy, and the United States. He feared that the Senate might adjourn for the summer without a vote on it. Vandenberg told Hoover the treaty could be ratified if the right senator—Borah—led the fight. Hoover doubted this could be done but asked Vandenberg to find out. "I saw Borah at noon," Vandenberg wrote in his diary. "He promptly stated that he felt the treaty should be ratified before the Senate quits for the summer; and said he would take command if asked." At 6 p.m. Vandenberg was back at the White House to report his success. Hoover was much relieved.[23]

Vandenberg proved adroit in knowing when to let Borah take the lead and when to do the work himself. Supporters hoped the naval treaty would slow the most expensive arms race of the era. Vandenberg argued not only that the fixed ratio of battleships and heavy cruisers worked in favor of the United States, but also, more significantly, "that progress for the theory of arms limitation by international agreement spells safe and rational progress in the stabilization of peace." He warned that failure of the London Conference would loose "an atmosphere of international suspicion and unrest."

Such a treaty, free of interlocking overseas commitments, struck Vandenberg as sound foreign policy. It was "cooperation without entanglement"—a way to work for peace without running afoul of the Founding Fathers.[24]

When the Senate approved the treaty, Vandenberg took a share of the credit. If the Young Turks as a group made little headway, their leader was becoming a noteworthy solo operator.

Neither Arthur nor Hazel ignored the social responsibilities that came with his rising status. Hazel "poured" at congressional teas, dined with Amelia Earhart, and interviewed novelist Mary Roberts Rinehart. The rest of the family was busy as well. Nineteen-year-old Barbara made her debut in the Florentine Room of the Wardman Park four weeks after the stock market crash. One year later, she announced her engagement to wealthy playboy Johnny Knight of Kalamazoo, on probation after his arrest in a liquor raid at his cottage in northern Michigan. They were married in Washington in February 1931 with only Arthur and Hazel present. Within a year, a first grandson was born.[25]

The big issues of the day demanded Vandenberg's attention, but he also savored smaller accomplishments. In 1933 sheets of parchment discovered in the files of the secretary of the Senate included an 1835 letter from President Andrew Jackson notifying Michigan legislators that their territory had met the qualifications for statehood, as well as the 1836 Senate bill granting statehood, and the credentials presented by the state's first two senators. Vandenberg won approval to transfer the papers to Michigan—the first time any state gained possession of its enabling documents.

Vandenberg had always been an ardent traveler. Now such exposure informed his work on the Foreign Relations Committee. In the spring of 1930 he and Hazel sailed to the Philippines. Because he was a member of the Territorial and Insular Affairs Committee, it was an official visit, but he could afford—and chose—to travel at his own expense, a rarity among senators that reflected his scrupulous commitment to government thrift.

They stopped in Hawaii to see nephew Hoyt Vandenberg, an Army Air Force captain commanding the Eighteenth Pursuit Group at Wheeler Field. The dapper aviator, tall, tan, with gleaming blue-gray eyes, was almost a second son to the senator. He was a Wisconsin native who moved in with the Vandenbergs as a teenager to win nomination to West Point from William Alden Smith. A decade later he was known as one of the best fliers in the fledgling army air corps. He strapped a leather helmet on Uncle Arthur, and soon they were lumbering down the runway in a biplane for a scenic flight over Diamond Head and Pearl Harbor. (In another highlight of his Hawaiian stopover, the senator could be seen for a millisecond emerging from his hotel, as an extra in the Charlie Chan movie *The Black Camel*.)[26]

After stops in Tokyo and Shanghai, Arthur and Hazel sailed on to Manila, capital of the Philippines. There, Vandenberg called for a timetable for granting the U.S. colony independence. In this white-suited world the senator was the visiting panjandrum, dispensing the wisdom of Washington.

The most contentious foreign policy issue since the League of Nations was the question of participation in the World Court. Vandenberg was slow to endorse American adherence—"We always owe more to the peace of America than to the peace of the world," he told a Hearst reporter—but like Hoover, he did support it, with reservations. At the other end of the spectrum were isolationist irreconcilables such as Borah and Hiram Johnson, who occupied senior seats on the Foreign Relations Committee. When the treaty came up for consideration, Johnson said, "I have only one idea on the court. That is to smash the hell out of it whenever it appears."[27]

Hoover needed Vandenberg's help, and Vandenberg was eager to give it, even as he, too, proposed some limiting protocols. In November 1930, Vandenberg asked Hoover to delay a treaty vote until 1931 so that he could marshal support. With the president's verbal assurance, he persuaded pro-court groups to hold off and informed the press that no action would be taken in the short December session. He thought the delay was assured when he left Washington for the Thanksgiving recess. Then, with no warning, Hoover changed course. "I READ IN THE PAPERS," Vandenberg fumed, that the president planned to send the court treaty to the Senate in December. "My first news was from the papers. My only notification is from the papers. The President's decision is his own business."

But he plainly felt it was his business too. Hadn't Hoover needed him? "I am one of the members of the Foreign Relations Committee upon whom he must particularly depend in matters of this nature," he wrote. "It's not particularly good 'team ball' not to let members of the 'team' know in advance when the game is to be played under different rules." His ego was bruised. "One less personally attached to the president . . . might resent such an episode," he said. "I wonder if this explains why many others are 'less attached.'" He saw little hope for passage of the treaty in the short session, "which means another needless 'black eye' for both the court and the president."[28] Vandenberg began to share in the widespread disillusion with the president he had tried so hard to help.

Reconvening in December, Congress confronted a growing economic crisis. Senators returned to the capital with the anguish of stricken constituents much on their minds. And there followed what Vandenberg in his diary labeled "another needless war" between the executive and the legislature. This time the issue was drought relief in the South. In exchange for Hoover's support, Senator Joe Robinson of Arkansas, the Democratic leader, had pledged to cooperate with the administration on other matters. When Robinson proposed a $60 million loan—for "food and feed for destitute farmers"—Hoover responded with $45 million. "He won the skirmish," Vandenberg wrote, "but he lost Robinson's cooperation and precipitated a far more serious war."

The drought precipitated a dust bowl in America's heartland. For the first time, Congress debated the wisdom of federal funds for disaster relief. Hoover was leery of government handouts—he had pieced together mostly private help in 1927, when, as secretary of commerce, he took charge of Mississippi River flood relief. In what was becoming his accustomed role, Vandenberg offered a compromise. He proposed a $25 million loan to the American Red Cross—though only when that agency's resources were exhausted. Watson, the Republican leader, quickly agreed, and Robinson said he would go along if Hoover would. Watson phoned the White House, laid out the situation for Hoover, and put Vandenberg on the line. This compromise sacrificed none of the president's principles, Vandenberg argued. But Hoover refused. "It must be his ideas or none," Vandenberg wrote in his diary. "Thus he rides for a needless fall. Thus ends, for the time being, another fruitless attempt at 'cooperation' with a non-cooperator."[29]

With the slide into depression, the president and Congress floundered. Weary, bitter, Hoover could do nothing right; his turn to activism was too little too late. Public men deserved respect, he told the junior senator from Michigan one night after a White House dinner. When Vandenberg departed, he gave Borah a ride home. Hoover was not the only despondent politician. Earlier in the day, the Lion of Idaho had captivated the Senate gallery with a speech on the plight of American farmers. Now he slumped in his seat. If he could live his life over, Borah sighed, he would practice law. "In public life a man spends his years beating out his energies against a . . . wall." He can rebound, "but only with a scar."[30]

For Hoover there was no rebound. He and so many Republicans soon had little choice but private life. As a member of the GOP senatorial campaign committee in 1930, Vandenberg spoke across the country, glossing over the growing depression. Voters were not impressed. Republicans lost forty-eight seats in the House and eight in the Senate. This left slender majorities in both, until a handful of special elections shifted control of the House to Democrats for the first time in a generation. Hoover vetoed eleven bills in the last session of Congress—a Congress still run by Republicans. Emotions in the GOP cloakroom were as bitter as those across the aisle.

In 1932, Michigan Republicans walked a tightrope between progressive and stand-pat factions. It was enough to turn a young senator's hair—what was left of it—gray, and that would be a shame, *Collier's* observed, because "the junior senator . . . looks so much like a future president that one would regret to see carking care upon his handsome brow." To preserve his own prospects, perhaps Vandenberg would move a little to the left—"cousin up to Couzens." But how, *Collier's* wondered, "move to the left and toward the White House at the same time?"[31]

Indeed, Vandenberg's efforts at compromise blurred his image. On

Prohibition repeal, he had fudged the issue and hoped it would go away. A reporter for the *New York World* noted that Vandenberg had been an ally of the president in tariff battles, but that "he has done nothing else of particular distinction. He does look well in evening clothes. He has a nice repartee with ladies. As a senator, no one in Washington would think of ranking him with the top-notchers." Drew Pearson was equally blunt: Vandenberg was the "blatant and ambitious would-be leader of first-term Republican mediocrities."

Vandenberg had arrived with great advance billing: the young editor who helped Lodge defeat the League of Nations, Warren Harding's speechwriter. But there was also the sense that he was all dressed up and not quite sure where to go—"a minor-league publisher," sniffed Westbrook Pegler, "up on his feet, swishing his coattails, and shooting his cuffs." He had a marketer's instinct for the clever phrase and was credited with popularizing "fiddle-faddle." When he said that Democrats had "hitch-hiked" on a Republican bill, the press found the verb noteworthy. Reporters loved his criticism of an opposing senator for being as "consistent as a chameleon on plaid." He was developing a style, said the *Tulsa Tribune*, "which should be pleasing to all those who can see nothing in any political statement except words." But his ideas, the commentator added, were also not so bad, nor was his growing reputation as a master of compromise—the flip side of the vacillator.[32]

Whatever he was, he was not a populist. He despised the Bryanites and agrarians; gold was his standard, not silver. But he had also lost patience with the partisan narrowness of the Hoover administration. As the depression deepened, the president's desperate jawboning sounded more like whistling in the wind. Although Vandenberg himself, late in 1931, called the economic collapse "temporary and transient," his words were as hollow as Hoover's. He helped coin the party's wishful slogan for the 1932 campaign: "Prosperity is returning—don't throw it in reverse."[33]

Hoover was carrying "the heaviest load of any president since Lincoln," Vandenberg said, facing "a vicious conspiracy of circumstances—the crash, world depression, the worst drought in history."

But Hoover's prospects only grew dimmer. In the summer of 1932, unemployed veterans of the Great War converged on Washington to press for long-deferred bonuses. Congressman Wright Patman proposed a $2.4 billion appropriation to accommodate them. Thousands of ragged men, many with wives and children, gathered at Anacostia Flats on the south bank of the Potomac, "billeted in old and abandoned buildings, billeted in self-improvised camps," as Vandenberg wrote in his diary, "usually creating their own shelter out of stuff from junk piles." The House passed Patman's bill. In the Senate, populists and panderers took up the veterans' cry as the old soldiers crowded the streets.

Opponents argued that the government could not afford such a vast obligation, nor should it favor even this constituency when millions of Americans faced dire straits. "It was all but heart-breaking—because these were soldiers of the Republic who believed (however erroneously) that the government owed them," Vandenberg wrote. They were "pathetically clad, some with the highest medals on their ragged shirts——yet all of them behaving splendidly (with very few exceptions) and (despite a particularly bad week of cold rain) uncomplaining about subsistence in veritable mud-holes."

The bill came before the Senate on the morning of June 17. Squads of vets were deployed to buttonhole their senators, who ran a gauntlet in the crowded corridors of the Senate office building. Unable to reach his office, Vandenberg went directly to the Senate chamber. At 9 a.m. he peeked through the cloakroom door. The galleries were filled with veterans, who waited with a quiet that seemed ominous. The marchers planned a mass meeting on the Capitol steps. Capitol police called the White House. Vice President Charles Curtis called out the Marines.

Protest leaders called for calm. "But pent up feelings repeatedly broke loose when some speaker urged that the men should 'stay in Washington until we get the bonus,'" Vandenberg wrote. The debate took all day. Populist Democrats played to the galleries with fiery speeches. Chants and cheers from outside filtered into the chamber. Vandenberg thought of the Continental Congress in Philadelphia, once similarly besieged. "I thought a 'good many things' before the day was done," he added. "I thought, among other things, that no job on earth is worth this mental torture; I thought how easy it is for smug editorial writers to set [*sic*] in their swivel chairs and 'tell' the Senate what to do."

By evening, ten thousand veterans had gathered outside the Capitol. Police raised a Potomac River drawbridge to turn back many more. By nightfall the crowd had doubled anyway. The tension was terrific, Vandenberg wrote: "It seemed inconceivable that so great a throng of desperate men could be trusted with the news of the Senate's inevitable rejection of their Bill."

Vandenberg saw no way to relieve the distress of veterans by direct payment. The spending would only fan inflation in a world already witnessing the tragedy of "printing press" money. (The senator carried in his wallet a million-mark note from the Weimar Republic.) And a mob was a mob, no matter how well behaved. The Senate would not surrender to intimidation. To do so, Vandenberg wrote, "would be the beginning of the end in orderly legislation and Washington would be a permanent armed camp."

The bill was defeated, 62–20. "I was never prouder of the Senate," Vandenberg reflected. "But I never did a harder job. And I never felt sorrier for anybody than for those rejected Vets. . . . Their commander told them the news. A bugle sounded. En masse they sang 'America.' And in orderly fashion, they swang away—tattered, disheartened—to return to their mud billets."[34]

In July, after Congress adjourned, General Douglas MacArthur led cavalry and tanks onto the Anacostia campground. They moved through the tents and makeshift shelters with a callousness that provided a bitter coda to the heartbreak of the Hoover years.

Some days it surely seemed as if everything were melting into air. In October 1932 came the death of Vandenberg's mentor, William Alden Smith. "For a quarter century our lives have been linked together," he wrote. "I have lost my greatest friend and my greatest inspiration." He was no longer a Young Turk, and he was soon to be without a friend in the White House.[35]

On Election Day, as expected, voters rejected Hoover in favor of the ebullient governor of New York, Franklin D. Roosevelt. The winner spoke of facing a national emergency with a confidence Americans hungered for. That reassuring voice struck a deft note of empathy in stark contrast to the tin-eared rhetoric of the incumbent. A big change was coming. Was this also a referendum on the politics with which Vandenberg had been most at home? He was ready to suspend his partisan predilections—a task made easier by FDR's landslide. What choice, after all, did he have?

· · · · · · · · · · · ·

SUCH A
PERILOUS HOUR

· · · · · · · · · · · ·

On the eve of a grim Christmas recess in 1932, a Michigan fruit grower appeared in Vandenberg's office. Fire had destroyed Adolph Belter's farmhouse. He stood before the senator clutching two charred rolls of unrecognizable paper money from the Mason jar to which he had entrusted his life savings. Vandenberg studied the sad little bundles. There wasn't much hope. But he put on coat and hat and led Belter to the currency redemption bureau of the Treasury Department. To Vandenberg's surprise, the experts there succeeded in identifying each of the fragments. Farmer Belter was issued a check—a rare happy ending in the waning days of the Hoover administration.[1]

On the afternoon of February 9, 1933, less than four weeks before Franklin Roosevelt's inauguration, a page rushed to Vandenberg's desk on the Senate floor. Two bankers from Detroit's Guardian Trust and its twenty-one-bank holding company, Guardian Union Group, were waiting outside the cloakroom. They also represented Wolverine Mortgage, a newly formed holding company to which Guardian had transferred nearly $90 million in hopes of securing a loan of $65 million from the federal Reconstruction Finance Corporation. By law, however, the RFC needed more collateral from Guardian before it could make the loan.

The bankers described their plight: without the loan, Guardian would run out of money to cover its normal deposit activity. Its largest deposits, from Henry Ford and his auto company, as well as the savings of thousands of smaller depositors, were endangered. Bad loans, real estate deals collateralized by properties of rapidly declining value, and big withdrawals by affiliated banks had left the bank insolvent. Henry Ford felt that he had done his part, investing more than $16 million; his son, Edsel, was on the board.

Although wilting collateral and mounting withdrawals plagued banks everywhere, Guardian was the largest institution in jeopardy. But this was perhaps no surprise: Detroit's banks epitomized the shaky financial structures of the day, having been among the most aggressive in forming holding companies—webs of banks—so that the failure of one could mean the failure of all.[2]

When word of the crisis reached the White House, Hoover summoned Michigan's senators. For two hours, the starch-necked Hoover, brusque Couzens, and somber Vandenberg mulled their choices with Treasury Secretary Ogden Mills. "Sucking our thumbs," said Couzens, who was afraid the RFC would approve the loan without adequate collateral. He vowed he would "shout against it from the rooftops." (He had become rich as Ford's partner in the motorcar company but had fallen out with the automaker.)[3]

Hoover and Mills wanted to piece together enough capital from Ford and other Detroiters to cover the shortfall in Guardian collateral. The president had pledges from General Motors chairman Alfred P. Sloan and rival magnate Walter Chrysler. He asked Couzens, one of Michigan's wealthiest men, to deposit $2 million. Couzens refused.

Hoover pressed the senior senator. "If 800,000 small depositors in my home town could be saved by lending three per cent of my fortune even if I lost it," he said, "I certainly would do it." But Couzens was in no mood for a lecture about civic duty. No, he told the president, this was Ford's bank. Let him come up with the money.

Vandenberg was horrified. A Detroit bank collapse could spark a national calamity. On February 12 Hoover's undersecretary of the Treasury, Arthur Ballantine, and secretary of commerce, a Detroiter named Roy Chapin whose appointment Vandenberg had helped secure, called on Ford at his Dearborn estate. Edsel Ford had earlier agreed to subordinate nearly half of the $16 million in Ford Motor deposits to the needs of other depositors. Just a little more help from his father would be enough.

The auto pioneer kept the president's envoys waiting for an hour. Then he again said no. Moreover, he threatened to withdraw his deposits altogether. And if Guardian failed to return his money, he vowed to send representatives to every Detroit bank to "draw my personal balances and the balances of the Ford Company from them without any further notice." Ford's deposits were large enough to bring down the other major Detroit holding company as well. Ballantine and Chapin warned of widespread bank failures. "Let them fail," Ford replied. "Let everybody fail."[4]

Treasury officials informed Vandenberg and Couzens of Ford's intransigence. Finally, Couzens agreed to curb his own choler long enough to ask Ford for help. He offered to come up with half the $20 million collateral if Ford would provide the other half. Still Ford balked.

Just after midnight on Tuesday, February 14, after an all-night meeting between federal and state officials at the Detroit Club, Governor William Comstock walked around the corner to the *Detroit Free Press* to announce that he would sign a proclamation calling for an eight-day bank "holiday." No Michigan bank would open that morning. (Vandenberg placed an early call to a friend at the Old Kent Bank in Grand Rapids. His hometown bankers had, he wrote later, "no inkling of the crisis.")[5]

That morning, Detroit was in shock. The only cash in town was in the till or in someone's pocket. The dean at City College cashed faculty checks for five dollars or less until the money ran out. Business was paralyzed. To Father Charles Coughlin, the populist radio priest broadcasting from the Shrine of the Little Flower in suburban Royal Oak, the money changers had torn down the temples.

For Vandenberg, the first task was to get the banks open—fast. He told Hoover he needed a congressional resolution authorizing emergency powers for the comptroller of the currency. Hoover was still angry with Couzens; Vandenberg tried to play peacemaker, allowing Couzens exclusive sponsorship of the resolution. But this proposal had to overcome the opposition of Senate Banking Committee chairman Carter Glass, who feared "national hysteria." Governor Comstock told Vandenberg that the federal government "won't save us and yet they won't let us save ourselves."[6]

In Detroit, Secretary of Commerce Chapin was alarmed by the paralysis. "I foresee by the first of the week the possibility of very serious disorders," he warned Vandenberg and Couzens. If the banks failed, he said, "we shall have a riotous Detroit and a prostrate Michigan facing us." Couzens demanded that RFC emergency funds be sent to Detroit banks immediately to "avert a threatened climax in disorder."

As Couzens issued his ultimatum, Vandenberg—who had scarcely slept for days—joined Mills, Ballantine, and the RFC board for an emergency session. The RFC approved a stopgap loan allowing depositors to withdraw up to 30 percent of their funds. The measure hinged upon Ford providing $11 million in new capital; this, in turn, would give the auto magnate control of both Detroit bank groups. And to this, at last, Ford agreed. By Monday, a *Free Press* headline boomed: "Banks Open Wednesday under Control of Fords." Washington gave a sigh of relief, as did Detroit's depositors. In Dearborn, a parade followed banners urging residents to "Bank with Hank."[7]

Then, new troubles set in. New York's Hanover Bank, as wary of Ford as he was of Wall Street, employed a technicality to cancel its $20 million loan to the reorganized Detroit banks. Outstate bankers opposed the deal because a state law requiring them to deposit at least half their reserves in other Michigan banks meant a substantial portion of their assets remained frozen in the Detroit institutions. The state supreme court ruled it illegal for those banks to receive preference over other depositors. Finally, when the cautious RFC reduced the amount of its proposed loan, Ford informed Couzens he was backing out. Under pressure to broker a solution, Couzens departed for Detroit with a plan of action that Vandenberg had hastily composed, calling for uniform standards for all Michigan banks.

As Franklin Roosevelt was sworn in on March 4, Washington was consumed with more widespread woes. On March 5, taking a page from Governor Comstock's book, the new president declared a national bank holiday. The legality of this action was open to question, and banks in many states were already closed, but Vandenberg had witnessed enough pettiness and vacillation to welcome FDR's bold stroke. Roosevelt "has asked for dictatorial powers," he wrote to a Detroit banker the next day. "I think we need a 'dictator' in this particular situation."[8]

Vandenberg's bias for action made him sound a lot like the incoming president. Calling for "bold experimentation—bold without being foolish—novel without being insane," the senator said, "we must end hoarding, release currency, relax and multiply credit, stabilize trade, facilitate new business, build morale, and break the vicious circle." These sentiments were echoed days later when Roosevelt was wheeled up to White House microphones for his first fireside chat. "When people find they can get their money, the phantom of fear will soon be laid to rest," he told Americans huddled by their radio sets. "I can assure you it is safer to keep your money in a reopened bank than under the mattress."[9] But Americans had every reason to be wary of FDR's soothing words. In the previous two years, five thousand banks had been declared insolvent.

The Detroit crisis convinced Vandenberg of the need for a fundamental change in the nation's banking structure: in particular, for the provision of federal insurance on savings deposits. He had tried this before. As recently as December 1932 he had proposed a "Time Deposit Insurance Fund" to protect small depositors. Hoover and Mills had rebuffed him. The governor of the Boston Federal Reserve declared that healthy banks would not buy insurance because they would see it as a subsidy for weak banks. The bill died in committee. On the eve of the Detroit crisis, in the face of Federal Reserve hostility, Hoover still shied away from even the mildest deposit protection. But the new upheaval reinforced Vandenberg's conviction: Only some form of insurance would restore confidence in the banks.[10]

He hoped a new administration would be more sympathetic, yet Roosevelt immediately rejected deposit insurance as "quite impossible." He warned of a dangerous drain on the Treasury and an invitation to lax bank management. He had seen states try and fail to protect deposits. What irony that at the very outset of the New Deal, the Republican Vandenberg ran into stiff resistance from the Democrat Roosevelt as he fought for what proved to be perhaps the most effective reform of the era.

The senator saw a glimmer of hope when Roosevelt appointed Jesse Jones as the new chairman of the RFC. Jones had favored bank insurance since the days of William Jennings Bryan. Another Texan, vice president–elect John Nance Garner, convinced Congressman Henry Steagall to add deposit insurance to his 1932 banking bill. Garner even lobbied Roosevelt at the Mayflower Hotel shortly before their inauguration. Hoover was finally coming around, Garner told Roosevelt. If FDR agreed, he could have a bill by the time he took the oath of office.

"It won't work, Jack," Roosevelt said. "The weak banks will pull down the strong." Garner, not for the last time, challenged his future president. "They are about all down now, anyway, the weak and the strong," he replied. "You will have to come to a deposit guarantee eventually, Cap'n."[11]

On March 10, two days after Roosevelt repeated his opposition at a press briefing, Vandenberg attached a bank-deposit guarantee provision to the proposed Banking Act of 1933. To finance the insurance, participating banks would contribute annually a sum equal to 1 percent of their deposits. Roosevelt and new Treasury secretary William Woodin dismissed Vandenberg's plan.

But Jesse Jones, who had just returned from Detroit, met with Vandenberg. "We are going to get you some new banks," Jones told him. Then he added a caveat: "I am not certain what they are going to do about getting depositors, unless you give the man who wants to open an account some assurance that he will get his money back." Vandenberg was ready. He sent Jones a copy of his bill. "Give us some legislation like that," the RFC chairman told him, "and the people will put their money in the banks instead of stuffing it in their socks."[12]

Although Congressman Steagall pushed for a similar version of deposit insurance, Carter Glass of Virginia, the seventy-seven-year-old chairman of the Senate Banking Committee and father of the Federal Reserve system, favored a liquidating corporation to pay off depositors. Glass wanted only Federal Reserve member banks or qualified applicants for membership to participate in the insurance plan. Steagall favored certified state banks as well. The two chairmen conferred and moved toward a compromise. The Senate had not yet acted on the Glass bill when the House approved Steagall's version. Roosevelt told his cabinet that he hoped both would be defeated—and that he was especially troubled by inclusion of a deposit guarantee.

But public sentiment and congressional opinion were on Vandenberg's side. He wrote an amendment to the Glass bill that incorporated Jesse Jones's suggestion for insurance of all deposits up to $2,500, effective July 1. Participating banks would pay assessments well above the estimated first-year loss before the Treasury Department would contribute more than its initial grant of $10 million. Vandenberg placed the temporary program under the authority of the Federal Reserve Board until a Federal Deposit Insurance Corporation could be established. His proposal provided immediate coverage for deposits in all banks: nearly fourteen thousand in total, unlike the Glass version, which was limited chiefly to the five thousand national banks belonging to the Federal Reserve System.[13]

Because the Senate was sitting as a court for the impeachment of a federal judge, Vandenberg had to postpone the introduction of his amendment. Vice President Garner was presiding late on the afternoon of May 19 when he climbed down from the rostrum and approached Vandenberg's desk. Garner's customary greeting for the ambitious junior senator was "Hello, Dynamite," but today the ruddy-faced, bushy-browed vice president had urgent business.

"Arthur, how fast can you get on your feet?" Garner asked.

"As quick as any man in the Senate, I think."

"You'll have to do a damn sight better than that," Garner whispered. "Where's that deposit-insurance amendment of yours?"

"It's never been out of my pocket."

Garner said he would suspend the court and gavel the Senate into session, recognizing Carter Glass to bring up the banking act legislation. "I want you to be on your feet and get your amendment out of your pocket," he told Vandenberg. "And I think we will get it in the bill."

Minutes later, with the Glass bill on the floor, Garner came to Vandenberg again. "Next to me," the vice president said of Carter Glass, "he is the most cantankerous man in the world; but he is in good humor now, and I don't think he will fight your amendment too hard." At that, Vandenberg leapt to his feet.[14] The amendment was attached to the bill, but could it pass? In the House, Steagall feared that covering deposits in all banks immediately was impossible. Yet Vandenberg refused to back down, arguing that his amendment would not only restore confidence in the banking system but also stimulate the economy, as hoarding ended and deposits returned. Seldom had he fought for a more popular cause. On May 25 Glass announced that the Senate finance and banking subcommittee would accept Vandenberg's amendment. The bill passed the next day by voice vote.

Roosevelt continued to oppose all deposit insurance proposals, but especially Vandenberg's, with its broad and immediate coverage. In a White House meeting with Steagall, Glass, and Treasury officials on June 1, the president pounded his desk as he vowed to veto the bill with Vandenberg's amendment. In a subsequent note to the conference committee, he said he saw no modification that he could accept: "the Vandenberg amendment must be rejected as proposed *in toto*."[15]

The source of his unwavering hostility remains unclear. He brought to the White House a Wall Street bias toward traditional banking practices. But Vandenberg nursed partisan suspicions, later given more credence by Roosevelt adviser Rexford Tugwell, that FDR resented the idea because it was not his own. Indeed, the president's opposition was uncharacteristic. After all, as the *Detroit Free Press* observed, the amendment favored Roosevelt's "Forgotten Man"—the average citizen—and "nobody has advanced any tangible argument against it."[16]

Confidence in the banks could not return without addressing the plight of the small depositor, who gauged the strength of the system by the fate of his savings. It was that plight that Vandenberg understood. With Glass and Huey Long, whose Louisiana banks had been closed before Michigan's, he lobbied colleagues. Still the White House refused to yield. Eastern bankers called on to their Michigan counterparts to get Vandenberg to back off. Vandenberg warned colleagues that if they dropped his amendment from the banking bill he would simply add it to the National Recovery Act legislation, the next big

New Deal proposal. He was not going away, and neither was the need for deposit insurance. He challenged the president to veto the bill, confident that both houses would vote to override.

It went, finally, as Garner predicted. On June 13 Roosevelt saw the popular will reflected in the Congress and reluctantly agreed to a modified version of the Vandenberg amendment, providing that insurance coverage would begin in January 1934, rather than July 1933. Vandenberg accepted the compromise, hoping only that the president might exercise his prerogative and put the guarantee in place before the end of the year after all. "This bill has more lives than a cat," a reluctant Roosevelt sighed. But he signed it into law on June 16, 1933.[17]

This was the breathtaking season of the first hundred days, when lawmakers approved one bold bill after another. The deposit guarantee, described by a prominent Democrat as "the most important legislation to be enacted by the present Congress," was the only major initiative not on the president's program. Within a month of its creation, the Federal Deposit Insurance Corporation extended insurance to more than 98 percent of the nation's depositors in more than thirteen thousand banks. Hoarding dropped sharply; deposits soared.

Before the year was out, Franklin Roosevelt performed an adroit about-face. He lauded the FDIC for managing a "gigantic task which the pessimists said could not possibly be done." When, early in 1935, Congress took up banking reform once again, Roosevelt told Glass, "I am only interested in two things." One was a better system of bank examination. The other was "to get the Federal Deposit Insurance Bill through."[18]

Success bred revisionism. Raymond Moley, a member of FDR's original "brains trust," later observed that Roosevelt, "despite his last-ditch opposition, in later years claimed credit for the legislation." Once Roosevelt became a convert, Vandenberg found himself forever reminding others of his role. When FDIC chairman Leo Crowley lauded Vandenberg as the "father of the FDIC," the administration pressured him to retract his remark. J. F. T. O'Connor, Roosevelt's comptroller of the currency, told Vandenberg, "You have rendered a great service to the country in connection with the Banking Act." Yet O'Connor helped write a 1936 radio address for Steagall denying Roosevelt's opposition and omitting Vandenberg's role in the bill's passage.[19]

While the New Dealers wounded his pride, Vandenberg allowed that the president was entitled to credit, once the bill passed, for his "vigorous and sympathetic" administration of the law. Vandenberg would make his name in foreign policy, but founding the FDIC was his most significant feat of domestic legislation. His safeguard for savings has been in place ever since.[20]

Over the course of a dozen years, the relationship between the Republican senator and the Democratic president passed from uneasy cooperation to fierce antagonism and back again. The first stage was occupied with domestic affairs and the early days of the New Deal, with which Vandenberg was not unsympathetic. The second phase saw Vandenberg's hardening opposition to the later New Deal and his emergence as a bitter foe of Roosevelt's foreign policy on the eve of a second world war. The third phase was dominated by the realization on both sides that the postwar world would require new ways of thinking and acting.

This Washington three-step began with the hundred days. Once past the frustrations of the deposit insurance debate, the first year of the new administration reflected a fair degree of the bipartisan cooperation Vandenberg cherished. Vandenberg supported FDR's Emergency Banking Act, of course, and he approved of austerity measures. He was the lone Republican to support the Economy Act of 1933 as Roosevelt called for "repairs to a capitalistic society" through a balanced budget and a willingness to adhere to the prevailing orthodoxy.[21]

"Too often in recent memory, liberal governments have been wrecked on the rocks of loose fiscal policy," Roosevelt declared— and Vandenberg cheered. The senator voted for reduced government spending and advocated tax increases. He declined to accept his full Senate salary until other government employees saw their pay restored. (He also subscribed to Will Rogers's acerbic suggestion that Congress cut its pay in half, "since it formerly had to vote either 'yes' or 'no,' whereas now it has only to vote 'yes.' ")[22]

Roosevelt aimed that first year to restore faith in the established order. As a member of the minority, Vandenberg was reacting to administration initiatives. He voted for the Truth in Securities Act and the Securities Exchange Act, bills to reduce the danger of stock market speculation. He was a champion of the Civilian Conservation Corps, which suited his impulse to employ people in public works. Its reforestation program would help heal the scars of Michigan's cutover timberlands.

Vandenberg stayed with Roosevelt when the president tried at first to preserve the gold standard. He voted against free silver and currency inflation. When FDR's Gold Reserve Act allowed for a degree of inflation, Vandenberg backed that, too. While conservatives accused the president of debasing the dollar, Vandenberg reckoned the measure a moderate attempt to resist the pressure for greater inflation.

"We must deal with things as they are and not as we might wish them to be," he wrote, early in 1934. He was a pragmatist who saw in the president's bill an effort to stabilize the monetary system. "If he were not permitted to proceed in this fashion with the sanction of Congress," Vandenberg noted, "he would be driven squarely into the arms of the *real* inflationists."[23]

Vandenberg's reactions to other New Deal measures were mixed. He backed emergency relief but balked at "semi-socialistic" experiments—such as allowing the secretary of agriculture to restrict farm production under the Agricultural Adjustment Act of 1933. And Roosevelt's far-reaching National Industrial Recovery Act, or NIRA, with its byzantine system of voluntary regulation, was harder to swallow. Giving sweeping powers to code-making agencies did not square with Vandenberg's interpretation of the Constitution. He was one of thirty-nine senators who voted against the final version of the bill in June 1933.

His opposition during the early New Deal generally turned on constitutional questions. Congress, with its power to tax, should be

responsible for setting tariff rates, he argued. He had never been a proponent of free trade. Allowing cheaper imports to depress prices on
American products appeared to conflict with administration efforts
to raise prices through the NIRA and the Agricultural Adjustment Act.
Roosevelt seemed like-minded, finally, in placing quotas on imports.[24]

Vandenberg approached labor questions with an open mind. Still
stirring were the progressive impulses reflected in his response to a
furniture strike in Grand Rapids in 1911, a pamphlet called "The Right
of Industrial Petition." He maintained ties with labor leaders even as
he tended to side with employers. He was anxious about the union-
ization of autoworkers, and he supported an amendment that would
have nullified the automatic right to collective bargaining guaranteed
in the NIRA.

Parochial interests also made Vandenberg an early critic of first
lady Eleanor Roosevelt. She proposed to improve living conditions
in Appalachia by developing a planned community in West Virginia
known as Arthurdale. Among the cottage industries contemplated,
there was furniture, and, while the scale was small, Vandenberg saw
this as government-sponsored competition for the most important
employers in his hometown. He detected a whiff of collectivism as
well. "Social responsibility and socialism," he said, "are entirely different things."

Despite his intermittent support for Roosevelt's programs, Vandenberg was on the outside looking in. His access to the White House van-
ished. This confidant of the previous president became just another
junior member of an endangered minority. Washington, he said, is "a
queer place for a Republican today."[25]

Outnumbered Republicans fell to fighting among themselves. Vandenberg led the campaign in the Senate to prevent the Sanitary District of Chicago from diverting more Lake Michigan water into the
Chicago River. This meant enduring editorial harangues from Robert
McCormick's *Chicago Tribune*. He also drew McCormick's wrath by
promoting construction of the St. Lawrence Seaway, a clear boon to
Michigan interests but opposed by the railroads and Huey Long, be-

cause it would compete for shipping with the Mississippi River and the Port of New Orleans. McCormick's Illinois senators were opposed not only because Chicago was a rail hub but also because McCormick was an Anglophobe who thought that relying on Canadian—and therefore British—cooperation on the seaway was an "abject surrender of sovereignty." A *Tribune* cartoon pictured Vandenberg as a toady of John Bull.[26]

Where Vandenberg and McCormick did agree was in their opposition to diplomatic recognition of the Soviet Union. Vandenberg was one of only two senators opposed to sending an ambassador to Moscow. (He did, however, as a member of the Foreign Relations Committee, escort Hazel to the lavish reception thrown by the Soviets to open their new embassy. The Vandenbergs were amazed at the mounds of caviar, the fiery vodka—"a bewildering elegance so incongruous with Russia," Hazel wrote.)[27]

The senator found himself on the defensive with Republicans who faulted his support for much of the early New Deal. He was no partisan martyr: "Dead heroes can be of little assistance in holding the line." But he was increasingly disturbed by what he saw as anti-business bias in FDR's administration. (Distaste for the self-interested behavior of the stereotypical businessman was "a badge of ardent New Dealers of all ages," Alger Hiss said later, suggesting a snobbery that offended Vandenberg, who instinctively identified with the nation's much-maligned Babbitts.) And he was not optimistic about the future. "It is going to be just one damn 'hot spot' after another as Franklin bats up his further legislation," Vandenberg noted in his diary, "because there's a lot of it I simply cannot swallow."[28]

At the White House correspondents' Gridiron Club dinner late in 1933, Vandenberg, the GOP spokesman, exhibited his mix of respect for government institutions and dismay over the people running them. "I rise with trepidation," he began, "in the presence of these new conquerors who first possessed the capital last March and who continue, with feverish pay-roll activity, to garrison it with their ever-multiplying legions." He glanced down the dais at the president, warming to his subject as he swept that stray forelock back across his balding scalp. "But I rise with supreme respect for our guest of honor—the chosen leader of our people . . . the captain-general of America's war on the depression . . . a man of gallant heartfulness and high adventure—the courageous, colorful and entirely too persuasive President of the United States."

Poor Thomas Jefferson, Vandenberg continued. "The great decentralizationist," foe to oligarchs, bureaucrats, and overlords, was today's "Forgotten Man"—a poke at FDR's campaign theme. Even Vandenberg's hero, Hamilton, "would be a rather anemic Federalist . . . in this day of new bureaucracy when our destinies are concentrated in a dozen alphabetical commissars which sound like the call letters of a radio chain." An excellent test of "post-prohibition sobriety," he added, "would be to quiz a suspect on the NRS, the REF, the AAA, the FCA, the CCC, the FCT, the TVA, the PWA, the CWA, the FERA, the HOLC, the FDIC—not to mention the embattled Ph.Ds."

Vandenberg was wary of this frenzy in the name of economic recovery. "We deflate, unflate, reflate and inflate. We flate, and counterflate. We close banks and open saloons. . . . Once we had just one 'noble experiment' [in democratic government]. Now we have a litter." He acknowledged, at the dawn of the welfare state, that "rugged individualism never can mean what it once did with its piratical 'laissez faire.'" But the United States had been built on a vision of cooperation, not regimentation.

Then the president rose to speak, bracing himself against the podium. Washington was flooded with alphabet soup, he acknowledged with a smile, but there were two ways of taking your soup: "One is the noiseless way, dipping softly with a spoon and conveying it gently to the lips. The other . . . is accompanied by gurgling and dribbling and other loud noises of the mouth." Unlike some Republicans, he concluded, the vast majority of Americans were using good manners. Vandenberg laughed politely.[29]

The Republican Party was in shambles. Vandenberg saw three choices for his GOP. It could continue to identify with Hoover's reactionary policies—though there lay the road to oblivion. It could follow its progressive wing into liberalism as thoroughgoing as that of the administration itself—but that was to deny the party's traditional and philosophical conservatism. The senator, not surprisingly, favored a middle way, which he offered at the Lincoln Day banquet in Grand Rapids in February 1934, invoking that day's icon: "Lincoln Liberalism."

Occupying the "middle ground where sanity and vision thrive," Vandenberg told his audience, meant that "as patriots, long before we are partisans, we owe all possible support to Franklin D. Roosevelt." It meant distinguishing between "constructive vigilance and cheap obstruction." The role of the loyal opposition was to moderate the excesses of more radical New Dealers, to guard the Constitution, and to offer solutions. "We owe the American people a wider and fairer distribution of prosperity when it is reclaimed," he declared. "We owe the American people protection against their exploiters. We owe labor and agriculture the square deal, and the full economic partnership which originated in the philosophy of an earlier Roosevelt"—Theodore, who by then served as a wistful reminder of an era when Republicans were the party of action, and of progress.[30]

Vandenberg was anxious about his chances in 1934. Roy Chapin, back in Detroit as an auto executive, organized an informal committee to plan the senator's campaign. The incumbent won renomination without opposition, but the general election would be a different story. From the auto industry to outstate farmers, Michigan had been sorely afflicted by the depression.

Vandenberg worried that his opponent might be the charismatic Frank Murphy, governor-general of the Philippines and former mayor of Detroit. Polling pioneer Emil Hurja argued that the popular Murphy was the only Democrat who could beat the Republican senator—a matter of national significance to party leaders who feared Vandenberg more than any other Republican challenger to Roosevelt in 1936. A Washington correspondents' poll named him the GOP's best presidential prospect—as well as the "most ambitious" senator. This was the year to derail him.[31]

Vandenberg was afraid of a pro-Roosevelt landslide. The relentless anti-Roosevelt rhetoric within his own party, as when the chairman of the Republican National Committee accused Congress of rubber-stamping the plans of a dictator, would not play well in Michigan. And a gubernatorial primary battle between former Governor Groesbeck and Secretary of State Frank Fitzgerald had split the state GOP. Already, more than a few wealthy Republicans had closed their depression-depleted wallets to a party with such bleak prospects. Vandenberg did have the influential support of Father Coughlin, but others were less enthusiastic. Veterans remembered his vote against the bonus. Opponents of Prohibition recalled his lack of enthusiasm for repeal. Labor leaders lined up with the Democrats. Farm groups never warmed to him. Couzens, having become a New Deal enthusiast, refused to endorse his colleague.

Vandenberg's own selective cooperation with the New Deal seemed to leave him neither fish nor fowl. One pol's moderation was another's opportunism. Vandenberg had learned, one columnist noted, "to pussy-foot aggressively." As a Hoover aide wrote of another senator fighting for his political life, "I had a thousand times rather see him go down fighting and true to his beliefs than doing a Vandenberg." A reporter at the 1934 Gridiron dinner spoofed Vandenberg as a baseball player in a uniform half black and half white, who said, "You got to play with both sides out in my state this year."[32]

Still, he was a formidable candidate. By virtue of his initial short-term appointment, he enjoyed seniority normally accruing to a two-term senator. He could boast of two big accomplishments: the FDIC and the census fight that brought Michigan four new congressional seats. He had successfully fought the closing of the Army Air Force's Selfridge Field near Detroit, sponsored the creation of Isle Royale National Park in Lake Superior, and pushed plans for a bridge across the Straits of Mackinac. He had won approval of the St. Lawrence Seaway treaty. And if he had few zealous followers, he had avoided making too many enemies.

"He is much stronger than is generally supposed," a friend warned Frank Murphy. "He has a large amount of a favorable kind of publicity that impresses a great army of voters who do not know the inside, and whose political opinions are unconsciously absorbed from newspapers." In other words, Vandenberg's fellow publishers spread the helpful impression that he was effective.[33] Certainly he had become better known. When a schoolboy was asked to name Michigan's state bird, he replied, "the Vandenbird."[34]

Then came a big break. Murphy decided to stay in Manila. Democrats nominated Frank Picard, chairman of the state's Liquor Control Commission. He was a colorful character from vote-rich Detroit who benefited, Vandenberg charged, from "a brazen alliance of politics and liquor,"[35] but he was no Murphy, and little known outstate. Picard assailed Vandenberg for riding "two horses in different directions." "Vacillate with Vandenberg," read one Picard slogan—"Fifty-fifty, hot and cold Artie," another. On the national level, Democratic Party chairman James Farley tried to turn the election into a choice between Roosevelt and "Hoover-Vandenberg old guard Republicanism." But Michigan voters knew Vandenberg as a Young Turk, a prod to Hoover, and, of course, a selective supporter (he said "constructive critic") of Roosevelt's programs.

Embarking on what he described as "the most strenuous speaking campaign I have ever negotiated"—quite a statement coming from the Jackie Band bond salesman—he addressed seventeen audiences in one day in Detroit. By November he had delivered his stump speech, poking that index finger aloft as his crisp phrases jabbed the air, in fifty-three Michigan cities. Where the relief rolls were high, however, he may have done himself no favor campaigning in a shiny new Packard.[36]

Borah declared with the credibility of a progressive Republican that a Vandenberg loss would be "incalculable." Most newspapers in Michigan and elsewhere agreed. "Mr. Vandenberg is one of the best-informed, most studious, conscientious and high-minded members of the Senate," said the *New York Times*. "There will be Democratic fledglings enough . . . without the absence of this old bird" (who had just turned fifty).[37]

Vandenberg waited in the *Herald* office on election night as returns rattled across the Associated Press wire. "I did not think there was a ghost of a chance," he recalled later. At midnight, in fact, as he trailed Picard in the early returns from Detroit—and then lost his home precinct—he thought of conceding defeat. By sunrise, however, Picard's lead was slipping. When all returns were tallied the following afternoon, Vandenberg had squeaked through by a margin of little more than fifty-two thousand votes—51.3 percent of those cast, down dramatically from the 71.8 percent he had seen in 1928.[38]

He was lucky it was not a presidential year, with Roosevelt on the ballot. He was lucky, too, that Murphy stayed in Manila. (Murphy would coast to victory in the race for governor two years later.) But Vandenberg had also been smart: his shrewd moderation gave voters too few reasons to vote against him.

Yet across the country, the GOP was reeling. Vandenberg was the only Republican senator returned by an industrial state. The Old Guard was finished. Reed went down in Pennsylvania, Fess in Ohio, Robinson in Indiana. Roscoe Patterson of Missouri was beaten by Democrat Harry S Truman. From the Alleghenies to the Rockies, only two Republicans won gubernatorial races: Fitzgerald in Michigan—whose popularity buoyed Vandenberg—and, in Kansas, Alfred M. Landon.[39]

Democrats gained seats in both House and Senate. In the House they outnumbered Republicans three to one. In the Senate their majority grew by ten, to sixty-nine versus twenty-five—the widest margin for any party in the history of the republic. Only seven states retained Republican governors. Pundits wondered whether the party had a future.

Vandenberg returned to a very different Washington, amid a depression that despite all the New Deal bustle seemed almost intractable. From Father Coughlin's broadcasts to Dr. Townsend's clubs to redistribute income came a clamor for more radical solutions. In Louisiana, Huey Long's regime offered programs only a dictator might prescribe. And for those who looked beyond American shores, the world was becoming a menacing place. Real dictators—Hitler in Germany, Mussolini in Italy, the ruling clique in Japan—grew more bellicose. They threatened new conflict even as Vandenberg struggled to understand what had gone wrong twenty years before—who was to blame for the Great War that had bankrupted Europe and sown the seeds of the Great Depression.

CHAPTER 8

INSULATION

For a politician raised in a big Republican tent, 1934 was an awkward year, to say the least. The world of Grand Rapids, of Michigan, of the United States, in which a striver's road to greatness ran through the Republican Party, had disappeared. The statesman of the age was Franklin Roosevelt. Vandenberg could support New Deal legislation that appeared useful or irresistible, and try to block what he opposed, but to move ahead he had to make better sense of the world. What had gone wrong that had led to the present moment?

Woodrow Wilson had painted American involvement in the Great War as a crusade. Vandenberg joined its nonpartisan legions. In war's aftermath came depression, the rise of dictators, a new belligerence abroad. Vandenberg came to believe that his elevated sense of American exceptionalism had been violated. After Versailles, Wilson's cause looked far less noble. Lodge had been right to fight American entanglement in the League of Nations.

In 1930 Vandenberg had been appointed by President Hoover to the War Policies Commission, created to review the roles of government and business in wartime. The commission's modest recommendation to give government greater authority over munitions sales and put mild limits on profits went nowhere in Congress. But Vandenberg would not let matters rest. Every year after that, he proposed legislation to impose an excess-profits tax in time of war. He still nurtured a suspicion of the role bankers and munitions makers had played in plunging America into the war. After all, the great Hamilton had counseled against private speculation in matters of defense.

In 1933 the Senate's Pecora investigation into the causes of the 1929 stock market crash revealed low behavior in high finance. Public interest in such malfeasance was piqued, and easily transferred from bankers to arms makers. A prominent article in *Fortune* described how the munitions industry had profited from the Great War. So did a much-heralded book, *Merchants of Death*. The cause was taken up by the *Nation* and the *New Republic*. The American Legion resented the profiteering associated with munitions contracts. Conspiracy theorists began to swarm. Eastern bankers had been among the most ardent interventionists—they had loans to protect.[1]

Pressure for a Senate investigation had been gathering steam since 1932, and Senator Gerald Nye of North Dakota became the cause's torchbearer. Nye was every inch a man of the people, a lean, chain-smoking plainsman—yet in many ways a perfect match for Vandenberg, who was none of those things. Nye had helped uncover the GOP's Teapot Dome scandal and had opposed the World Court. He had never been east of Chicago before his arrival in Washington in 1925. Sensitive about his provincialism, he deemed both sides of the Atlantic suspect.

When Nye's proposal early in 1934 to investigate the arms industry was referred to an unsympathetic Military Affairs Committee, Dorothy Detzer of the Women's International League for Peace and Freedom urged him to collaborate with Vandenberg, who had support from the decidedly not pacifist American Legion. In March 1934 the two senators submitted a combined resolution, S. Res. 206, to investigate the munitions industry and to review the findings of the War Policies Commission. Nye wanted a 98 percent tax on all incomes greater than $10,000 during wartime. Vandenberg wanted a permanent committee to study what would later be called the military-industrial complex. They submitted the requests as amendments to a hotly debated tax bill. Finance chairman Pat Harrison was furious as Nye lined up support and Vandenberg talked on and on, rising from his desk, taking his big, black-rimmed spectacles on and off for dramatic emphasis. Finally, Harrison asked the Senate to interrupt the debate for a vote on S. Res. 206. Nye asked for unanimous consent. He and Vandenberg leaned forward, tense as runners in the starting blocks. The press gallery stood and waited. The gavel fell—no objection.[2]

After years in which he had found himself first retreating from the League of Nations, then questioning the World Court, Vandenberg assumed leadership of an effort to affix blame for American involvement in the Great War—and to prevent a recurrence. His approach combined the "no-entangling-alliances" nationalism of Hamilton with the moral sense of America as exceptional, a "city on a hill." How, he demanded, "can we bankrupt the God of War?"[3]

Where Nye was the more reflexive isolationist, Vandenberg was the intellectual backbone of the new committee. Together they recruited members of both parties. The name of a chief investigator came from Dorothy Detzer. When she presented herself in Vandenberg's office, he greeted her with a smile. "What kind of hell are you proposing to raise with me today," he asked her.

"You malign me, Senator," she replied, also smiling. "I've come to make one of my usual constructive suggestions."

"You needn't send us any wild-eyed radicals," he warned.

"Certainly not, not with you on the committee, Senator," came the reply.[4]

Thirty-eight-year-old lawyer Stephen Raushenbush—a lanky, self-effacing academic, son of a noted theologian, witness to the slaughter on the Western Front—became chief investigator. His staff included a young attorney on loan from the Agriculture Department: Alger Hiss, who, though an ardent New Dealer, was impressed by Vandenberg's "forthrightness and intellectual vigor."

At first Vandenberg insisted that the subject of American neutrality was beyond the scope of the investigation. Fiscal questions were paramount. Had an international arms lobby sabotaged disarmament conferences? Why were European nations, in arrears on their war debts, spending so much on their military? Roosevelt cautioned the senators, in a letter drafted by the State Department, that the issue was international, that it was impossible "effectively to control such evil by the isolated action of any one country."[5]

The panel convened in September 1934 in the high-ceilinged Senate Caucus Room. Anticipation ran high. Records were subpoenaed from munitions makers and arms dealers. Vandenberg helped lead the questioning of some fifty executives, including the four Du Pont brothers and legendary financier Bernard Baruch. This was front-page news: along with the arms industry, the seamier side of American diplomacy came under scrutiny. Vandenberg and Nye were subsequently attacked for suggesting that the House of Morgan may have influenced Wilson's policies. Carter Glass, his raspy voice quavering, denounced their "shocking assault." "Oh, the miserable demagogy," he cried, challenging their "mendacious suggestion" that Wilson could be bought.

Secretary of State Cordell Hull met with Vandenberg and his colleagues, then issued a statement reassuring friendly governments that the Senate meant no offense after the committee probed bribes from American firms to Latin American politicians. When foreign indignation grew, so did speculation that the administration was pressuring the senators to soften their criticism. Hull and Roosevelt asked the senators to refrain from examining wartime correspondence between foreign governments and American financiers. Nye told the press they had only scratched the surface.

For all the publicity attending these revelations, it was Vandenberg's aim of limiting war profits and perhaps even nationalizing the arms industry that most alarmed Roosevelt. It was hard to refute the senator's clever mantra that if young men were to be conscripted, so too capital. He wanted patriotism expressed in the sacrifice of treasure as well as blood. He explored the profits of shipbuilders and compared the cost of purchasing gunpowder and ammunition from private firms with that of government production. When Vandenberg heard arguments favoring an efficient government arsenal, Alger Hiss noted the senator's lack of bias in admitting that the finding was contrary to his expectation. When critics questioned the radical ties of Raushenbush, Vandenberg rose to his defense.[6] *Time* declared Vandenberg the "best of the senatorial inquisitors." Rimless spectacles had replaced the thick black frames. As one reporter noted, "his quizzical glance, his trick of shrouding the lower half of his face with his hand and his extreme patience in questioning witnesses often creates the feeling of an extraordinarily kindly professor."[7]

Witnesses testified to the pernicious influence of the arms industry on foreign policy: how loans to Allied governments may have added to pressure for American involvement in the war. Roosevelt, afraid the committee's findings would raise pressure for neutrality legislation that could constrain his conduct of foreign affairs, soon conjured his own watered-down version of the bill he expected from the Nye Committee. Transparent as it was, the maneuver pleased those in finance and industry who feared the Nye-Vandenberg "inquisition."[8]

At the same time, the committee was in need of additional funding to continue its work. The public was in no mood to see it disband. Thousands of letters and wires poured into the offices of Vandenberg, Nye, and the committee's other senators. One reporter suggested a Nye-Vandenberg ticket in 1936. In the event, funding was extended. Subsequent hearings exposed the bonuses paid to executives of firms profiting from wartime sales—$2 million to the president of Bethlehem Shipbuilding, for example. Committee adviser John T. Flynn proposed to "conscript" through taxation all individual income greater than $10,000 per year during wartime.

Yet Roosevelt was not the committee's only opponent. Flynn's proposed "conscription of capital" even troubled some union leaders, who feared conscription of labor would follow. Others charged that revelations of capitalist greed played into the hands of communist propagandists. "I am about as far from being a communist or a socialist as any man in the world," Vandenberg declared. "But I refuse to subscribe to the absurd philosophy that I immediately become one if I happen to hit a war system that has crucified this world for a thousand years."[9]

The committee's work seemed increasingly urgent as world events took on a darker cast. Adolf Hitler had decreed universal military service in Germany and would soon have a standing army of more than half a million men. Benito Mussolini was preparing to attack Ethiopia. No one knew whether the League of Nations could respond to these threats. The president surprised Vandenberg and his colleagues by suggesting they bring the issue of American neutrality within their purview. Vandenberg readily agreed.[10]

On April 1, 1935, the committee's 2,000-page report endorsed Flynn's recommendations. Bernard Baruch blasted the proposals, arguing that "business wouldn't do its share of the fighting . . . when profits were so restricted." Vandenberg was indignant at the implication that his ideas might undermine free enterprise. He was "everlastingly opposed to the collectivist state," he declared, but "God help capitalism if it won't defend a common national crisis without its pound of flesh."[11]

A week later, on the anniversary of American entry into the world war, fifty thousand veterans staged a "march for peace" through the streets of Washington. College students across the country declared a one-hour "strike against war" and demanded the abolition of campus reserve-officer training programs. In a flurry of pacifist oratory, the House of Representatives passed the administration's mild bill. When that bill reached the Senate, Nye and his colleagues introduced amendments transforming it into Flynn-type legislation. But Roosevelt pushed the House bill, which doomed the Nye-Vandenberg proposal. Nor did Congress approve legislation Vandenberg proposed to prevent collusive bargaining and profiteering in shipbuilding.

In late April the committee called its final witnesses. Nearly twenty years after the Great War, with public interest waning, the hearings that began with a bang concluded with a whimper.

Or did they? Events abroad meant that Roosevelt's impulsive request for neutrality legislation was coming home to roost. Here was a subject Vandenberg and his frustrated colleagues could fix on that had immediate relevance. Americans were anxious to immunize themselves from foreign wars. Bills were introduced prohibiting loans to belligerent nations and requiring the president to embargo arms shipments to warring states. Vandenberg argued that the lack of a neutrality law before the Great War made American involvement inevitable. The United States need not take sides in a conflict in which it was not engaged.

This was not what Roosevelt bargained for. The arms embargo would go into effect automatically if the president declared a state of war. The only chink in the neutrality armor the administration could get was a House amendment placing an expiration date of February 1936 on the embargo. With that proviso, the measure passed both houses of Congress overwhelmingly. Roosevelt signed the bill at the end of August 1935, applauding its intent and lamenting its inflexibility.

Vandenberg's experience on the committee reinforced his notion that American involvement in the world war had been a mistake. Although business greed had been the target of initial investigations, committee members increasingly shifted their concern to the role of government. The senator had begun the hearings by declaring that neutrality questions were beyond their scope, yet thanks to Roosevelt himself, he came to conclude that the United States might have avoided war with Germany if Wilson had maintained neutrality. The hearings had bolstered those who were predisposed to have America steer clear of "foreign entanglements."

When Italy invaded Ethiopia in October 1935, Vandenberg wrote Hull in the hope that "we may be able to maintain our complete and effective detachment." He had just returned from England. Despite fears of Hitler and anger with Mussolini, neither the Chamberlain government nor the man in the street had any stomach for conflict, he said. The League of Nations was confirmed in its fecklessness when pleas for help from Ethiopian emperor Haile Selassie drew only a tepid response.[12]

In a speech to the Michigan Press Club in November, Vandenberg noted that since his return, "two nervous questions" had been asked: Will there be war in Europe? If there is, can we stay out? On the first he refused to speculate. But the second? Yes, he wrote, "we can and will stay out if we have sense and courage enough to maintain a real neutrality and protect it, on the one hand, against international emotionalism and, on the other hand, against the appetites which love commerce in spite of casualties." The latter concern had inspired his work on the Nye Committee. The former loomed ever larger, and pushed the senator further into isolation between the passage of the temporary act and the reconvening of Congress in January 1936.[13]

Vandenberg countenanced American intervention only if the

national interest dictated. Preparedness now meant something far different than in 1917. Security would be best served by complete "insulation" against any involvement in European hostilities. No longer should the United States even cooperate with the impotent League of Nations. No longer should the United States insist upon a neutral's right to freedom of the seas or make loans to belligerent states. The president should have no discretion to even inadvertently bring the nation closer to war.

Rigid neutrality "may deny us an expression of natural sympathies in a given dispute," Vandenberg admitted, "but it substantially insulates us against the dreadful consequences which otherwise could embroil us in alien wars. The loss of incidental commerce is infinitely less important than a maintenance of American peace."[14]

In February 1936, the committee formally adjourned. With the first neutrality law expiring, Vandenberg endorsed a bill so strict that even Borah and Hiram Johnson were taken aback. These legendary isolationists still believed in America's right as a neutral to trade with belligerents, and resisted any encroachment upon the country's freedom of the seas. Vandenberg abandoned that brand of nationalism and demanded a ban on the export of *any* goods to any nation at war.[15] The administration offered a bill that gave the president discretion in applying a trade embargo. As a compromise, Vandenberg joined in approving an extension until May 1937 of the temporary act that added a ban on loans and credits to belligerents and reduced the president's leeway in determining when a state of war existed.

By spring of 1936, Mussolini's conquest of Ethiopia was nearly complete. An uneasy calm settled over Europe. Japan consolidated its occupation of Manchuria. In this election year, the issues of the Nye Committee had come to seem rather abstract. The public had its neutrality bill. The committee's work came to a close with just a whiff of failure for leaving loose ends.

But Vandenberg found his own views clarified. He assumed that a future war would present the nation with the same dilemma as the last one. And he therefore signed on to—indeed, became a leader of—the isolationist cause. When he talked of the nation minding its own business, radio journalist H. V. Kaltenborn asked him point-blank, "Does that make you an isolationist?" Drawing on his concordance to the Bible, Vandenberg quoted Timothy: " 'If any provide not for his own, and especially for those of his own house he hath denied the faith and is worse than an infidel.' If that makes Timothy an isolationist, so am I."[16]

· · · · · · · · · · · ·

IT CAN'T
HAPPEN HERE

· · · · · · · · · · · ·

A *Washington Post* profile once listed Vandenberg's chief amusement as "watching Long perform." He was referring to Huey Long, the Louisiana senator with the garish neckties and gun-toting bodyguards. Long offered a spectacle the sacred chamber had never seen before. He was, said Vandenberg, "the most amazing character I have ever known. . . . He had an interest for the common welfare which he pursued to dangerously radical extremes." Tourists clamored for seats when the "Kingfish" took the floor. This dictator-in-waiting was cunning in his guise as an eloquent buffoon, strong on Holy Scripture.[1]

When the senators sparred in debate, reporters scurried to their Bibles. Long wound up a peroration against the St. Lawrence Seaway treaty with a quote from Ezekiel chiding those "which have eyes to see and see not; they have ears to hear and they hear not." Vandenberg leapt to his feet to declare that Long's observations reminded him "of nothing quite so much as the language in the thirteenth verse of the tenth chapter of Ecclesiastes, and I will leave it there." Someone in the gallery found the passage: "The beginning of the words of his mouth is foolishness; and the end of his talk is mischievous madness." In that debate, madness prevailed, with the seaway treaty falling twelve votes short of ratification. (How many senators caught the gist of Vandenberg's riposte is unclear, but bracketed after it in the *Congressional Record* is the word *laughter*. Long was mum.)[2]

In the first days of 1935, Franklin Roosevelt was looking over his left shoulder, apprehensive about a convergence of demagogic voices tapping into growing disillusionment with the two major parties. At the forefront of this challenge were the dimple-chinned Long and the fiery radio priest from Royal Oak, Michigan, Father Coughlin. Their overlapping followers threatened to weaken Roosevelt in the 1936 election and perhaps even form a third party. That was the message one Republican activist had for former Michigan governor Fred Green early in 1935. He mentioned not only Long and Coughlin, but La Follette in Wisconsin, radical young Minnesota governor Floyd Olson, the pugnacious mayor of New York Fiorello La Guardia, and the eminent Borah himself. This nexus of opponents on the Left might create an opportunity for a Republican to challenge Roosevelt, the activist suggested: "They're talking Vandenberg—nobody ever heard of him until you sent him to Washington."

Indeed, Vandenberg was increasingly spoken of as a dark-horse candidate for 1936. Long's cheeky comment that he preferred Borah generated a *New York Post* cartoon showing him pushing aside Vandenberg and other worthies to drag the elderly senator toward the GOP nomination. But Long would soon announce his own intention to challenge Franklin Roosevelt in 1936.

FDR also came under assault on his right flank. The Supreme Court rejected a key provision of the National Industrial Recovery Act, casting into doubt the constitutionality of its myriad regulations. This set the stage for further rulings, culminating in "Black Monday," May 27, 1935, when the National Industrial Recovery Act itself was unanimously declared unconstitutional, invalidating the National Recovery Administration. An audacious Roosevelt had sought to regulate the economy, from wages to production, to inoculate nearly every industry from the vagaries of a laissez-faire marketplace. It was the boldest intrusion ever by government into private enterprise.

To Vandenberg, the Court's ruling signaled a "welcome repose" from the tyranny of a planned economy. To Roosevelt, basking in his 1934 mandate, it was the reactionary response of nine old men and a threat to other New Deal legislation. "All the smart people [Vandenberg among them] think that what we should do is compromise and temporize with the situation," the president declared, "but I am inclined to fight."[3]

In June 1935 FDR summoned congressional leaders to the White House. They were greeted not with that wide smile that even Republicans had come to expect, but with a grim, desk-thumping president who insisted Congress stay in session until he got action. This was the beginning of Roosevelt's Second New Deal, his "turn to the left." He wanted social security, a labor bill proposed by Senator Wagner, a new banking bill, a holding company bill—and finally a tax bill, derided by the GOP as a scheme to "soak the rich."

The Social Security Act introduced government old-age pensions. The Wagner bill, which Roosevelt had not favored at first, became the National Labor Relations Act, which guaranteed the right of workers to organize and to bargain collectively. The Utilities Holding Company Act was designed to break up networks of power companies. The tax bill targeted wealthy Americans, who represented what Long and Coughlin supporters claimed was a nefarious concentration of wealth. Congressional Democrats, enjoying strong majorities, obeyed their marching orders. The Second New Deal was on its way.

Vandenberg drew a line between the first and second New Deals, between reform measures that a "Lincoln liberal" could support and a federal government reaching for too much power. Legislation that merited months of study was rushed to the floor amid high heat and higher tempers. From spending to labor policy to bureaucratic expansion, Roosevelt was proposing a vast increase in federal authority. Toss in contempt for the constitutional guardians on the Supreme Court, and a world in which authoritarian regimes were consolidating their power, and the climate was ripe for cries of dictatorship. A line had been crossed.

Vandenberg moved from tentative support of parts of the president's agenda to full-throated opposition. He led the fight against the most ambitious of FDR's second New Deal programs, the Works Progress Administration. The WPA, a relief agency with a $5 billion budget, employed millions of Americans on projects large and small. To Vandenberg it was a pork barrel "pot luck" on a vast scale, "a blank check for the biggest sum of money ever appropriated in a single transaction." After he charged that the WPA favored allies of the president, director Harry Hopkins was forced to promise publicly to root out political bias in his agency.

Leading Democrats lined up to blast their Republican colleague. Black, Byrnes, Wagner—each took a turn. "When the old GOP elephant again gets to its feet it will find Senator Vandenberg astride its back," predicted influential Kansas editor William Allen White.[4] "He is capable of the quick strategic shifts generally deemed necessary to political survival," the *New York Times* observed, and was, "roughly speaking," liberal. He represented a middle state, industrial and agricultural, poised between east and west, right and left. Michigan may have been home to Father Coughlin, but in most respects it was fertile soil for a man of the middle. Vandenberg was as conventional as he was conservative.[5]

As a counterproposal to the WPA, he suggested allocating funds to states on the basis of their unemployment levels, hoping to keep the central government smaller while trusting the states to innovate—and to spend more wisely. The Second New Deal conceded too many legislative prerogatives to "alphabetical commissars who deeply believe the American people need to be regimented by powerful overlords in order to be saved," Vandenberg warned. Federal subsidies would leave states' rights and individual initiative "beguiled or bludgeoned into coma."[6]

He delayed the relief bill, but there was no stopping it. Roosevelt was in control. "The big boss is sending in so much revolutionary legislation and it is being pressed for such early consideration that no one dares be absent," he wrote. He found a label for this flood of proposals: the "New Ordeal."[7]

Vandenberg did support the Social Security Act, and the Banking Act of 1935, which included his cherished FDIC. Otherwise, he stood with a coalition of Republicans and Southern Democrats opposed to this more radical Roosevelt. They were most roused by the Revenue Act of 1935, which, along with adding stiff inheritance taxes and a steeply graduated levy of up to 75 percent on the highest incomes, increased taxes on corporate incomes over $50,000 and imposed an excess-profits tax. This, Vandenberg declared, was an appeal to "mass prejudice" which made no economic sense. It would fail to raise enough revenue to balance the budget while discouraging private enterprise and recovery. Vandenberg had always supported inheritance taxes—until this bill. Roosevelt was reaching for more revenue—and more power—than any president before him.

Under the proposed bill, the enormous Ford Motor Company, Michigan's largest employer, could not survive as a family company upon Henry Ford's death, given the burden of its estate tax. Edsel Ford dispatched his attorney to confer with Vandenberg. Vandenberg contended that Henry Ford had long "preferred creation of a vast and effective instrumentality of employment and commerce rather than disbursement of personal dividends." The tax would force the company "into the hands of Wall Street." Vandenberg refused to jeopardize Ford's "continuity as an employment reservoir." The bill passed the House, but the Senate coalition managed to remove the estate tax provision—enabling Ford to maintain its status for another generation.[8]

The Wagner Act went too far for Vandenberg's mild progressivism on labor issues. He was afraid that its proposed National Labor Relations Board would function not as a balance between employer and employee but as a defense of labor against "unfair labor practices." It allowed a closed shop and imposed no restraints upon coercion by union organizers. He conceded that in the past "industrial employment was a one-way street, on which workers were to be exploited at the discretion of the employer." But this was the other extreme, "with labor holding the whip." Unions that grew too powerful were no more deserving of government protection than monopolies or trusts. Vandenberg was one of only eight Republicans opposing the bill. He backed every amendment—adding some of his own—that tried to cripple it, all to no avail.[9]

Sometimes it was the smaller fights that soured him the most. Immediately after convening in January 1936, Congress approved a big bonus bill for veterans that Roosevelt had vetoed as wasteful the year before. Roosevelt vetoed the bill again, but, in what Vandenberg declared a "pre-arranged pantomime," tacitly agreed to the veto's override. Vandenberg, one of only nineteen senators voting to sustain the veto, spoke with contempt of reelection-obsessed colleagues who supported paying an additional $1.5 billion "out of an empty treasury." As for GOP senators who had voted with the majority, Vandenberg reflected, how could they pillory the president for reckless spending when they were party to the extravagance? "This is the most depressing day I have spent in public service in eight years," he wrote in his diary. "It marks the first great surrender of the Congress to minority group pressure. If this surrender becomes a habit, the days of the Republic are doomed." Not for the last time, Vandenberg found himself contemplating the future in apocalyptic terms.[10]

Hazel Vandenberg was her husband's boon companion and partner in Washington society. She may also have been conscious of the allure his increasing stature gave him in the eyes of other women. She may have been painfully conscious, as well, of how much the distinguished senator enjoyed the flattery and attention.

On December 31, 1934, New Year's Eve, Hazel suffered a searing pain in her abdomen. The senator called A. B. Smith, who caught the next train from Grand Rapids. He performed an emergency appendectomy the next day. Smith also looked after his best friend, prescribing digitalis to stimulate an irregular heartbeat and lending a sympathetic ear. Vandenberg's older daughter, Barbara, and grandson Johnny Knight were staying in Washington after the breakup of a four-year marriage. Arthur Junior was a puzzle to his parents. He was nearly thirty, his father's trusted aide and confidant, playing the eligible bachelor even as he concentrated more of his energy on the meticulous renovation of a tiny house in Georgetown.[11]

Despite his evident vanity, Vandenberg did precious little to look after himself—although he may have been the only senator who carried a pedometer. He walked two miles toward work along Connecticut Avenue—never was the term *constitutional* more happily applied—after which he would, at precisely the same corner, hail a cab for the final mile to Capitol Hill. (Sometimes he walked home as well. Most memorable for him was the summer night when Hazel was back in Michigan and his route took him through a rougher neighborhood. He was accosted, he wrote his wife, "by a big buck" who "stuck something in my tummy that *felt* like a gun." Told to put up his hands, he recounted, "I could see that he was just as scared as I was." Vandenberg started to raise his arms, then said, "Listen, pal, you've overlooked something—a cop just came around the corner behind you and you'd better beat it." And "he did beat it, faster than anyone I ever saw run," the senator continued. "But I'm not telling this around Washington. The police would get excited. So would the newspapers."[12]) Nor was his diet conducive to good health. He went days without a complete meal and then favored potatoes and pie. He smoked cigars constantly.[13]

Invitations to gatherings at the Wardman apartment were coveted. In the wake of the Republicans' 1934 election debacle, talk of dissension in the Democratic ranks was a welcome topic of cocktail conversation. H. G. Wells came to dinner in the spring of 1935. In a voice so low his companions in the green and gold living room strained to hear, he described a series on the New Deal he was writing for *Collier's*. Hazel noticed "a quiet humor and a twinkle in his eyes that have not been dimmed by his almost seventy years."[14]

Hazel had mastered the pitiless protocol of a Senate wife. On New Year's Day she served eggnog at her annual brunch. She complained of the "keyed-up-ness" of the social pace and welcomed the Senate's spring recess. Summer meant a sojourn by Lake Michigan. The senator was back and forth to Michigan more often, claiming he was the best customer of Pennsylvania Air Line flights between Washington and Grand Rapids.[15]

When Congress recessed in that sweltering summer of 1935, the Vandenbergs repaired again to the beachfront estate of George Getz, former treasurer of the Republican National Committee. The Chicago coal tycoon's Lakewood Farm featured a zoo along with several guest cottages. While Vandenberg was in residence, Frank Knox came up from Chicago, fueling press speculation about Vandenberg's presidential prospects. Vandenberg dismissed talk of his candidacy. "The idea doesn't even bring an extra pulse-beat," he said. But in Grand Rapids, a reporter began to assemble clippings for a campaign biography.[16]

That September, the Vandenbergs embarked on a voyage to England. It was a private trip, but with Long and others raising fears for democracy at home, and Hitler and Mussolini growing more bellicose, a lengthening shadow of menace accompanied them. Vandenberg said he had no official business across the Atlantic. "I just want to refuel for the 1936 marathon," he told reporters.

Would he meet with foreign leaders? Hitler was rumored.

"I have definitely not planned any interviews," he insisted.

"In spite of previous reports to the contrary?"

"In spite of erroneous reports." He smiled.

He was, he said, "minding my own business and I hope America will do the same."[17]

They were greeted in London by the daughter of Scripps-Howard newspaper executive Milton McRae. They visited 10 Downing Street— "modest and small," Hazel reported. The American ambassador hosted a lavish luncheon in their honor. They saw the Magna Carta at the British Museum. In Oxford the senator found the grave of a maternal ancestor. In Hyde Park they heard, in Hazel's words, "all kinds of wild speeches." They visited H. G. Wells and also Gertrude Atherton, the author whose fictionalized life of Hamilton was Vandenberg's idea of the great American novel. At the Cheshire Cheese, the senator made himself comfortable in the seat once occupied by Dr. Johnson. At Lord Beaverbrook's townhouse, he struck up a friendship with the press lord while lamenting that only in the international edition of the *Herald-Tribune* could he find World Series scores.[18]

As the SS *Aquitania* departed Southampton for the return to New York, the Vandenbergs received an invitation to cocktails from a fellow passenger, Sinclair Lewis. Hazel, more than her husband, was curious to meet the Nobel Prize winner, who expressed his admiration for the senator. Vandenberg thought he knew Lewis well enough. From *Main Street* to *Elmer Gantry*, with the boorish George Babbitt in the middle,

Lewis offered a caustic view of the America that Vandenberg held dear. But Lewis had since married the flamboyant journalist Dorothy Thompson, a good friend of Hazel.

Thompson had interviewed Hitler and Mussolini, then sailed back to New York with her exclusive stories, so Lewis was alone when the Vandenbergs met him in the ship's lounge. "S. L. *tight,*" Hazel wrote. But the surprise was that the two nearly exact contemporaries, the ponderous senator and the acerbic novelist, found much in common. Each was in his way a sentimentalist about their Midwestern world. Each looked at the unfolding drama of European politics with a jaundiced eye and fear for American involvement.[19]

Lewis had delivered his latest manuscript to his publisher earlier in the summer. Written in a white heat early in 1935, at a time when throngs of the discontented hung on every word of Coughlin's talks and cheered Long's plan to "share the wealth," *It Can't Happen Here* envisions an America that wakes up with a dictatorship after a demagogic Democrat wins the presidency in 1936. ("What was the New Deal but pure Fascism?" one character asks.) Lewis's novel opens with a list of presidential prospects who had not been elected in 1936, including Franklin Roosevelt, Herbert Hoover, and "Senator Vandenberg."[20] Rather, voters chose a folksy New Englander, "Buzz" Windrip, who invokes, echoing Long, patriotic principles to justify a fascist regime. His fictional Republican opponent is a Midwestern senator who becomes the unlikely hero of a popular revolt. Walt Trowbridge, "loyal, yet strangely honest . . . a man with a touch of Lincoln in him," appears to be one part George Norris, the Nebraska progressive, and two parts Arthur Vandenberg, the "Lincoln liberal," Thompson recalled.

The "bulky, placidly defiant" senator, thought also by Arthur Schlesinger Jr. to be modeled on Vandenberg, conducts a confident campaign against the Democrat Windrip, who courts the poor and disaffected with populist bromides. Trowbridge, writes Lewis, "did not moan over the Forgotten Man (he'd been one himself, as a youngster, and didn't think it was so bad)! Speaking on the radio and in a few great halls, he explained that he did advocate an enormously improved distribution of wealth, but that it must be achieved by steady

digging and not by dynamite that would destroy more than it exca-
vated."

Vandenberg also could identify with the novel's protagonist, small-
town editor Doremus Jessup, a cynic with a big heart. Jessup pounds
out editorials that challenge the utopian visions of central planners.
"Is it just possible," he muses, "that the most vigorous and boldest
idealists have been the worst enemies of human progress instead of
its greatest creators?" Such opinions have become subversive in the
Lewis story, but that doesn't stop the editor from "furiously rattling an
aged typewriter, typing with his two forefingers"—as Vandenberg did.
"Scorned by all the noisier prophets for refusing to be a willing cat for
the busy monkeys of either side," Jessup is arrested by the new regime.
He finds himself in good company. Lewis lists prominent reporters
who have been imprisoned, names of real people, some of them
friends of Vandenberg. (The droll exception: "Few writers for Hearst
were arrested.") Hope comes from the heartland, where Trowbridge
leads a rebellion that breaks out in Michigan. The novel ends with Jessup on the run, dreaming of a Trowbridge triumph.

But aboard the *Aquitania*, Vandenberg may not have known that
his name appeared on the first page. Although it was soon to be a best-
seller, *It Can't Happen Here* was just arriving in American bookstores
as martinis were shaken in the first-class lounge. Over several days the
Vandenbergs, with Lewis, screenwriter Gene Markey, and a boxer—
perhaps George Godfrey, "Negro," noted Hazel—had "just a hilarious
happy time in spite of the rough weather." When they reached New
York after midnight on October 15, daughter Betsy was there to meet
them, as well as Dorothy Thompson and the actress Joan Bennett,
Markey's wife. "Much excitement," wrote Hazel. Lewis was rather less
articulate, so drunk he had to be hospitalized. The Vandenbergs departed for Michigan with Arthur telling reporters that he was not a
candidate for "anything on earth."[21]

Nor would Huey Long be a candidate. In early September he had
returned to Baton Rouge predicting that a third party would soon
emerge. On the night of September 7, 1935, his handpicked governor

convened a special session of the Louisiana legislature. Among the bills awaiting votes was one that empowered state authorities to fine or imprison anyone who interfered with the state's rights—a challenge to Roosevelt and federal officials wishing to conduct programs in Louisiana—and another that would gerrymander out of office one of his most powerful enemies. Long was on hand to ensure passage of the measures. As he strode from the House chamber, the son-in-law of his enemy stepped from behind a column and fired a pistol at his chest. The Kingfish lingered for a day, but the shot proved fatal.

Long's death allayed fears of what could "happen here," yet from Royal Oak, Father Coughlin broadcast to a growing audience. The persuasive radio priest had turned hostile to Roosevelt, promoting populist nostrums and grumbling about Wall Street's influence. In California, retired doctor Francis Townsend launched his wildly impractical crusade to revive the economy by distributing government checks to elderly Americans with the mandate that they spend to stimulate commerce. Thousands of "Townsend Clubs" sprang up to promote this redistribution of income. These threats from the left only emboldened the president.

The threat on Vandenberg's mind was the mirror image of Roosevelt's: an executive branch gathering to itself unprecedented power. His duty in loyal opposition was to thwart such power if it threatened the public good. He saw an opportunity to drive a stake through one proposal described by a reporter as "the most expensive, most economically unsound and completely futile project yet undertaken by the government"—a ship canal across the peninsula of Florida. Interior Secretary Harold Ickes had rejected the idea, so Roosevelt turned to Harry Hopkins's Works Projects Administration, which earmarked an initial $5 million for it.[22]

In hindsight, the project might have proved fatal to the Everglades. The canal, said the *New York Herald Tribune*, was "the New Deal's experiment to find out, by spending a trifling $150 million or so, whether turning Florida into an island will also turn that fertile state into a desert." But the environmental impact of the project was decidedly secondary in a decade when the Roosevelt mantra was jobs and the Vandenberg mantra was fiscal prudence. On that score, nowhere was the line between those contending interests more sharply drawn. And in Congress, Roosevelt usually had the votes.[23]

Indeed, Republicans in northern Florida, eager to benefit from federal largesse, warned Vandenberg to lay off. The senator joked that henceforth he might have to travel through Jacksonville incognito. But he pressed on. Canal advocates claimed that the project would cut shipping time significantly between Gulf Coast ports and the Atlantic Seaboard. Vandenberg obtained statements from shipping lines that the canal would see little use by their vessels, but the administration bulled ahead. It would be a miracle if the project were stopped, Vandenberg told the *Miami Herald*: "The *merit* of our opposition . . . will have little to do with the outcome." He marshaled facts from scientists and the Army Corps of Engineers. George Getz, wintering in Miami, apprised him of sentiment there: southern Florida citrus growers indeed feared that seepage of salt water might ruin their groves.

By March 1936 Vandenberg's efforts began to pay off. The Senate voted 39–34, across party lines, against a $20 million appropriation, a move that to Vandenberg marked a "new turn in the spending epoch." (Each senator who voted no received a case of celery from grateful growers in southern Florida. Vandenberg gave his to a Washington hospital.) Roosevelt resubmitted the request, but even with a full-court press, the appropriation was defeated, 36–35. Finally, in 1937, the administration resigned itself to terminating the canal project. Vandenberg had almost single-handedly—and by a single vote—defeated the president's costliest pet project.[24]

Some northerners feared that by fighting the Florida canal, Vandenberg jeopardized appropriations for the St. Lawrence Seaway. Michigan backers of the bridge across the Straits of Mackinac were also anxious—and found Vandenberg willing to do no more than study the idea, lest it become another boondoggle.

Despite his alliance with south Florida farmers, Vandenberg also launched a devastating attack on the New Deal's Agricultural Adjustment Act, an example of federal largesse by which he was affronted on principle. Congress approved a resolution demanding that his Ward-man Park neighbor, Agriculture Secretary Henry Wallace, provide a list of farmers who had received federal payments of more than $10,000. When Wallace resisted, Vandenberg made hay. His investigation revealed that the chief beneficiaries of the farm support program were corporations and large-scale farmers and planters. (The administration counterattacked by suggesting that the trimming of farm benefits might begin with Michigan sugar-beet growers.) Vandenberg objected to Agriculture Department schemes paying farmers not to grow crops where a surplus would depress prices.

His effectiveness in opposition—and a dearth of attractive candidates—only burnished his prospects for the GOP nomination in 1936. "Between the Alleghenies and the Rockies, he seems to be the only Republican who offers any haven, however distant, to the shipwrecked G.O.P.," wrote *Collier's*. The president was still riding high, teasing Vandenberg that he had "a spare White House dress suit awaiting your use, even though it is the one I wear to funerals."

Coyness was the senator's customary response to presidential politics, even as he reveled in rumors of his candidacy. In the spring of 1936, he came off the Senate floor through a swinging door and nearly collided with Vice President Garner, who had begun to distance himself from the White House. As Vandenberg apologized, Garner gave a low bow. "It's quite all right," he drawled. "Don't mention it, Mr. President."

Vandenberg, in a grave tone, shook his head. "That's all over, Jack," he said. "They say Hoover is backing me." A Cheshire Cat smile creased his face: "That's enough to whip anybody."[25]

At a dinner in his honor, Washington friends turned their home into the "Dark Horse Inn." Guests included Wardman neighbor and Supreme Court justice Harlan Stone and the indomitable Alice Roosevelt Longworth, whose barbs laid low Vandenberg's rivals. Old progressive Donald Richberg, former head of the NRA and once Roosevelt's "assistant president," entertained the party with a song about the senator's prospects—strong to win the nomination, weak to beat FDR. The last lines: "There's a moral to this story—keep it dark / If they want it, may they get it! / But we still would not regret it / If next fall should find them back at Wardman Park."

Vandenberg sensed that the country was at a crossroads, and so was he. Long's assassination had ended one threat to the republic, but the concentration of power in Washington was only increasing. One of the New Deal's most maligned programs, the Federal Theater Project, contributed in its own way to the unease, and not just as an example of federal extravagance. On one night, in eighteen cities, the curtain rose on the theatrical adaptation of *It Can't Happen Here*. In New York, Lewis himself appeared as Doremus Jessup. Vandenberg attended the Washington premiere. It was "positively shattering," he wrote. "I didn't sleep all night. . . . I can't decide what the mass psychology of the thing will be—whether it will stiffen patriots to protect their heritage or whether it will encourage the mongrels to reach for power."[26]

The Vandenbergs had dined not long before at the apartment of Lewis and Dorothy Thompson. Through Lewis, Vandenberg became friendly with the liberal journalists Herbert Agar and Heywood Broun. Lewis himself was something of an enigma. He ate little, drank much, and fell asleep before dessert. "It is said he never drinks while he is writing, but when he isn't busy, he doesn't eat, just drinks," Hazel wrote.[27]

At a book party the Vandenbergs hosted for Lewis, their housekeeper handed each guest a place card for a table bearing the title of one of his novels. Alice Longworth, society columnist Martha Blair, Arthur Krock of the *Times*, the Italian ambassador, and Attorney General Homer Cummings helped themselves to Hazel's famous oyster bar. (On another occasion Lewis was invited to dinner but never showed— "too tight" was the note in Hazel's diary.)

Amid talk of a presidential nomination, the Vandenberg social calendar was full. Not unusual was a dinner at *Times-Herald* publisher Cissy Patterson's for the young Randolph Hearsts—Hazel would not be the only Washington wife who might remark, as she did, that Cissy greeted her husband "affectionately." Arthur and Hazel joined the Sulzbergers of the *Times*, tycoon Joe Kennedy, columnist Joe Alsop, and the odd cabinet member. When Hazel wasn't pouring tea with senatorial wives or dining at yet another embassy, she enjoyed lunch with Katherine Dayton, coauthor with George S. Kaufman of the new Broadway hit *First Lady*, and attended lectures by Pearl Buck and the mother of movie star Katharine Hepburn, the latter speaking on birth control.[28]

When Roosevelt delivered his State of the Union address, Vandenberg sat grimly, hands folded in his lap, never applauding. If Couzens broke ranks and clapped from time to time, and Borah did as well, Vandenberg was more partisan, ready for war on New Deal programs he judged mistaken or mismanaged. "This is not the opening of the Congress," he declared. "It was the opening of a political campaign which, judging from the tenor of the speech, promises to be hot, rabble-rousing and intolerant."[29]

Vandenberg filled a void in GOP leadership: a center-right voice of moderation around which New Deal critics might rally. Walter Lippmann thought him the one man shrewd enough and conservative enough to build a coalition with anti–New Deal Democrats. The columnist liked his plan to abolish the WPA and make cash grants directly to the states. As Vandenberg said, "You can't boondoggle your way to economic safety." The economic security that Roosevelt and Vandenberg, each in their way, looked for was still elusive. The New Deal's bold experimentation was having a wholly inconclusive effect. Democrats and Republicans debated whether improvements in the economy owed more to federal activism or cyclical change. Disgruntled bureaucrats, fed up with changes they disliked and administration infighting, fed Vandenberg anti–New Deal ammunition. Sly suggestions came in the mail, and no one could use them more effectively.

Vandenberg's willingness to cooperate with Roosevelt ended, he said, "at the point where emergency was used to permanently remodel our institutions." In *Fortune* magazine he presented a sixteen-point "Republican indictment" of the New Deal. He attacked everything from swollen federal payrolls to bad management of social security to a farm program based on a "philosophy of scarcity." And public dollars were buying votes for Democrats who controlled relief funds. He had found an effective approach: hit administration policies, but tiptoe around a popular president.[30]

As the election year unfolded, Vandenberg seemed to be everywhere. In May he was on the cover of *Literary Digest*, with cigar, of course. The story quoted Hazel: "He can't even drive a nail in the wall; why he'd starve if he didn't have someone to look after him. . . . But I have never known anyone who had such a great capacity for hard work and intense concentration." In *Redbook* his byline appeared on a story that asked, "Is the republic slipping?" (He called the Florida canal project "an affront to prudence.") "Senator Vandenberg more than anyone is keeping alive the two-party system in the Senate," wrote the *Christian Science Monitor*.[31] His "ability to needle Roosevelt without wearing the cloak of an old guard has made Vandenberg very popular on the minority side . . . indeed, its *de facto* leader," noted *Barron's* weekly.[32]

He knew how to break down complex New Deal programs into comprehensible bits. He chose his targets carefully—"symbolic episodes," he called them, with a writer's knack for narrative: "I've hunted out a few of the most thoroughly understandable atrocities and tried to visualize them for the benefit of public opinion." Then, with "steel-jacketed nouns and dum-dum adjectives," as *Literary Digest* put it, he turned to his trusty Smith-Corona, "the machine gun with which the Michigan marksman has been sniping away" at every New Dealer who stuck his head above the parapet.[33]

Did it really matter who the party nominated in 1936? Comedian Ed Wynn summed up the GOP dilemma with the tale of a tourist in Egypt who asks workmen digging in ancient ruins if they were looking for King Tut's tomb. "'No,'" one replies, "we are trying to dig up a Republican to run against Roosevelt."

Early in the year, Governor Alf Landon of Kansas, Chicago publisher Frank Knox, and even Borah were jockeying for position, Vandenberg seemed to be everyone's dark horse.[34] Lurking in the shadows, Herbert

Hoover hungered for vindication, but no one else wanted a reprise of 1932. Knox was positioning himself for second place on the ticket. Vandenberg had a soft spot for seventy-year-old Borah, but party regulars had little interest, and the maverick Lion of Idaho fared poorly in primaries. Better positioned and far better organized was Landon. Like Vandenberg, he had been reelected against the Roosevelt tide, a sturdy partisan with a moderate image. And unlike Vandenberg, he thought this might be his year.

Vandenberg was hardly an eager grassroots organizer, even were the timing more propitious. He suggested leaving the choice of a nominee to the convention. He wanted a moderate platform, not a reactionary document. The only hope he could find for a Republican victory lay in attracting Democrats disillusioned with the New Deal. If Roosevelt veered further left, more middle-class voters might become disheartened, but they would need a moderate alternative.

And why not him? Before announcing his own bid, Borah had touted Vandenberg. Legendary liberal lawyer Clarence Darrow declared that if the GOP chose Landon, he would back Roosevelt, but if Vandenberg were nominated, "I'll have to stop and think it over." Couzens had swung round again to say he would help finance his colleague's candidacy. Henry Ford, growing fonder of his longtime critic after Vandenberg's attack on the 1935 Revenue Act, also offered to put up money. Vandenberg's hope that most delegates might remain uncommitted until the convention was the wishful thinking of a man whose ambition had practical limits. "This is not a 'pose,'" he told a friend, regarding his disavowal of interest. "I have been solicited from all over the country—and frequently by thoroughly worthwhile people—to let them initiate a movement on my behalf. Of course I deeply appreciate all of these expressions of confidence (or is it desperation). But in every instance I have made the same reply."[35]

It was not hard to understand why. He had only the beginnings of a national reputation, with low poll numbers to prove it. He carried the baggage of a senator's record. He would struggle with farmers— indeed, had the temerity to admit, when asked about his agricultural policy, "I haven't any; I don't know enough about it." (In an exchange on the Senate floor with South Carolina's "Cotton Ed" Smith, Vandenberg challenged a procedural question during a debate on an agriculture bill. ("The Senator thinks it is a matter of supererogation to inquire about that?" he asked. Came Smith's reply: "The Senator should not use that sort of word in a farm bill.") He alienated organized labor by opposing the Wagner Act. The Old Guard distrusted his Nye Committee probe of Wall Street and the Du Ponts. As Harold Ickes observed, the party preferred a candidate "whose record is most colorless, whose views on the burning issues of the day are least known, and whose convictions are most accommodating." Landon better fit that bill.[36]

While Vandenberg was a gifted phrasemaker—the press swooned over "Dr. Jekyll and Mr. Hyde Park" and "The New Ordeal"—radio was hardly his friend. His flights of oratory—he could "go into the south and talk the boll weevils out of the cotton," one writer observed—were chiefly platform wonders.[37] Despite help from Hazel in trimming the five-dollar words, his rhetoric was ill suited to the intimacy of the microphone. "Sounds raspy, lacks oil," said one pundit.[38]

The shortcomings of any candidate are easy to enumerate, but Vandenberg's ambivalence was genuine. He loved being a senator. He might have wished to be president, but Drew Pearson quoted him as saying, "The Republican Party hasn't got a chance this year. . . . I've got my eye on 1940." He confided as much to a Michigan congressman: "He thinks the Republican nominee is likely to lose this year, but that four years hence there will be a violent conservative reaction."[39]

Vandenberg arrived in Cleveland for the convention ahead of any of the announced candidates. Michigan delegates were pledged to their favorite son on the first ballot. For a non-candidate, he was curiously active, receiving a stream of visitors in his red-carpeted suite at the Statler Hotel. There were no Vandenberg signs or buttons in evidence, yet the suite soon became a center of stop-Landon speculation. Vandenberg fretted that he was "frankly afraid of the Landon nomination"; he still favored Borah. And if the convention turned to him? "I am not interested in bandwagons," Vandenberg told a reporter, as he sank into an armchair and lit another cigar. Yet a deadlock was possible.[40]

Talk of an anti-Landon coalition grew. Vandenberg basked in stories that he might be chosen. "Two conflicting psychologies took possession of Cleveland," he wrote. "The paradox is that most delegates believe *both* of them. One: Landon will be nominated on the first ballot. Two: If he isn't by the third ballot, I will be." The California delegation flattered him with an offer of support. Before the opening-session gavel fell, he anticipated 150 first-ballot votes. If Knox and Borah delegates both turned to him along with enough of the uninstructed, he could find himself the nominee. He created a stir when he walked arm in arm with Borah through the crowded lobby of the Statler. But he was careful to say, "That was Borah's idea from start to finish."[41]

He learned of a meeting between Knox and Borah at which Knox had proposed to support Vandenberg in exchange for the vice presidency. It would have been a ticket without precedent: two Grand Rapids boys, former colleagues in the same newsroom. But negotiations came to naught when the Pennsylvania and New York delegations declared for Landon. Borah, Knox, and Vandenberg all released their delegates, and Vandenberg asked to second Landon's nomination. "I belong to but one bloc and it has but one slogan," he announced: "Stop Roosevelt."[42]

He barely knew the Kansas governor—indeed, referred to him at first as "Langdon." But Landon knew of Vandenberg. The candidate had been hoping a prominent Democrat might join him on an anti–New Deal ticket. Short of that, he wanted the Michigan senator, who could appeal to northeastern industrial interests in combination with a Kansan who spoke for the agrarian west. But only with Borah did Vandenberg have any interest in the second spot. His early mentor, Dawes, had tried to make the vice presidency more influential in the Coolidge years and got nowhere. Vandenberg watched Garner up close and saw the frustration.

Party leaders pursued him nonetheless. He would bring "unbelievable" strength to the ticket, the *Chicago Tribune* insisted in a front-page editorial. Eventually Vandenberg told Landon's manager, John Hamilton, that he might consider a nomination by acclamation, convinced it was his duty to the party. When Knox learned of Vandenberg's assent, he thought it trumped his own aspirations and left Cleveland.

"If they just plain draft him—well, I'm philosophical," Hazel Vandenberg confided to a friend, "in a dispirited way." That night Vandenberg was in the Statler suite, incommunicado as far as the GOP leadership was concerned. Two national committeemen paid him a late-night visit. Hazel knew her husband was "being argued with." The publisher of the *Kansas City Star*, acting as Landon's intermediary, tried to inform Vandenberg that plans were under way for the acclamation that the senator had insisted upon. He could not get through. Hamilton claimed that he also was unable to put through a call— though Vandenberg did take one from Arthur Krock of the *Times*. Vandenberg finally dictated a telegram to Bertrand Snell, the convention chairman: "If my name is proposed for vice president, please say to the convention that I wish it to be withdrawn. I am deeply convinced that I can serve more effectively . . . on the floor of the Senate during the next Landon administration." With that, he retired for the night and left a message that he not be disturbed.[43]

Hamilton knocked on his door with the news that forty-five states were prepared to support him, but Vandenberg told the Landon man of his telegram to Snell. Selection of a vice presidential nominee has often been a chaotic business. Somewhere between Hamilton's phone call and Vandenberg's, time slipped away, and with it the ticket the party wanted. "After forty-eight hours of pressure," Vandenberg told Frank McKay, the Grand Rapidian who controlled the Michigan delegation, "I think I know how a fellow feels when he has had the 'third degree' in a police station." Knox was en route back to Chicago when Vandenberg called with his decision. The Rough Rider doubted his friend could resist the appeal of the party. But Vandenberg was emphatic, and soon Knox was on the ticket.

"Let us proceed to battle and to victory," Vandenberg told delegates when he seconded Landon's nomination. The happy talk was obligatory—miracles could happen—but Democrat Bennett Clark applauded Vandenberg for choosing not to ride in "the back seat in a hearse."[44]

In August Vandenberg met with Landon in Topeka. The senator still hesitated to attack Roosevelt personally. He preferred to blame James Farley, Rexford Tugwell, Henry Wallace, Hopkins, and others for New Deal excesses. He happily invoked Jefferson to court conservative Democrats, suggesting that an activist government was encroaching upon the rights of the states. The faults of the administration were manifold, from reckless spending and a tangle of regulation to unfair taxes, the political misuse of relief funds, and a disregard for anti-monopoly laws. By executive decree the "alphabetical commissars" of the bureaucracy had assumed far too much power. Democrats were exploiting a politics of class and scarcity, moving toward regimentation, away from the Constitution. Vandenberg had been deft enough at avoiding direct attacks on Roosevelt for the president to suggest, at a meeting of Midwestern leaders discussing drought relief, that he wished the senator might have been his opponent. If he had been, Roosevelt quipped, they might have saved money and campaigned together.

But the gentility did not last. Other forces were at work to ensure that the next four years would see a widening breach. As the campaign progressed, Vandenberg stepped up his criticism. In October he conducted a "debate" on a radio broadcast sponsored by the Republican National Committee. He brought a recorder into the Columbia Broadcasting studio and proceeded to replay Roosevelt's 1932 acceptance speech, offering searing replies to the president's taped campaign promises. To Roosevelt's 1932 call for a balanced budget, Vandenberg sneered: "Red ink flows across your ledgers in a sinister stream." He derided the "swivel chair infatuations of the overlords of Washington," and a president who "flirts openly with socialism." Midway through the program, CBS chairman William S. Paley ordered his network to pull the plug.[45]

The fight was uphill in Michigan as well. Murphy returned from the Philippines to challenge the Republican governor, Frank Fitzgerald.

Couzens, who had supported the Wagner Act and other programs of the Second New Deal, endorsed Roosevelt while seeking his own reelection as a Republican. When former governor Wilbur Brucker challenged Couzens in the GOP primary, Vandenberg stayed neutral as long as he could. On the eve of the primary, he went along with the state machine and endorsed Brucker, who defeated the incumbent. In Grand Rapids thirty thousand residents massed downtown to hear Vandenberg and Landon attack the administration. Landon was backed by sugar-beet farmers and auto magnates, cereal makers and celery growers, but it was not enough.

The Republican platform did not help its candidate. Party doctrine appeared little changed from 1928. Acceptance of some relief measures and a temporarily unbalanced budget was too little too late. Landon sounded slightly apocalyptic when he said voters faced a "question of whether our American form of government is to be preserved," but in fact the expansion of federal authority was not a trifling issue.[46]

In the end, Republicans slid further toward what seemed like oblivion. Murphy ousted Fitzgerald and Democrat Prentiss Brown defeated Brucker. Landon carried only Maine and New Hampshire—eight electoral votes. Vandenberg proposed that Michigan Republicans distance themselves from the national party. The trend toward liberalism and a less obstructionist opposition was clear.

Yet he was still no insurgent. Neither the maverick criticism of Borah nor the crusading impulse of Norris or La Follette agreed with him. He needed respectability and security. But he was a party man without much of a party, and more on the outside than ever.

He had at least avoided a role in the crushing defeat. But he would be returning to Washington as one of only seventeen senators on the Republican side. When a New York columnist called him a "sure G.O.P. presidential choice in 1940," he could only laugh: "That just shows how decimated our ranks are." It was easy to stand out in such a small crowd. Seventeen senators? How could one hope to wield influence or resist the Roosevelt juggernaut? Even if the party survived, Vandenberg would have little voice—unless the partisan landscape changed, or the world did.[47]

CHAPTER 10

· · · · · · · · · · · ·

THE NEW ORDEAL

· · · · · · · · · · · ·

It might have been the Lord's way, Vandenberg said later to Chief Justice Charles Evans Hughes, "of warning us that Constitutional Amendments are dangerous." One had passed in 1933, moving up the presidential inauguration from early March to late January. That January morning in 1937 a damp chill had settled over the Capitol as Franklin Roosevelt stepped out on the East Portico to take the oath of office for his second term. From inside, Vandenberg watched with Democratic senator James Byrnes as the elderly justices of the Supreme Court gathered near the president. The shivering cold of the ceremony was just the thing, Byrnes observed, to "shove the Judges out into the storm and thus perhaps get rid of a few of them from exposure."[1]

Roosevelt called on his fellow citizens to help the one-third of the nation that was "ill-housed, ill-clad, ill-nourished." Vandenberg found the rhetoric "amazingly effective," but as chilling as the driving rain that blurred the president's glasses. Roosevelt further declared that his administration had reined in big corporations whose "heedless self-interest" had "been challenged and beaten." With a shudder, Vandenberg heard in such phrases "a direct emotional appeal to the class consciousness of the underprivileged—well calculated to further enflame their passions," but with no way to answer "their aroused appetites."[2]

For Vandenberg—as it may indeed have been for Roosevelt—the challenge was to help a market-driven society respond to the needs of the poor. "We make an ominous error if we fail frankly to confront these realities and deal with them accordingly," the senator acknowledged. If capitalism were to survive, new ways were needed to "demonstrate our social-mindedness as distinguished from Socialism."

He feared that the lopsided Democratic majorities in Congress would do the president's bidding. Indeed, the administration "can do anything it wants to do hereafter," Vandenberg wrote, perhaps aware of rumors around the White House, "including the emasculation of the Supreme Court." He recalled Benjamin Franklin's warning that "those who seek security at the expense of liberty are likely to lose both." That, he said, as he contemplated the emaciated GOP, "is precisely what America is doing under FDR."[3]

Successive landslide defeats had left the Republican Party adrift. Although Charles McNary was leader of the Senate minority, the more forceful Vandenberg was its de facto voice. But what did that amount to? Of seventeen GOP senators, nearly half were insurgents, who followed no lead but their own, or New Deal Republicans, such as Nye and Norris. "We do not deserve to even exist as an opposition party," Vandenberg wrote. "*How* we do need a few more aggressive, industrious Republican senators."

He stepped into this vacuum determined to rebuild the GOP. Caution and patience were the watchwords, he counseled colleagues, with the minority acting principally as a "sentry service" to meet each New Deal program with constructive criticism rather than denunciation. The Senate Finance Committee, in response to his resolution, convinced the Social Security Board to employ experts to evaluate the entire system—a welcome departure, wrote Arthur Krock in the *New York Times*, from the Republican response in Roosevelt's first term, when the first impulse had been to "hamstring, harass and embarrass." The opposition would gain little by attacking a popular president. Nor did it have enough votes to pursue its own agenda—"an exceedingly perplexing problem," Vandenberg admitted. It needed the approach he had often embraced: coalition.

Even though the Second New Deal alienated many "Jefferson Democrats," they would cooperate with Republicans only discreetly. Certainly no Southerner wished to be seen as an ally of a party still alien to the former Confederacy. Vandenberg would have to tread lightly; a coalition could form only with the stimulus of a compelling issue. The senator refused to deliver a partisan address at Lincoln Day speeches in February. That might "interrupt the strategy which we are using in Congress—namely, to wait for the Administration to create a major issue before we start talking politics again."[4]

Only the Supreme Court appeared to stand between the administration and its ambitious agenda. In 1935, the court had declared key New Deal measures—most significantly, the National Recovery Act—unconstitutional. That same day had seen two other unanimous verdicts: against a law granting mortgage relief for debt-ridden farmers and against the president's authority to remove a member of the Federal Trade Commission—the latter a bid by Roosevelt to force the FTC to adhere to his policies. "Extraordinary conditions do not create or enlarge constitutional power," wrote Chief Justice Hughes. He referred to the NRA, but the implications were clear: "The code-making authority thus conferred is an unconstitutional delegation of legislative power." Suddenly seven hundred pages of NRA codes were presumed void, including those covering working conditions that affected nearly twenty million Americans. Justice Department prosecutors had upward of four hundred business-related code violations pending when the decision was rendered. Roosevelt had to drop the charges. Far from imposing a rigid new order, the administration felt checkmated at every turn by a conservative court.

The president had been furious then. Now, reelected with the largest majority ever, he saw no reason to accept the court's rejection of his legislation. Just three weeks into his second term, Roosevelt summoned reporters to the Oval Office and detailed a plan to appoint an additional Supreme Court justice, up to a total of six, for each sitting judge who chose to remain on the bench past the age of seventy. He cited the court's increasing workload, but his goal was transparent: to dilute the influence of the "nine old men" who had thwarted him.

Vandenberg's response was immediate and apocalyptic. To say he "most emphatically" disliked it "expressed only about 1% of my opinion," he confided in his diary. "If the President has a sufficient grip on Congress so that he can force it to give him an equivalent grip on the

Supreme Court, then all Constitutional checks and balances are gone; he can run his personal standard to the masthead of every flag-pole in the land." The president was trying to "kidnap" the Supreme Court, "to control its decisions and warp them to the Roosevelt idea."[5]

His actor's sense of the dramatic did not always come with an actor's sense of timing. Vandenberg's first impulse was to shake the Senate chamber with a thundering blast of indignation. Then he realized that this was the issue he had been waiting for. Democrats were also taken aback. Even many who supported the New Deal had no stomach for so radical a change in the structure of the judiciary. Vandenberg did something that was, for him, rather new and remarkable—he held his tongue.

Instead, he called the GOP chairman and talked him out of making any reference to Roosevelt's proposal. He told an inquiring reporter to talk first to Carter Glass "or some other big *Democrat.*" He met with McNary and Borah. Hoover was outraged and eager to blast the proposal he termed *court packing.* Yet he, too, was persuaded to join the "conspiracy of silence," Vandenberg wrote in his diary. "But what a bitterly unfair contemplation! That an ex-President must efface himself."[6]

The senators played a shrewd game. Vandenberg knew he was on the right track when a Democratic colleague cautioned him, "I am inclined to vote NO; but your Republicans and particularly Mr. Hoover must not make it too hard for me." Within a day of the president's address, Republican senators were united by a commitment to yield for a week or more to their opposite numbers, "and let the revolting Democrats make their own record," as Vandenberg put it. "In other words, we are putting the good of the country ahead of the good of the Party." This was enlightened self-interest as well. "We think, tonight," he confided at the end of a long day, "that the President can be beaten on this issue."[7]

Montana Democrat Burt Wheeler became the Senate's most vocal opponent of the proposal. Republicans supplied him with arguments as he prepared an enormous speech in the event of a filibuster. Vandenberg, finally growing impatient with his own discipline, wanted to add his voice to radio attacks on the scheme. Wheeler and Borah counseled him to yield to Nye, who had supported Roosevelt in the last election and was less identified with the Republican leadership. "I shall wait a while longer," Vandenberg confided, expressing his orator's agony. "Silence is the hardest job of self-control I ever undertook because this assault upon an independent Court utterly burns me up. But the time will come! And the main thing is to win!"

Deference to Democratic opponents of the court plan was for Vandenberg a first taste of bipartisan strategy within the legislative branch. Something could be achieved "by robbing the presidential gang of their best talking point . . . by not giving them a Republican target at which to shoot." Roosevelt's support was slipping away. An invincible Democratic majority was splintered, perhaps irrevocably, by a president whose legendary finesse failed him. Opposition was a visceral thing, born not only of resistance to change, but also of apprehension over social discontent and an economy sliding back into depression. Vandenberg received more than fourteen thousand letters opposed to court packing—and only seventy-five in favor. "I believe," he wrote in his diary, that "we can win this battle against the President—although I still have profound respect for his push buttons, his patronage, his personality and his pap."

When the coalition agreed it was time for a Vandenberg speech, the senator consulted columnist Joseph Alsop, a Roosevelt cousin, who urged him to offer not merely criticism, but an alternative. Vandenberg spoke in support of a constitutional amendment proposed by Wheeler that would enable Congress, after a minimum of three years, to pass again, by a two-thirds vote, any legislation that had been declared invalid by the Supreme Court, provided it did not compromise guarantees in the Bill of Rights. This was a short speech, not the 12,000-word manuscript that stayed in his desk, but it marked the first formal Republican reply, nearly four weeks after Roosevelt threw down the gauntlet. Vandenberg calculated that the substitute plan could not take effect until 1945, even if it were adopted soon. By then, he argued, "we will either have lost America to the mobs or to the Fascists, or we will have regained our senses after the departure of F.D.R."[8]

In the meantime, the Court itself undermined Roosevelt's campaign. By upholding the pro-labor Wagner Act in April, the justices showed themselves amenable to an important New Deal bill. Roosevelt expressed pleasure, yet inwardly he might have wished for a veto, to galvanize support for his plan.

Hazel Vandenberg, plagued by sinus trouble, spent much of that winter in Arizona. She returned to Washington in the spring, and by June was ready to decamp to Grand Rapids and Lake Michigan. The Senate, however, still wrestled with the court proposal as Washington began to steam up. Vandenberg wore his white summer suit in a chamber that offered no relief from the heat. The White House had air-conditioning, but not the Capitol. In the gallery, visitors waved white cardboard fans supplied by a funeral parlor.[9]

Then came the July morning when Senate Majority Leader Joe Robinson, the president's chief champion in the court fight, slumped to the floor in his apartment. He died of a heart attack, clutching the *Congressional Record*. A week later the Senate voted 70–20 to send the bill back to the Judiciary Committee. "We have won the long battle to defend an independent Judiciary and to defeat an executive dictatorship," Vandenberg wrote.[10]

Roosevelt's Senate majority, so lopsided on paper, not only had failed in practice, but also was irretrievably fractured. And for perhaps the first time in Vandenberg's experience, Republicans had acted in concert with Democrats on a major issue. With an uncharacteristically deft touch on the part of the minority, bipartisan indignation worked its magic. FDR overreached, Vandenberg waited, and Vandenberg won.

Not long after, Arthur and Hazel were invited to lunch at the Rock Creek Park estate of the blind former senator from Oklahoma, Thomas P. Gore. Long a crusty oracle of populist wisdom, the old Democrat had fought Wilson over the League of Nations. He turned to Vandenberg as they sat on the terrace and declared, "It's time some of you youngsters saved the country from the New Deal." Vandenberg agreed. Saving the country—an ambitious man, particularly when he was so much on the outside, needed a mission, and that had an aw-fully nice ring to it.[11]

Despite the court-packing victory, the Republican side of the Senate was so small that it was hard not to feel embattled. And occasionally Vandenberg led a traditional charge against the dominant president. Sit-down strikes in Michigan auto plants had become a national sensation; Roosevelt seemed to condone them—even though they were anathema to conservatives in his own party. After Vandenberg attacked Roosevelt in a speech on the Senate floor, Vice President Garner came down from the rostrum to pump his hand. "It was about time somebody said that," he declared.[12]

Roosevelt, who had rarely reached out to his opposition, had less incentive than ever. As the country slipped back into the depression from which, in fits and starts, it had seemed to be emerging, all the governmental activism of the last half decade appeared to have ac-complished little—except to concentrate more power in the execu-tive. Vandenberg's politics reflected his principles. He quoted a pas-sage from his galley copy of Walter Lippmann's *The Good Society*:

> We are trying to operate a capitalistic system under a government that dislikes the system, and would, if it had the courage and power, replace it with a collectivist system. This inner conflict between the nature of free capitalism and the real purposes of the government has created a deadlock. Business cannot proceed because it is ter-rorized by New Dealers. The New Dealers cannot proceed because, being only half-hearted collectivists, they dare not follow out the logic of their own ideas.

Lippmann argued for smaller government: "The dynamics of human capacity follow the rule that the more complex the interests which have to be regulated, the less possible it is to direct them by the coercion of higher authority." The National Recovery Act, with its myriad marketing boards and price schedules, had been the pre-eminent example of this rationale. The fantasies of Sinclair Lewis were an extension of the logic Lippmann employed when he said of incipient collectivists: "They must not complain, then, if men look at Russia, Italy and Germany to see where the cult of the state is leading them. There, in deeds visible to all, the idea is incarnate."[13]

In a November radio address, Vandenberg asked, "Where do we go from here?" The economy was stalled, the Congress deadlocked. Authoritarian regimes threatened their neighbors in Europe and Asia. Channeling Lippmann, Vandenberg blamed the administration for the nation's ills: "Business must not be permitted to run the government," he acknowledged, "but unless it is permitted reasonable latitude to run itself—free from an ambitious collectivism which creates more problems than it solves—prosperity will die on the vine." Private enterprise, he said, depended on consistent policies. The administration needed to abandon "anti-constitutional activities and intrigues which shatter democratic faith. Candid communists or fascists in a democracy are bad enough. But wolves in sheep's clothing are worse."

Emboldened by victory in the court fight, Vandenberg harbored dreams of a permanent conservative alliance. Just as Roosevelt speculated about a realignment that would bring liberals together under one banner, Vandenberg could imagine a new era of competition between a Roosevelt party and a conservative one that might forsake the Republican name in the interest of coalition. The party needed to rebuild. He was looking ahead to the midterm election in 1938, "but I think it would be absurd for us to shut our eyes to the cold hard fact that some such coalition may be absolutely indispensable in 1940 if we are to save the Republic."[14]

Vandenberg saw the next election as a defining moment for his dream of coalition. Missouri Republicans supported Democrat Bennett Clark's reelection. Other Democrats who had broken with FDR might also expect GOP support. Vandenberg predicted that 1938 elections would offer "laboratory demonstrations of the means by which a new coalition (built around the Republican nucleus) can produce a triumphant realignment of political parties." To Alf Landon he envisioned "some sort of a fusion or coalition or union ticket," adding, "It would not shock me at all to find myself in 1940 supporting the right kind of Democrat."[15]

The economic downturn only added to a sense of urgency. In late summer of 1937, a torrent of sell-offs had washed over the stock market. Many stocks dropped to their lowest point in four years. The administration spoke of a "corrective dip" and sounded like Hoover. In three months the Dow Jones index dropped from 190 to 115. As inventories of steel and autos backed up, two million people lost their jobs. New Dealers blamed conservatives who had forced reductions in public works and relief programs, but Vandenberg charged that this was "Roosevelt's Recession."

FDR still expected Congress to pass some of his more important proposals, but a special session late in 1937 was a washout. "No runs, no hits and a lot of errors" was how the *Grand Rapids Press* characterized Roosevelt's performance as the bipartisan band of conservatives became a force to reckon with. The coalition rejected a wages-and-hours bill, "little Tennessee Valley Authority" power projects, new antitrust regulations, expanded housing programs, and a new agriculture bill. They slashed spending for relief and public works and refused to allow the president to set the price of silver. They pushed through the Hatch Act, which limited the administration's patronage powers and outlawed political activity by civil servants. They fought for lower corporate taxes to spur investment, repealed the excess profits tax, and slashed the tax on capital gains.

When the Senate could not stop FDR's plan for a reorganization of the executive branch, the House did. This rather benign effort at greater efficiency, involving a reshuffling of agencies, roused Father Coughlin and other critics to cries of dictatorship. The plan was "more sinister as a symbol than a reality," Vandenberg admitted, but "we are dreadfully sensitive these days to symbols—whether they be fasces or swastikas or hammer and cycles [*sic*] or new blue eagles over the White House."

Late in 1937 Vandenberg and North Carolina Democrat Josiah Bailey drafted a confidential manifesto calling for a balanced budget, states' rights, and other old standards that might pull together anti-Roosevelt forces. Yet the coalition was never more than an ad hoc alliance of convenience. It found consensus only on domestic issues.

For Vandenberg, as for Roosevelt, there would be no realignment. The senator was left with the task of rebuilding the GOP. He was ever the pragmatist.

"The Old Guard dies but never surrenders," one pundit wrote. "Vandenberg surrenders, but never dies."[16]

CHAPTER 11

· · · · · · · · · · · ·

CROSSROADS

· · · · · · · · · · · ·

At diplomatic gatherings, ambassadors hung on Vandenberg's accounts of congressional intrigue. Foreign ladies looked upon the man their husbands courted: pompous, yes, but powerful in the way he spoke so expansively. He seemed outsized—the hands, the height, the dome of a head—a conspicuous figure, almost dashing, the white silk scarf drawn from his neck with a flourish as he stepped into an embassy foyer, the black brows furrowed above the big dark eyes. If the flair of a tailored suit—Hazel's doing—was part of the senator's image, so was a good line for the ladies, a wry smile, a knowing gaze wreathed in cigar smoke. He was attractive enough, by virtue of posture and position, to court trouble.

Hazel's reputation was built on a broad smile and down-to-earth good cheer. She may have been a little too self-consciously Midwestern not to feel the rivalry of other women in the more sophisticated legations of the capital. She fell so easily into the big sister role, had no concept of herself as an object of attraction, while her husband exuded importance and was growing toward gravitas.

As they returned from a party in April 1937, the Vandenbergs were invited for a nightcap by their upstairs neighbors, Harold and Mitzi Sims. He was a wealthy Canadian in his sixties attached to the British embassy. Long a Washington bon vivant, he had married late. Mitzi was younger, a native of Denmark. Arthur and Hazel stayed until 4 a.m. "Never do that again," Hazel wrote the next day. "Can't take it." But she found Mitzi, with her quick wit, to be "some gal."

A society columnist wrote a feature entitled "These Fascinating Ladies!" Most of the prominent wives had their turn, including Hazel.

When Mitzi was profiled, Hazel pasted the item in her scrapbook with a notation: "And How!" (Years later, her daughters would withhold that page when they released the Vandenberg Papers.)[1]

Mitzi was no matron: "She is like a luscious peach that has been ripening in the sun," the columnist wrote. Her expressive face framed big blue eyes, "a strong, determined nose which turns up unexpectedly at the tip," a dimpled chin, "warm, rosy skin," light brown hair. "Her curves are distracting," the columnist continued, and a deep, throaty voice was "one of her real fascinations." Mitzi "personifies the meaning of the term 'joie de vivre,' " the columnist gushed.

Another society writer found Mitzi "one of the few social notables in Washington who need never rely on the weather as a topic of her repartee." She was as much fun at a picnic as in a ballroom, loved to gamble and dress luxuriously. And she had "a prankish side which she can't keep down and which sometimes gets her into trouble." Perhaps that was a way of saying she was a flirt. "Mitzi Sims, Mitzi Sims," one eminent rake recalled long after. "I always wanted to meet her, but I never did."[2]

Arthur Vandenberg was smitten. His gaze followed Mitzi when she entered a room. Hazel was also charmed. The couples became a foursome. But Hazel was not always around. In the winter her sinuses tormented her. In 1938 she disappeared for a few weeks of dry air on a Tucson ranch. The year before, elder daughter Barbara stayed with her father in the wake of her divorce. Now Arthur had the apartment to himself.

Even in rapture a little discretion is advisable. Arthur and Mitzi employed a post office box for their communication. From fragmentary evidence in Hazel's diary—caustic asides, sad hints—it appears that when she returned to Washington in the spring, she found a husband she could not trust. Her ebullience evaporated. She attended the opening of a new play, *Once Is Enough*, but did not join Arthur for dinner with the cast. In the play the wife gives her husband freedom. "Made to order for present situations," Hazel noted, "only I wouldn't want the same denouement." The Vandenbergs were in a social maelstrom. When Hazel had a headache, a friend "guaranteed" to act as chaperone for Arthur at a Sims party. The friend later "made some very revealing remarks," Hazel confided. "Family difficulties put me in a dither."[3]

When she took a three-day trip, alone, to Atlantic City—"to get the fuzziness out of my head," Hazel said, the small cadre of Washington newspaperwomen paid attention. "When Mrs. Vandenberg ceases to be enthusiastic about what is going on about her," a friendly columnist reported, "we do agree that it is time for her to take a rest, for there are few people who are so imbued with genuine enthusiasm." The year before, Hazel spent time with General Pershing, the elderly hero of the Great War, who wintered near Tucson. Now Pershing was gravely ill. Newspapers carried a photo of Hazel and the general attending a rodeo. "Far happier then!!" Hazel scrawled alongside the clipping pasted in her scrapbook. "Ha! Ha! What can happen in a year!"[4]

Hazel's torment stoked gossip. The solon and the siren were seen about town in Mitzi's convertible. Walter Winchell slipped an item into his column in the Hearst papers, then repeated it on radio in his staccato style: "The Senator Vandenbergs of Michigan have their intimates wondering."

While it is clear what attracted Vandenberg to Mitzi, one might wonder why the object of the senator's passion responded as she did. Part of the answer may have been spy craft.

The role of Harold Sims at the British embassy was rather vague. He was an attaché of independent wealth and perhaps of no particular consequence—except that his friend, William Stephenson, had set up the British spy network in the capital and Sims was rumored to run the embassy code room. It would have been quite a coup to have a source who was well placed to report on the strategies—and more—of Senate isolationists. Yet there is no suggestion that Vandenberg's infatuation influenced his position or blunted his zeal for neutrality. Nor could he not have been aware of her connection to the British embassy, or of its interest in American policy. Still, people talk. The romance, wrote Arthur Krock, years later, "led to gossip at Washington hen parties where the hens have teeth and the teeth are sharp, that Vandenberg had been 'converted' from isolationism by the pretty wife of a West European diplomat, a lady of whom, as the saying goes, he saw a lot."[5]

The senator's seduction may have been sanctioned by British intelligence and perhaps even accepted by her husband, but the romance was real. He loved Mitzi, and his children knew it. Their father faced a stark choice of whether to stay in his marriage or go—and on that choice hung his political career.

Early in 1938, the Vandenbergs attended Mitzi's birthday party for Harold. Arthur composed a poem for the guest of honor, which Hazel pasted in her scrapbook:

Hearts across the border
Hands across the sea,
Here's to Harold's birthday
And many more to be.

Hearts across the border, indeed! Hazel reported rather cryptically that Harold, upon reading the verse aloud, "responded very much to the point."[6]

Vandenberg's own birthday in 1938—his fifty-fourth—was celebrated with hundreds of guests in top hats and tiaras at the Sulgrave Club. Daughter Betsy, a concert pianist, played Chopin, Debussy, Brahms, and Wagner. Her encore of "The Beautiful Blue Danube" brought some of the audience to tears with thoughts of the recent *Anschluss*.

"That was a Viennese waltz," one guest told German ambassador Hans Dieckhoff.

"I know, I know," he laughed. "Didn't you understand—they played it in my honor." (The next morning the ambassador sent the young pianist a bouquet of gardenias and daisies. "No matter what Washington thinks of Nazi politics," wrote one society columnist, "everybody likes the Dieckhoffs.") Later everyone sang "Happy Birthday" as the tuxedo-clad senator cut the cake.

Soon after, against her parents' judgment but also in part to escape the tension of their Washington life, Betsy Vandenberg married Edward Pfeiffer in New York City. "Awful day," Hazel wrote in her diary.

The awful days were just beginning. Barbara's divorce, Betsy's hasty marriage, her own distress over Mitzi—Hazel's world was coming apart. "Downbeat again! Hell is nothing!" she wrote in early June. When her husband left for New York to collect an honorary degree, she stayed at the Wardman, "desperately blue."[7]

Vandenberg himself, however, was flying high, and never more so than later that year, after the elections. His tactical mastery helped spell the end of Roosevelt's domestic policy revolution. In the 1938 election, Republicans picked up eight seats in the Senate, eighty-one in the House, and thirteen governorships—including Michigan's, where Frank Murphy was ousted. Robert Taft reached the Senate from Ohio, Harold Stassen became, at the age of thirty-one, governor of Minnesota, and young prosecutor Thomas Dewey nearly upset Roosevelt's successor as governor of New York. If not an outright rejection of the New Deal, wrote Arthur Krock, the results meant that "the New Deal has been halted; the Republican Party is large enough for effective opposition; the moderate Democrats in Congress can guide legislation. . . . The country is back on a two-party system . . . and legislative authority has been restored to Congress." The Senate was recovering a little pre-Roosevelt swagger.

So complete was the triumph of the conservative coalition in the 1938 election, one journalist declared, "President Roosevelt could not run for a third term even if he so desired." Voters wanted neutrality, opposed packing the court, and were rattled by the stubborn Roosevelt recession—oh, how the president loathed that phrase! Vandenberg, as a leader of the conservative coalition as well as the isolationist bloc, drew considerable attention. These were the last days of the American Pericles, when what a senator said made news. Although the imperial presidency was emerging with the swift growth of federal power, the speeches of certain senators were important pronouncements. Vandenberg was always quotable, and it didn't hurt that the ranks of senior Republicans remained thin—still only twenty-three senators in 1939.[8]

In 1940 Roosevelt would complete his second term. No president had challenged the two-term tradition. But who would challenge his successor? A poll after the 1938 election showed that Vandenberg had slipped from first to third among potential candidates, trailing ambitious newcomers Robert Taft and Thomas Dewey. In his diary, he professed not to care. The party "wants and needs new names, new ideas, new blood," he wrote. "I have 'carried the flag' through the 'lean years,' so it is a great relief to me to have the Gallup Poll bring forward some new names." For two years, the only names had been Hoover, Landon, and Vandenberg—two losers and the senator: "It has been a pathetic confession of weakness."

And yet, Landon, titular head of the GOP, considered Vandenberg a favorite for the party's 1940 nomination. So did Lord Beaverbrook, the British press magnate, who referred to his friend as the "next president." Asked if Vandenberg would be the Republican nominee, Democratic Party chairman James A. Farley replied, "undoubtedly." Though a dark horse no longer, Vandenberg was coy about his prospects. "The Senator is not lifting a finger to get the nomination," one columnist wrote. "He is just working quietly to make himself the most available candidate." He met quietly with Michigan party chairman Howard Lawrence and former Governor Frank Fitzgerald to lay the groundwork for an organization later dubbed the "Vandenberg Movement."[9]

When a reporter asked Roosevelt if he had seen reports that Vandenberg might run, he replied that he had, then changed the subject. He had, however, instructed FBI director J. Edgar Hoover to open an office in Grand Rapids. The agent in charge told a friend that he had been assigned to this placid Midwestern city to keep an eye on Arthur Vandenberg.[10]

Vandenberg's ego, capacious as it was, rebelled against an overt display of ambition. He was uncomfortable announcing plans that risked the embarrassment of defeat. There was also the practical fear that by appearing too eager to move up from the Senate, he might jeopardize his seat, which would also be contested in 1940. An appearance of detachment was important, he had told Lawrence late in

1937, "lest someone think I have started another campaign for myself," rather than for the entire anti–New Deal movement. He discouraged speculation: "The moment we begin to organize for 1940 in terms of individual candidacies we shall at least partially dilute our unity and dissipate at least some of our strength in internecine warfare." He did not want a presidential campaign to "nullify" his usefulness in Congress.[11]

In that capacity, he helped stop Roosevelt's second attempt to build the Florida ship canal, and he claimed his biggest victory in March 1939 when Treasury Secretary Henry Morgenthau backed away from a proposed 50 percent increase in social security taxes. Vandenberg called for a freeze on payroll tax rates. "This evidently drove the administration to the point of capitulation," he wrote, another instance "of how a political minority can render constructive service." His fickle friends at the *Chicago Tribune* praised him in May 1939 as "the Most Useful Senator." His ease and good humor tempered the increasingly strident edge of his hostility to the New Deal.

When Harry Hopkins appeared before the Commerce Committee for his confirmation as secretary of commerce, Vandenberg greeted this fellow son of a harness maker with "God bless you, Harry; may we always be friends." The senator opposed the nomination but left the niggling questions to Hiram Johnson and to Democrats Roosevelt had tried to purge. He challenged the political activities of Hopkins aides in the massive relief program overseen by the onetime social worker. Hopkins defended his chief assistant, who had been outspoken about working to keep Roosevelt in power, by suggesting that the man was entitled to an indiscretion. "Do you reserve a few for yourself, as we all do, I assume, in the same connection?" Vandenberg asked, to the amusement of the audience.[12]

Speaking of indiscretions, in February 1939 the Winchell item—"The Senator Vandenbergs of Michigan have their intimates wondering"— was picked up by gossip columnist Igor Cassini. "That leading Midwestern candidate for the 1940 Republican presidential nomination won't get it after all," Cassini wrote. "His wife will divorce him shortly, and the party has turned thumbs down for that reason." Then came a story in *Look* magazine by, in Vandenberg's words, "those two jackals of American journalism," Drew Pearson and Robert Allen. *Look* carried a photo of Arthur and Hazel taken at a Washington Senators baseball game the year before. The caption said he was "too shopworn to arouse enthusiasm even if he could live down his nickname, 'the senator from Mitzigan,' earned by his friendship for Mitzi Sims, charming wife of a British diplomat. Democrats would rub their hands in glee if Vandenberg were nominated." Vandenberg suspected Democrats of stoking this fire. After all, had not Jim Farley so recently declared him the strongest candidate the Republicans could field? This was "obviously part of a deliberate 'smear' for political effect," Vandenberg wrote in his scrapbook diary. "It shows, once more, the depths to which mud-campaigners will go."

Vandenberg's scrapbooks were assembled with an awareness that they might come under scrutiny from history—or Hazel. He noted that it must have annoyed "these vultures" of the press that the Vandenbergs and the Simses shared a box at a recent concert. "We ALL happen to be great friends," he typed below the scandal reports. "And that's that."[13]

Others remembered it differently. Arthur could not conceal his love for Mitzi. For Hazel, though schooled in lovelorn advice on the faithlessness of men, this was a staggering blow. She had watched her husband's passion grow, a friend said, seen "the kettle boiling over," and then quietly taken him back. But she was humiliated and hurt. Said her friend, "Something warm went out of her heart."[14]

Chicago Tribune reporter Walter Trohan remembered the evening in 1940 when he and John T. Flynn, the journalist who had advised the Nye Committee, joined Nye, Wheeler, and La Follette in the Vandenberg apartment. Hazel was away. Mitzi came by, and Vandenberg introduced her to the Senate ringleaders of American isolationism. As she left, she turned to Vandenberg and said, "Good night, you great big statesman, you." In a low voice, Trohan—who considered Hazel "a real lady"—whispered to one senator, "Where does one go to throw up?" He was never invited back.[15]

Vandenberg would admit to nothing. "I do not want the nomination," he protested to reporters. "I do not want the presidency itself. This is unequivocal. Perhaps I know too much about the job. Perhaps I am too familiar with my own limitations." Vandenberg's ambivalence is only partly believable. He hardly felt shopworn; indeed, he felt as though he were just hitting his stride. But he could live without being president, and the emotional toll of life at home just might have trumped the drive of an ambitious man.[16]

There remained the remote prospect that a conservative coalition might lead to a realignment of the parties. "If the Democratic Convention splits wide open and there is a complete breach between the left and the right wings," Vandenberg wrote, in thrall to his melodramatic sense of history, "it will be of vital importance that *our* Convention should join forces with the sound Jefferson Democrats to save the national situation. The thing may be required (as was the case in 1864)." The wise course was "to subordinate all personal aspirations and personal booms." He hoped for a convention of uninstructed delegates—then who knew what might happen?

If wisdom counseled discretion, the political situation in Michigan called for more forthright plans. In February 1939, Republicans endorsed Governor Fitzgerald for the vice presidential nomination while making no mention of Vandenberg for the presidency. His waiting-to-be-wooed posture was wearing thin. Too many expressions of disinterest and he might be taken at his word. "Your independent attitude toward the presidential nomination . . . has been misunderstood by some of our Michigan friends," Howard Lawrence warned.

The state party boss, Frank McKay of Grand Rapids, was leaning toward Thomas Dewey for president. Longtime Vandenberg supporters in the press were also tiring of their Republican Hamlet. Vandenberg's son, running his office in Washington, agreed. His father could not spurn Michigan Republicans every time the presidency was mentioned and still rely on their enthusiasm for his senatorial candidacy. He owed them, Arthur Junior wrote, "at least acquiescence . . . especially when it involves such highly complimentary activities as are currently discussed."[17]

Vandenberg finally agreed that he would no longer object to others working on his behalf, although he was not yet prepared to pursue the nomination. Lawrence started a "draft Vandenberg" campaign, lining up prominent endorsements and sending Republicans across the country copies of his pamphlet "Why Michigan Believes in Arthur H. Vandenberg." Lumber magnate John Blodgett provided financial support, with Detroit bankers and industrialists joining the effort as Lawrence set up shop on a budget of $100,000.[18]

Vandenberg's high-minded but clumsy response was to pledge himself to one term and to accept the nomination but not campaign for it. He was merely allowing his name to be circulated to increase Michigan's leverage—and his own. "But when the smoke clears," he told Lawrence, "I fully expect to be thumping up and down Michigan again in an effort to succeed myself in the Senate."[19]

In May 1939 the Vandenberg movement became public, with an endorsement by the Hearst papers and favorable coverage elsewhere. A majority of congressional Republicans named him their favorite. By June he had climbed to a distant second in the polls, the choice of 19 percent to Dewey's 47 percent. By early August, Lawrence had Vandenberg organizations in every Michigan county. The Grand Rapids chapter received permission from the city commission to build a "mini–White House" on Campau Square.[20] Lawrence assured the senator that his supporters were mindful that he would otherwise be seeking reelection in 1940. In the crisis of Arthur Vandenberg's middle age, that was the security that seemed to matter most.

CHAPTER 12

REPEAL

Arthur Vandenberg listened carefully as Franklin Roosevelt braced himself at the lectern. The president's 1939 State of the Union address responded to war clouds in Europe and Asia by asking for "methods short of war" to discourage Hitler and Mussolini and the Japanese cabinet. Roosevelt wanted to repeal the embargo on selling arms in the 1937 Neutrality Act so that the United States could help friendly nations threatened with attack.

For Vandenberg, neutrality remained the holy grail of American foreign policy. The temporary bill he had engineered in the wake of the Nye Committee had expired in May 1937. That year, Democrats, led by Foreign Relations chairman Key Pittman, had proposed a bill that continued an arms embargo against belligerents and also imposed an embargo on export of any other goods which might endanger the "peace or neutrality" of the United States. Vandenberg liked this — except for the provision allowing the president to choose what goods were to be banned from shipment on American vessels. With his Nye colleagues, he offered a substitute, which required the president to re- strict all trade with belligerents. But the Pittman version had the votes to reach the floor.

Vandenberg tried an amendment preventing American ships from carrying goods to belligerents. Again he lost, but the Pittman bill, ap- proved overwhelmingly, was strict enough for most — though too strict for the House, which was more hospitable to Roosevelt. It watered down the final version by giving the president a degree of discretion. That was more than Vandenberg could abide, for it transferred "a sub- stantial portion of the war-making power from the Congress to the

Chief Executive." Still, Vandenberg claimed partial victory. The revised Neutrality Act repudiated the principle of freedom of the seas, banned both travel and loans to belligerents, prohibited the arming of merchant ships, and, fundamentally, enshrined neutrality as a permanent law of the United States.[1]

As Roosevelt wrestled with ways to check the dictators, France and Great Britain demonstrated their willingness to appease them. Hitler marched into Austria and encountered only diplomatic protests. When the Czechs refused to submit to German demands for annexation of the Sudetenland, war seemed imminent. British prime minister Chamberlain flew to Munich to win Hitler's assurance that his appetite for land would be satisfied with a piece of Czechoslovakia. This wishful negotiation late in 1938 gave an illusion of relief, of "peace in our time"—and only reinforced the American desire for distance from the European maelstrom.

What was going on across the Pacific was also disturbing, even if the ocean was wider and Americans, by interest and ancestry, generally less engaged. The Japanese army marauded through China as its government, in November 1938, slammed shut the vaunted American Open Door policy of trade with the Chinese and proclaimed a "new order" in Asia under Japanese domination.

With the world teetering on the verge of war, the president wanted the latitude in foreign policy that he enjoyed on domestic issues. He also wanted more money in the budget for defense. For Vandenberg—by this time unquestionably the leader of the isolationists and increasingly the president's bête noire—Roosevelt's ambition was doubly dubious. It threatened to undermine the senator's cherished neutrality, and, with the country still in the "Roosevelt recession," who was to say that the president wasn't hoping that preparing for war would stimulate the economy? Distrust ran deep. Was this the ultimate government intervention to relieve hard times? The strong hand in foreign policy that Vandenberg might have granted Theodore Roosevelt was not to be ceded to his Hyde Park cousin, this wily disciple of Woodrow Wilson barely a generation removed from Wilson's ill-starred crusade. The president was saying that he wanted to keep America at peace. But he had also said that America's frontier began on the Rhine. What were his true intentions?[2]

If Roosevelt's aim was preparation for war—Vandenberg seemed to have forgotten his old mantra of "preparedness"—the people should know. And surely such a course should be pursued only after all hope of negotiation had been exhausted. Nor should defense spending grow as a means to scare off potential adversaries. A foe who equated an aversion to war with "peace at any price," Vandenberg emphasized, "misunderstood the American determination and ability to defend itself and to wage war if the people and the Congress decided to go to war."[3]

Perhaps it *was* time to review the mandatory character of the arms embargo, Vandenberg conceded. But the power to make war was a congressional prerogative not to be usurped by the executive—nor by a national referendum, as some isolationists advocated. Congress looked to public opinion for direction, but not for action. There was a whiff of urgency in the air.

Early in the sultry summer of 1939 Roosevelt pressed again for repeal of the arms embargo. "Day and night, neutrality is the issue . . . not only on Capitol Hill but everywhere else in Washington," wrote one columnist. "Even at society teas the women defend or condemn the isolationist block. After all, a lot of these women would be enjoying cool breezes at some summer resort if their husbands in Congress would take final action on neutrality."[4] (Among the women was Hazel Vandenberg. She looked forward to a summer escape to Lakewood.)

Repeal of the embargo would enable the United States to become, as Roosevelt later phrased it, "the Arsenal of Democracy." Pressing the issue at a meeting with Senate leaders, he recounted his fruitless peace overtures to Hitler and Mussolini. "I've fired my last shot," he said, pleading for repeal. "I ought to have another round in my belt." But the meeting ended when Vice President Garner told FDR: "We might just as well be candid about this, Captain, you haven't got the votes."[5]

On July 7 Vandenberg and thirty-three colleagues declared unalterable opposition "to repeal or modification of the present Neutrality law." If the White House persisted in seeking repeal, neutrality advocates would filibuster for the rest of the summer. On July 11, the Foreign Relations Committee voted 12–11 to postpone consideration of the issue until the next session of Congress—in January 1940. The Congress—a minority of senators, in this case—had tied the president's hands in the shadow of war.[6]

While most eyes were on Europe, where Hitler commanded the headlines, reports from China were also grim. American resentment of Japan had been growing since 1931, when the imperial army engineered a coup in Manchuria and installed a puppet state. Many Americans regarded China with almost paternalistic affection, even as Asia generally had never been more than a peripheral concern in the great neutrality debates. The United States seemed to treat Japanese ambitions less seriously than those of Nazi Germany, with a bluster that was almost cavalier.

Yet bluster, though a mark of Vandenberg's political style, had no place in his foreign policy. If neutrality was the right policy in Europe, it was the best way to keep out of war in Asia as well. He sensed that the balance of power was shifting in the Far East and that too many Americans, including many of his colleagues, were ignorant or indifferent to these changes. Administration policy toward Japan was harsh. Economic sanctions imposed after the invasion of China were a powerful weapon against an island nation with few natural resources. Vandenberg was uneasy. "No American citizen," he had written in 1932, "has a right to urge an anti-Japanese boycott unless he is deliberately prepared to take the next subsequent step and engage in an anti-Japanese war."[7]

Again, Vandenberg suspected Roosevelt of the worst. The Nye senators—Vandenberg, Borah, Bone, Clark, Nye himself—had long insisted that Roosevelt maintain neutrality in Asia. When Japanese planes sank the American gunboat *Panay* in Chinese waters in 1937, Vandenberg shared the general demand for an apology and financial compensation but refused to go further. Let it not be a pretext for abandoning neutrality, he argued, or for an "excursion into collective security." He opposed the naval expansion bill in 1938, arguing for a new effort at naval limitation rather than an arms race with the Japanese. The reality was that Japan was a major Asian power, and the security of American possessions in the Pacific did not justify naval competition with it. In that spirit, Vandenberg welcomed the refusal in 1938 of the House of Representatives to fortify Guam.[8]

In the midst of the Foreign Relations Committee's debate in the summer of 1939, China protested that the neutrality bill would require the president to declare that a state of war existed between it and Japan. Thus trade with both nations would be placed on a cash-and-carry basis—to the advantage of Japan, with its naval and economic power. The State Department did little to mask its sympathies for China. In April 1939, Senator Pittman, with administration approval, offered a resolution authorizing the president to embargo trade with any nation that violated the Nine-Power Treaty of 1922, which guaranteed the Open Door and the territorial integrity of China. The United States had already accused Japan of treaty violations. The same day— July 12, 1939—that Vandenberg and his colleagues beat back Roosevelt's bid to repeal the arms embargo, Pittman predicted that the Committee on Foreign Relations would soon deliver a resolution for an embargo on trade with Japan only. Such a measure, Vandenberg believed, amounted to a declaration of war. It also violated provisions of the Japanese-American commercial treaty of 1911—a questionable step when the United States was denouncing Japanese treaty violations. Yet popular support for action against Japan made it likely some measure would pass. Before it could, Vandenberg stepped forward with a two-part resolution of his own.

He proposed that the United States give six months' notice, as called for by the 1911 treaty, of its intent to abrogate the trade agreement— while simultaneously expressing its intent to negotiate a new treaty "of commerce and amity" in which the United States would seek Japanese guarantees of specified American interests in return for recognition of a new modus vivendi. Vandenberg hoped to satisfy embargo advocates while negotiations for a new agreement might defuse tension between the two countries. He was convinced that there were no American interests in Asia worth a war.

His resolution also tried to find a way for the United States to fulfill its obligations to China under the Nine-Power pact. He knew that the Europeans were too preoccupied to do anything but appease the Japanese, and he did not want to see the United States embroiled in a conflict with Japan without their participation. Nor did he want the United States to defend European imperial interests. Unless others went along, the wiser course was to accept Japan's new status as the dominant Asian power. But sentiment at State and on Capitol Hill favored pressuring the Japanese, not appeasing them.

Two days later, to Vandenberg's surprise and dismay, Secretary of State Cordell Hull announced support for his resolution to renegotiate the Japanese treaty—surprise because the bill ran counter to what had been administration policy, dismay because the resolution reduced the threat of war only if it was accompanied by a serious intent to renegotiate the trade treaty. Vandenberg feared that was not the case. Hull said that State was waiting for a vote on Vandenberg's resolution before setting a future course for American-Japanese relations.

Other Democrats were not so inclined and pushed for a stronger anti-Japanese statement. Then, the very day the committee took up the bill, Hull made a surprising announcement. The State Department formally notified Japan that it intended to abrogate the 1911 trade treaty within six months, in January 1940. Diplomatic events ran ahead of congressional deliberations. Roosevelt was still smarting from the rejection of his bill to repeal the arms embargo. Canceling the treaty without waiting for senatorial advice and consent served his impulse to spank Vandenberg and the isolationists—and suggested his readiness to confront a nascent Axis power with or without congressional authorization.

The American ambassador to Japan, Joseph Grew, counseled against terminating the trade agreement. Echoing Vandenberg, he warned Roosevelt that "if we once start sanctions against Japan, we must see them through to the end, and the end may conceivably be war." This was a step, Roosevelt adviser Adolph Berle Jr. wrote in his diary, "which might very well be a material day's march on the road to a Far Eastern War." Hull's response, when Japanese diplomats repeatedly asked the intent behind abrogating the treaty, was to "keep them guessing." State was determined, he said, "to give them no enlightenment."[9] But Japan needed oil and would have to get it somewhere. In late July came news of a British agreement with Tokyo recognizing a Japanese role in China.

Vandenberg was caught in a crosscurrent. He wanted to make plain, he told Hull in August, that his "theory of abrogation" was "predicated upon earnest efforts to agree upon a new engagement. I do not need to tell you that I would not be interested in a mere arbitrary prelude to a subsequent one-sided embargo." If an embargo were ever judged essential to protect American interests, he added, "and if the American people are ever deliberately and consciously ready to take what might thus be the first step toward war itself, we can meet that situation when the issue is unavoidably precipitated." Such a "sinister step" should be avoided "until we have exhausted every pacific recourse." He pleaded with the White House to inform Japan that the United States was "anxious to negotiate a new treaty of commerce and amity."[10]

The administration's reply came from Sumner Welles, the undersecretary of state, who coyly assured him that the termination notice reflected essentially the same intent as the Vandenberg resolution. Regarding his plea for a new treaty, Welles said nothing. Vandenberg realized he had inadvertently given the president a new way to intimidate Japan. He had played into the hands of the interventionists, and that made him look like one of them. The White House had played him.

Walter Lippmann, who rarely misread the subtleties of a situation, may have done so on this occasion. He contended that Vandenberg's proposal "was the longest step on the road to war" since Wilson announced in 1915 that the United States would hold the German government accountable for its actions. Vandenberg fumed. It was "impossible for the United States to police the world," he told the columnist; he agreed that this embargo was the first step toward a war he wanted less than anyone.[11]

As senators debated neutrality, much of Washington society wondered whether American women should curtsy to the visiting king and queen of England, whose hugely publicized state visit in June was the social event of the year. Senate wives who received coveted invitations to the garden party at the British embassy debated the need for long skirts. Populists wished not to be seen kowtowing to royalty. Isolationists regarded the visit as a public relations ploy timed to build sympathy for Britain and intervention.

Arthur and Hazel wrestled with all of these issues. They also took on an assignment. With reporters denied access to the event, they agreed to be *Chicago Tribune* "legmen." After an Associated Press photographer snapped their picture at the Wardman—Arthur in white suit and Hazel in a long floral-print dress—they set out for the embassy with a reporter's notebook in Hazel's purse. Harold Sims made sure they were escorted to a good spot. Describing the fashions was Hazel's duty—who wore short dresses, who long. "All this detail about clothes to prove that it was a toss-up between the longs and the shorts, after the controversy that has raged," she noted.[12]

Arthur met the queen on one side of the lawn; Hazel shook hands with the king on the other. "We all followed them around like a bunch of kids," wrote Hazel. She was struck by the queen's charm. The king was gracious as well, "evidently trying his best to live up to her democratic manner." They were a simple couple, "obviously in love with each other, and anxious to have everybody like them. No more perfect goodwill messengers could have been found by Great Britain, whatever her ulterior motive may have been."

There was bedlam when the sky darkened with a sudden downpour. Arthur Sears Henning of the *Tribune* waited outside the embassy gates, where Hazel passed along her notes to him. The senator and his wife gave "a damn good account" of the event, Walter Trohan recalled.

The afternoon showers left the evening steamy as the Vandenbergs arrived at the White House for a "musicale" in honor of the royal couple. Members of the Senate, the Supreme Court, and the cabinet moved through a reception line to greet the monarchs and the Roos- evelts. At the head of the line, the president, supported by two of his sons, made introductions to the king. When Vandenberg approached, Roosevelt turned to King George and said, "This fellow thinks he's going to succeed me, but he's mistaken." FDR's sarcasm was delivered "without even a smile to make it seem facetious," Hazel wrote later. The king looked puzzled. Roosevelt proceeded to the next guest, never mentioning Vandenberg's name. "As we went on down the line and shook hands with the Queen and Mrs. R," Hazel recalled, "we heard the Roosevelt sons in the back break out in a loud ha ha!"[13]

Roosevelt seemed to enjoy his rival's discomfort. For Vandenberg the breach of etiquette hit a nerve. "It was unbelievably rude and quite upset Pops," Hazel said. A reporter noted that the president had spo- ken "seriously and with unconcealed bitterness."[14]

Emotions were raw. Vandenberg had once tried to cooperate with FDR, but by June 1939 their relationship had all the earmarks of a feud. After the Senate refused to revise the Neutrality Act, Roosevelt vented his fury in a late-night telephone call with Treasury Secretary Henry Morgenthau. "I think we ought to introduce a bill for statues of Austin, Vandenberg, Lodge and Taft," he grumbled, "to be erected in Berlin and put the swastika on them."

From that fetid Washington summer of high humidity and low poli- tics, Vandenberg returned to Michigan in early August, flush with suc- cess. "This is my first time in Grand Rapids in nine months, the longest separation since the day I was born,"[15] he told reporters at the Union Depot. He returned to the brick and stucco Tudor Revival on Morris Avenue. It was here that he had written the books about Alexander Hamilton. And he took to heart Hamilton's warning: "The greater part of our foreign politics ought to be to have as little political connec- tion with foreign nations as possible."[16] It was here that he would plot his defense of American neutrality. "If I disappear from time to time," he told reporters, "forgive me, because I think I owe myself at least enough of a vacation and a rest so that I can refuel for 1940."[17] But the world would not wait until 1940. German troops were massing on the Polish border. With two million men under arms, the Wehrmacht was staging dress rehearsals for war all over the Reich. Hitler was preparing a pretext for an attack on Danzig.

"This so-called war," Vandenberg said, in a speech to the American Legion, "is nothing but about twenty-five men and propaganda." In the western Michigan town of Ionia, he addressed a sunbaked crowd at the big Free Fair. Although the turnout had been greater that morning for the heavyweight horse-pulling contest, more than seven thousand constituents filled the wooden bleachers of the grandstand to hear their senator. "America wants nothing of Europe's wars, troubles or fears," Vandenberg declared. "Our hearts and souls are not burdened with gloom as over there. . . . If there should be war, there is no reason why we should become automatically involved."[18]

War, on that sweltering August afternoon, might still have been a hypothetical proposition for spectators at a Midwestern fairground. When Vandenberg thrust his forefinger in the air and vowed that "we want mandatory neutrality,"[19] the crowd roared its approval. Even in Ionia, however, the cheers mingled with an undercurrent of booing.

Later that month, Hitler and Stalin startled the world with news of their nonaggression pact. For Vandenberg, this was old-style European power politics at its most brazen, and it deserved a response as clear as the bright summer sky over Ionia. For Roosevelt—who was then on a getaway of his own, sailing to Nova Scotia aboard the USS *Tuscaloosa*—the future was a dangerous muddle. Newspapers reported the president's ship fogbound off the coast of Maine. And, in a sense, so was he, groping "through pea soup"[20] as he fretted over Hitler and the intransigence of his isolationist foes.

For many Americans, the German capacity and motivation for war, once the humiliation of the Treaty of Versailles had been redressed, seemed implausible. Awareness of the degree of Hitler's malevolence was slow to build. American newspapers reported food and clothing shortages in the Third Reich but were sure they would not be tolerated. Vandenberg's *Grand Rapids Herald* suggested: "The Germans are good feeders, notoriously so. They also like to wear good clothing, especially the women, for they are no different than women in other countries."[21] But Germany's neighbors were in no position to comfort themselves with such bromides.

The day V. M. Molotov and Joachim von Ribbentrop signed their treaty, the Vandenbergs arrived at their beachfront cottage. A heat wave gripped the Great Lakes. Lake Michigan was a warm bath. The senator could change from his flannel trousers and tennis shoes, set aside his rimless spectacles and ubiquitous cigar, and go for a swim below the dune. Posing in black trunks, he is shapeless but not entirely unfit-looking, his thinning hair swept carefully across a balding pate, no hair on his chest. Standing waist-deep in fresh water, he could look west across an immense inland sea.

But the crisis intruded, with calls for a special session of Congress to reconsider its refusal to amend the neutrality law. Vandenberg was not opposed to the notion—"if war breaks out." In his mind, however, that was not a foregone conclusion. "It's all a big bluff," sniffed Henry Ford, reflecting a widespread opinion. "If they do have a war in Europe they are crazy."[22] Forty-eight hours later, on September 1, 1939, German bombers appeared over Warsaw.

Interventionists argued that the neutrality act had strengthened the hand of Hitler. Panzer divisions quickly overran Polish cavalry. In Berlin, the British and French ambassadors declared their readiness to honor mutual assistance pacts with the Poles, and on September 3, Britain and France declared war.

Roosevelt, back in Washington, told reporters crowded around his cluttered desk that he believed the United States could stay out of the war, but only by aiding the European democracies in their hour of crisis. In a radio broadcast he told his countrymen that the United States' neutrality was born of reason, not of emotion. "Even a neutral," he declared, "has a right to take account of the facts. Even a neutral cannot be asked to close his mind or his conscience."[23]

Vandenberg might have agreed with the president's sentiments, but he argued, in effect, for the closing of the mind to the temptations of the heart. The alternative, which he suspected was Roosevelt's intention anyway, was a wedge of uncertainty, of something less than *absolute* neutrality, which was not really neutrality at all. But neutrality was the only security he could imagine. He was ready to fight for it. In a world awash with treachery, Vandenberg found his ideological high ground behind the levee of unrelenting neutrality. English economist John Maynard Keynes worried that Americans such as Vandenberg seemed to find "some sort of moral beauty"[24] in this stance—which was exactly right. The mind could fix itself upon this concept and avoid altogether the slippery slope of partial involvement. "I propose to be wholly neutral until American sovereignty is challenged," Vandenberg said, "and then I propose to be wholly unneutral." Or, as he put it on another occasion, "It's like taking the first drink of whiskey. After a while you're drunk."[25]

Roosevelt called upon Congress to convene a special session to revise the Neutrality Act by repealing the arms embargo, allowing belligerents to buy supplies from the United States on a "cash-and-carry" basis. That sounded innocuous enough, conjuring up the image of an up-to-date grocery store. To an isolationist, however, it was better to keep the lid clamped tightly shut and not tamper with neutrality than to open Pandora's box. From the dust and heat of the Michigan State Fair in Detroit, Vandenberg quickly countered: "This is not our war. It should not be. Pray God it never needs to be."[26]

But Vandenberg must have been conscious that the onset of war doomed the isolationist cause. The fall of Warsaw was imminent. With Britain and France committed to war, isolationism meant withholding aid from traditional allies who were in jeopardy. Vandenberg cut back his sojourn by the lake. He canceled all speaking engagements save one—a GOP "homecoming" rally in Grand Rapids—and announced that he would return to Washington thereafter "to remain for the duration of the war."[27]

Hugging the shore of Reeds Lake in East Grand Rapids, Ramona Park was the regional venue of vaudeville shows and roller coasters. Kent County Republicans grilled hamburgers and NBC technicians installed broadcast cables as the temperature rose to eighty-seven degrees. On the pitcher's mound of the baseball diamond, before three thousand party faithful, Governor Luren Dickinson introduced Vandenberg as "first-class material for president."[28] In his last speech before the special session, the senator, in shirtsleeves, issued a "battle cry of peace and democracy." The Neutrality Act, he told his friends and neighbors, "represents our best thoughts."[29] The United States could not become an arsenal for one side without becoming a target for the other. Such was the irrefutable logic of his position.

But Vandenberg had left behind Lake Michigan only to find himself swimming against the tide. His audience had liked his attack on Roosevelt's anti-business domestic record, but now it was business, in Michigan as elsewhere, that often supported repeal of the arms embargo. The opposition was finding more appeal among reactionaries than progressives. It included Father Coughlin, whose listeners flooded Senate mailboxes. It ranged from populist demagogues to pacifists, from Soviet sympathizers, in the wake of the Molotov-Ribbentrop Pact, to those who, cynically or sincerely, cried: "America First." From the middle of the country, Vandenberg claimed that he spoke for the "prayerful heart of America."[30] His allies, from Herbert Hoover to the socialist Norman Thomas, made strange bedfellows indeed.

Senator Borah had fought foreign entanglements since the League of Nations. "If in a few months we can tear up a law which a nation almost universally approved, how long do you think it will take to put across the proposition of sending our young men into the trenches?"[31] he asked in a radio address. For years the isolationists had smothered the chief executive under a blanket neutrality law. Now, with the first reports of combat, the blanket began to fray. Roosevelt wished to fling it off altogether. "Pressure and propaganda,"[32] Vandenberg wrote in his diary, were pushing America into war.

Unlike the *Chicago Tribune*, his own *Grand Rapids Herald* offered Vandenberg little comfort. Frank Sparks speculated on the chief source of his friend's opposition. "Were it not for distrust as to what the President, given a little power, may do," he wrote, "were it not for our suspicions as to just how far we already may be involved in the European situation, I don't believe there would be much opposition to the cash-and-carry plan which he now favors."[33] Even Vandenberg would have conceded that his insistence on absolute neutrality derived not only from its potential to "insulate" the United States from conflict, but also from an almost paranoid fear of what Roosevelt had up his sleeve. As a sympathetic columnist wrote, "The President of the United States will become a military dictator in hard economic fact as well as political imagining under legislation framed for governing the U.S. in the event of our entry into the European War."[34] If the First World War were any guide—and for Vandenberg it certainly was—the pace of centralization would accelerate as prices surged and liberties shrank. Dreams of Lippmann's *Good Society* would disappear as surely as troop ships on the horizon.

The rector of St. Mark's Episcopal Church in Grand Rapids, whose flock included many of the town's leading citizens, also felt the shadow of the First World War. He sermonized against the profit motive he detected in calls to repeal the arms embargo. One could discern the influence of the Nye hearings, as well as the moral beauty of a willfully simplistic rationale: "The more complicated the international situation becomes, the more strictly neutral we should render ourselves."[35]

Neutrality had always seemed a logical response for those, like Vandenberg, who said, "I am afraid we do not know all that is going on in the mystifying cabinets of Europe. . . . Frankly, I think we would be the prize 'suckers' of all time to become involved in this latest game of European power politics at all."[36] Vandenberg challenged "the easy and complacent assumption that England automatically 'stands for the things we stand for' "—a criticism that could not have gone down well with Mitzi and Harold Sims. Had not His Majesty's government, for example, signed a trade agreement with the Soviet Union just weeks after Stalin conspired with Hitler in the "rape of Poland"? Global relations are inevitably complex and perplexing, which is why Vandenberg believed that "the only way you can have a neutral attitude is to define it in advance of its application."[37]

But in the face of news from Europe, public opinion was shifting. A month after the German invasion of Poland, Gallup reported that Americans, once evenly divided over maintaining the embargo, now tilted 60 percent toward repeal.[38] According to *Time*, that was particularly true in Michigan, home to one of the nation's largest Polish communities, which "could be the most feverishly pro-repeal of all U.S. states."[39] Automakers and other manufacturers could anticipate a boom. Already, Britain and France had placed orders for four thousand warplanes. The British wanted four hundred thousand feet of fire hose.[40] In Grand Rapids, civic leaders, including the mayor and many longtime Vandenberg supporters, placed full-page advertisements in both newspapers imploring the senator to support repeal.[41] What most Americans wanted, observed the *Herald*, did not lend itself to a neat solution: "The people are almost unanimous to keep out, yet most want to thrash Germany."[42] No politician in the land knew how to do both.

On September 21 in a front-row seat in the House chamber, Vandenberg sat with his chin cupped in his hand, "conspicuously present," in the words of *Time*, "as captain of the willful opposition."[43] Now it was his turn, as it had been the senior Bob La Follette's with Wilson a generation before, to sit motionless as a somber president addressed a joint session of Congress. Slumped in a black leather chair, he never took his deep-set eyes off Roosevelt, who gravely and calmly asked Congress to repeal the arms embargo. "I regret that Congress passed that act," the president said. "I give you my deep and unalterable conviction that by repeal of the embargo the United States will more probably remain at peace than if the law remains as it stands today."[44]

Vandenberg did not believe that for a minute. After Roosevelt spoke, he joined two dozen other anti-repeal senators—fourteen of them Republican—in Hiram Johnson's office to map strategy. Afterward, Robert La Follette Jr. called the president's proposal "the road to war," adding, "We are going to fight this thing from Hell to breakfast."[45] Vandenberg then "went into solitude for three days . . . locked the door in his apartment, shut off the telephone."[46] He sat down at his typewriter to pound out phrase after phrase in defense of the embargo. Even as the repeal measure was voted out of the Foreign Relations Committee, he tried to put his cause in perspective: "Our battle (though a losing one)," he wrote a friend, "has made it impossible for the President to misunderstand the national attitude toward war itself."[47]

On October 2, the first day of Senate debate, ten thousand people stormed the Capitol hoping for a place in the gallery. Borah, aged and visibly tired, led off for the isolationists. Vandenberg rose on the second day, clutching his manuscript, and spoke "good, clear, and loud,"[48] as *Time* put it. "Consciously or otherwise," he observed, shaking his fist and tossing his long wisp of hair, "we are asked to depart from our neutrality policy in behalf of one belligerent whom our personal sympathies largely favor and against another belligerent whom our personal feelings largely condemn. In my opinion, this is a road that may lead us to war and I will not voluntarily take it."[49] There came the sweeping sidearm swish, punctuating the air, *Time* reported, something like the windup of pitcher Carl Hubbell.[50] "There are those who would mend our faltering economy—even the President's recent message plaintively touched the rim of this cash-register suggestion—by reaching for war orders and war profits behind a shield of technical but highly transparent and fictitious neutrality." Americans, he concluded, should "husband all our resources and perfect our own unassailable defense on this side of three thousand miles of sea, rather than dissipate our strength . . . in advance."[51]

Time hailed the ascendance of the "Big Michigander." He had in his grasp, their cover story noted, "the kind of issue politicians dream about: national, emotional, impeccable, honorable." He was standing up to the "Praetorian Guard of his party—Big Business," which, Henry Ford notwithstanding, supported the president's position.[52] (So did *Time* publisher Henry Luce, who would play a role in determining the Republican nominee in 1940.) Vandenberg's growing stature seemed paradoxical. A *Muskegon Chronicle* editorial offered one explanation: "He is entitled to supreme credit for his sincerity, even from the multitudes that will disagree with him as the days pass." Remarkably, his standing in the polls also rose. The *Detroit News* editorialized: "People in the long run often will approve the more highly the man who dares take the unpopular side when, after study and deliberation, he believes it to be right."[53]

Vandenberg conceded to a friend that "it is silly to be dogmatic on either side" of the neutrality question. Yet he refused to soften his stance, "For I happen to think I am completely right about it. . . . Perhaps that is Dutch stubbornness"—an ethnic defense he shared with Roosevelt—"or perhaps it's a sense of deep conviction."[54]

The isolationists had pledged not to filibuster. Instead, in mid-October, they proposed a three-week "peace recess" so that Roosevelt might try to mediate the European conflict. Their proposal was roundly defeated—a harbinger of the repeal vote to come. As the suspense waned, so did the crowds.

Vandenberg took solace, on the eve of defeat, in the way in which Roosevelt's presumed intentions had been circumscribed. The repeal fight forced the administration to declare its aim to keep out of war, he wrote to John Blodgett. "This is a hundred per cent change from the atmosphere in Washington four weeks ago when it was being fatalistically accepted as inevitable that we must go into the war in the near future."[55]

War fears served the president's cause. He placed American troops in the Panama Canal Zone on a state of alert. There was talk of experimental blackouts—to Vandenberg, more evidence of an administration trying to stampede public opinion. "The only thing lacking," he wrote later, "was a distribution of gas masks."[56] Once the embargo was repealed, Vandenberg wrote, the president "will interpret this as a 'go' sign for him to 'help' the allies in any way he can (and plenty of ways will be found). Having authorized him to be *unneutral*—and that is the essence of this contemplated action—he will impulsively proceed to be *very unneutral*. This will result in an increasingly sharp issue between the United States and Germany."[57]

But events would not sustain the political strategy or moral beauty of Vandenberg's position. When war became fact—a reality many isolationists had difficulty acknowledging—the hollowness of the symbolic gestures, the amendments and resolutions over which they fretted, stood revealed. The Episcopal bishop of Detroit wrote Vandenberg that he could not support a candidate of the senator's stripe in 1940, preferring "a man who has the moral and political discernment to guide this nation along those paths that alone offer the hope and assurance of peace with liberty and justice." The clergyman may have given Roosevelt more than his due, but the message was clear: even as Vandenberg offered the most cogent defense of neutrality and the arms embargo, the moral high ground was shifting.[58]

On October 27 the Senate voted 63–30 to repeal the arms embargo section of the Neutrality Act. "It is a tribute to the American heart, not to the American head," Vandenberg wrote beforehand in his diary. "The same emotions which demand repeal of the embargo will subsequently demand still more effective aid for Britain and France and Poland just as soon as it is evident that the embargo repeal is of no material consequence." He was right, of course, yet to an increasingly unneutral public that was as it should be. "The flood comes," he had prophesied the month before, "when the first breach in the dike is permitted." The breach had come.[59]

The repeal of the embargo broke the backs of the isolationists. Their position had become an increasingly inadequate response to the conflict, a response ill-suited to a great power. Their hold on public opinion waned as neutrality took on the air of an unachievable pretense. The vision Vandenberg cherished was a fading one: an America safely situated an ocean away from war.

. . . .

DARK HORSE

. . . .

In January 1940 in the *American Mercury*, Arthur Vandenberg set forth his domestic agenda in an article entitled "The New Deal Must Be Salvaged." He argued for "conservation of basic American institutions" and "the prudent notion that all change is not progress just because it is a change." Judged by its own standards, he wrote, the New Deal was an economic failure, even if not all of its ideas were bad. "The hands upon the clock of history cannot be turned back, no matter how we itch for the so-called good old days," he declared. "Eight years of the New Deal have launched certain social concepts which, in their objectives, cannot and should not be reversed." He called for a guaranteed pension system for Americans not covered by social security, and a welfare system run by the states, but with federal standards and matching funds. But he railed against expanded presidential power, the excesses of federal spending, and "the persistent and deliberate calls to class divisions, class hatreds, and class warfare which dynamite the national unity."[1]

The article and Vandenberg's philosophy of constructive engagement found widespread favor—more, Vandenberg wrote, "than any other single thing I ever did." Outspoken New Dealer Harold Ickes viewed Vandenberg as "a sounder and safer proposition for the country, even from a New Deal point of view, than anyone else on the Republican side." Vandenberg, declared the Democratic National Committee's Chairman Farley, "is the Republican to defeat." A *Newsweek* poll in December showed Vandenberg leading all contenders. A survey of nearly five hundred editors showed a majority predicting Vandenberg as the nominee. Much of the establishment agreed, from

Scripps-Howard columnist Raymond Clapper to Joe Kennedy, who said he would "back Arthur against half the Democratic candidates."[2]

In January 1940, William Borah died of a brain hemorrhage. "He was the greatest friend I ever had in public life," Vandenberg lamented. As an honorary pallbearer, he accompanied Borah's body to Boise and delivered a eulogy. In Washington, he asked Robert La Follette, whose seniority outranked his, whether he might take over Borah's desk—he already had his former office. La Follette agreed. "It is with deep but humble joy that I shall move to his vacant seat," Vandenberg wrote.[3]

Vandenberg saw the vacuum in party leadership, yet was torn, reluctant to campaign for the high office he aspired to but did not lust for. He was tired too. "By twenty I was where most fellows are at thirty-five," he told a female dinner companion, "and I have not had even so much as fifteen minutes in which to relax and play." He insisted he did not want the presidency: "I am fifty-six years old, and have burned up my energy and driven myself so hard all these years that I don't think I have more than ten years to live." Big head shaking, big eyes shining behind big glasses, waving a big cigar—"for everything about Arthur is big," that companion observed—he insisted he could make a lucrative income with a lecture bureau or writing for the *Saturday Evening Post*. He also recalled the superstition that the president elected every twenty years since 1840 had died in office.[4]

If 1940 were to be his year, he would actually have to make himself available—indeed, maybe stir himself to *run*. Urged to enter some of the handful of primaries, he refused New Hampshire, New Jersey, and Illinois. He liked his chances in Wisconsin, though. The *New York Times* reported he was a three-to-two favorite against Dewey there. His response was the same for Nebraska, where his name also went on the ballot. Yet he resisted pleas to campaign. If he lost his resolve, there would be no end to the requests. It was a curious logic, a half-hearted commitment, justified by the wishful notion that if he won without campaigning, victory would be all the more impressive.[5]

For Dewey, beating Vandenberg in the Midwest would go a long way toward establishing his credentials as a national candidate. The prosecutor was as organized as he was eager. "He gave the impression that the campaign was an extension of the district attorney's office, subject to rational conduct and personal dictation," wrote Dewey's biographer, Richard Norton Smith. Voters might find him cold, but they could find him. Vandenberg barely lifted a finger, while Dewey delivered twenty-two speeches in fourteen counties in two days. On April 2 nearly 62 percent of Wisconsin's Republican voters chose the young prosecutor. He swept all but four counties and the entire slate of delegates.[6]

Vandenberg continued to wow the Washington crowd. At the annual Gridiron Club dinner-cum-roast soon after the Wisconsin vote, Roosevelt's delivery struck listeners as tired, while Vandenberg's riposte for the GOP soared. It had been seven "dreadfully long years" since he had stood at the same rostrum to welcome the new chief executive, the senator noted. Now he had the "exquisite pleasure of speeding this departing Administration upon its skidding way." By the time the club reconvened in 1941, he predicted, "America will have convalesced." With Roosevelt, most of the Supreme Court, the cabinet, Taft, and Dewey looking on, "The hawk-beaked, thin-haired shadow of William Alden Smith had everything," one columnist observed. "His fast ball had a mean hop and his slow curve had the white ties and tails convulsed. . . . A little poetry, a little classical prose, a little soft speaking and some stump raving, in the perfect mixture, brought gales of applause." This was, Vandenberg noted in his diary with characteristic modesty, "the greatest speech in Gridiron history." How seductive the purr of the insiders![7]

In Nebraska the Senate establishment rallied to his side. Nye, Capper, McNary—all made speeches. But Dewey, outspending Vandenberg nearly six to one, was again well organized and actually campaigned. He won by a four-to-three margin. "Senator Vandenberg simply does not speak the language of anybody under the age of 40 in this country," wrote Dorothy Thompson. Yet Dewey's delegate count stalled far short of what he needed, and odds favored a convention fight. Kansas City publisher Roy Roberts called on Vandenberg in the company of a charming utility executive named Wendell Willkie. Maybe the party was ready for a fresh face. Even as shrewd an observer as Franklin Roosevelt predicted a Taft nomination, conceding that the convention could also turn to Vandenberg. Dewey was an upstart and Willkie stood little chance.[8]

Through the early months of 1940, the world was in suspense. In Washington, Vandenberg was on the outside looking in. Suspicious of Roosevelt, he insisted that Congress be informed of plans for national security. Senators were "earnestly seeking to cooperate," Vandenberg wrote Roosevelt in May. He asked for "confidential access" to a recent report of the War Resources Board. But the White House snubbed him. "Dear Arthur," FDR replied, the report was already out-of-date. "If I were a judge I would tell you that it is 'not germane' to the pending case."

In May the waiting, the "phony war," ended in a dizzying barrage of news bulletins, armored columns, and screaming dive-bombers. Germany invaded Norway, France, Denmark, and the Low Countries. Kings and queens fled their thrones. The map of Europe was being drawn and quartered. Arthur and Hazel might dine at a European embassy, only to have the host called away for news that his country had been invaded. Their Norwegian friends, Ambassador and Mrs. Morgenstierne, were "quite composed," Hazel reported in her diary. They planned to stay in their legation "until ordered out. . . . They are still unbelieving in the stories of treachery that have come from the homeland." Tales abounded of Nazi brutality.

A British expeditionary force, rushed to France to resist the Germans, was forced onto a slice of beach at Dunkirk and evacuated helter-skelter back across the channel. Luftwaffe bombers began night raids on English cities; an invasion of the British Isles appeared imminent. Yet when the American undersecretary of state, Sumner Welles, threw a party, German consul Hans Thomsen and his wife were among the guests. "One can't understand why they came," Hazel mused, "except as they now feel so superior to everyone else."

Vandenberg conceded that the United States had become a nonbelligerent ally of the British, with little pretense of neutrality left. That gave "the clear conception that America is safer if the allies should win." He seemed to be accepting the status quo and squirming under the "isolationist" label. He maintained that the two oceans offered the U.S. "insulation" and that an Allied defeat need not be fatal to American interests. Even as reality closed in, he was reluctant to send more aid to Great Britain.[9]

His opposition to foreign entanglements persisted. "An overwhelming percentage of the American people (regardless of their sympathies) insist that we shall never export another American soldier," he told a constituent that spring. He opposed involvement, "directly or indirectly," he said, "and since I do not intend to take the 'last step' in this bloody direction, I also do not propose to take the 'first step' or any other step."[10]

Beyond the news of Nazi conquests, beyond the primary defeats, May was also a month of loss at the Wardman Park. Harold Sims came home ill one noon from the embassy. Hazel helped Mitzi get him upstairs and into bed. "When I saw Harold," Hazel wrote, "I telephoned Pops and told him if he wanted to see Harold alive, he'd better come right home." The Vandenberg housekeeper found a nurse. A doctor was summoned. Sims slipped into a coma and died that night. Hazel reported, "There was nothing to do but for dad and the doctor to make burial arrangements." It was the next day before anyone from the embassy arrived.

While his professional role was never clear, Sims was described in one news account as "Great Britain's first casualty of war to occur in this country." Even as Hazel joined her husband to look after a distraught Mitzi, both must have wondered what this meant for a relationship that had nearly destroyed their marriage.

Wendell Willkie came out of nowhere. The Wall Street lawyer and utility executive had gained prominence as a foe of the Tennessee Valley Authority and other federal forays into fields normally the province of the private sector. He combined his sallies against Roosevelt with a willingness to align the United States with Great Britain in the fight against Germany. This set him apart from Vandenberg, Taft, and Dewey—and endeared him to East Coast publishers and financiers who could abide neither the New Deal nor isolationism. Willkie's well-funded campaign combined a sort of grassroots elitist enthusiasm with the power of Time-Life and the *New York Herald Tribune*. With his curly forelock dancing as he spoke, he barnstormed the country, quickly amassing more delegates than Vandenberg, although fewer than Taft. The front-runner, Dewey, stalled at 360 delegates, 140 shy of the 500 needed for the nomination.

On the eve of the convention, Roosevelt startled the Republicans by nominating Henry Stimson, secretary of state under Hoover, and Frank Knox, Vandenberg's old friend and former GOP vice presidential candidate, to lead the departments of war and navy. Inviting Republican stalwarts into a coalition cabinet gave a bipartisan gloss to FDR's foreign policy. Arthur, Hazel confided, was "so wrought up he proceeded to entertain us thoroughly."

In late June the Vandenbergs arrived in Philadelphia for the convention. The senator strolled through the lobby of the Hotel Adelphia in his linen suit, brandishing a smile and a cigar and predicting that if the convention battle reached a sixth ballot, he would be the nominee. He met with delegation after delegation, hoping to be everyone's second choice. After breakfast with Willkie came hints he might be invited on a Willkie ticket, should one come to pass. These were exhausting days, Hazel reported, but her husband looked "fit and fighting though he feels there isn't a chance outside of a miracle which we hope won't happen."[11] Her ambivalence reflected his.

Dewey might have gone over the top had he picked up Vandenberg's seventy-six delegates. He offered Vandenberg the vice presidency. Vandenberg wrote later that Dewey could have controlled the convention "if he had been willing to take a sporting chance." Vandenberg first suggested that Dewey take the second spot while the senator pledge to serve a single term and support him in 1944. If that were "too much to swallow," he would meet Dewey in half an hour and "flip a coin to see which end of the ticket we take." Not surprisingly, Dewey declined.[12]

Michigan congressman Roy Woodruff placed Vandenberg's name in nomination as a candidate willing to end "seven socialistic years" of Democratic rule. He described Vandenberg as a master of coalition politics, capable of drawing support from "Jefferson" Democrats as a fiscal conservative. Moreover, he would keep the United States out of war.[13]

After four ballots, Dewey's delegates were defecting. Conservatives rallied round Taft. Willkie supporters had been given tickets to pack the galleries. As the sergeant-at-arms let them in, the chants of "We Want Willkie!" that had been heard from outside the hall began to re-sound within. (Somewhere in that full-throated legion stood a young Grand Rapidian who would be vice president and president, too: Gerald Ford.)[14]

On the fifth ballot, Taft reached 377 votes. Dewey was collapsing as his East Coast delegates moved to Willkie by the score. The dark horse soared to 429 delegates, but his lead looked precarious. Willkie's managers turned to Frank McKay, Michigan's GOP kingmaker. Willkie had pledged to cut no deals. Now he agreed to give McKay control of judges and other patronage in the state. As McKay swung to Willkie, Michigan's favorite son agreed to release his delegates. On the sixth ballot, the Michigan delegation gave thirty-five votes to Willkie. The galleries roared. "The die was cast," Vandenberg wrote.[15]

In the end the isolationist had tacitly thrown his support to the most interventionist of Republican candidates. Taft's views were closer to his own, but he felt Willkie had a better chance. He hoped, however, that Willkie would defer to the platform on foreign policy, which approved extending only such limited support to the Allies "as shall not be in violation of international law or inconsistent with the requirements of our own national defense." Despite his wishes for greater "insulation," he admitted that the platform acknowledged the United States as a "nonbelligerent partner of the allies." Willkie shared Roosevelt's interventionist impulse, and his nomination muted campaign season debate on foreign policy.

From the beginning, the stigma of the Hoover years and his own isolationism clouded Vandenberg's appeal. Yet there were other factors that contributed to his eclipse. He may have owed some of his ambivalence to gossip surrounding his affair with Mitzi Sims. He had never raised much money. But more than anything, the rush of events eroded his standing. The Nazi onslaught in the weeks preceding the convention gave him an air of futility and estranged him from wealthy Detroit manufacturing interests. By June 1940 the Blitzkrieg dominated the headlines, and it became ever harder to imagine a rigid isolationist in the White House. Dorothy Thompson had it right; her friend "had made serious mistakes so far as gauging the mind of the country on foreign policy." His oratory was old, his words had "the unfortunate associations which harken back to a time that no one wants to see restored."

And how much of a chance had he ever had? Vandenberg was naïve to think that he might prevail at the convention without winning so much as a single Midwestern primary. He had struggled to hold even some Michigan delegates—Dewey, after all, was another native son. As Vandenberg wrote later, "The Willkie *blitzkrieg* hit me just like it hit everybody else."[16] On the train back to Washington, Vandenberg asked a female friend, "What has Willkie got that I haven't got?" The reply: "A mop of unruly, curly, black hair that to most women is almost irresistible." Said the balding senator, "I haven't thought of that."[17]

When Democrats convened soon after, they nominated Franklin Roosevelt for a precedent-shattering third term. Many delegates booed his selection of Agriculture Secretary Henry Wallace to replace Garner on the ticket. But no Republican underestimated the president's political skills—or the sweep of his coattails.

When Congress adjourned in August, Vandenberg rushed home to fight for reelection. Even as the Battle of Britain raged and public opinion shifted further from isolation, he overwhelmed a razor-blade salesman in the Republican primary. More jobs helped. A war-driven economic recovery, including foreign orders pouring into Michigan factories, seemed to increase voter comfort with the status quo. Vandenberg was the antiwar candidate, but by then he supported providing Britain with "every material assistance which can flow from our industrial munitions productions." This was what the autoworkers and their bosses wanted to hear.

Democrats chose Detroit attorney Frank Fitzpatrick to challenge the incumbent. Blessed with a name that played well on a Michigan ballot, he attacked Vandenberg for opposing so much of the New Deal and the needs of American defense. Although Fitzpatrick had some help from labor, the national party gave him little support.

Vandenberg had struggles, too, as Detroit Republicans focused their financial support on Willkie. The senator was still bitter about the loss of his home precinct in 1934 and told Arthur Junior not to look for help "from anybody in Grand Rapids." A Gallup poll in Michigan gave Roosevelt 54 percent support. If that margin held, Vandenberg noted, the president would carry the state by 130,000 votes—it would take a miracle for a Republican to overcome that margin. He persuaded Willkie to suggest that Roosevelt had confidential understandings with the British that would commit the United States to war. FDR's response was the famous promise voters wanted to hear: "Your boys are not going to be sent into any foreign war." With that brazen assurance, Roosevelt tempered public anxiety. "That hypocritical son of a bitch," Willkie fumed. "This is going to beat me."[18]

Vandenberg avoided public disagreement with Willkie's interventionism. He even withheld comment on Roosevelt's offer to Churchill to trade destroyers for bases, a deal he regarded privately as a lethal blow to neutrality and quite beyond the constitutional prerogative of the president. He prodded Willkie to denounce Roosevelt's "dictatorial" use of executive power.[19]

"By 1940 I began to wonder," the *Tribune*'s Trohan said of Vandenberg: "He wasn't hitting as hard" at Roosevelt's policy. Mitzi Sims might have been a factor, Trohan hinted. In an era when such affairs were usually treated with discretion by the press, Vandenberg's private travail was public fodder. More important were the senator's election-

year calculations—the ambitious politician's governing imperative—
and a dawning recognition of a new reality.[20]

The soft-pedaling paid off. While Roosevelt swept to a third term,
Michigan alone among the major industrial states gave its presidential
vote to Willkie—and Vandenberg's coattails probably made the difference. His margin of victory was 113,000 votes, while Willkie edged
Roosevelt by fewer than 7,000 and Governor Dickinson was swamped
by Democrat Murray Van Wagoner.

The senator's presidential balloon had not hurt. Although the Congress of Industrial Organizations, known as the CIO, worked for the
Democrat, Vandenberg even showed strength among union members,
with endorsements from the Detroit Federation of Labor, United Mine
Workers President John L. Lewis—a rabid anti-Roosevelt isolationist—
and American Federation of Labor President William Green. Indeed,
Vandenberg won the support of twenty-three unions and swept all but
ten counties—the CIO hotbeds of Wayne, Genesee, and Muskegon,
and seven in the traditionally Democratic Upper Peninsula.

He weathered the storm. War was on and the United States was
gearing up to play a crucial role. Yet his own was more open to question than ever.

· · · · · · · · · · · ·

WAR

· · · · · · · · · · · ·

Like millions of other Americans, Vandenberg sat by a radio as the last year of peace ended with a fireside chat. Franklin Roosevelt spoke of helping Great Britain much as you might help your neighbor—if his house were burning, you would loan him your hose. After the collapse of France, not only were the beleaguered British running out of arms; they lacked the money to buy more. They were winning the air battle, but they would need more help to fend off a German invasion.

In his State of the Union speech, the president asked Congress to approve a $7 billion loan and grant him authority to "sell, transfer title to, exchange, lease, lend" armaments to any country whose defense he deemed vital to the security of the United States. This was "lend-lease"—a way to provide Great Britain all aid short of American troops.

There was polite applause, though seldom from Republicans. The administration's response to war had moved, in the later words of Walter Lippmann, "from large promises carried out slyly and partially by clever devices to substantial deeds openly and honestly avowed."[1]

Vandenberg saw it otherwise. The speech "was a flop," he wrote. He denounced lend-lease as "war-by-proxy." A furious Eleanor Roosevelt, displaying "more raw anger than ever before," declared at her press conference the next day that Vandenberg had no right "to play with words when the world is on fire." This was a symptom of the very war fever Vandenberg feared. Taken aback by the personal attack, he found even among Democratic colleagues a consensus that "the Roosevelts do not relish facing the reality of what they are trying to do."[2]

Lend-Lease was a turning point. Defeat of the bill might hasten Britain's defeat, but passage would presage American entry into the war. Vandenberg made a passionate case for keeping out while there was still time. For years, his son wrote later, the senator had been carefully creating a "Portrait of an Isolationist," symbolizing in himself "the lessons of a century and a half of protected democracy, the yearnings of a hundred and fifty million Americans [for peace]. . . . Nothing had been omitted that might catch the eye or stir the emotions." He drew on the counsel of the Founders—Hamilton first and foremost. He took cues from Borah. But Vandenberg felt increasingly isolated, facing a bill that allowed the president "to make undeclared war on any country he pleases . . . at any time he pleases, and almost in any fashion he pleases."[3]

Hazel, accompanied by Mitzi—or was it the other way around?—observed the Foreign Relations Committee hearings on Lend-Lease. More than a few attendees had come to see the opposition's lead witness, Charles Lindbergh, who spoke for America First, the strident isolationist organization. Chairman Walter George threatened to clear the vast room when applause for the handsome aviator took so long to subside. Lindbergh argued that all-out aid to Britain would compromise America's ability to defend itself. He urged a negotiated peace with Germany. Witnesses supporting the cleverly numbered H.R. 1776 included Wendell Willkie and the Republican mayor of New York, Fiorello La Guardia. They raised the issue of Nazi barbarism, which America Firsters tended to brush aside.

Vandenberg proposed an amendment permitting the president to dispose of military equipment only after the army and navy certified "that such equipment was not essential to the defense of the United States." He lost, and Mitzi's team prevailed, as it were. The committee reported out Lend-Lease, fifteen votes to eight.

On the Senate floor, Vandenberg was "generalissimo," in *Time*'s words, of the coalition opposing the bill. Democrat Burt Wheeler led off the attack with a notorious assertion. Playing on the crop reduction programs of the New Deal's Agricultural Adjustment Act, he accused the president of proposing "to plow under every fourth American boy." Vandenberg would not go that far. He quoted the apostle Paul, writing to Timothy, about providing for his own house first. Had not Roosevelt won reelection with a vow to keep us out of war?[4]

Vandenberg reminded colleagues of his own campaign vow: "We must not lose democracy at home in an effort to save it abroad." The Lend-Lease bill, he charged, authorizes the president "to become power politician number one of this whole, mad world." In passing it, Congress would be telling the president, in effect, "You pick our allies; you pick our enemies. . . . You lend, lease or give away what you please (with only casual limitations) out of our own defense facilities or out of the reservoir of our resources; you are the monarch of all you survey."

He sensed the end of an era. "There may be no such thing as isolation left in this fore-shortened world," he declared, "but there still is such a thing as relative detachment and magnificent independence." He feared "negation" of a "life-saving foreign policy" that had served the republic since its founding. On Saturday, March 8, 1941, the Senate found Vandenberg's fears less compelling than those laid out by Roosevelt. The senator slouched in his seat, his dark eyes darting about the chamber. When the storm of rhetoric subsided, his colleagues approved Lend-Lease, 61–30.

Vandenberg retreated to his diary. He recorded the time of the roll call: 7:10 p.m. "If America 'cracks up' you can put your finger on this precise moment as the time the crime was committed," he wrote. Lend-Lease "passed because it wore the popular label of an aid-to-England bill and because the Roosevelt Administration left no stone unturned to drive its votes in the Senate in a goose-step—backed by a nationwide emotion and a nationwide propaganda of amazing proportions."

Vandenberg did support Taft's simple resolution, approved overwhelmingly, which would give immediate aid to Great Britain. This was sufficient, he argued, to demonstrate American commitment. The Lend-Lease bill was open-ended. "I had the feeling," Vandenberg wrote right after the vote, "that I was witnessing the suicide of the Republic."[5]

With H.R. 1776, Vandenberg further charged: "We have torn up 150 years of traditional American foreign policy. We have tossed Washington's Farewell Address into the discard. . . . We have taken the first step upon a course from which we can never hereafter retreat. . . . We have said to Hitler and Mussolini and Japan: 'We are in an undeclared war with you, and we will never sheath the sword until you have suffered a *conclusive military defeat.*'"[6] As Henry Kissinger observed, "Vandenberg's analysis was correct, but it was the world that had imposed the necessity; and it was Roosevelt's merit to have recognized it."[7]

The senator was beaten. Unilateral isolationism—the dominant theme in American foreign policy since the founding of the republic—had come to an end for Arthur Vandenberg. When the time came to approve Lend-Lease appropriations, he voted with the majority. "If we stand *any* show, it will be from pursuing this new, revolutionary foreign policy to the last limit with the swiftest speed," he wrote. "Our fate is *now* inseverably linked with that of Europe, Asia and Africa. We have deliberately chosen to 'sit in' on the most gigantic speculation since Time began."[8]

He did not fully capitulate, however. He opposed Secretary of War Stimson's plan for American escorts to convoy British merchant vessels across the Atlantic. That could quickly lead the United States into a "shooting war," he warned, in May 1941. In July he denounced Roosevelt's decision to station troops in Iceland as a move that invited an attack by the Axis. He unsuccessfully opposed renewal of the Selective Service Act in August, citing the power it gave to administration "warmongers." And in November he opposed, again without success, an amendment to the Neutrality Act of 1939 that allowed the arming of merchant ships.

But this opposition masked increasing doubts about the wisdom of his position. As his son and chief apologist observed, "If conditions changed for the worse through no fault of his own, Vandenberg was not a man to keep on defending an outpost when the enemy had overrun him and was attacking the fort." The fort was under siege. Ideas that had animated Vandenberg throughout his adult life appeared discredited in a world dominated by Roosevelt and Churchill and Adolf Hitler.[9] He found himself ever more on the defensive. "It is dangerous to attempt to lump all of us (who oppose intervention in the war) into one standard isolationist bracket,'" he wrote in November. "If I had to choose between being an isolationist or an internationalist I should unhesitatingly proclaim myself to be the former. But the path of wisdom and prudence lies somewhere in between."[10]

The best he could do was hope for more favorable circumstances in the future, writing of the need for "some rational formula under which the next peace agreement can be underwritten by all the major powers of the world, including the United States. In other words—although I continue to be wholly opposed to any sort of foreign entanglements for America—I would very much prefer to join in guaranteeing a just European peace than to join in a European war." The pragmatist prone to dealing with "a condition, not a theory" was clinging, in this rearguard view, to the latter.

Entanglements were the order of the day. The Senate authorized seizure of German and Italian ships in American ports—and rejected a Vandenberg amendment to prevent their transfer to Great Britain. Roosevelt denounced the sinking of the American freighter *Robin Moor* by a German submarine as "outrageous and indefensible." Vandenberg was more ambivalent, having heard that the vessel carried cargo on the German contraband list—a list similar to that of the British: "If that is anywhere near the truth, it puts a totally different light on the episode (although it would not excuse the utterly unexplainable fact that the sub-commander did not take off all the passengers and crew before the sinking)." Country and Congress were entitled to "all the facts"—and did not get them. Vandenberg pressed Hull for information but received no reply. When he pressed further, the State Department said it was uncertain whether war materials had been aboard.[11]

Vandenberg had fallen a long way from being a White House insider. Ever eager to be consulted, he groused to his newspaper friend Lord Beaverbrook that Roosevelt welcomed only "Republicans who are *known in advance* to be 'yes men.' . . . I have not been invited into the executive office in eight years."[12] Sometimes he felt as though he learned more from foreign visitors than from the White House or the State Department. He was learning more as well from his nephew,

Hoyt Vandenberg. The dashing pilot had become a senior officer in the Army Air Corps. While the two Vandenbergs were discreet, they were also close—had been since Hoyt's teenage year in Grand Rapids living with the widowed editor. The senator regarded his nephew with almost paternal affection. Hoyt used the Wardman's underground entrance to avoid notice on social visits with Uncle Arthur and Aunt Hazel. While their wives were in with the children, Vandenberg and his nephew retired to the kitchen. Major Vandenberg, a student of Royal Air Force tactics in the Battle of Britain, brought a strategic understanding of modern warfare.

On the afternoon of Sunday, December 7, Vandenberg sat hunched over scrapbook and glue pot at a card table in his living room. He wielded scissors through half a dozen newspapers, pasting in any item that mentioned his name. When the phone rang, he set aside a cigar and lifted the black receiver to his ear. The Japanese were bombing the American fleet at Pearl Harbor. He turned on the radio and did not have to wait long for a news bulletin to crackle through. This was not the distant conflict of Old World rivals. These were American sailors, American ships—American soil. He rang up the White House and reached press secretary Steve Early. "Despite all differences on other things," he told Early, he supported the president without reservation. Minutes later, another aide was on the phone relaying Roosevelt's thanks.

On December 8 the president addressed a joint session of Congress. Citing the preceding "day of infamy," he asked for a declaration of war against Japan. Perhaps war was inevitable, Vandenberg acknowledged. But that inevitability owed something to American policy. As he noted in his diary, "We 'asked for it' and 'we got it,' the interventionist says today—as the President virtually did in his address to the nation—'See! This proves we were right and that this war was *sure* to involve us.' The non-interventionist says (and I say)—'See! We have insisted from the beginning that this course would lead to war and it has done exactly that.' "

His ambivalence had a powerful whiff of defensiveness. "In a sense, we are *both* right," he conceded. "But I do not see, on the face of the record, how it can be denied that *we* certainly have been right." Had not the United States, as the arsenal for one belligerent, become a target for another, just as he had predicted? His old friend Frank Knox, by then secretary of the navy, had been particularly bellicose in 1940, calling for the defeat of Germany "by proxy."[13]

It may have been the *right* course to help Britain, he admitted privately. "God knows I have wanted Britain to win and win conclusively. . . . The point is that we did everything we could—by proxy—to help defeat Germany, and said so." The American navy had been instructed to shoot at German aircraft on sight, and "Roosevelt and Churchill sealed what they called 'The Atlantic Charter' for Germany's doom. . . . I do not here question the *justification* of these policies. . . . But I say that when, at long last, Germany turned upon us . . . it is no contribution to 'historical accuracy' (to put it mildly) for us to pretend to say that this war has been '*thrust upon us.*'" The thrusting, he concluded, had begun two years earlier, before the repeal of the arms embargo, and it continued when a few concessions to Japan might have averted the fatal surprise attack.[14]

With these thoughts in mind, Vandenberg, on the Senate's return to its own chamber that day, asked for the floor. Democrats objected. Foreign Relations chairman Tom Connally was on his feet, trying to dissuade his colleague; then he sat back down. "Of course," he muttered, "the Senator has a right to speak if he insists."

Vandenberg insisted, and his was the only speech that preceded a vote to declare war. "I felt it was absolutely necessary to establish the reason why our non-interventionists were ready to 'go along,'" he wrote in his diary. "I felt it was necessary, too, in order to better swing the vast anti-war party in the country into unity with this unavoidable decision." He and opponents of administration policy were postponing debate, he argued, not abandoning their beliefs. As he finished, the chamber was quiet. Then old Carter Glass of Virginia, on outspoken interventionist, crossed the aisle to extend his hand. No one else rose to speak—tacit acknowledgment that Arthur Vandenberg not only spoke for, but also embodied, the loyal opposition.[15]

"In my own mind," Vandenberg wrote later, in a simplistic formulation that glossed over many halting steps along a road that ran from the seductive Mitzi Sims to the strategic Air Force nephew, "my convictions regarding international cooperation and collective security for peace took firm form on that afternoon of the Pearl Harbor attack. That day ended isolation for any realist."[16]

As the war spread around the world, Washington, DC, was blacked out for brief periods for civil defense, but the darkness might as well have been constant for Vandenberg, so remote was he from the lights of the White House Map Room. He proposed a joint congressional-executive committee to keep Congress informed of military needs and policy decisions. The president brushed him off. Isolationism had once had an aura of rugged American individualism—the self-reliance of the Founders. Now it was coming to be seen as a cowering anachronism.

An anguished year after the death of Harold Sims—would Arthur stay with Hazel? Would he choose Mitzi?—Mitzi, "a siren all of her life," moved back to Montreal. After she left, British intelligence was quick to ensure that Vandenberg received flattering attention from its most famous agent, Betty Pack. "She singled out men and seduced them," wrote her biographer. While her wiles enabled the Allies to steal code books from the Vichy French and the Italians, however, there is no evidence that she ever had more than fleeting contact with the senator.[17]

For Hazel, a friend observed, there seemed to be hope of "a new era" after the Sims affair, When she visited Grand Rapids, friends at the Women's City Club welcomed her with sympathy.[18]

"A bomb dropped on Grand Rapids," intoned narrator Jimmy Stewart in a short documentary directed by Garson Kanin early in 1942. Filmed in the wake of Pearl Harbor, *Fellow Americans* was intended to rally the home front. It singled out four towns around the country to bring home the consequences of war. In each locale, everyday life was interrupted by news of a hometown sailor killed in the Japanese attack. While no record exists to explain the choice of locations, it is not difficult to imagine why the home of Roosevelt's most formidable isolationist foe was the only Midwestern setting.

Meanwhile, Washington became the capital of the free world before anyone had a chance to think about what that meant. "None of that easy-going Southern atmosphere of the past," Hazel noted. "Crowds in the buses and street-cars that are being used by everybody, even justices of the Supreme Court. Crowds in the restaurants where you wait interminably to be served. Crowds in the stores where the service has been equally disrupted. . . . Young girls by the hundreds who have poured into town to do war work. It really seems as if the world and his brother have landed here." Here came the nobles and diplomats of occupied nations. The streets bustled, not only with American soldiers and sailors, with women in uniform, but also with the uniforms of allies and the accents of refugees.

In 1941 it had still been possible to saunter onto the White House grounds without showing a pass. Now, the buildings along Pennsylvania or Constitution Avenues—Treasury, the White House, the old State Department—were cordoned off. Jeeps and troop trucks, sentry boxes, and khaki-clad guards with white gloves and cartridge belts were everywhere. Headlines spoke of cataclysmic events half a world away, but when H. L. Mencken looked in vain for news of a local snowfall, he learned that his newspaper was complying with an order against giving weather information that could be of use to an enemy.

The war was not going well. Japanese forces swept through southern Asia. They seized the British fortifications at Singapore in February 1942. Malaya, Burma, and the Dutch East Indies fell. General MacArthur retreated from the Philippines. In North Africa, German armored columns under Erwin Rommel threatened Cairo. Most crucially, Hitler turned on the Soviet Union. The Wehrmacht drove deep into Russia, reaching the outskirts of Stalingrad, laying siege to Leningrad.

"The typical week of a senator's wife . . . is no more," wrote Hazel. "Gone are the formal Cabinet and White House receptions where tea was dispensed by the gallon. Formalities have completely disappeared along with striped trousers and tall silk hats." Ambassadors of occupied countries refused to hand over embassy keys to their Axis conquerors. Hazel described poignant visits with the Czechs and Poles, and "the effort they are all making to keep alive the spark of patriotism." The Netherlands was "living on hope. And we complain of our lot!" The White House canceled most of its diplomatic entertainments. But the Cave Dwellers of old Washington held to their rituals. Cissy Patterson and the Guggenheims threw big parties; the Latin American legations felt less constrained than those from war-torn regions. "And so the social pace goes on, regardless of war," wrote Hazel. "The Capital's heterogeneous population must play."[19]

The Senate Ladies Luncheon Club transformed itself into the Senate Red Cross. Hazel took up a regular post at a sewing machine every Tuesday and Thursday, with a half-hour break for lunch. Hoyt Vandenberg rose to brigadier general after organizing the Twelfth Air Force in Great Britain. Arthur Vandenberg Junior—thirty-five years old and newly the winner of an award for the tasteful remodeling of his tiny Georgetown house—pitched in, too. He declined an army commission to enlist as a private.[20] All Arthur Senior could do was speculate. In the House of Commons in January, Churchill intimated that the United States might have entered the war in the Far East even without the attack on Pearl Harbor. Vandenberg wondered if Roosevelt had given the British some assurance, at the time of the "Atlantic Charter," that *we were slated for this war*," that "Pearl Harbor merely precipitated what was 'in the cards.'" Churchill's remarks received little attention in the United States, leading Vandenberg to fret that some hint of censorship was in the air.

Worse, after the fall of Singapore, Churchill declared American involvement to be "what I have dreamed of, aimed at and worked for, and now it has come to pass."[21] In other words, Vandenberg wrote, "the major objective of British diplomacy all through these recent years (when all our British co-operation was supposed to be for the purpose of *keeping us out of the war*) has been to get us into the war. I don't blame 'em. But if any non-interventionist, prior to last December 6th, had accused Churchill of 'working to *get us into the war*' he would have been condemned by the interventionists as a pro-Nazi. 'Just give us the tools and we will finish the job' was what Churchill was saying then."[22]

More than ever, labels mattered. Vandenberg preferred "non-interventionist" to "isolationist." He was "simply scared to death," the *Tribune*'s Trohan reported to Colonel McCormick, who was trying to assess where his erstwhile ally stood. He quoted Vandenberg: "We isolationists before Pearl Harbor are liable to be smeared any time."[23]

Those who accepted that label in private kept their thoughts mostly to themselves. One was Taft, McCormick's new favorite. His son had married a Grand Rapids woman. It was a small world of isolationist presidential hopefuls. Taft later quipped, "I may not be Michigan's favorite son, but I hope to be her favorite father-in-law."[24]

Vandenberg and Taft's nemesis of 1940, Wendell Willkie, was about to embark on a highly publicized fact-finding trip around the world—his effort, as Roosevelt's representative, to build awareness at home of the need for greater international cooperation. It was also, as Vandenberg surely recognized, a symbolic act of bipartisanship from the titular head of the Republican Party. The journey would result in the publication, early in 1943, of *One World*, a slender best seller that proselytized for a new world order when the war ended. In his introduction, Willkie described the land he had left behind: "America is like a beleaguered city that lives within high walls through which there passes only an occasional courier to tell us what is happening outside," he wrote. "I have been outside those walls. And I have found that nothing outside is exactly what it seems to those within." The implication for Arthur Vandenberg was that he was one of those within who did not understand the shifting reality. Though for him the villain was Roosevelt, who had walled off congressional Republicans from the White House, and whose occasional couriers shared precious little.[25]

Vandenberg complained loudly. Secretary of State Hull finally assigned an assistant as a liaison between Congress and the State Department. Witnesses appeared before the Foreign Relations Committee. When American troops landed in North Africa, General George Marshall briefed Vandenberg and a handful of others on the need for a cease-fire with the pro-Nazi Vichy French. Marshall had "turned on the light," Vandenberg said. It was welcome insight from one of the rare voices Congress knew to trust. Such sharing was the exception, however, not the rule.[26]

At the outbreak of war, wrote columnist Mark Sullivan, Vandenberg "was spokesman and symbol of an especially strong segment of Republican opinion." Yet he was carrying a banner few wished to follow, and he knew it. Even though four out of five Americans had agreed with a policy of "non-intervention" before Pearl Harbor, Sullivan wrote, Vandenberg "probably recognizes that the extreme quality of his view . . . would be, in the light of present conditions, a handicap to a presidential aspirant."

Sullivan's assessment drew a rebuttal from the senator: "In my own section of the country pre-Pearl-Harbor-non-interventionists won some of their most spectacular political victories as recently as last November. Those 'four out of five Americans' of whom you speak have gone through a perfectly simple and obvious mental process under the impact of war." Wasn't everyone opposed to a shooting war before—including the president? Then war came—"historians can someday unravel the underlying reasons why"—and soon five out of five insisted that the war "must be fought to a conclusive finish and to a peace-for-keeps." That, he declared, was "my own relentless course." He was a patriot then and a patriot now. "I do not believe," he insisted, "it is a handicap to have been one of the 'four out of five' then and one of the 'five out of five' now."

He was offering his early intimations of a changed world. It was clear "that the fact of global war itself . . . shatters any chance for America to view her world responsibilities in any such isolated pattern as followed World War Number One." He turned to a new phrase to describe his approach: "It would not even be enlightened self-interest." He was thinking aloud for the "first and only time," he confided to

Sullivan. "The mistakes of Versailles must not be repeated. We must find an ultimate peace-unity to match our war-unity with the world's friends of freedom." No one knew, he continued, "what that post-war pattern will be," but "America must accept her full responsibilities."[27] He would not lead that charge, though. He let it be known, two years in advance, that he would not be a candidate for president in 1944.

But what *would* follow the war? Vice President Henry Wallace declared that from the war would emerge the "century of the common man," and he only half-jokingly added that the war's object was "to make sure that everybody in the world has the privilege of drinking a quart of milk a day." For the Wheelers and the Tafts, the imperatives of war were temporary. They would, said Vandenberg, "simply insist upon consulting the best welfare of 'America First'—and *that* sort of 'isolationism' will be found very much alive (despite all these Willkie funeral orations) *when the time comes* to deal with the post-war world." The senator himself would wait and see what peace would bring, fervently hoping that America's "enlightened self-interest" would coincide with his own.[28]

Vandenberg, Wallace, and much of official Washington took a "night off from work and worry," Hazel noted in her diary, to celebrate the New Year of 1943 at Friendship, the estate of Evalyn Walsh McLean. Here were Lord Halifax and Senator Wheeler, socialites and Supreme Court justices and Cave Dwellers, and probably a British agent or two. Washington society, same as it ever was, except in that year five courses instead of eight, paper flowers for centerpieces, and a guest list that included not only the top tier of government and the diplomatic corps, but also twenty servicemen chosen by lot from a nearby canteen.

Hazel talked with a private from New York who studied his right palm. "I don't ever want to wash it again after shaking hands with such famous people," he said. Roosevelt's postmaster general and his wife gave the Vandenbergs a ride home, proving, Hazel noted, "how the political picture works at a party"—and displaying the only sort of bipartisanship that had been in evidence.[29]

The president conducted the war with scant regard for congressional egos, Republican or otherwise. For Vandenberg, distrust as much as ideology, FDR's arrogance as much as partisan division, governed his fears for the future. He was bitter; confusion reigned: "Even we in the Senate," he wrote, "can't find out what's going on. This is Roosevelt's private war."[30]

. . . .

THIS INEXPLICABLE MAN

. . . .

As the war raged on and the tide appeared to be turning against the Axis, a different world was beginning to take shape. Willkie's *One World* prophesied a new dawn. A new term gained currency when Roosevelt described the Allies as the "United Nations."

Arthur Vandenberg was worried about falling through the cracks of history. The best he could do was claim to speak for the American everyman, neither isolationist nor internationalist, who "wants justice rather than force to rule the postwar world; who is willing to take his full share of responsibility . . . ; but who is perfectly sure that no one is going to look out for us." He was the best of Babbitt, contemplating a new world.[1]

The end of the war was coming, sooner or later, and most every senator wanted to do—or at least to say—*something*. In February, Iowa Republican Guy Gillette introduced a resolution calling upon the president to convene an international conference to formalize the principles of the Atlantic Charter—the right of all peoples to choose their form of government. The proposal was referred to the Foreign Relations Committee, and to a new subcommittee of Gillette, Walter George of Georgia, and Vandenberg. Then nothing happened. Vandenberg did not know what hand to play, or even what game was being played, but he did know that to show his cards too soon was to sacrifice leverage.

In March, a bipartisan quartet—Senators Ball, Burton, Hatch, and Hill—expanded on Gillette's resolution. They proposed committing the United States to five objectives: coordinate Allied resources to defeat the Axis, establish temporary administration of liberated lands until permanent governments returned, administer relief, establish procedures for peaceful settlement of disputes between nations, and, finally, provide for a United Nations military force to suppress future aggression by any nation, with member nations committing themselves not to seek "territorial aggrandizement." The bill reflected a chorus of such ideas pouring forth from politicians and pundits, so many of whom, wrote Vandenberg, seemed determined to announce to the world that American "isolationism . . . is dead."[2]

Vandenberg understood the Ball resolution to have the tacit support of the administration, though Roosevelt demurred. To Vandenberg, suppressing aggression and forbidding territorial aggrandizement collided with Stalin's announcement that "Russia intends to keep Latvia, Estonia, Lithuania, eastern Poland, Bessarabia, parts of Finland, etc." Perhaps it collided as well with Britain's hope to retain its colonies.

More proposals kept coming, and, as much as the Senate lusted for action, inaction was beginning to seem wise. When British Foreign Secretary Anthony Eden appeared before the Foreign Relations Committee, Vandenberg asked if agreeing to postwar plans might be premature—whether that might "disunite our war effort." Eden said he feared so. Vandenberg and a handful of colleagues also met with Hull, who said he "would have given *anything*" to avoid a congressional debate of postwar plans. Since the subject of postwar planning had "unfortunately" been raised, however, "it was probably necessary for the Senate to do *something*"—but for God's sake, to keep it simple and vague.[3]

Hull suggested avoiding debate by having all senators sign a general statement of postwar intentions. Vandenberg decided to "see what chance there was to write a general resolution" that would "avoid all the yawning pitfalls." The senator was feeling his way, explicitly saying that the United States "must be a far greater cooperator after this war," but with no specific commitments—no foreign entanglements. Especially not without something concrete from Churchill and Stalin: "We cannot afford the luxury of quarreling with Russia *now* unless we are prepared even to drive [Stalin] back into the arms of Hitler and to take

on the balance of this war alone." Vandenberg drafted a brief resolution to that effect—win the war, aspire to a world in which justice
prevailed among cooperating and self-governed peoples, promote
through constitutional means American cooperation commensurate
with American responsibilities—and nothing more. That was keeping
it vague all right. Vandenberg passed his proposal to Hull.[4]

In the meantime, a new Foreign Relations subcommittee—
Vandenberg and seven others—convened at the end of March to
ponder all the proposed resolutions. This was the start of the Senate's
formal deliberations on what the world would look like once the war
was over. No one on the committee liked the Ball resolution. The consensus, wrote Vandenberg, was to go slow. The Ball group demanded
action. So did Willkie. Such pressure, Vandenberg noted privately,
"had no effect whatever except possibly to slow us down still more;
these gentlemen evidently do not know what fire they are playing
with in the war situation." Gillette withdrew his resolution, but others
waited. One "great vice" in the situation, Vandenberg wrote, was that
the Senate had set itself up as the president's foil. If debate caused
trouble, FDR could blame the Senate. If issues festered, FDR could
blame the Senate for that, too. Wrote Vandenberg, "I do not think he
has overlooked these possibilities."[5]

Poor Hull just wanted the whole thing to go away. That wasn't going
to happen. There was tension within the executive branch. FDR relied on his Groton friend, Undersecretary Sumner Welles, more than
on the aging secretary of state. Who spoke for the administration?
Vandenberg suspected that Hull might not be long in his job. The beleaguered secretary likened the senators' predicament to that of the
army plane that had recently developed engine trouble over the South
Atlantic. The pilot had to decide whether it was safer to make for Africa
or turn back and try to reach Brazil. "You are in the same fix," Hull told
Vandenberg and his colleagues. "You'll have to decide which of your
courses offers the lesser danger."

Something was happening, a feeling, a sensation almost, that Vandenberg had not experienced since the days when Hoover turned to
him for help. He had a role to play: not in reaction, as he had with

the New Deal, but in shaping what came out of the committee. Such decisions rippled out in widening circles. What the committee determined would shape the action of the Senate, how the Senate acted shaped American policy, American policy would affect how the world emerged from the current catastrophe—and what it might look like for years to come. No one was inviting him back to the White House yet, but he was engaged within the Senate chamber. And the stakes were higher than ever.

Hull warned the senators that the Allies were beginning to ask, in Vandenberg's words, "whether America will withdraw unto herself after this war, as she did in 1920?" While pleading that the Senate avoid "tender subjects," Hull wished for a pronouncement that "we have a 'cooperative state of mind.'" Vandenberg suggested senators delay debate and join with the State Department to say that nothing specific should be written at the moment. He also proposed that a permanent Senate liaison committee meet with the State Department to monitor developments.[6]

Senators of all stripes were relying on rumor and supposition. An "intimate discussion" with a handful of committee colleagues was "the gloomiest morning I have had since Pearl Harbor," Vandenberg wrote. "Grapevine" reports suggested that the war was in an "utterly dangerous" phase. Gillette had heard that Germany had approached Russia through Japan with peace proposals "which *might* detach her from the war." There were also fears of a Russo-Japanese pact, allowing Japanese armies to divert south to fight the British and Americans. Rumors of Japanese reinforcements at the tip of the Aleutians seemed to belie the claim of Secretary Knox: "We can drive the Japs out . . . anytime we wish." Walter George had heard that relations between Churchill and Stalin were worse than ever, and that American raw materials were being depleted too rapidly. La Follette raised fears that "we may bleed ourselves so white that we become a second-rate power."

Hearing all this, Vandenberg contended "that the Senate *dare* not start 'resoluting' on any phase of the war (or subsequent peace) without far more *accurate* information than we have now." Until then, there could be no action on Ball or any other resolution—"If we are stopped in these directions," Vandenberg predicted, "there may be explosive action."[7] More Senate resolutions were proposed, some withdrawn. Maybe, said Vandenberg, "if we just continue to 'sit' on the lid of this Pandora's Box, the situation will take care of itself."[8]

The war raged on. Germany reported unearthing mass graves of thousands of Polish officers murdered by the Russians. The Poles asked the Red Cross to investigate. The Soviets blamed German propaganda and broke relations with the London-based Polish government-in-exile. Suspicion grew of Russian intentions, even as Vandenberg realized that Soviet withdrawal from the war "would cost us a million needless casualties." He blamed Roosevelt for equivocating with the Russians over their territorial ambitions.

The British appeared unequivocal in their goals. General Marshall met with the committee in May after Roosevelt's Casablanca conference with Churchill. He reported that his British counterparts arrived with clear plans and support from Churchill down, "including, frequently, a 'softening up' of our own American situation through the activity of all the British 'Secretaries' here in Washington"—whether this included Mitzi Sims and her confederates is not clear. By contrast, the Americans were not similarly united on their strategy. Some in the military chafed over commitments Roosevelt may have made to Churchill without their knowledge. Marshall, said Vandenberg, "left us with an uneasiness about who makes our decisions."

A *Washington Post* columnist described Vandenberg and his colleagues as "the eight silent senators" charged with an "awful responsibility." Their job, wrote Bob Devore after a long talk with Vandenberg, "is to remain silent" on matters "about which secrecy is of utmost urgency—saying nothing . . . while in every section of the country editors are editorializing and citizens are adopting resolutions calling upon the eight silent men to act."[9]

In mid-May 1943, Churchill addressed a joint session of Congress, then met in closed session with the Foreign Relations Committee. Vandenberg pressed him on whether premature peace plans might disrupt the Allied war effort: "He replied emphatically 'YES.'" Vandenberg asked further whether Britain needed Senate resolutions for assurance of American cooperation after the war: "With tears in his eyes and with great eloquence he answered in the negative." Vandenberg asked whether Senate debate over the meaning of "territorial aggrandizement" and its application to Russian intentions in Eastern Europe might endanger Allied unity. "He said 'YES,' his 'attitude' arguing against Ball or any similar resolution."[10]

At a reception later at the British embassy, Churchill took Vandenberg by the arm. As they walked down the lawn, the prime minister said he hadn't meant to object to a vague "general resolution" of postwar goals. But when the senator noted that even that might invite "any sort of inflammatory amendment which any member of the Senate might offer on the floor," Churchill hesitated. He, too, feared "opening Pandora's box," particularly on subjects that might affect Britain's imperial interests.[11] (Many Americans were sympathetic to colonial aspirations for independence. The prime minister told Vandenberg he preferred to speak of "commonwealth" rather than "empire," suggesting that it was a matter of branding: "We keep trade labels to suit all tastes.")[12]

In the Senate, Vandenberg groped for the right approach. In the House, in June, Democrat J. William Fulbright introduced a one-sentence resolution "favoring creation of appropriate international machinery . . . to establish . . . a just and lasting peace and as favoring the participation of the United States therein." This was a bill Roosevelt could postpone. Besides, approval of any "international machinery" was the Senate's job. As Connally expressed it, the Senate would be glad, when the time came, "to have the views of the House on this matter."

Vandenberg finally decided to test the waters. He proposed to Democrat Walter George that the two of them introduce a bipartisan resolution. When George demurred, Vandenberg teamed with Maine's Wallace White to introduce "the first all-Republican" resolution.[13] It differed from all the others his committee reviewed because it spoke only for the current Congress. It pledged postwar cooperation between "sovereign nations"—a rebuke to "World Staters" like

Wendell Willkie and others—while "assuring the continuance of the American Flag over the Capitol." It limited "exploration of peace aims to such acts as will not disrupt the united military war effort." It demanded that postwar plans follow "due Constitutional process," a rebuff to what Vandenberg described as "the Roosevelt habit and desire to by-pass Congress." When Ball and his co-sponsors warned the committee that it must act soon on their resolution, Vandenberg noted that "these gentlemen will find that *their* resolution is *not* 'the only pebble on the beach.' "[14] Vandenberg was moving slowly toward some degree of international cooperation. Events of spring and summer 1943 showed that an American consensus might be needed sooner rather than later. On the Eastern Front, the Soviets broke the siege of Stalingrad. The scorched-earth tactics of retreating Nazis did little to slow the Red Army's advance. British and American troops landed on Sicily and soon began their long march up the Italian Peninsula. Mussolini fled Rome. In the Pacific the previous summer, a great clash of navies at the Battle of Midway had dealt the Japanese a mortal blow. American troops recaptured the Aleutians. It would be a long road, but victory looked increasingly inevitable.

Addressing postwar objectives might be deferred, but the rollback of Axis forces confronted the Allies with a more immediate issue—hunger and devastation in newly liberated territories, from North Africa to southern Italy to eastern Russia and the Pacific islands. Here, as Vandenberg was wont to say, was a condition, not a theory. He did not know that British and American diplomats had been meeting secretly for months to plan for this situation. The State Department had shared its plans with the Soviets and Chinese, but no one had bothered to brief Congress. Hull warned Roosevelt of the danger of neglecting to consult congressional leaders. Roosevelt paid no heed.

In June, Roosevelt unveiled the new United Nations Relief and Rehabilitation Administration. With American participation by executive agreement, there would be no need for the Senate to advise or consent. Yet it sounded to Vandenberg quite like an entangling alliance. He read about it in the newspapers. He sputtered about the president flouting the Constitution. "Nothing is more frustrating," wrote Dean Acheson of Vandenberg's situation, "than not to know what is going on."

The State Department maintained that the UNRRA pact was not a treaty but an agreement to contribute funds for relief as Congress might from time to time authorize. House leaders, who generally felt excluded from Senate treaty making anyway, would have a say when they exercised their control of the government purse. But the upper chamber was a different matter. Publication of the draft, wrote Acheson, "set the cat among the pigeons. And it was Vandenberg who indefatigably kept them aflutter."

Vandenberg spoke from the depths of his own resentment. Was Congress to be confronted with a fait accompli? Did the president think he could get away with pledging "our total resources to whatever illimitable scheme for relief and rehabilitation all around the world our New Deal crystal gazers might desire to pursue?" He strode the halls of the Capitol in high dudgeon. He demanded of Hull that the agreement be submitted to the Senate. Two weeks passed; he heard nothing.[15]

In July he introduced a resolution calling for a Foreign Relations Committee investigation of the agreement. "This episode," he wrote, "poses the question as to the extent to which the Congress is to be a constitutional partner in the plans and decisions which shall liquidate this war; [or] to what extent, on the other hand, the President and his administration shall settle these war and post-war problems to suit their own discretion." Hull told Vandenberg that Roosevelt had met with congressional leaders who agreed with him. Vandenberg queried the GOP leaders and was assured that they had not endorsed an executive agreement. Roosevelt told them no legislation was needed, simply approval of appropriations. Somehow, neither Senate nor House members of the Foreign Relations and Appropriations Committees had been invited.[16]

For Vandenberg, this was the stuff of which precedents were made. He was not alone. The *Washington Times-Herald* called it "a strange and sinister document," a backdoor way into "a postwar League of Nations" for the thirty-one countries who comprised the Allies' "United Nations," and "a postwar, world-wide WPA." Even Connally, a Roosevelt ally, felt the president had overreached. The Texas senator joined a subcommittee with Vandenberg and three colleagues to meet with the State Department.

They summoned Hull and Acheson. This was, Vandenberg proclaimed, "a first showdown as to where President Roosevelt's treaty-making power leaves off and that of the Senate begins." Or, as *Time* put it, it "conjured up all the specters of the Executive-Senate disagreement that thwarted ratification of the Treaty of Versailles." Connally berated Hull for not consulting the Foreign Relations Committee. Hull "bitterly accused Connally of impugning the department's motives," grabbed his hat and nearly stormed out, then stayed long enough to tell the senators "in cold fury" that it wasn't his plan anyway. After he left the hearing, "Vandenberg and the equally suave Dean Acheson" were left, in Acheson's words, "to restore peace."[17]

Vandenberg was deputized to investigate the UNRRA plans. It wasn't UNRRA per se that he objected to. The more he learned about it, the more he looked for ways to make the program work. The need was incontrovertible, and only the United States had the resources to prevent starvation. Moreover, State wasn't the adversary. Hull hinted—and Acheson confirmed—that it was the White House that wanted UNRRA approved by executive agreement.

After a short summer break in Michigan, Vandenberg sat down with Acheson, one other senator, and one other diplomat—men of two parties, of two branches of government. One spoke on behalf of the Senate, the other on behalf of the administration. They were tinkering with language. They were brokering a deal. They were negotiating in a politics as old as the republic, and they were starting something utterly new.

When the dust settled, Vandenberg and Acheson found language that allowed the UNRRA to come into being through agreement, not treaty, after Acheson acceded to Vandenberg's demand that the draft come before Congress as a joint resolution. Both houses could debate and approve it, but without requiring the Senate's two-thirds majority. "I do not consider this to be the 'surrender,' " Vandenberg told one skeptic. "I consider it to be the 'triumph' of constitutional procedure."[18]

Whether UNRRA was the stalking horse for an executive dictator-ship or the benign beginnings of the American Century, Vandenberg was slipping almost unnoticed into new territory. He foresaw, in sub-mitting such agreements for congressional approval, "a pattern for other post-war problems short of the actual treaty of final peace." He was optimistic, a man at home with compromise.

Other critics of the president were less sanguine. While Vanden-berg argued that the administration had caved in to his pressure to put the resolution to a vote, his isolationist colleagues accused him of negotiating the surrender of the Senate. Critics took no comfort in a *New York Times* editorial hailing Vandenberg's consensus building on UNRRA as "the most significant accomplishment in the field of American foreign relations for a generation."[19]

More predictable than this eventual victory was the calendar of American politics. In 1944 Republicans and Democrats would again contest the presidency. With so many young men in uniform, Vanden-berg tried to steal a march on the Democrats by calling for the voting age to be lowered from twenty-one to eighteen—despite the fears of other Republicans that younger voters favored the New Deal. And for whom might they vote? Vandenberg floated the name of General Douglas MacArthur—"incomparably our most available leader"—for the Republican nomination.[20]

The GOP was still smarting from 1940, and party leaders feared an ugly fight over foreign policy when they wrote their platform for 1944. Hoping to avoid that, chairman Harrison Spangler created the Repub-lican Post-War Advisory Council. The choice of Vandenberg to chair its committee on foreign policy looked like a nod to the isolationists.[21]

Pearl Harbor may have ended isolationism in a symbolic way. Entangling alliances were formed in the heat of battle, driven by expedience and executive actions of the commander in chief. But whatever replaced isolationism for Vandenberg and the millions of Americans who saw the world as he did—more often than not a siz-able majority—would evolve more slowly, in a world fraught with new dangers.

Postwar Artist

I must be able to be a postwar artist . . .
to perform the paradox of being hard
and yet soft.

Tennessee Williams,

Notebooks,

1942

CHAPTER 16

. . . .

HUNTING FOR
THE MIDDLE GROUND

. . . .

By the summer of 1943, the Allies appeared to be winning the war. But what would they do with the peace? In Congress and in the country, there were growing calls for some concrete expression of how to organize the world once the guns fell silent.

There was no clear direction from the White House, where "Dr. Win the War" professed but one objective.[1] For Roosevelt, to speculate on postwar security arrangements was to risk dividing not only the American public but also the Allies. This was no time to court conflict with Britain over the future of its empire, or, more imminently, with Russia over the future of Poland. And what if the Soviets felt compelled to make a separate peace with Germany? FDR, ever the exquisite hedger, had no wish to gamble his prestige on a messy Senate debate before he sat down with Churchill and Stalin.

Among Republicans, wartime unity papered over a great divide. On one side stood Wendell Willkie, spinning visions of global harmony in his best-selling paean *One World*. On the other stood Robert Taft, son of a president, a rising freshman senator from Ohio. As a leading voice of the party's unreconstructed isolationists, Taft supported the war effort as a matter of national necessity, but he blanched at talk of a global organization after the war. And Thomas Dewey? Perhaps he was the early favorite for the 1944 nomination in part because no one knew exactly where he stood.

If the Republicans were to win the White House back in 1944—or, short of that, reduce the dominance of Democrats in Congress—this divide had to be addressed. The GOP needed a platform it could agree on, one that would persuade voters to entrust it to meet the demands of the postwar world.

With proponents of a global New Deal to the left and isolationists to the right, one of the latter, Arthur Vandenberg, was charged with finding a compromise. He harbored few regrets about his role in help- ing scuttle American membership in the League of Nations two dozen years before. But the world, and America's place in it, had changed dramatically. The old answers that had served him so long no lon- ger sufficed. If, in the public mind, he still personified isolationism, he also understood the requirements of leadership. As one colum- nist observed, he was advancing postwar proposals that were "rather startling and courageous for one who has an 18-year investment in the isolationist way of thinking."[2] Charles Eaton, ranking Republican on the House Foreign Affairs Committee, told friends he was amazed by Vandenberg's turnabout.[3]

That turnabout was still in its infancy as the senator rode north through the Michigan forests to a Labor Day retreat of Republican elected officials (thus sans Wendell Willkie) at the venerable Grand Hotel on Mackinac Island. The Post-War Policy Conference had been organized by party chairman Spangler to create a plank for the GOP platform setting out peace plans in advance of the 1944 campaign. But as one reporter noted, "The Republican Party is going to be lucky if it comes back from Mackinac Island without having split itself right up the back." Some delegates were determined to press their posi- tions even if they wrecked the party. Vandenberg worried most about Senator Warren Austin of Vermont, an outspoken internationalist. Austin contemplated putting his views before the conference and let- ting the side with the most votes win, leaving the defeated "to submit gracefully or sulk."[4]

That was not Vandenberg's way. He wanted a foreign policy posi- tion that all delegates could accept. "I am hunting," he said, "for the middle ground between those extremists at one end of the line who would cheerfully give America away and those extremists at the other end of the line who would attempt a total isolation which has come to be an impossibility."[5]

His challenge was how to agree on something like a new League of Nations without resurrecting the old schism that had ruined Woodrow Wilson. Soon he was circulating a draft statement among party leaders. To "all world staters," he vowed there must be "continuance of the American flag over the capital." But he was also determined to bury "the miserable notion (so effectively used against us in many quarters) that the Republican Party will retire to its foxhole when the last shot in this war has been fired and will blindly let the world rot in its own anarchy."[6] Inching toward compromise, he wrote Dewey: "You will note that I have left in the magic word 'organized,' " modifying a proposed commitment to "post-war cooperation." As the Mackinac meeting approached, he thought both Taft and Dewey approved.[7]

At the ebb of summer 1943, ferries carried delegates across the choppy Straits of Mackinac toward the island and its great hotel. Up on the bluff, American flags fluttered as if celebrating a perpetual Fourth of July. Between soaring Doric columns on the Grand's famous porch—said to be the longest in the world—guests gazed out over red geraniums and formal lawns. Beyond the treetops lay Lake Huron and Lake Michigan, inland seas with a thinning late-season traffic of sailboats and freighters. Farther away, in the mist, was the forested tip of the Lower Peninsula, a land out of Longfellow.

As unofficial hosts, the Vandenbergs were among the first to arrive. On the sunlit porch, the senator, reclining on a chaise longue and smoking his inevitable cigar, listened to stately hoofbeats as carriages bearing new arrivals came to a stop below. He weighed potential allies and adversaries, whom to buttonhole and when.

The press knew where to find him. A young reporter named Liz Carpenter shared the main-floor governor's suite, with deep windows opening on the western end of the porch. Vandenberg's lobbying on behalf of his proposed declaration was typically performed one on one, often on a stroll that paused at the far end—right outside the reporters' window. "We flattened ourselves on the floor of the suite and heard a good deal of Vandenberg's persuasiveness," Carpenter recalled. "He was there to persuade [his party] to give up isolationism."[8]

Vandenberg had arrived, *Time* reported, with a "marvelously vague" document, each word "planed and sandpapered down to political harmlessness." Converging from all corners of the country, nineteen Republican governors had other ideas. "They had come to participate in a deliberative assembly," said the *New York Herald Tribune*, "only to find they were expected to rubber stamp plans already drafted by others."[9]

Among the last to arrive was Thomas Dewey. With his election the year before, the dapper New York governor had vaulted to the front rank of Republican hopefuls for 1944. At a press conference in the lobby, he gave the knot of newsmen something to write about.

What was that old Washingtonian injunction against entangling alliances? "We have had a de facto military alliance with Great Britain ever since the War of 1812," Dewey declared. "In the two principal cases since, when war was made on Great Britain, we went to her defense." Echoing Walter Lippmann's new treatise, *U.S. Foreign Policy: Shield of the Republic*, Dewey said, "The American people never before had such a shock as the one they had when they realized that Germany might capture the British fleet. You in this room remember as I do how everyone was chilled."[10] Reporters were soon "scribbling notes at top speed."

Did Dewey favor an alliance with Great Britain after the war? Yes, he said. Would he include Russia and China? Here he beat a cautious retreat to the passive voice: "It would be hoped that in the working out of the peace, Russian and China might be included." Was he afraid of compromising American sovereignty—the precious concern upon which Vandenberg had long hung his hat? Again, the answer was pure Lippmann. "No," said Dewey. "Making treaties or entering a group of nations determined on international action would not impair American sovereignty. Such acts were merely the way nations had to live together." All night, teletypes rattled on the remote island. On Monday, front-page reports said Tom Dewey was calling for a postwar alliance of the United States and Great Britain. This was the stuff of Churchill's dreams, but not of many Republicans.[11]

"A damn fool utterance," huffed Taft. "Anti-American," roared the Anglophobic *Chicago Tribune*: "He has finished his pilgrimage to Downing Street by way of Wall Street."[12] But in Willkie's absence, Dewey had sent a message to Vandenberg and the conference organizers: the status quo was not acceptable. Vandenberg may have agreed, but he still sought unity—not ultimatums rooted in excessive certainty—over how the party ought to address the most important question of the day.

Delegates got more privacy than they had bargained for when high winds knocked out telegraph service connecting the island to the rest of the world. The only link was a private telephone line controlled by the Associated Press and the *Detroit Free Press*.[13] Nonetheless, the conference opened as planned in the spacious hall called the casino, filled now with a forest of baize-covered tables. Bunting hung from the balcony.

Front and center sat Vandenberg, who soon learned that his backroom preparations had failed to bring early accord. Frustrated governors, led by California's Earl Warren and Connecticut's Ray Baldwin, said they would not accept Vandenberg's preconference draft—it was too mild, too milquetoast. According to *Time*'s reporter, it was clear that "GOP leaders, as individuals, if not *en masse*, are willing to go further than anyone would have guessed a few years ago."[14]

The debate turned on just a few words. The need for postwar "cooperation"—which sounded harmless enough—was the inevitable starting point. Vandenberg, long the preacher of "nationalism, not internationalism," insisted that the word *sovereign* accompany any mention of American "cooperation." Austin, Congressman Eaton, and a clutch of governors demanded inclusion of the word *organization*—but that suggested something akin to the discredited League of Nations, which the Senate had spurned for fear of compromising American sovereignty.

By the second day, the politicians had reached an impasse.

Vandenberg and a dozen colleagues retreated to a small conference room. Guards were posted and sandwiches sent for. In midafternoon, Taft stepped out to ask for a bottle of scotch and a bottle of bourbon. They were having trouble reaching agreement, the dour Ohioan hinted. Maybe some lubrication would help. After another two hours—"fighting with our coats off,"[15] according to Austin—the weary delegates opened the door.

The result was more specific than anyone expected. At the heart of the 500-word declaration was a call for "responsible participation by the United States in postwar cooperative organization among sovereign nations to prevent military aggression and to attain permanent peace with organized justice in a free world."[16] The party took a deep breath. Vandenberg had agreed to *organization*, but he had won his battle for *sovereign*, too—Wendell Willkie, Henry Wallace, and fans of *One World* take note. Even Colonel McCormick resisted condemning the final language. Vandenberg also kept his cherished caveat that any action by an international organization including the United States would have to respect American constitutional processes. That meant respecting the Senate.

Vandenberg and Austin collaborated on the final text. There was, said Austin, "not a weasel word in it." How did they do it? Both had compromised. Said Austin, "There were some specific things I wanted to put in but I don't think that the failure to include them hurts. Van was a prince." And he said, "Yes, I think Willkie will be satisfied with it."[17]

When Vandenberg presented the compromise to the full assembly, Maine governor Sumner Sewell asked what the senator meant by *sovereignty*. Vandenberg's classic equivocation was that sovereignty "possessed within itself the right to part with some elements if that becomes necessary to effectuate an international organization."[18] His point was as inarguable as it was incomprehensible. Commentators had fun with it. But Vandenberg's elasticity disarmed his critics. In the spirit of FDR's Atlantic Charter, outlining an alliance of "United Nations," the Republican declaration was dubbed the "Mackinac Charter."[19]

In two days the party that had killed the League of Nations had committed itself to supporting a world organization. Reporters cynical about the value of this remote gathering suddenly realized that the GOP had filled a vacuum. "As the declaration sank in," *Time* noted, "it became clear that this was the greatest tactical advance . . . by the Republican Party in years. For once, the party had not set itself up as a helpless punching bag for Franklin Roosevelt. Temporarily, at least, it bound up all quarrels. . . . It put the next move for enunciation of U.S. foreign policy squarely up to the Democrats."[20]

Vandenberg had found his safe harbor. Dewey was happy. The uninvited Willkie grumbled only a little. At first he called the declaration "vague and meaningless," but he soon conceded it was "a very distinct step in the right direction."[21]

Roosevelt shrewdly avoided direct comment. Yet he could not resist a swipe at Vandenberg's ambiguous prose. He grinned as he told reporters, "Well, I always have my thesaurus handy on my desk." However Roosevelt might try to diminish Vandenberg's achievement, most of the press praised it. The *Washington Herald*'s analysis suggested the nature of his breakthrough: "The Resolution was so carefully hedged about with qualifications that both hard-boiled isolationists and ardent internationalists clapped hands and chanted, 'That's what I wanted all the time!'"[22] Vandenberg was hailed as the architect of a grand compromise; he had finessed an issue that could have torn his party apart.

In a radio address, he acknowledged that the charter was a partisan project. But he also declared that "partisan politics, as such, should stop at the water's edge." Americans could be "faithful to the primary institutions and interests of our own United States and still be equally loyal to essential international cooperations which are required to end military aggressions for keeps. . . . This is what the average American has been waiting to hear." He knew Americans would endorse a policy that recognized the "limited liability" of U.S. global responsibilities, but not one of "general and unlimited liability." This was "the great middle course of sanity and reason to which 95% of our people can subscribe."[23] Luxuriating in his new role, he began to grasp its potential. "When I succeeded in putting forty-nine prima donnas together at Mackinaw," he crowed to Henry Luce, "I discovered the necessary formula."[24]

When Congress reconvened, the House passed the Fulbright resolution with plenty of Republican support, thanks to the Mackinac declaration. All of a sudden, Republicans were doing the talking. "It is the wise voice of American intelligence and enlightened American self-interest which [says] that a bad world for others cannot be a good world for us," Vandenberg told a national radio audience. The U.S. had to recognize its role in sustaining peace and progress after the war. "So long as both of these objectives remain inseverably linked we can *unite* America on foreign policy," he continued. "When they are divorced we inevitably fall apart."[25]

Vandenberg's success was stirring Democrats to action. When young congressman William Fulbright convinced Roosevelt that Republicans were stealing the show, the president agreed that the time had come for the Senate to act. As Vandenberg wrote, "the general agitation for *some* sort of Senate action has reached a point where it may be even *worse* to longer keep the subject bottled up."

Vandenberg had a tricky course to navigate for a Senate resolution, in the absence of which the secretary of state would be left to cite the Mackinac Charter to British and Soviet counterparts as evidence of support for a postwar organization.[26] The Senate was no more unified than Republicans had been. Foreign Relations chair Connally favored a mild resolution echoing the Mackinac language but calling also for military and economic sanctions to maintain peace. That was too specific for Vandenberg's taste, so the section was deleted before the full Senate took up Connally's proposal. Yet the mild language was not specific enough for the two Republican and two Democratic senators of the Ball group. Led by Minnesota Republican Joseph Ball, they wanted the resolution to go beyond merely endorsing an international "organization," calling for a permanent international "authority" for peacekeeping, with an explicit call for military force.

The Connally resolution looked to be in jeopardy until Vandenberg's subcommittee added two compromise paragraphs. To appease the Ball group and draw upon what Hull had been negotiating in Moscow, the resolution called for the proposed organization to maintain "international peace and security." To keep old isolationists in the fold, American membership in the new organization would require a two-thirds vote of the Senate.

In early November 1944, the resolution was approved with only five dissenting votes. After Vandenberg's adroit compromise at Mackinac was repeated by both parties in the full Senate, the *Detroit Free Press* observed, "He will have participated as much as any man in high position next to Churchill and Roosevelt in writing such declarations."

Hull was encouraged, Roosevelt dismissive. "The water is going over the dam very fast these days and what language is used today may be wholly out of date in a week or two," the president wrote. "Frankly, I am paying very little attention to the language of the debate."

There was an element of truth in FDR's hauteur, but the president with the finely tuned political ear missed something bigger than the precise words of the Senate resolution. When Vandenberg and Connally worked out language on which both parties could agree, bipartisan foreign policy was born.[27]

Coincident with these first stirrings of bipartisanship, representatives of forty-four nations met at the White House to sign the United Nations Relief and Rehabilitation Administration agreement. The Senate was called upon to approve the measure on terms that Vandenberg had negotiated with Acheson months before. He had agreed that it might be treated as an agreement rather than a treaty, but it required Senate consent nonetheless. Hull and Acheson took to heart his advice to consult Senate leaders "before instead of after the fact." And Hull conceded that the size of the United States' financial commitment to world relief was entirely up to Congress. Vandenberg knew some senators would insist that UNRRA was a "treaty." Indeed, after the resolution sailed through Foreign Relations, recalcitrant isolationists attacked it on the Senate floor. To some observers, this debate was a precursor of bigger ones to come over peace treaties and the United Nations itself. The fate of the Versailles treaty—"Death by Reservation"—might await the UNRRA, wrote Allen Drury of the *New York Times.* Taft went along with the agreement, but he criticized FDR for imposing it by executive fiat, since "exactly the same thing could be done in the case of a League of Nations."

Old Burt Wheeler "indulged in one of the sharpest colloquies of the entire debate," wrote Drury. Not so long ago, Wheeler and Vandenberg had been allies. Now, said Drury, "Van is for it and Burt is against it, and the cross fire with which they mowed down isolationism's opponents heretofore was directed at each other." Vandenberg's consensus was fragile. "There is a tremendous latent 'suspicion' of this entire enterprise in the Senate," he told Acheson. The UNRRA was a test. Senators approved the resolution 47–17, but with little enthusiasm and a lot of absences. What might that portend for a final peace treaty?[28]

Vandenberg had moved with careful steps, using cautious language, into uncharted territory. He was negotiating—if not yet making—policy in concert with the executive branch. He was also conscious of his new distance from the isolationists. But he was no internationalist either. His uncharted territory could become a no-man's-land. He waffled a little, advancing and retreating, in subsequent debate over postwar preliminaries, allowing observers to consider him a potential leader of the opposition even as he drew closer to the administration. Helping both sides at once seemed safer than siding with one or the other. And it was a new source of power.

. . . .

COMMITTEE OF EIGHT

. . . .

As 1943 drew to a close, with Allied forces on the offensive around the globe, the president embarked for Teheran and his first meeting with both Churchill and Stalin. This, everyone knew, would be the opening discussion at the highest level of how the Allies were to finish the war and manage the peace. Vandenberg saw danger in such a summit. His distrust of Roosevelt was reflexive. And Churchill, much as Vandenberg admired him, had his fraying empire to protect. The senator had no faith whatsoever in Stalin. The new internationalism was starting to take shape, and Vandenberg was as uncertain as anyone about how it would play out. Was Roosevelt the right man for the job? Vandenberg had doubts.

A fracas over domestic policy only increased the tension between the White House and Capitol Hill. When senators blocked the president's call for higher corporate and social security taxes, Roosevelt blasted them as fiscally irresponsible—a charge that struck Vandenberg as the height of irony. Roosevelt's high-handedness throughout this debate was so obvious that Democratic majority leader Alben Barkley quit his post in protest. (Vandenberg teared up as his friend took the floor. He rose after Barkley finished, but, unable to complete his opening sentence, he sat back down before crossing the aisle to offer congratulations.) Roosevelt apologized to Barkley, who was quickly reelected, but the damage had been done. The president's rank partisanship, Allen Drury wrote in his diary, was fomenting a "real, deep and ugly hatred that can have the most serious consequences for the country."[1] Roosevelt could blame Senate Republicans for sowing discord, too, but none of this augured well for a nation facing perilous choices about its future.

With that ugly backdrop, Roosevelt directed his secretary of state to proceed with planning the United Nations. Despite his fear of premature publicity, he accepted Hull's recommendation that plans be shared with key senators. In an echo of the UNRRA dustup, Roosevelt told the State Department that he preferred to see the United Nations organization set up informally, as a wartime tool, before June 1944. In that case, he told Hull, congressional approval would not be necessary.

Hull was stunned. With the League of Nations fight fresh in the collective consciousness of American leaders, and a growing coalition challenging FDR over a host of issues, he thought it downright dangerous to ignore the Senate's mandate to advise and consent. Reluctantly, Roosevelt accepted the need for congressional consultation. But he told Hull that Republicans could not be trusted. The onus was on Hull to prove the process could work.

From the Mackinac Charter to the Connally resolution, it was clear that Congress was willing to pursue American membership in a new world organization. But the League of Nations had failed to prevent global war. How would a new body be different?

The precedent of 1919 was much on Hull's mind. In that year, as a young congressman, he had seen Senate approval of the League of Nations crushed by the rancor between his hero, Woodrow Wilson, and the Republican leader Henry Cabot Lodge. Now, at seventy-two years old, Hull was determined that this new organization avoid the fate of the League.

But to what extent would the United States commit itself to a new world body? What would be the role of the great powers? Would the new league have its own military force to prevent aggression? If it were to have the authority to settle disputes, would member nations have to relinquish a degree of sovereignty? These were profound questions. *Organization* sounded benign and constructive, but it would be devilishly difficult to define its *authority* or *machinery*. Each word carried the weight of great hope and anxiety.

In March 1944, Hull asked Connally to select a small group of senators from both parties to meet informally with the State Department about plans for a new association of nations. Connally asked Vandenberg both to serve and to recommend other Republicans. Although Vandenberg was then only the third-ranking minority member of the Foreign Relations Committee, none of his colleagues approached his stature on foreign policy questions. If he was serious about cooperation between Congress and the executive branch, he had no choice but to sign on. But he did say he would resign if consensus could not be reached on the issues that arose. He further said he would not speak formally on behalf of his party; he intended to serve simply as a liaison between White House and Senate.

Hull's plans hinged on Vandenberg. If the two of them could work together, bipartisanship might mean something. In April, with Vandenberg on board, Connally announced the formation of a committee that included Democrats Barkley, Gillette, and George, Republicans White and Austin, and the progressive La Follette, an unrepentant isolationist upon whose involvement Vandenberg had insisted. The group was quickly dubbed the Committee of Eight.

In Hull's office the senators received copies of the secretary's proposal for what Vandenberg referred to as a "world security organization." The plan called for an executive council made up of Great Britain, China, the Soviet Union and the United States, plus four nations chosen annually by a general assembly of all members. The assembly was to be the forum from which recommendations flowed to the council, which would decide issues by majority vote. Each of the Big Four would have veto power. In addition, there was to be an international court of justice, a general secretariat, and agencies to oversee former colonies and social and economic initiatives. At the request of the executive council, member nations could contribute to a joint military force to maintain peace—although this highly controversial concept remained vague.

Vandenberg was heartened by what he heard. The striking thing, he wrote in his diary, "is that it is so *conservative* from a nationalist standpoint. It is based virtually on a four-power alliance. . . . Hull's whole theory is that there must be continued agreement between the

Big Four or the post-war world will smash anyway. Also, to his credit, he recognizes that the United States will never permit itself to be ordered into war against its own consent." Hull had even gone so far as to suggest that consent could come only by an act of Congress: "This is anything but a wild-eyed internationalist dream of a world state." Nor, with its deference to the Senate, was it necessarily a dream shared by President Roosevelt.[2]

Despite his enthusiasm, Vandenberg hesitated when Hull asked the senators for preliminary approval so that he might negotiate with the Allies. He thought the fate of a new world body depended on an acceptable peace settlement, lest member nations be pressured to uphold an unjust peace. Hull, more sanguine since his Moscow meeting with Stalin, suggested that concessions to Russia mattered less if the Soviets were active in the new organization. Indeed, an international organization would be the place to correct deficiencies in any peace settlement. Vandenberg conceded the point, agreeing to help "perfect the document."

But Vandenberg did not trust the Soviets. He insisted that a functioning security organization reject any territorial aggrandizement. "We are all disturbed," Vandenberg wrote in his diary, "by Russia's unilateral announcements from time to time as to what she intends to 'do' for example, with Poland and the other Baltic States." Buffer states and "spheres of influence" ought to become relics of an old order. The peace would create some kind of new status quo. Therefore, "final consent to membership in the organization cannot precede the final and conclusive disclosure of the terms of the peace itself," Vandenberg told Hull after their second meeting. "Otherwise we would be signing the most colossal 'blank check' in history."[3]

Four weeks passed before Hull replied. With all due respect, he said, State disagreed with the senator: creating the peacekeeping organization and negotiating a peace treaty were separate issues. He further clarified how he saw the role of the Committee of Eight. While he wanted a nonpartisan approach, that was distinct from "bipartisanship." In his conception, nonpartisanship meant Republicans would offer support or remain silent while the administration went about its policy making. *Bipartisanship* implied more active cooperation—in which Hull had little interest, and Roosevelt even less.

To Vandenberg, this looked like a one-way street and more of the same from the president. Worse, the actions Hull was proposing could hamstring future presidents—including whatever Republican might succeed him in just a few months. Hull had to recognize, Vandenberg said, that by meeting with State to discuss postwar plans, Republicans were vulnerable to "considerable political embarrassment to ourselves because we are largely silenced in our public criticisms." This was the delicate balancing act behind any sort of bipartisanship.[4]

Hull was encouraged by the committee's overall reaction. But he wanted the senators to go on record backing his proposals. Vandenberg refused. He advised the secretary to meet with the Russians and British and Chinese. In the meantime, he said, the senators would confine any public statement to "renewed assurance of our desire" to cooperate. Any commitment beyond that would be premature. Hull dispatched Assistant Secretary Breckenridge Long to Capitol Hill to rewrite the senators' tepid statement. When a revised letter had the committee promising "to cooperate further in the development of *this* proposal," Vandenberg balked. That was too close to the "blank check."[5]

At the next meeting of the Committee of Eight, Austin backed Hull on the need to establish an international organization without worrying about eventual peace terms. Vandenberg, in a spirit of compromise, suggested giving Hull a note praising the draft and urging its circulation among the Big Four, but withholding an actual endorsement. Otherwise, Connally told Hull, the committee had reached an impasse. It would produce either a split report—which would defeat Hull's objective entirely—or no statement at all. The senators would only agree to give the administration their tentative and oral approval of ongoing negotiations. They would not issue a written statement.

At this, Hull badgered Connally for some kind of letter from the committee. The chairman proposed a statement more "prolix" than ever, Vandenberg observed, "but which still fought shy of any *real* reservations." (*Reservations*—the loaded word from the old League of Nations debate was on everyone's mind.) There had to be wiggle room for the loyal opposition before it would join with an administration it did not trust.[6]

At the end of May, the committee reassembled in Hull's office. On the secretary's desk lay a copy of the *Saturday Evening Post* with an article purporting to tell the inside story of the Tehran conference. It suggested that Roosevelt had yielded to Soviet and British demands regarding spheres of influence—Eastern Europe for the former, a colonial empire for the latter—and agreed essentially on a three-power alliance to dominate the world. The report only reinforced Vandenberg's anxiety about the nature of the impending peace.

What had transpired between the president and the other leaders? "Hanging like a cloud over all these negotiations," Vandenberg wrote in his diary, "is the fact that *none* of us knows what personal commitments may have been made by Roosevelt to Stalin and Churchill." Indeed, wrote Vandenberg, for all he knew, peace terms "may have already been agreed upon" among the three leaders, and not necessarily to America's benefit. If Roosevelt would not stand up for American interests—as Churchill did for Britain's and Stalin for Russia's—then somebody else had to.

Suspicion of Roosevelt ran through more than a decade of Vandenberg's career. Indeed, it was more than suspicion. Vandenberg hated Roosevelt, Breckinridge Long wrote in his diary: "The word 'hate' is used advisedly. He thinks Roosevelt stands for everything bad and for nothing good." Roosevelt may have been the subtlest politician of the century, but he treated Congress not as a respected antagonist or co-equal partner, but as a rival, and not a very worthy one at that.

Hull professed a cooperative spirit, but if the White House was making policy, the secretary's intentions might not matter. Vandenberg thought it significant that the committee had "not seen the Chief of State himself in respect to these matters concerning which he is supreme."[7] As it happens, Roosevelt *had* offered to meet with the Committee of Eight, starting with Vandenberg. But Hull did not encourage him, nor, in sharing the offer with the committee, did he make it sound as if the president were terribly interested. Hull thought his negotiations with the senators would go better if the White House were not directly involved. His approach allowed Vandenberg's fears to fester, losing an opportunity to bridge the divide between the president and the senator. The result was that election-year calculations came to the fore. "I confess that I cannot escape the feeling," Vandenberg wrote, "that the persistence with which we are being pursued to sign what could virtually be a blank check has its definite *political* implications in connection with the approaching campaign." This was no time, he said, for Republican senators to " 'sign up' *in the dark*."[8]

Hull insisted that that wasn't the right way to look at the issue. If they postponed a world organization until the war was over, he warned, they would run the risk that "everything will blow up."

"You totally misunderstand me, Mr. Secretary," Vandenberg replied. Go ahead with the discussions, but "I do not think you have any right to expect this Senate Committee either to endorse your plans in advance or agree that your League shall bind us regardless of whether the peace satisfies the American conscience or not." Vandenberg refused to be "driven into a blind alley," and La Follette backed him up.

At the end of the meeting, Connally turned to the two Midwestern senators and said, "Well, the tail wags the dog."

In fact, Hull's hope for an early endorsement from the Senate had been no more than wishful thinking—and an oddly backward approach. It was June 1944 before Roosevelt himself formally endorsed Hull's United Nations Organization plan. Perhaps the secretary of state, in his own uncertainty about where Roosevelt stood, hoped that an endorsement from key senators would strengthen his hand with the president. Certainly he hoped to cap his career with the peacemaking success that had eluded Woodrow Wilson. Yet even within the State Department, there were doubts about the wisdom of creating an international organization to maintain peace before the nature of the peace had been determined.

Although the Committee of Eight withheld the endorsement Hull had wanted, it provided something that turned out to be more important: greater influence for Arthur Vandenberg in foreign policy. He moved closer to a commitment to international cooperation, building on the foundation he had labored over at Mackinac, and gained the ear of the State Department.

This was a pivotal moment for Vandenberg, Dean Acheson wrote later: "The experience brought out all his many and great talents." And it led to "a unique service not only to his own country but, ironically enough, to peoples whose affairs and interests he had believed only a short time before to be of no concern of his or his country's." Had the disagreement between Hull and Vandenberg played out on the Senate floor, rather than behind closed doors, their positions might have become entrenched and opportunities for compromise might have evaporated. Instead, they did their work in secret, with the contentious back-and-forth known only to a few.[9]

In the wake of the D-Day invasion of Normandy, Hull issued a bland statement about congressional support for an international organization. Vandenberg wrote in his diary. "No one would ever know—from Hull's general statement—what has gone on. . . . But there is plenty of discussion coming before this thing is finished."[10]

· · · · · · · · · · · ·

BROTHERS UNDER
THE SKIN

· · · · · · · · · · · ·

In the 1940 presidential race, Vandenberg had gone from dark horse to front-runner and back again, swept aside by Wendell Willkie in a stinging rebuke to his iconic isolationism. Willkie wanted the nomination again in 1944. So did Dewey. The young governor certainly seemed to have a bright future, but he lacked the gravitas of a wartime leader. Vandenberg, with his lifelong penchant for heroes, had another idea. He argued that only one figure possessed the leadership and name recognition that might attract independent voters to the GOP: General Douglas MacArthur.

MacArthur, the commander of Allied forces in the Pacific, had come to symbolize much that Vandenberg and other armchair generals in Congress resented about Roosevelt's conduct of the war. The chief priority of Roosevelt and his military chiefs was defeating Germany, a strategy that forced MacArthur to plead for men and matériel. Was this the right strategy? Who knew? "Even in the Senate we can't find out what's going on," Vandenberg wrote in his diary. "This is Roosevelt's private war! He sends out troops where he pleases—all over the map—and meanwhile MacArthur fights alone! *Ugh!* If he gets out alive, I think he will be my candidate for President in 1944."[1]

Early in 1943 Representative Clare Boothe Luce invited the senator to her apartment to meet a pair of MacArthur's staff officers. The general had abandoned the Philippines to the Japanese with his famous vow, "I shall return." Now he was directing the Pacific theater from Australia. Meanwhile, the War Department issued an order barring active-duty members of the armed forces from seeking public office. When Vandenberg objected, Secretary Stimson was forced to acknowledge that MacArthur, called out of retirement, was exempted.

Vandenberg's comments in Luce's apartment were relayed to the general, and soon the senator received a cable—personal and confidential—from the South Pacific. "I am most grateful to you for your complete attitude of friendship," MacArthur wrote. "I only hope that someday I can reciprocate. There is much that I would like to say to you which circumstances prevent. In the meanwhile, I want you to know the absolute confidence I would feel in your experienced and wise mentorship." Further, MacArthur was grateful for the "prompt repudiation" of the War Department order.

Vandenberg pasted the cablegram in his scrapbook beneath a characteristically hyperbolic note. "The following message *might* be supremely historic," he wrote. " 'Mac' is certainly not 'running away' from *anything*. It is typical of his forth-right courage."[2]

Vandenberg began quiet preparations for a MacArthur campaign. He published an article in *Collier's* titled "Why I Am for MacArthur." He dampened talk of a boom, however: "Our primary obligation to the General is to protect him against any untoward political activities." He wanted a spontaneous draft for MacArthur—"certainly without the appearance of any connivance on his part (of which he would never allow himself to be consciously guilty)." Vandenberg kept it low key. "It just happens by fortuitous circumstances that the MacArthur movement seems to find me as its focal point," he wrote, "because I am the only Senate Republican who has spoken out unequivocally on his behalf.

"It would be obviously impossible for the General to recognize [the] movement," he added, "unless and until he is actually drafted by the next National Convention." MacArthur attracted the attention of other party notables, including publisher Frank Gannett and the retired general Robert Wood, chairman of Sears Roebuck. Vandenberg acknowledged a certain fairy-tale quality to this "gigantic speculation." The effort depended on "the evolution of events" that no one could foresee.[3]

The general owed his popularity to shrewd public relations as well as a shrewd defensive campaign in the Pacific. "It seems to me that the

American people are rapidly coming to understand what the General is up against in the Far East," Vandenberg wrote. "These people can easily *martyrize* him into a completely irresistible figure." Or perhaps it was Vandenberg himself who found the notion irresistible. Yet he was no kingmaker orchestrating party machinery. He knew that heaven helps those who help themselves. MacArthur was hardly in a position to do that, and in the political arena time was running out.[4]

More critically, however, heroes can have feet of clay. Early in 1944 Vandenberg began to hear returning soldiers mock the preening general with the corncob pipe. A "very intelligent Grand Rapids boy" in the South Pacific polled some of his comrades. "He reports growing unpopularity for our friend," Vandenberg wrote. "What does this mean?"[5]

In the meantime, Thomas Dewey built an impressive string of primary victories, leading Willkie to withdraw. The chance of a deadlocked convention that might turn to MacArthur seemed remote. Still, Vandenberg, typically, hesitated. "I think we should wait until at least the first of May before we take any active step toward joining the Dewey parade," he advised his colleagues. "I have written Australia [MacArthur's staff] and frankly presented this picture."[6]

Then the "evolution of events" took a more definitive turn. Congressman A. L. Miller of Nebraska published correspondence in which MacArthur praised Miller's diatribes against the New Deal. Such approval of a partisan rant was unseemly for a hero. Subsequently, the general announced that he did not "covet" the nomination and would not accept it. The adventure was over. Miller, said Vandenberg, had, "in one inane moment, crucified the whole MacArthur movement (and MacArthur with it)." MacArthur "would have been our most eligible President," he mused, "especially in his spokesmanship for America at the peace table." But the general's questionable judgment seemed to vindicate his ex-wife, who, when asked to assess him as a dark horse, replied, "It depends which end you look at."[7]

With his candidate out of the running, Vandenberg pressed his foreign-policy agenda ahead of the GOP convention in Chicago. He was comfortable with Dewey, who reflected his own centrist tendencies. His chief concern was to enshrine the Mackinac Charter as the basis of the Republican platform. Willkie objected to some of the charter's "phony phrases," but Vandenberg insisted that the language committed the party to an international organization. A *Washington Star* cartoon reinforced this interpretation. It showed a confident Vandenberg leading an anxious elephant across a "Mackinac" plank and toward the Republican platform. "Come on, old girl," says the senator, "if it can hold me, it can hold you."[8]

To placate isolationists, Vandenberg stressed that nations would retain their independence and sovereignty in spite of international "cooperation." The United Nations would be no "world state" or step toward global federalism. And approval of any treaty committing the United States to an "association of nations" would require a two-thirds vote of the Senate. To internationalists he offered support for "peace forces to prevent or repel military aggression."

Secretary of State Hull wanted an explicit Republican commitment to *his* plan for an international organization. When Vandenberg refused, Hull detected a threat to State's postwar planning. "The 'foreign policy' problem is still dynamite," Vandenberg wrote in his diary. "But, once more, we got unanimity by sticking to the 'Mackinac Idea.'" He took heart from the more internationalist Senator Austin, who worked with him to build consensus on the party's Resolutions Committee. "We always felt that if we (who had been so far apart in pre–Pearl Harbor days) could agree," Vandenberg wrote, "it ought to be possible for others to do so too. And that's the way it worked."

He was also careful to consult the Dewey campaign. The New York governor dispatched his foreign-policy guru, the formidable John Foster Dulles, to visit with the senator. After one congenial evening, Vandenberg found himself in complete harmony with the tall, bespectacled international lawyer who had worked with Wilson at Versailles. Thus began a friendship crucial in its influence on American policy. Dulles, the obvious choice for secretary of state in a Dewey cabinet, praised Vandenberg's "assiduous and painstaking advance work" that allowed the delegates to find common ground. Vandenberg was careful to consult Taft as well. "The job was just about done before we ever got to Chicago," he noted. "Thereafter, it was fairly plain sailing."[9]

At the convention the other contenders all withdrew in favor of Dewey before the first ballot. But Vandenberg learned that a MacArthur delegate from Milwaukee still planned a thirty-minute nominating speech. The senator made his way to the Wisconsin delegation after warning Chairman Joe Martin "to rush the program into the quickest possible roll call if the unwelcome orator could not be stopped." This lonely holdout of the MacArthur boomlet would only embarrass the general and provoke catcalls. Vandenberg pushed across the crowded floor to the Wisconsin stanchion, where delegates pointed to a man headed for the stage. Vandenberg caught him by the steps. "I greatly admire your loyalty," he told the errant delegate, "but General MacArthur has asked that his name should not be brought up here at all; and I make that request of you in his name."

The Wisconsinite was adamant: "I've been instructed by my people to vote for MacArthur and I intend to keep the faith."

Vandenberg saw that his only hope was to hold the man in conversation "until Chairman Martin could start the roll call. And that's what happened. Before he could get to the platform, 'Alabama' had been called and had voted. But it was a narrow escape."[10]

The senator kept a low profile in the Dewey campaign, though not entirely by choice. Over his objections, Dewey and Dulles had decided, at Hull's request, not to publicly discuss the issue of international organization. Yet Dewey's silence may have worked to Vandenberg's advantage: it provided an incubation period for the concept of bipartisan policy. It proved, Vandenberg recognized, "the first formal and formidable exercise" of a policy under which, in his favored phrase, politics stopped "at the water's edge."[11]

Dewey's decision had come at Hull's request. Roosevelt felt no such constraint. He attacked Republicans as isolationists who had helped bring on the war. To Hull's discomfort, he insisted that "the question of the men who will formulate and carry out the foreign policy of this country is an issue in this election—very much an issue." Vandenberg was furious that the president treated efforts at bipartisanship so cavalierly, and he was more broadly bitter about the way the world esteemed the incumbent. He often recalled Roosevelt's 1940 vow: "I have said this before, but I shall say it again and again: your boys are not going to be sent into any foreign wars." Roosevelt, Vandenberg wrote, "totally failed in the stated objectives of his statesmanship," and this failure was being paraded as "the consummate proof of his wisdom and vision!" After all, *he* had been the one who was serious about avoiding war in 1940; Roosevelt had been just another pandering politician.[12]

The isolationist label stung Republicans, and they had other problems as well. Some GOP liberals—including Senator Ball, whose resolution had helped motivate the Mackinac Charter—endorsed Roosevelt. Dewey didn't know what to do, fearful as he was of renewing "the old cleavage" in Republican ranks between western isolationists and eastern interventionists. Although the New York governor made a respectable showing that November, he was, as Vandenberg predicted in frustration, no match for the experienced commander in chief. Roosevelt, with his new vice presidential nominee, Senator Harry Truman, won decisively.

And yet, his coattails were short. Republicans gained ground in Congress. The party could still have hopes for real influence once the war was over. For Vandenberg there was another tangible gain—the friendship of Dewey's shadow secretary of state. "I feel that we are already 'old friends,'" he wrote to John Foster Dulles right after the election. "I look forward to working intimately with you in the great 'peace adventure.'" He confessed a feeling of loneliness as he looked ahead—where did he fit in this rapidly changing world?

With Dulles, who was leading the World Council of Churches, he shared a worldview—as well as a ponderous Republican gravitas. "I suspect you will find me knocking at your door more than once," he said. "I really think it is little short of amazing that our views on foreign policy should have proved to be so emphatically harmonious." It felt almost like a revelation to Vandenberg "that so called 'isolationists' and so-called 'internationalists' are not *necessarily* very far apart and *really* may be 'brothers under the skin.'"[13]

CHAPTER 19

· · · · · · · · · · · ·

THE SPEECH

· · · · · · · · · · · ·

The presidential race had been very nearly a sideshow to another conflict. A quarter century after Versailles, idealism and disillusion were again locked in a battle that seemed to hold the fate of the world in the balance. Hull, Roosevelt, Vandenberg—each was haunted by the tragic mistakes of a previous generation, and each sought a better, safer world. But what chance did they have to unite other countries when they themselves did not share a vision of the United Nations and the future it presaged?

At a Georgetown estate named Dumbarton Oaks, Cordell Hull, wearing a beribboned pince-nez, convened a conference to set the ground rules for organizing the United Nations. His young but silver-haired undersecretary, Edward R. Stettinius, presided over three dozen diplomats from Great Britain, the Soviet Union, China, and the United States. This outgrowth of the Tehran conference was a step on the road from the Mackinac Charter—a step that Vandenberg and the Committee of Eight had encouraged—but a step toward what?

At the end of August, Hull briefed the Committee of Eight on the conference. He raised the subject of when and how American forces might participate in United Nations military action. Vandenberg opposed any plan that gave authority to the president and the American representative to the new "league"—the term he still used—to dispatch American troops. He insisted that the United States would veto any commitment not sanctioned by Congress. He agreed, however, that the general staffs of the Big Four might begin to study joint preparedness. He was, after all, in favor of preparedness—indeed, he had been all his life.

At the heart of these negotiations lay the most difficult question:

what power did the president have to deploy military force, and to what extent was that power circumscribed by Congress? "I do not know whether this distinction can be definitely described," Vandenberg wrote to Hull. "I should like to see the effort made."[1] While he emphatically did not want to be accused of working in bad faith or of "an attempt to 'wreck the League,'" he would never cede congressional power to an American delegate on the proposed Security Council. He allowed that the president might have some discretion in the use of force within regional security arrangements, as suggested by the Monroe Doctrine. "But if the dispute discloses an aggressor who cannot be curbed on a regional basis—if it takes another world-wide war to deal with him," Vandenberg told Hull, "I do not see how we can escape the necessity for Congressional consent."[2]

In a telling letter to Walter Lippmann in September 1944, he asked, as if of Roosevelt, "Why jeopardize 99 per cent of this great adventure . . . by stubbornly and blindly insisting upon asking for the final one per cent of totalitarian power which you do not need and which you would not dare to use in any major crisis if you had it?" Beyond constitutional concerns, he had political ones as well. "Why hand the President a blank check which in turn invites the American opponents of all international collaboration," he asked, to shout "on the Middle Western hustings—'Are you willing to let the President take you into World War No. Three without regard to the Constitution and without any consultation of your Congress?'" He knew that enemy—it had been himself. "It should not require very much imagination to realize what can be done with that sort of an appeal," he said.[3]

Two weeks before the election, as the Dumbarton Oaks negotiations came to a close, Vandenberg told Hull he wished to discuss "our mutual problem." He was reassured when the secretary suggested that any agreement on military force be dealt with separately and ratified by the Senate after the United Nations was established. Vandenberg welcomed the assurance that if any nation found the status quo unjust when peace arrived—"as seems clearly threatened by a new dismemberment of Poland"—it could press its claims before the new body. "If this *is* so," Vandenberg wrote, "it makes a great difference in my attitude; and under such circumstances I would welcome the earliest possible organization of the League."[4]

On the surface, Senate support for a world organization appeared widespread. Yet there were undercurrents of concern. The conference was barely under way when Allen Drury noted, "All of us are afraid of what the Senate will do. The press is afraid, the Senate itself is afraid. The responsibility is so great, and no one can be sure that the strength will be found to meet it." Democrat Claude Pepper of Florida feared that "the cabal between the Republicans and the Democratic isolationists is coming out of hiding. . . . The same crowd that defeated the League and obstructed preparation for war is getting ready to defeat the peace."[5]

But this time even Taft, perhaps the most thoughtful isolationist, was ready to go along, provided that veto power on the Security Council protected the United States from being drawn into new conflicts. Vandenberg was more ambivalent about the veto power. At first he had seen it as a way to protect American interests. But when the Russians demanded it as well, he objected. I wonder, he asked, "if we ever really speak up to Stalin, as is our great right and our equally great responsibility?" He was new to the business of power diplomacy, still feeling his way.[6]

Internationalists on both sides of the aisle wanted to go much further and create a United Nations police force to restrain aggressors. Vandenberg was deeply skeptical. "I doubt," he said, "whether any hard and fast international contracts looking toward the use of cooperative force in unforeseeable emergencies ahead will be worth any more . . . than the national consciences of the contracting parties."

The war continued to make and remake political realities. By late 1944, with a Nazi defeat imminent, the Soviet Union was showing no interest in restoring freedom to the Eastern European states it had wrested from German occupation.

Vandenberg was not alone in wondering what sort of peace might come in the months ahead. As his son wrote later, "Everywhere there was an urgent if almost unrecognized desire to believe, to be reassured that the future was not necessarily a hopelessly sinister mirage of political and military machinations, or, alternatively, a hazardous experiment in starry-eyed idealism." Before Christmas, Winston Churchill told the House of Commons that the United States had yet to step forward with its thoughts for the future, that he counted on that day arriving.

Franklin Roosevelt, said to be ill, did not appear at the Capitol for his State of the Union address. It was read by the clerk of the House. His urging of compromise and his attack on "perfectionism" seemed to be preparing his listeners for what he would face in upcoming negotiations with Churchill and Stalin. Roosevelt's words, Drury reported, "soured the idealists, confirmed the isolationists, and disturbed the middle-of-the-roaders."[7] Everyone wanted to believe in the promise of the future, but perhaps no one really did. Vandenberg was among the "disturbed."

As 1945 began, the president prepared for the February Big Three summit in the Crimean resort of Yalta. At this conference, postwar planning would supplant wartime strategy as the priority. For the sake of Allied unity, the deep schism between Western and Soviet ideologies had been suppressed for half a decade. The platitudes of Willkie's *One World* pervaded the public consciousness even as the urgency of brothers-in-arms was giving way to rival visions of the future. What would become of the liberated peoples of Europe? The president had broad support for some form of postwar cooperation, which was fine as far as it went. But there was widespread worry that it did not go far enough.

U.S. News had noted that Republican leadership in the Senate was virtually powerless on foreign policy. Connally's mood vacillated between disgust and pessimism. Democrats appointed three internationalists to the Foreign Relations Committee. "Certainly the White House," wrote Drury, "is doing nothing to counteract the growing . . . uncertainty on the Hill."[8] Clouds of distrust hovered over Washington.

Vandenberg abhorred the vacuum. *Somebody* needed to do *something* to stay the drift of policy. It was time to act. That meant a speech,

an address that would push the president to work with the Senate—
and let his colleagues, and the American people, know what he was
thinking. As *Time*'s Senate correspondent reported, "Vandenberg's
fingers fairly itched for a typewriter."[9] The senator said later that he
was placing before the president what amounted to a challenge—to
see if Russia would act in good faith.[10] Nothing more, nothing less.

At the Wardman Park Hotel, looking out across the leafless treetops
along Connecticut Avenue, Vandenberg hitched himself up to that
battered Smith-Corona—the same one he'd used before the war to
argue against repeal of neutrality. He lit one cigar after another. No
speech in his career was prepared with greater care. "I should think I
rewrote it at least a dozen times from start to finish before I was satisfied with its final form," he said later. He shared these drafts with
newspaper friends. Blair Moody of the *Detroit News* read at least two
versions.[11]

New York Times Washington correspondent James Reston saw
an early draft and said it was the worst speech he had ever read. He
argued that the senator had to do more than sound an alarm about
drift and secrecy in American foreign policy. He urged Vandenberg to
propose, of all things, an alliance. If the United States, Great Britain,
and France joined with the Soviet Union in a security treaty against
future German—or Japanese—aggression, the Soviets no longer
needed to expand their control of bordering nations as a buffer. The
Red Army would lose its pretext for occupying Eastern Europe. Vandenberg incorporated Reston's suggestion.[12]

On January 10, 1945, Vice President–Elect Harry Truman, presiding over
the Senate, recognized his friend, the big man in the double-breasted
suit who stood on the left side of the aisle. There were fifty-nine senators on the floor. Vandenberg, dark eyes bulging under beetling black
brows, was the Republican whose idea of the world mattered most. If
he was not always the eloquent orator he fancied himself, his dogged
intelligence and evident passion pulled along his colleagues. He was
sixty years old that winter. His gravitas was ingrained.[13]

With the even cadence and high-flown phrasing that were his trademarks, he proceeded to review the status of the Allied war effort. In bitter cold in the Ardennes forest, American troops held out against a German counteroffensive that became the Battle of the Bulge. In Budapest, Russians and Germans fought house to house as much of the Hungarian capital was reduced to rubble. In the Pacific, Americans fought island by deadly island to dislodge the Japanese. "We not only have two wars to win," the senator observed, "we also have yet to achieve such a peace as will justify this appalling cost." He called for a shared purpose among Democrats and Republicans, as elusive as that seemed, cautioning that without it, "we shall look back upon a futile, sanguinary shambles and—God save the mark—we shall be able to look forward only to the curse of World War III."

His words reflected contending impulses of hope and fear that Americans experienced as the end of the war approached. He believed in the need for an international security organization to promote and perhaps enforce peace. But this conviction was haunted by a deep disquiet, anxiety that the Allies might soon—at Yalta, if it had not happened already—betray the vaunted principles of the Atlantic Charter for the postwar aggrandizement so familiar from Versailles. Decisions could be in the offing that would force the United States to underwrite an unjust peace. It was necessary not only to sound the alarm, but also to flush out Soviet intentions.

What worried Vandenberg most was the opacity of Roosevelt's plans. Silence was a wartime expedient, but it had given birth to the misconception "that we in the United States dare not publicly discuss these subjects lest we contribute to international dissension." Why, he wondered, must the United States "be the only silent partner in this grand alliance?" Did Moscow worry about unity when its aims collided with American interests? Was Churchill timid about his determination to preserve the empire? Vandenberg could only wonder if "by our silence we have acquiesced. But that hypothesis would only make a bad matter worse. It would be the final indictment of our silence."

Worst of all, if silence meant acquiescence, then "our only role in this global tragedy is to fight and die and pay, and that unity for us shall only be the unity which Jonah enjoyed when he was swallowed by the whale." Without an understanding of their government's intentions, Vandenberg said, "too often a grave melancholy settles upon some sectors of our people. . . . [C]itizens, in increasing numbers, are crying 'what are we fighting for?' " With his classic overstuffed phrasing, the grandiloquent senator implored the administration to abide by "a new rule of honest candor . . . as a substitute for mystifying silence or for classical generalities."

The Atlantic Charter had enshrined the principles of national self-determination. While Roosevelt's commitment to the charter had been uncertain—he had recently called it "a mere collection of fragmentary notes"—he had said in the State of the Union text that the United States would not hesitate "to use our influence and use it now" to fulfill its principles. "That is the indispensable point," Vandenberg declared. Then he reached into his rhetorical grab bag for another lofty image: "These basic pledges cannot now be dismissed as a mere nautical nimbus." These pledges "march with our armies. They sail with our fleets," he said.

The United States faced a choice—and so did Arthur Vandenberg. The nation could approach the end of the war with a unilateral spirit or with a preference for joint action, whereby "we undertake to look out for each other." The first choice was the old way—his way, once— and it had twice now embroiled Americans in European wars. "The second way," Vandenberg insisted, "is the new way in which we must make our choice. I think we must make it wholly plain to our major allies that they, too, must make their choice."

With that, Vandenberg set the stage for what he called his "confession." It was a brief sketch of where he had come from. His thoughts had changed—since the private visits with his nephew in the Army Air Force; since Pearl Harbor, of course; since the Mackinac conference and the convening of the Committee of Eight. More important, America's relationship to the world had changed as well. Americans had not asked for the responsibilities of global leadership, but the task was upon them.[14]

The crowded galleries were hushed. More senators filed in, with seventy-five attending to their colleague's words. Vandenberg assessed the obstacles ahead. "I have always been frankly one of those who has believed in our own self-reliance," he said, with a timing and pitch that were just right. "But I do not believe that any nation hereafter can immunize itself by its own exclusive action. . . . Our oceans have ceased to be moats which automatically protect our ramparts." The solution was "maximum American cooperation, consistent with legitimate American self-interest." "We should tell other nations that this glorious thing we contemplate is not and cannot be one-sided," Vandenberg continued. "I think we must again say that unshared idealism is a menace which we could not undertake to underwrite in the post-war world."[15]

The question, he asked, "always becomes just this: Where does real self-interest lie . . . ? Russia's unilateral plan appears to contemplate the engulfment, directly or indirectly, of a surrounding circle of buffer states, contrary to our conception of what we were fighting for in respect to the rights of small nations and a just peace. Russia's announced reason is her insistent purpose never again to be at the mercy of another German tyranny. That is a perfectly understandable reason. The alternative is collective security. . . . Which is better in the long view, from a purely selfish Russian standpoint: To forcefully surround yourself with a cordon of unwillingly controlled or partitioned states, thus affronting the opinions of mankind . . . or to win the priceless asset of world confidence . . . by embracing the alternative, namely, full and whole-hearted cooperation with and reliance on a vital international organization . . . ? Well—at that point, Russia, or others like her, in equally honest candor has a perfect right to reply, 'Where is there any such alternative reliance until we know what the United States will do . . . ?' "

Was vague endorsement of a new world organization enough? There was no reason, said Vandenberg, to wait and see. American interests paralleled Russian ones in disarming Germany and Japan. Then came Vandenberg's clincher, via Reston. "I know of no reason," said the disciple of Hamilton, that pioneer of nationalist realpolitik, "why a hard-and-fast treaty between the major allies should not be signed today to achieve this dependable end. We need not await the determination of our other post-war relationships. This problem— this menace—stands apart." By acting on a treaty, Vandenberg argued, Americans would learn "whether we have found and cured the real hazard to our relationships." A treaty, along with an agreement to use a new organization to address injustices that might come with the peace, would also clarify future relationships.

In thirty-nine minutes the critic had shown the way, admitting, in the process, "how much easier it is to be critical than correct." There were momentous problems ahead, Vandenberg said: "We cannot drift to victory." Only through "plain speaking," which had been "too conspicuous by its absence," could the United States find "the only kind of realistic unity which . . . will best validate our aspirations, our sacrifices and our dreams."[16]

Vandenberg could not have created more of a stir, Frank McNaughton of *Time* reported, if he had walked in "wearing a loincloth and a g-string." Isolationism was dead—killed by none other than its greatest proponent, Arthur Vandenberg. The old isolationist stood naked before the world to confess the new truth.[17]

The speech "hit the Senate like a Caribbean hurricane," McNaughton added, "and when it passed the air was a lot fresher." Senators applauded. The galleries practically cheered. The press fawned. This was, Reston wrote, "a speech heard round the world." The *Washington News* compared it to orations of Clay and Webster and even, to Vandenberg's satisfaction, the great Borah. The *Boston Herald* declared rather hyperbolically that his address was the most significant to come from the Senate since the Civil War.[18]

"The important thing about the speech," Reston later reflected, "was not that Vandenberg made it but that the American people responded to it with such enthusiasm." Thousands of telegrams and letters poured into the senator's office. His phone kept ringing. Calls came from James Byrnes, Vandenberg's former colleague and the "assistant president" to FDR who thought he should have been in Truman's job, and from James Forrestal, secretary of the navy and champion of a hard line with the Soviets. At a diplomatic reception at the Mayflower Hotel soon afterward, Vandenberg was strutting around, according to Lippmann, "just like a pouter pigeon all blown up with delight at his new role in the world."[19] Allen Drury wrote in his Senate diary, "There is nothing phony about the great Van's conversion. He is tickled pink with it."[20]

The next morning, Vandenberg joined a White House meeting with Roosevelt. The puzzled president withheld public comment. Was Vandenberg's conversion sincere? Henry Cabot Lodge had feigned cooperation before the League of Nations fight, after all. At first blush, the *Washington Post* noted, the White House seemed "frightened rather than encouraged" by its adversary's speech. It was not long, however, before Roosevelt noted the public's support of Vandenberg's proposal.[21]

The next week, Stettinius, meeting with the Foreign Relations Committee, interrupted his remarks to praise the speech. The Office of War Information broadcast it to armed forces overseas. As the address was more widely analyzed, its significance grew. "I can't understand why it has been such an appalling sensation," Vandenberg told Hazel, not realizing how far his public image had trailed the evolution of his thinking.[22]

Vandenberg had sensed a collective national tension. By promising opposition support for the president while suggesting what the country was waiting for the president to say, his speech reduced that tension. An anxious public was galvanized. "What he did," Reston reflected, "was merely to express and symbolize their change [in outlook] and then stick single-mindedly to the *action* necessary to implement their will." "*Merely,*" said Reston—yet in that sentence lay the mystique of Vandenberg's leadership. His proposal set a direction that had been lacking; it was Mackinac writ large. For Allen Drury, "This placed the Republicans' most powerful spokesman on foreign affairs far out in front of both his own party and the leader of the opposition."[23]

The wave of enthusiasm set him on a new course. The momentum was his, and with it the strength to stamp his name on the crucial years when America's newfound leadership might be sorely tested.[24] Vandenberg may have been coming over to a position Roosevelt had long held, but he was saying things that the president, bound by the exigencies of the war, could not—and with the conviction of a sinner who had found his way. A British Foreign Office memo declared Vandenberg "a world figure overnight" who "may yet mould large international politics."[25]

Vandenberg explained to a young Canadian diplomat, future prime minister Lester Pearson, that he had deliberated at length before staking out his position, and that his success derived from having put into words what so many Americans were thinking. It was his argument, even more than his oratory, that swayed the nation—abundant facts, a logical presentation, and the occasional catchphrase. The typewriter, as well as the booming delivery, was a powerful weapon. He read and reread the text, just to see what he had said and why it had such an effect. "I still don't know," he admitted. It would not, in any case, have been easy for him to articulate.

And yet he had swept away the fear that Senate Republicans would obstruct the establishment of an international organization. After the First World War, Woodrow Wilson and Georges Clemenceau had suggested a three-power treaty to restrain German militarism. Had they lived, columnist David Lawrence wrote, "to read the great speech of Senator Vandenberg, nearly 26 years after their historic discussion in Paris, they would have considered themselves vindicated."[26]

"It cannot be said of many speakers that they affect the course of events," Lippmann wrote. "But this may well be said of Senator Vandenberg's speech if the President and his lieutenants will recognize promptly and firmly its importance."[27]

Timing was everything. If he had given the speech earlier, he might have drawn the wrath of fellow Republicans—just another late-blooming Willkie. Had he waited, with the drumbeat of collective security sounding louder, he might have been one more repenting isolationist. On the eve of Roosevelt's meeting with Stalin and Churchill, he was neither early nor late: he was right where most of the people were.

It was a good thing he was comfortable in that spot. The senator's friends at the *Chicago Tribune*, who had questioned his conduct since the UNRRA compromise and the Mackinac Charter, had closed off his avenue of retreat. Vandenberg spoke for himself, not his party, the *Tribune* insisted: "He is abandoning the principles of Americanism for which the party must stand if it hopes to regain the confidence of the voters." He appeared willing to bow to Britain and Russia, "pledging us to maintain a well-nigh permanent police force in Germany, in exchange for vague concessions." Republicans ought to have learned by then not to ape Mr. Roosevelt, Colonel McCormick warned. The *Washington Times-Herald* thought Vandenberg's speech foreshadowed the breakup of the GOP. Why, an editorial asked, "have two major political parties professing the same foreign policy?"[28]

Vandenberg's old friends were unnerved by the notion that politics might stop at the water's edge. So was the American Left. Communist leader Earl Browder tore into Vandenberg during a rally at Madison Square Garden. "He offers the carrot of a military alliance," Browder said. "Behind his back is the club of a wholesale revision of all European settlements after the war." Friendlier observers could not fault his sincerity. But the Canadian, Pearson, also suggested that "the approval itself is likely to have something to do with the continued advocacy of the cause for which he is speaking." Vandenberg had become the voice, on this important issue, of the many, and he seemed to inspire others: if he could change, they could, too.[29]

On January 20, from the South Portico of the White House, Vandenberg looked over Roosevelt's right shoulder at the shivering crowd on the South Lawn. He watched as the president was sworn in for a fourth term, listened with head bowed to the shortest inaugural address since George Washington's. In near-freezing temperatures, the little party was mostly bareheaded, but the senator in the white silk scarf had donned his black homburg.

Did the man who stood before him, gamely bearing the weight of braces on his legs and war on his shoulders, appreciate the power of the senator's address ten days before? An answer was not long in coming: when Roosevelt departed days later for his rendezvous with Stalin and Churchill, he brought with him fifty copies.[30]

DEAR ARTHUR

. . . .

As Roosevelt embarked for Yalta, one word captured the fear, the specter of appeasement, that haunted Arthur Vandenberg: Munich. The Red Army occupied Poland, Hungary, Bulgaria, Romania, Czechoslovakia, and the Baltic states—and had pushed on into Austria and eastern Germany. Refugees fled from America's erstwhile ally. Governments in exile wondered whether they had traded one brutal invader for another.

In early February, Roosevelt—looking drawn, alarming aides with his evident fatigue—met with Churchill and Stalin in a former summer palace of the czars. When they were done, several days later, the Soviets pledged to call free elections in Poland and other liberated areas. That seemed to be good news. The amicable tone of discussion and compromise among the Big Three felt reassuring. More encouraging still was the news that San Francisco would host a conference in late April to create the United Nations.

Vice President Truman and House Speaker Sam Rayburn summoned congressional leaders to the Capitol to hear the text of the leaders' joint communiqué read aloud. "Congressmen are so accustomed to having Roosevelt hand them an uninhibited skunk in an Easter basket," wrote McNaughton of *Time*, "that the product of Yalta was a tremendous and pleasing accomplishment." Vandenberg's formula to demilitarize Germany and Japan was part of the agreement, though not in the form of a treaty. The senator gave the talks his tentative blessing— though there was far less substance there than he had hoped.

Depending on the Senate nettled FDR. En route home from Yalta, he complained to his translator, Charles "Chip" Bohlen, that senators were "a bunch of incompetent obstructionists." The only way "to do anything in the American government was to bypass the Senate." But that could not happen. Roosevelt "could orate, dream, aspire, sermonize" with Stalin and Churchill, wrote James McGregor Burns, but he could not ignore "mean facts." These included the westward push of Russia's borders, Polish American voters in key states, and the U.S. Senate, where "the importance of one Arthur H. Vandenberg" was indisputable. Nor could Roosevelt forget, Burns wrote, "that it was not only bitter enders like Hiram Johnson and Henry Cabot Lodge, but also Republican moderates—men who were then much like Vandenberg now—who had destroyed Wilson's League." Roosevelt was cornered.[1]

One night while at Yalta, Secretary Stettinius had directed the president's attention to the question of who should represent the United States in organizing the United Nations. He wanted a bipartisan group, with Foreign Relations Chairman Connally, House Foreign Affairs Chairman Sol Bloom, House ranking member Charles Eaton, former Minnesota "boy governor" Harold Stassen, Barnard College dean Virginia Gildersleeve—and Vandenberg. Roosevelt said he hoped to find a place for Warren Austin, a Republican senator who backed his policies. Vandenberg was Austin's senior on Foreign Relations, Stettinius noted. Roosevelt acquiesced in silence.

In agreeing to the State Department's names, the president, wrote Drury, knew "the right men to get committed in order to embarrass the Republicans and also strengthen the peace." He had therefore "done a good job of picking with Vandenberg." Vandenberg himself wondered about his situation. As a Republican, "I shall occupy a particularly difficult role if I am to be of subsequent utility to this great adventure," he wrote the president. Were there specific commitments "implicit in my acceptance of this designation?" he wondered. He needed to be a free agent—and be seen as one—if he was to influence other Republicans. "I cannot go to this conference as a stooge," he told Dulles. But go he would: "I think I am called upon to put my head in this noose and take my chances."[2]

From Stettinius came a pro forma reply: "Your constructive and helpful comments in regard to our recent efforts are deeply appreci-

ated." Vandenberg needed more—from Roosevelt himself. He told reporters he was delaying his acceptance. He wanted freedom to oppose
the treaty, and he wanted it clear that he was in no way committing
the Republican Party. (The party, noted Allen Drury, "is reported to
be equally anxious to get a guarantee from Arthur on this last point.")[3]

Roosevelt dispatched a glib note: "Thank heavens this whole business is getting to be on a really non-partisan basis."

This was not the answer Vandenberg needed. Again he asked for
freedom of action: "Please forgive me for pressing the question."[4]

Roosevelt was finally reassuring. "Dear Arthur," he wrote in reply,
"Of course" he was to present his own views: "We shall need such free
expression in the delegation, and in America before and after the conference."[5]

Barely a day after his return to Washington, Roosevelt was wheeled
into the well of the House to address a joint session of Congress. He
was lifted into a deep chair upholstered in a bright floral pattern.
Under the glare of klieg lights, on a small mahogany table, were thirteen microphones—until an engineer removed a redundant one to
avoid the unlucky number. Flashbulbs popped; newsreel cameras
whirred. Roosevelt shuffled his notes, took a drink of water, and began
to speak in a soft voice—a voice too soft, almost hollow, coming from
a gaunt face, pale and weary. "The shadow of death was already on
him," Vandenberg said later, even as he and his colleagues in their
front-row seats admired the tired man's determination.[6]

First the good news: the Big Three had agreed to establish the
United Nations, following the outline sketched at Dumbarton Oaks.
They reiterated support for the principles of the Atlantic Charter.
But the fate of Poland was another matter. Stalin said he would support free elections (although there was no assurance that the Polish
government-in-exile would be welcomed back), but he also insisted
upon moving boundaries west. A vast swath of Polish territory would
be absorbed into the Soviet Union. A sizable piece of Prussia was to
be incorporated into a redrawn Poland. The new map set off alarm
bells in the west—all the more so since only the western boundary

would be settled in subsequent peace talks, leaving the new eastern boundary a fait accompli. Where was justice for beleaguered Poles? Worse, was this a harbinger of the treatment awaiting Eastern Europe's smaller states?

This news hinted at concessions that would betray Vandenberg's insistence on justice. "Where does this leave the Michigan Senator?" one pundit asked. "Must he turn a somersault?" Burt Wheeler opined, "They've got Vandenberg roped in now. He climbed way out on a limb in that security speech of his, and now he can't get back."[7]

Vandenberg had a sizable Polish constituency, though he was defensive about its influence. "Frankly, I should very much prefer to wind up my public career in a successful contribution to world peace than to suffer six more years in the Senate," he said, "if there has to be a choice."[8]

As he told the editor of Detroit's Polish newspaper, "I could get no greater personal satisfaction out of anything more than . . . in leading a public denunciation of Yalta and all its works as respects Poland." But was that the best way to win justice for Poles—"not merely for Poland's sake but also for a permanent World Peace which can never survive injustice?" A bad Polish settlement could turn public opinion against the United Nations. In fact, Vandenberg confided, if a UN treaty were to die in the Senate, "over its body will stand the shadow of Poland."[9]

It would not take much to "dynamite" the proposed United Nations, Vandenberg noted. But that would leave Russia "in complete possession of everything she wants. . . . There would be no hope left for justice except through World War Number Three immediately." Instead, he would make every effort at San Francisco to write the objectives of the Atlantic Charter into the charter of the new organization—would do all he could to give it "specific authority to examine at any time whatever injustice may have been inherited from the war era and to recommend correction."[10]

His warning that collective security might hinge on the fate of Poland drew the wrath of the Soviet press. He was denounced as an imperialist bent on obstruction. He became a lightning rod for anti-

American anger. On March 6, the prospective delegates met briefly with Roosevelt, and Vandenberg offered to resign. "We will have to deal with the Russians and I don't want to make it difficult," he said. "I can conveniently arrange to break a leg—if you wish."

"No—I want you to go and for that very reason," Vandenberg said Roosevelt replied. "At conference after conference I have been forced to agree to things which I do not agree with in fear lest Russia should make a separate peace. She will now blackmail us again by threatening to withdraw from our League." Roosevelt had his own concerns about Stalin. "If I could name only one delegate to the San Francisco conference," he told the senator, "you would be that delegate."

The Soviets heard in Vandenberg's obsession with "justice" a code word for meddling. *Justice* was not a code word for Vandenberg, but it was a shorthand counterpoint to *Munich*, meant to give smaller countries leverage, whether they were buffer states at the mercy of a great power or colonies longing for independence. And justice was his goal in San Francisco, especially after the Dumbarton Oaks draft charter did "not once mention 'justice' as a guiding objective or a rule of conduct." He vowed to present "concrete proposals . . . along these lines."[11]

Vandenberg submitted to Leo Pasvolsky, the Russian exile who was the delegation's State Department adviser, amendments to the draft charter that inserted references to justice. The rotund professor dismissed his worry that Soviet criticism might make him persona non grata among the UN delegates. The question on every delegate's mind, said Pasvolsky, was "the same one that plagued them in past experience, namely, what will the Senate do? Well—when we are pressing for something we don't seem able to get, we'll send you in to tell 'em that it has to be done if they expect to get their Treaty past the Senate."[12] This was the legacy of his speech: he had a credibility he had never had before.

On March 23 the delegates returned to the White House. A weary president informed them that Stalin had demanded six votes in the proposed general assembly—to match the six votes held by members of the British Commonwealth. Roosevelt said he had negotiated Stalin down to three votes, and he added that the United States was entitled to three as well. He assured the delegates that they would have a free hand but that he had told Stalin that if he were a delegate, he would support such an allotment.

Vandenberg was dumbfounded. "We began to get some of the inside 'bad news' from Yalta today," he wrote in his diary. "It is typical of the baffling secrecy which leaves one eternally uncertain of what 'deals' have been made." Vandenberg, "hot as a furnace flue," told colleagues he was ready to raise hell. "The delegates were rather stunned," he said. How would other nations react? Might the Chinese or French protest a lopsided setup? "This is going to be a 'tough nut.' It looks like bad business to me."[13]

The deal with Stalin threatened the pretense of equality in the proposed general assembly. Vandenberg tried to reach Stettinius, to "unburden" himself, but the secretary of state was on vacation. He suggested bringing the matter to Cordell Hull's attention in hopes that the former secretary, the United Nations' great champion, could impress upon the president "the importance of urging Stalin to drop the whole thing (since it *can't* be approved). Or, failing that, that Stalin be left to present his demand *de novo*—without any reference to any tentative agreement with F.D.R. or Churchill, and certainly without any reference to the fact that F.D.R. wants to 'horn in' on the scheme in behalf of the U.S."[14]

Dulles agreed, Vandenberg wrote, "that this effort to 'stack' the Assembly could easily dynamite San Francisco—or subsequent Senate approval of the entire treaty." When the *New York Herald Tribune* broke rumors of the deal, the White House was forced to confirm the substance of the story. Vandenberg quickly announced his objections, leading one reporter to conclude, "If this drives Vandenberg into opposition, then the whole project is doomed."[15]

Stettinius soon showed Vandenberg and Connally a compromise statement that, in Vandenberg's words, "*committed* our Government (and therefore our Frisco delegation) to 'three votes for Russia,' leaving us free *only* respecting 'three votes for the U.S.'" Had not Roosevelt told the delegates they were free agents on both propositions? Vandenberg unleashed all the righteous wrath he could summon. State agreed to check the wording with the president, who had departed for Warm Springs, Georgia.

Vandenberg and Connally decided to ask Roosevelt if the United States could renounce its claim to three votes, even if Russia insisted upon its own. This, Vandenberg wrote, would "establish our moral position" and "manifestly weaken the Russian claim." The American delegates were developing "a general disposition to *stop this Stalin appeasement*," Vandenberg added. "It *has* to stop *sometime*. Every new surrender makes it more difficult."[16] The senator was ready to force the issue, even if, as Frank McNaughton wrote, "to expect that Russia will bow to Vandenberg is stretching the imagination."[17]

To appease Vandenberg, Stettinius drafted a statement that put Stalin "out on the end of a limb" by announcing, on the eve of the conference, that the United States "is stuck with a bad bargain of which we want no part." Vandenberg was grateful that Roosevelt at least "had the guts to spurn his own deal," giving up the extra votes for the United States. Otherwise, "any further talk of the 'sovereign equality of (little) nations' would be a travesty. I feel we have accomplished *something*."[18]

He soon accomplished more. The State Department accepted his language giving the General Assembly power to promote human rights—a form of justice—in accord with the Atlantic Charter. "Thus we would end the war on the same note with which we began it," he wrote.

"Hold onto your hat!" he added in his diary. "Mrs. FDR endorsed my proposals!"[19]

On the afternoon of April 12 came news from Warm Springs. "President Roosevelt died today," Vandenberg wrote in his diary. "Thus a truly great and gallant spirit, despite all his flaws, was gathered to his fathers."[20]

Over a dozen years of sometimes bitter rivalry, Vandenberg had tried to distinguish between political and personal feelings. Speaking at the Gridiron dinner in 1940, he said, "I never knew a more gallant soul who has laughed triumphantly at the handicaps of life and given his country a superb example of *personal* courage and a *personal* challenge to 'carry on' to victory, no matter what the burden, no matter what the odds." And history would say of Roosevelt, "He made us *social-minded.*"[21]

On April 14 came the White House funeral—to Vandenberg a "simple, deeply impressive service." Sheets of rain washed the lawn as leaders of the government gathered in the East Room with diplomats and generals. When the new president filed in with his wife and daughter, no one thought to stand. Nor did Harry Truman seem to notice. No eulogies were spoken over the flag-draped casket. There were hymns, and then the Episcopal bishop recited the memorable lines from Roosevelt's first inaugural address: "Let me assert my firm belief that the only thing we have to fear is fear itself."

Grand Rapids Central High School, class of 1900. (Bentley Historical Library)

Editor of the *Grand Rapids Herald*, c. 1907. (Bentley Historical Library)

Courting Hazel
at a Lake Michigan
beach, c. 1918. (Bentley
Historical Library)

Ionia, Michigan Free Fair, 1939. (Bentley Historical Library)

Republican 1940 presidential hopefuls—before Wendell Willkie stole the show—with William Allen White (*left*), progressive GOP pundit and president of the American Society of Newspaper Editors. Ohio senator Robert Taft (*second from left*) and New York prosecutor Thomas Dewey joined Vandenberg at the event. (Harris & Ewing, photographers, Library of Congress)

On the porch at the Grand Hotel, Mackinac Island, Michigan, 1943: "Beginning to grasp the full possibilities of his role." (Getty Images)

Addressing the Republican policy conference on Mackinac Island, 1943: "Hunting for the middle ground." Seated to Vandenberg's left are Robert Taft and California governor Earl Warren. (Getty Images)

Hazel and Arthur, filling scrapbooks in their Washington apartment, c. 1945. (Getty Images)

Arthur and Hazel with nephew and Army Air Force general Hoyt Vandenberg (*left*) and Arthur Junior, c. 1944. (Bentley Library)

Writing the speech, c. 1945. (Getty Images)

Vandenberg (*center left, with cigar*) and fellow negotiators from the Big Five presumptive members of the UN Security Council, in the penthouse of the Fairmont Hotel in San Francisco, 1945. Vandenberg is flanked by Senate Foreign Relations Committee chairman Tom Connally of Texas on his left and House Foreign Affairs chairman Sol Bloom on his right. Secretary of State Edward Stettinius, at right in the window, presided, with Soviet ambassador Andrei Gromyko at his left. (Getty Images)

Signing the United Nations Charter, June 26, 1945, with President Harry Truman (*far left*) looking on. (Getty Images)

Vandenberg en route to London for the first General Assembly of the United Nations, in January 1946, with fellow delegates (*from left*) Eleanor Roosevelt, Edward Stettinius, and Tom Connally. (Getty Images)

At the peace table: Vandenberg in the Luxembourg Palace for the Conference
of Foreign Ministers peace treaty negotiations, Paris, 1946. (Getty Images)

Vandenberg with (*from left*) fellow Michigan senator Homer Ferguson, Governor Kim Sigler, and GOP national committeeman Arthur Summerfield, 1946. (Getty Images)

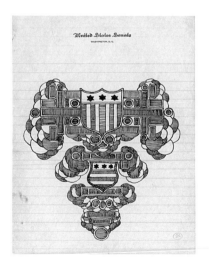

While presiding over the Eightieth Congress: Vandenberg doodle from the rostrum of the Senate, c. 1948. (Private collection)

Present at the creation: Secretary of State George Marshall and Vandenberg discuss the European Recovery Program—the Marshall Plan—in 1948. (Getty Images)

Arthur and Hazel and the press on the eve of the Republican National Convention, Philadelphia, June 1948. (Getty Images)

Vandenberg and a kindred spirit, the freshman congressman from Grand Rapids, Gerald R. Ford, c. 1949. (Gerald R. Ford Presidential Library)

Back to the Capitol, c. 1949. (Getty Images)

. . . .

CHAPTER 21

SAN FRANCISCO

. . . .

The day after Roosevelt died, his successor returned to the Capitol for lunch with Vandenberg and other congressional leaders. The senator marveled at this gesture. "It means that the days of executive contempt for Congress are ended," he said. Truman sent him the last box of cigars from the vice president's office. Vandenberg gathered Senate Republicans to send the new president "a message of trust and faith." The hasty statement "seemed to make a profound impression," he wrote. And he added a personal note to Truman: "Good luck and God bless you. Let me help you whenever I can. America marches on."[1]

Arthur Vandenberg was already a formidable figure when Harry Truman arrived in Washington in 1935. He grew fond of the junior senator from Missouri. Vandenberg was one of a small fraternity, including Majority Leader Barkley and House Speaker Rayburn, belonging to the "Lowell B. Mason Chowder, Marching and Baseball Club," which shared the best box at Griffith Stadium, and Truman joined their ranks soon after he took office. Yet there was a note of condescension in Vandenberg's private reaction to a Truman presidency: "Can he swing the job?" he wondered in his diary. "Despite his limited capacities, I believe he can."

Truman's first decision pleased him. The San Francisco conference would proceed as scheduled. Nor would the new president attend himself—as Roosevelt had planned to—but he would "leave Frisco to our delegation." With such freedom came responsibility. Not only was Truman unschooled in foreign affairs, his young secretary of state was a neophyte. Vandenberg, the Republican, was the delegate to whom others deferred.[2]

Hazel traveled to California on the "UNCIO [United Nations Conference on International Organization] Special." Cars of the Baltimore & Ohio, Rock Island, and Southern Pacific lines combined to transport State Department functionaries, journalists, and diplomats—French, Dutch, Iranian, Chinese, Russian. The Mexican delegation boarded in El Paso. Then it was on to Los Angeles and up the scenic coastal route to San Francisco, where delegates were greeted by military bands, popping flashbulbs, and Vandenberg ally Nelson Rockefeller, the undersecretary responsible for relations with Latin America. A cordon of soldiers and sailors stood at attention in the depot. Chauffeured cars from an Army-Navy motor pool followed a police motorcycle, siren screaming, up the steep incline of Nob Hill to the imposing Fairmont Hotel.[3]

Vandenberg and Connally had flown in on a bomber the day before. Stettinius was lodged in the hotel's penthouse. John Foster Dulles was across the street at the Mark Hopkins. Arthur and Hazel's flower-filled suite on the fourth floor overlooked the bay. When the fog lifted, the city, the harbor, and the gleaming Golden Gate Bridge spread out below them.

The streets filled with the costumes and accents of a global officialdom, the chaos and protocol of fez and turban, homburg and pinstripe. Andrei Gromyko, the dour young Soviet ambassador, crossed the gilded lobby of the Fairmont. There was Anthony Eden, handsome British foreign secretary, striding up Nob Hill with his overcoat flapping in the wind. Society invitations rained down on the VIPs. Hazel christened a ship, toured United Service Organizations facilities, and attended one splendid luncheon after another.

The Soviet foreign minister, Vyacheslav Molotov, arrived from Washington, where he met the new president. Truman's response to the Soviets' desire to seat Polish delegates from their puppet government had been blunt. Vandenberg got the "thrilling" news from Stettinius: "Not even *you* could have made a stronger statement than Truman did." A chastened Molotov arrived in San Francisco rather more cordial than expected.[4]

The conference opened on April 25. Plenary sessions convened at the San Francisco Opera House, a ten-minute ride from the Fairmont. Stalin had insisted at Yalta on voting membership for Ukraine and White Russia, along with seats for them in the plenary assembly. Roosevelt had yielded to the first demand, and Truman ordered the American delegates to vote that way. Regarding the conference itself, however, Vandenberg argued that Russia get no additional seats. "I don't know whether this is Frisco or Munich," he mused.[5]

After the opening ceremonies, the U.S. delegation repaired to the Fairmont penthouse to discuss the matter. Vandenberg was firm. It was one thing to keep Roosevelt's pledge, quite another to submit to new demands. "The decision is one of judgment," Vandenberg wrote in his diary. And, "At what point is it wisest to stop appeasing Stalin?" When Stettinius polled the Americans on seating the Soviet puppet states—in a compromise that would also seat troublesome Argentina—Vandenberg alone voted no.[6]

He was riled up again when Molotov proposed rotating conference chairs. The State Department thought Eden supported Stettinius as the host country's permanent chair, with the other powers designating vice-chairmen. Instead, the British proposed a compromise of four chairmen, with Stettinius presiding. A potential showdown became a three-ring circus. Though the fight was largely symbolic, Truman told his delegates to hold firm for the chairmanship. Vandenberg saw in Russian determination to win every point "a sort of 'rule or ruin' attitude."

On the third day the Americans met in the penthouse with Eden and Molotov. The Soviet foreign secretary, "a powerful fellow though not large," greeted Vandenberg with a smile and said he knew all about him.[7] The smiles ended when the talks began. The Soviets yielded on the conference chairs only when it was clear they lacked the votes. The steering committee went with Eden's compromise, a rotation—a "Soviet," said Vandenberg—with Stettinius chairing the steering and executive committees and generally responsible for overseeing the conference. On the question of three votes for the Soviet Union, the Allies kept the faith, "altho [sic] we *all hated* what we had to do."

There is no lack of choice for a moment that could mark the onset of the Cold War, but this would be high among them. To Vandenberg, "*This* is the point at which to line up our votes . . . and *win* and *end this appeasement of the Reds now before it is too late.*" The opening ceremonies were over, and so, in San Francisco, was the illusion, still prevailing in much of the land, that Americans and Soviets shared a bond that went beyond their wartime alliance. The lines were clearly drawn.

A pattern of Russian behavior seemed to be emerging. One demand led to another. Not only did Molotov want Ukraine and White Russia at the conference, the Czech foreign minister, Jan Masaryk, announced that his government supported admission of the Soviet-controlled Lublin Poles. Seated just behind Stettinius, Vandenberg whispered in the secretary's ear: "This move must be killed at once and in the open." He handed a note to Stettinius, who read it verbatim to the assembly: The United States honored its Yalta pledge. It expected Russia to honor hers, which meant a more representative Polish government. To recognize the Lublin communists, Vandenberg wrote, "would be a sordid exhibition of bad faith."

Molotov was taken aback. Eden promptly seconded the American position, expressing shock that the Soviets would renege on their commitment. Molotov knew he was beaten.

"Molotov and Vandenberg are the dominating figures," wrote the *Washington Times–Herald*. "It looks as if the entire history of the Conference may revolve around a battle of wits between these two men—it is the hand of Vandenberg that is generally discerned in U.S. moves on the Conference chess board."[8]

Molotov had learned the slang *OK* and employed it with relish whenever he agreed to a proposal. "And he agreed quite generally," Vandenberg wrote, "until we hit my key amendment to Chapter V B6." This was a revision of the Dumbarton Oaks draft allowing the assembly to investigate "situations arising out of any treaties or international agreements." Vandenberg told Molotov he needed the specific language reflecting the Atlantic Charter to win Senate approval.

Molotov countered that such language would weaken all treaty obligations. Vandenberg: it was the only way not to freeze the status quo and whatever may have flowed from wartime contingencies or peace-table machinations. Molotov: "No OK." The issue was tabled. The senator and the foreign secretary spoke at length. Vandenberg found Molotov earnest and able, "despite our disagreements."[9]

The solution lay in language. Vandenberg would drop references to "treaties" in favor of the general assembly having the freedom to consider situations "regardless of origin." He could live with that so long as justice was mentioned in the charter. "Regardless of origin" was a euphemism Molotov could accept. "Thus justice gets a forum and injustice loses its grip," Vandenberg concluded. When Stettinius issued a press release about the amendments that did not mention Vandenberg's favorite word, Vandenberg grumbled, "Is the State Department eternally allergic to . . . 'justice'?" The senator defined his duty by a determination to include it in the charter.[10]

Justice meant three things for Arthur Vandenberg. At a tactical level, it was cover for attacks from his old isolationist cohort. The isolationists thought themselves realists, alert to danger, resistant to the siren songs of treaties and foreign connivance—"power politics." *Justice* sounded hardheaded in the midst of utopian talk about world peace. Stalin was a murderer, not to be trusted, and "justice" was the cautionary, tough-minded key to holding him and others to account—while making Vandenberg's new role more respectable to old allies.

At a strategic level, *justice* put the Soviets on notice. It meant that the United Nations could look beyond the status quo at war's end. Although the big powers would call the shots, *justice* demanded that the smaller nations be heard. A commitment to justice would give the United Nations the opening to fight peace treaties and national boundaries that big-power compromises and the fait accompli of Soviet occupation might impose, particularly in Eastern Europe. Russia would resist him "from Hell to breakfast," Vandenberg predicted. But Poland would not be forgotten.

Finally, there was the moral dimension. It was not in Vandenberg's nature to understate his ambitions in San Francisco. This was a noble undertaking, or it was not worth doing. *Justice* had a righteous ring, with none of the wavering echoes of Wilson's failed enterprise. In a world where communism was the soulless foe, his goal, "in an allegorical word," Vandenberg confided to a friend, was to "give this new International Organization a 'soul.' "[11]

Midnight, May 4, was the deadline for filing the revised charter of the new organization. It was preceded by two days of marathon talks. Penthouse negotiators agreed on two dozen amendments. While issues remained regarding regional security arrangements and treaty revisions, Vandenberg got the references he wanted: "justice," "human rights," and "fundamental freedoms."

That very afternoon came word that sixteen members of the Polish government-in-exile—whom Americans hoped would be included in the new government—had been arrested in Moscow, where they had been invited for "talks." Stettinius and Eden demanded information. Molotov was visibly uneasy, and perhaps even worried, lest the prisoners be killed, although none was and several were soon released. "This is bad business," Vandenberg wrote in his diary.[12]

Beyond his other concerns, Vandenberg was occupied with the question of regional security under the charter. He feared that the Monroe Doctrine might be superseded by the deliberations of the Security Council, where Russia and the other powers could veto UN action. "The grave problem," he wrote, was to find a formula that protected regional arrangements without compromising the overall responsibility of the new body—and without inviting dangerous new "regional spheres of influence."

By what he termed a "significant coincidence," Vandenberg dined the evening of May 5 with Nelson Rockefeller. Neither Vandenberg nor the Latin delegates could imagine giving Stalin a say in a regional conflict that might well involve communist forces. Perhaps, Vandenberg suggested, the charter could grant a temporary exemption to signatories of the Act of Chapultepec, the existing regional security treaty.

Rockefeller called the Colombian foreign minister and the Cuban ambassador, who liked the proposal. By midnight, Vandenberg had written it up for morning delivery to Stettinius.

On Monday, May 7, Germany surrendered. Hitler was dead in his bunker. Russian and American troops embraced on the banks of the Elbe. This was the news that mattered most to the rest of the world. But in San Francisco, Vandenberg was so preoccupied that he barely seemed to notice.

That morning, when Stettinius circulated his letter, "hell broke loose," reported Vandenberg. Pasvolsky argued that if defensive military action in the Western Hemisphere were vetoed by the Security Council, the United States would act anyway—why sanction regional pacts in the charter? Because unilateral action would be a bigger blow to the United Nations than a specific exemption, Vandenberg countered. But even Dulles objected, saying that allowing nations to bypass the Security Council might emasculate the new organization. Vandenberg understood: "The Monroe Doctrine is protected only if we kick the daylights out of the world organization." What to do?[13]

As resistance mounted, Vandenberg "served notice" to his colleagues. If the charter failed to address the issue to his satisfaction, he expected to see a Senate reservation when it came time to ratify—a reservation he would support. He would not sacrifice inter-American defense pledges to a Security Council veto.[14]

When Latin Americans insisted on recognition of their mutual-defense treaty, Australians wanted the same recourse. Potential blocs began to emerge. Arab states, worried about the future of Palestine, talked of organizing that tinderbox region. The great problem, Vandenberg wrote, was to find a way to protect existing regional groups without inviting new balance-of-power alliances. Moreover, the United States had to satisfy its Latin neighbors to win their votes on other issues. If not, Vandenberg predicted, "we are surrounded by trouble."

Stettinius, a former steel executive who had competently run Lend-Lease operations but rarely contributed to policy decisions, was not a visionary diplomat. He was not *really* secretary of state, Vandenberg observed, more the "general manager" of the State Department, able enough to get things done but nothing more. "There is no longer any strong hand on our foreign policy rudder—neither Truman nor Stettinius nor [Undersecretary Joseph] Grew."[15]

He urged Stettinius "to take hold of this [regional security] problem with a firm hand and *to be Secretary of State* in fact as well as name." The issue demanded a clear statement of the administration's policy toward Latin America. It could not be settled "by us Republicans" alone.

The secretary offered Latin American delegates the idea promoted by Vandenberg and Rockefeller: an amendment to the charter that reserved to member states the right to take individual or collective action to defend themselves against aggression. Stettinius also promised to call another Pan-American conference after the UNCIO to enact the Act of Chapultepec "within the framework" of the United Nations. Latin American delegates agreed, and so did Truman. Eventually, the Russians did, too. Smaller nations found a measure of security in this path to collective self-defense. This was the breakthrough Vandenberg had been working for.[16]

In little more than two weeks of roller-coaster negotiations, the issue had been resolved harmoniously. Concepts, terms, words had been refined to suit disparate tastes. The process had been a dry run for the "town meeting of the world" Vandenberg envisioned. Amid laudatory speeches and applause, the Regional Security Committee gave the senator's draft resolution unanimous approval. The world had hunted for a middle ground and had found one.[17]

There were subsequent negotiations, of course, but Vandenberg shone in those, too. When the Soviet delegate said that the Pan-American treaty was a poor model of a regional arrangement, Vandenberg "immediately" countered that the Pan-American Union was "the finest flower of pacific relations for fifty years." The cheers of his Latin American friends, he wrote in his diary, "took the roof off."

He drew another ovation two days later, when the regional committee produced a unanimous report, three weeks after many had predicted that the dispute over regional arrangements might wreck the conference.[18]

Regional security was hardly the last nettlesome issue, however. There were arguments over whether a nation could withdraw from UN membership. Was a withdrawal clause necessary? Vandenberg was the only American delegate who thought so. If a big power, particularly, wished to leave the organization, it ought not be blocked from doing so—not least because its unwilling presence would almost guarantee divisiveness. The same reasoning applied whether it was the Soviets, turning recalcitrant, or the Americans, whose Senate might insist on a way out.

Moreover, he argued, including such a clause would actually show confidence on the part of the world body. "In the long run," Vandenberg said, "if it cannot hold them on a voluntary basis, it cannot hold them at all."[19] He took up the debate with the Russians, dealing in "blunt, plain realism." He spoke sardonically of a budding "peace partnership" that gave a potential adversary a veto upon "our freedom of action all round the globe to a substantial degree." Yet even since the conference began, "our relations with Russia have worsened all over the world (as well as here)." The United States needed a way out because no one could foresee the future, Vandenberg wrote, "plus the fact that a World Organization *without* a right of withdrawal is too much like a Super-State paraphrasing our own 'indestructible' union."

Compromise was possible. Delegates agreed that members could withdraw under certain conditions—although these were not specified—if the organization were unable to keep peace, "or could do so only at the expense of law and justice." There it was again: *justice*—or the lack of it—working to Vandenberg's ends.[20]

The question of veto power for the five permanent members of the Security Council—including France—also nagged the conference. There was near consensus that any of the Big Five could veto any enforcement action against an aggressor state, thus allowing the powers to control a decision that would involve their forces or otherwise lead to war. At Yalta, the Soviets, British, and Americans had agreed that the veto could also be exercised to stop the Security Council from attempting to settle a dispute. Vandenberg found this absurd but went along with the Yalta understanding.

Then the Russians insisted that the veto could be used to keep a dispute from even coming up for discussion. The Americans balked. This was a restraint on freedom of speech. As distasteful as Americans found this prospect, smaller nations found it even more so. Latin Americans threatened to bolt. Commonwealth nations bristled. A vote on the proposal likely would be 45–5, with only the Czechs and Yugoslavs joining the three Soviet votes. And yet no one wanted to alienate the Russians.

"It means in plain language that the Russians can raise Hell all over the world, through satellites and fifth columns, and stop the new League from even inquiring into it," Vandenberg wrote. "It is the worst of our legacies from Roosevelt. What a tragedy that F.D.R. could not have lived through this. . . . I do not doubt for an instant that he would force a show-down with Stalin." Vandenberg pressed Truman: get Stalin to drop his demand, "lest our stubborn adherence to this repugnant thing may either wreck the Conference or ultimately shock the moral conscience of the country and the world."

Nothing posed a greater threat to the birth of the United Nations than this disagreement. The Russian proposal was unacceptable to nearly everyone else. But Gromyko would not drop it without Stalin's say-so. "It *might* be argued that when all the rest of us agree on an interpretation of Yalta, *our* view ought to govern rather than Russia's," Vandenberg wrote. "On the other hand there is much to be said for *not* giving the Russians *any* excuse for running out on Yalta itself." He clung to fragile hopes for Polish democracy, for example, and shared a general inclination to satisfy the Soviets if they might somehow be shamed into keeping their end of the bargain.

Days passed; delegates motored down the coast or dined with Nob Hill society while the conference waited for word from Stalin. Irony abounded. The very open-ended quality of the veto that Vandenberg wished the Soviets to surrender held a certain appeal for Americans suspicious of their country's entanglement with the new organization. The greater the veto power, Vandenberg noted, the easier it would be to fight off critics in Congress: "Every cloud has a silver lining."[21]

At the end of May, the Big Five reconvened for an evening meeting in the Fairmont penthouse. Gromyko brought word that Russia must have a veto that encompassed even debate before the Security Council. "It is 'Yalta' carried to the final, absurd extreme," Vandenberg declared. When the Soviet ambassador, in his careful English, delivered the news, "we all knew that we had reached the 'zero hour' of this great adventure," he said. The Russians could not accept open discussion; the Americans could not accept the Soviet approach.[22]

Two bad choices loomed: breakup of the conference or a charter rejected by Russia. Stettinius wisely adjourned the meeting before rancor dissolved it. Then he phoned Truman. From Washington came instructions as firm as Stalin's: reject the Soviet position. The British, French, and Chinese all agreed.

Truman dispatched the ailing Harry Hopkins to Moscow, where he would join Ambassador Averell Harriman to inform the Russian dictator of the danger of a "wholly new and impossible interpretation" of the veto. The fate of the United Nations was tied to Stalin's response.[23]

In San Francisco, the anxious diplomats turned to other matters. Even lesser issues, however, brought frustration. "Any 'conference' in the true sense of the word is impossible when the Russian delegates dare not come to *any* agreement, however trivial, without referring the matter to Moscow," Vandenberg wrote in early June after another fruitless afternoon in the penthouse. From regional security to charter drafts or even choosing chairs, Gromyko needed "more time to study" or was "not ready."

Meanwhile, the press waited and delegates were loath to explain the impasse. Delay invited speculation. Morale sagged. Nearly everyone but Gromyko waited for Stettinius to say something. Then, to top it off, Gromyko announced that he would be glad to forward to Moscow any proposed press statement for "instructions." More delay—did that mean another week to get an answer? Vandenberg suggested that the United States at least declare its opposition to the Soviet veto demand.

An American adviser took Vandenberg aside to propose another forty-eight hours of silence—to deprive the Russians of any excuse if the veto controversy led to an open break between the two countries. "And so-o-o," Vandenberg lamented, "we again adjourn while the Soviets push us around."

For eleven days the main conference had been adjourned, waiting for news. Some forty-five other delegations could not be counted on much longer "to twiddle their thumbs while the Big Five impotently palaver," Vandenberg said. The senator wanted a charter, whether the Russians signed it or not, but he also knew how important it was that they sign—provided "that *we* should not stultify our souls."[24]

On the afternoon of June 5, Stettinius summoned Vandenberg to the penthouse for a meeting with Connally and Undersecretary James Dunn. Washington wanted him to join in a message to Hopkins and Harriman telling Stalin that "*if* he could not back down on his 'veto' stand," the conference might simply enter on its record "the *different* interpretations which we put on the Yalta 'veto' formula." Vandenberg refused. This was a way of giving Stalin what he wanted, leaving the charter itself in doubt and embarrassing the United States. When Connally seconded Vandenberg's response, Stettinius said his department had come to the same conclusion.

Stettinius then shared his cable to Harriman. "It would not have been stronger if I had written it myself," Vandenberg said. "After *that* message it would be *impossible* for us to yield, or even compromise, if we *ever* expect Stalin to *ever* have the slightest respect for our American word again." The meeting ended with no "weasel words," just a note to Hopkins and Harriman to stand firm.[25]

Vandenberg was delighted when Bert Andrews wrote in the *New York Herald Tribune* that the two men in San Francisco fighting most consistently against any weakening of the American position were the Michigan senator and his adviser John Foster Dulles.[26] If the United States were unwilling, "on this issue and at this juncture and with all of the support that is available, to stand firm," the senator argued, less powerful nations could hardly be expected to resist Soviet pressure.

"The result," he declared, would "be to leave the United States in a position of greatly increased and dangerous isolation."[27]

This was the Cold War coming, isolation going. Vandenberg and Dulles were worried about the return of isolation as a consequence of a stillborn successor to the failed League of Nations. But isolationism was unsustainable in the world as it then stood. The expanding American economy depended on global markets. The United States was the dominant power, but if any power could veto all debate, any hope of justice for those who resisted was out the window.

Finally, Gromyko asked Stettinius for another meeting of the Big Five. The secretary of state summoned Vandenberg and Connally. "The 'Veto' crisis broke today—and it broke our way," Vandenberg wrote in his diary. The Soviets yielded: "*America wins!* . . . It is a complete and total surrender. This ought to clear the track for a quick and successful conclusion of the Conference." He was convinced that the blunt message to Moscow had been decisive. "I *hope* some of our people have learned a lesson," he said of those in Washington who might waver under what he described as the "war of nerves." He was careful to note in his diary, "We did not *gloat* over a victory." (The term *Cold War* had not yet come into vogue, but the analogy between Soviet-American tensions and outright hostility seemed apt. The vocabulary of conflict heightened the drama of the confrontation.)

The veto resolution was no mere procedural win, the American bow tie over the rumpled Russian suit. Rather, it restored "a sinking American prestige at home and abroad." It gave the new "Peace League" a chance. It argued, finally, for "an American foreign policy which stands up for our viewpoints, our ideals, our purposes," showing "just how we *can* get along with Russia." Holding firm, pushing back—what came to be called "containment"—worked.[28]

And yet, Gromyko wasn't finished. In mid-June he objected to the right of the General Assembly to "discuss any matter in the sphere of international relations." But there was no stopping Vandenberg. "I fought him vigorously," he said, adding soon after, "The wonder grows as to what Russia is aiming at."[29] When Gromyko threatened to bring the issue before the conference steering committee, Vandenberg thought he was bluffing. The senator misjudged the ambassador.

Gromyko told Stettinius he had "instructions" not to sign the charter without a change in language: the Russians preferred a phrase the General Assembly committee had thrown out weeks before that limited discussion to issues affecting "the maintenance of international peace and security." Vandenberg had already inserted in the charter a more universal paragraph allowing for the assembly to address the "peaceful adjustment of *any* situations, *regardless of origin*, which it deems likely to impair the general welfare." This was about justice.[30]

The executive and steering committees met in the hotel penthouse to hear Gromyko's protest. From Moscow, Molotov sent his young ambassador a new text confining debate in the assembly to specific sections of the charter. Vandenberg acknowledged that a compromise might be found, but this nitpicking rankled him. When the Big Five met again, he insisted that issues under any section of the charter could be debated in the assembly. Gromyko bristled. Vandenberg prodded Stettinius, who "stood up like a concrete column," the senator wrote. "It is this sort of thing that endears him to me." Stettinius gave the Soviets two days to accept one of three alternative texts. If they did not, the Americans planned to proceed with a motion of their own.

"My personal feeling," Vandenberg wrote, "was two-fold; first, that we dare not abandon 'free speech'; second, that, for the sake of future relations with Russia, we *must* make them understand that the United States *means what it says* and that we cannot forever be bluffed down." When the Big Five reconvened, Gromyko, "all smiles and sweetness," said he had been instructed to accept one of the American texts. Vandenberg was fond of quoting Marshal Foch, Supreme Allied Commander in the First World War: "Whoever holds out for the last fifteen minutes wins the battle."[31]

Gromyko again needed time—three full days—for Moscow to study the completed text of the charter. The signing ceremony, for which Truman had come west, had to be postponed. The president cooled his heels two states away while the American delegates held their final meeting. Although Vandenberg praised Stettinius, one suspects that his generosity came from the secretary's near-total deference. Meanwhile, Dulles, nominally an adviser, had been "at the core of every crisis," Vandenberg wrote. "He knows more of the foreigners here personally than any other American. . . . He would make a very great Secretary of State." Vandenberg liked Nelson Rockefeller and had kind words for Stassen, too. Not coincidentally, this team shaping policy on behalf of a Democratic administration was all Republican.[32]

On June 26, 1945, Truman looked on as the American delegates took their turn onstage to sign the charter. The flutter and click of movie cameras were the only sounds as Vandenberg sat down at the round table covered in light-blue baize to affix his signature. Helping write the charter for the "town meeting of the world," he wrote, was "the crowning privilege" of his life. "It has an excellent chance to save the peace of the world *if* America and Russia can learn to live together and *if* Russia learns to keep her word." Those were daunting questions to ponder as Vandenberg, Connally, and a host of diplomats shared an air force flight back to Washington.[33]

An army band and colleagues from the Foreign Relations Committee greeted the returning senators, who were whisked to Capitol Hill with a motorcycle escort and a cushion of warm feeling. Vandenberg described an immediate "explosion" when they reached the Senate floor. A recess was declared while senators crowded round, slapping their backs, pumping their hands.

Connally spoke the next day, Vandenberg the day after. This was the culmination of a metamorphosis that began at Mackinac. Sixty-four colleagues were in their seats when the balding senator rose at William Borah's polished mahogany desk. The gallery was full. Diplomats occupied the center section, over the big gilt clock. Lean and pale Lord Halifax, the British ambassador, bent over the rail. Vandenberg, his starched white cuffs shooting from the sleeves of a powder-blue summer suit, rocked forward in his black-and-white shoes, a white handkerchief flowing from his breast pocket. He recounted the tense and heady days in San Francisco when partisanship had been absent among the American delegates.

"For fifty-five minutes his fist thrashed the air," wrote *Time*. Twice he blew his nose. He supported ratification of the charter, he said, because "we must have collective security to stop the next war, if possible, before it starts; and we must have collective action to crush it swiftly if it starts in spite of our organized precautions."

The chamber was hushed. "You could have heard a pin drop all the way through," Vandenberg told Hazel later. He drew a breath and reached for words that expressed his passion, concluding, in a paroxysm of hyperbole, that the charter represented "a new emancipation proclamation for the world." He blew his nose again with the honk of a foghorn. The Senate suspended business. As other senators lined up, he eased to the aisle to receive their handshakes, mopping his brow with that white flag from his pocket.[34]

Although the war in the Pacific dragged on, the impulse for peace and security after half a decade of global conflict was overpowering. Opposition evaporated. Even Bob La Follette and Burt Wheeler were expected to support the United Nations, as the apostate Vandenberg told colleagues, "You won't be able to find a maggot in this charter if you use a microscope."[35] Indeed, debate was brief and confined chiefly to details. The charter had anticipated its critics.[36]

The vote came in July. "89 to 2!" Vandenberg reported to Hazel. Privately he boasted that his opposition could have killed the charter, but that negative power never suited him. "I must confess, now that it's over," he wrote, "that I am very proud to have been at least one of the fathers. . . . The things we did at Frisco to remove potential Senate opposition have paid rich dividends." He tempered his pride with the realization that the world's troubles would never be so neatly resolved. Yet, he wrote, he had justified his "senatorial existence."

The night the Senate consented to ratification, Connally called Vandenberg at the Wardman Park. Truman wanted the two senators to help negotiate the Allied peace treaty with Germany. "That's one job I don't want," Vandenberg told Hazel, "but I don't suppose any man is entitled to decline such a request." Not least, he might have added, the voice of Republican foreign policy.

The world was embarking on a new era. The president replaced Stettinius with James Byrnes, the former senator many thought more qualified than Truman to succeed Franklin Roosevelt. Byrnes had been an advisor at Yalta, an experience that cut both ways in the wary eyes of Arthur Vandenberg. In August, Truman and Byrnes flew to Potsdam, outside Berlin, to meet with the British and Soviets and take the measure of Stalin. (Word reached Truman there that an atomic bomb had been detonated in the New Mexico desert—did that mean the end of the war was imminent?)

In Britain, voters rejected Churchill, their wartime leader, in favor of a Labour government. Vandenberg was stunned. "Here is one of the few men in 2,000 years of history upon whom you could put your finger and say—'he saved a nation!' And then the nation slits his throat!" This was bitter medicine. "Nothing has done more to make me *seriously* consider getting out of this miserable business in 1946," he told Hazel. "I guess the whole world is on a leftward march. I want no part of it."

Nor did he want any part of an American "surrender" to leftward pressures. He returned from San Francisco with convictions forged in close contact with Molotov, Gromyko, and the deputy minister of foreign affairs Andrey Vyshinsky. He had faced off with the Soviets while so many of his countrymen still accepted the "one world" bromides of wartime alliance and the vague promise of a new United Nations. Stalin was an enigma. Successive presidents could delude themselves that "Uncle Joe" might be wooed. But it wasn't hard to find menace in the maneuvers of his emissaries. Vandenberg had looked them in the eye.

From a distance it appears the Soviets survived their grinding and ghastly battle with Hitler to suddenly find themselves "liberating" the eastern half of Europe. They had neither capacity nor inclination to help these devastated lands restore civil societies. Their ideology gave convenient cover to do what their survival instincts and imperial impulse favored. From Moscow, George Kennan saw it coming. They wanted plunder and control. The question for American policy makers was, what next? Vandenberg saw no early end to the struggle. "Everything, in the final analysis, depends on Russia," he wrote, "and whether we have *guts* enough to make her behave."[37]

· · · · · · · · · · · ·

CHAPTER 22

WHAT IS RUSSIA
UP TO NOW?

· · · · · · · · · · · ·

When Vandenberg had last met with Franklin Roosevelt, on the eve of the president's departure for Warm Springs, a copy of his famous speech of January 10 lay amid the clutter on the Oval Office desk. One passage was underlined: "If World War III unhappily arrives, it will open new laboratories of death too horrible to contemplate." The president had nodded toward the text. "Senator," he said, "you have no idea how right you are, but I think you'll discover that before the year is out."[1]

This reflection came back on August 6, 1945, with news that the *Enola Gay*, an Army Air Force B-29, had let slip from its bomb rack "Little Boy," an atomic explosive that obliterated the Japanese city of Hiroshima. Days later, another bomb destroyed Nagasaki. On August 14 the emperor and his cabinet agreed to unconditional surrender. The mushroom clouds that ended the war were the result of a project so secret that even Truman, until he became president, had been unaware of its existence.

As if overnight, the bomb made the case for the United Nations all the more compelling. Atomic power underscored the urgency of everything Vandenberg had been preaching about a mechanism for the pursuit of peace. It also posed no end of arguments over international cooperation versus national interest. Many scientists were eager to exchange atomic information with colleagues worldwide. Most of the military saw secrecy as paramount and wanted tight controls over atomic research. From Congress came bills calling for everything from military control of atomic energy to forsaking military nuclear research. Senators could not even agree on where oversight belonged. Foreign Relations and Military Affairs both claimed jurisdiction. Why not the committee on the District of Columbia, one senator joked, for that was where "most of our explosions occur."[2]

Vandenberg was again at the forefront, pushing through a resolution calling for a joint congressional committee on atomic energy, composed of six members from each chamber. While the House stalled at the urging of the White House, the Senate created its own nine-member committee. Vandenberg and his colleagues were tutored in atomic science by Lieutenant General Leslie Groves, head of the Manhattan Project. Their instruction included a field trip to the laboratory at Oak Ridge, Tennessee.[3]

"I am frank to say that I do not yet know what the answer is to the awful problem which we have brought upon ourselves," Vandenberg confessed to his minister at Park Congregational Church in Grand Rapids. He was a nationalist first, and his impulse was to keep the secret. But he knew that once other nations did possess atomic weapons, international control of some sort would be essential. The next step, then, was to develop through the United Nations a system of worldwide inspection. Its aim would be to ensure that no nation employ atomic energy as a weapon of war: "I know of no other *logical* answer."[4] Even with proper inspections, he said, "we shall be at the mercy of any brutal aggressor who may suddenly decide to use the atomic bomb against us. So the prospectus is appalling under *any* circumstances and under *any* controls which we might conjecture. I sometimes wonder whether the wit of man is competent to deal with this murderous discovery."[5]

Truman may have agreed with Vandenberg's call for transparency in inspections, but his atomic diplomacy was opaque. He failed to keep the Senate abreast of his plans, perhaps out of fear of giving Vandenberg too much say. When the new British prime minister, Clement Attlee, and Canadian prime minister Mackenzie King came to Washington to discuss atomic energy, Vandenberg and Connally were invited only to listen to the visitors' public statements. The senators stood stone-faced as Truman outlined a joint program for outlawing the bomb through the United Nations. Immediately afterward they left, not waiting for the customary photographs. Reporters observed a "state of strain."[6]

Vandenberg had a speech to give. That day on the Senate floor he introduced a term he thought might catch on. It was the vivid image by which demarcation between east and west, between free and oppressed, between Adam Smith and Karl Marx, would come to be most powerfully expressed: the Iron Curtain.

Winston Churchill had employed the phrase a few months earlier, in a note to Truman and then in a Potsdam session with Stalin. In August he uttered it in a speech before Parliament. But it had yet to reach American ears on November 15, 1945, when Vandenberg rose to express the frustration of many Americans over the fate of Eastern Europe. With press blackouts and rigid censorship, he said, the needs of millions went unreported behind an "iron curtain" of secrecy imposed by the Soviet Union. The old newspaper editor was appalled by the veil that had fallen across countries under Soviet occupation, and his "Raise the Iron Curtain" speech (later mailed out in envelopes printed with that title) urged Russia to allow for the open flow of information.[7]

His rousing remarks received little notice. Headlines were dominated by the talks on atomic energy and by General Dwight Eisenhower's triumphant return from Europe. John Foster Dulles, expressing himself "delighted" with Vandenberg's speech, offered his friend this comfort: "It is too bad that it came on such a bad day, but I have no doubt that the ideas and the phrasing will catch hold."[8]

Dulles was right. Timing can be everything. Six months later, in April 1946, Churchill used the term publicly for the first time on this side of the Atlantic in a speech at tiny Westminster College in Fulton, Missouri. The phrasing indeed caught hold.

In December, Vandenberg and other senators were summoned to the State Department. Byrnes was leaving for Moscow to meet with his Soviet and British counterparts. He planned to ask for an exchange of atomic scientists and to push for the establishment of an international atomic energy commission under the United Nations.

Vandenberg was shocked. This was late in the day for advise and consent. He wished to be consulted, not merely informed. He borrowed the words of Harold Stassen regarding a tenet of bipartisanship: "I don't care to be involved in the crash landing unless I can be in on the take-off."[9]

A crash landing is the least of what he feared. "This is the crux," Vandenberg wrote, outraged. "We want to banish atom bombs from the earth. But it is impossible unless Russia agrees to a total exchange of information, instead of hermetically sealing herself behind 'iron curtains.' " Until then, sharing atomic secrets was "sheer appeasement." Get safeguards first, Vandenberg insisted, *before* sharing vital data. The indignant senators asked for an audience with the president.[10]

The next morning Truman suggested contritely that the lawmakers may have misunderstood the secretary. But Byrnes was already in the air. Could he be reached by radio? Could his agenda be modified? Truman appeared unconcerned. "For some inscrutable reason," Vandenberg noted in his diary, "the President seemed to fail to grasp our point."[11]

In the event, the foreign ministers called for a four-part role for a UN atomic control commission: oversee the exchange of basic atomic information for peaceful purposes, ensure peaceful uses, eliminate atomic weapons, and develop inspection procedures. This struck Vandenberg as the very sequence to which he had objected. How could the United States disclose secrets without assurance that the Soviets would not begin building nuclear weapons? He found the Moscow communiqué "one more typical American 'give away' on this subject." Dean Acheson, the acting secretary in Byrnes's absence, assured Vandenberg that complete security *had* to accompany each stage of disclosure. And the Senate would have to approve the whole package.[12]

The strain over atomic secrets was only one piece of a global postwar puzzle. The administration had also proposed a massive loan to prop up the battered British economy. "This was a tough conundrum," Vandenberg told Dulles. Something had to be done, but other Europeans would be standing in line. Precedents might be set. To grant a loan to Britain and deny one to Russia because of the Iron Curtain might make further cooperation among the Big Three impossible. Someone would have to work overtime to supply answers if the United States were to embark on an ambitious worldwide aid program for war-wracked nations. "I have no present inclination," Vandenberg told Dulles, "to volunteer for any such night work."[13]

He supported the British loan by reason of "intelligent American self-interest," as well as "some nebulous affinity which the English-speaking world must maintain in mutual self-defense." The loan was not popular, but Vandenberg felt that postwar conditions were forcing the United States to accept "the economic as well as the moral leadership in a wandering world which must be stabilized just as necessarily for us as for others." Only narrowly did Congress approve. Mail from the senator's constituents did not, by a wide margin.[14]

The first regular session of the United Nations General Assembly was scheduled for London in January 1946. Truman asked Vandenberg to join the American delegation. The senator was unsure whether he could work with Byrnes, "but it may be my duty to go along," he said. First, however, he again wanted the administration's assurance that he could speak his mind. Indeed, time and again as he embraced bipartisanship, Vandenberg was alert to having what would later be known as an exit strategy. He never had to use it, but he wasn't leaving home without it.[15]

The Vandenbergs embarked on the *Queen Mary* with fellow delegates—Stettinius, Connally, and an old nemesis, Eleanor Roosevelt. The Michigan senator, wielding his ever-present cigar, found a warm reception from the moment he stepped off the gangplank to be greeted by the mayor of Southampton in full ceremonial garb. Back home, opponents of the British loan—including the *Chicago Tribune*—caricatured Vandenberg as a Midwestern hick in the den of the British lion. But he was protective of his baby. "Having helped at the birth of the United Nations in 'Frisco," he told reporters, "I wanted to be in on the christening. And I have a desperate feeling that this is the only thing left to save the world."[16]

Peace brought relief from bloodshed, but not from tension. Indeed, with so much of Europe in ruins, the Soviet Union appeared to pose an increasing threat to a peace whose details were yet to be negotiated. The end of the war found the Soviets flush with success on the battle-field, despite the devastation they had suffered. The Red Army had no rival on the continent's central plains. The atom bomb was an intimidating achievement, but Russia had the boots on the ground. The Soviets sponsored insurgent communist parties in Western Europe. Desperation in France and Italy, both gripped by depression, might tip one or the other into the Soviet orbit without a fight beyond the ballot box.

Into the vacuum of postwar power sailed two goliaths. One, a republic, possessed an extraordinary new weapon but functioned through a maddening cacophony of voices. The other, a dictatorship, compensated for its lack of economic might and technological prowess with a single-minded mission and an enormous army. These were the superpowers that sat down with ministers of fifty other nations in the damp chill of a London January.

Vandenberg's task had less to do with the conceptual role of the international organization than with its mechanics. He served on the Administrative and Budgetary Committee, which established a bank account, provided for staffing, and oversaw the budget. He was a voice for frugality, favoring some college campus for a permanent headquarters rather than a new office complex on high-priced real estate. He cautioned against mistaking "pomp for power" and warned that the United Nations must never become a "rich man's club."

His prudent ways extended to the scope of possible UN action. A Filipino resolution calling for a conference on freedom of the press—a campaign to draw back the Iron Curtain—should be postponed, he insisted. He was apprehensive about exacerbating differences. But a resolution was approved unanimously to establish the Commission on Atomic Energy. And a committee was set up to address relief in war-ravaged regions.

Vandenberg's maiden speech, aimed at persuading other nations to cap U.S. support at one-third of the total budget, was a humbling experience. "I never saw anything like it," he told Connally. "I got all ready for an enjoyable swim. I put on my swimming trunks; I walked out to the end of the diving board; I took a deep breath; I held my nose and jumped. And I'll be dog-goned if the pool wasn't empty!"[17] On the other hand, "Mrs. Roosevelt is doing a splendid job," he told colleagues. "I want to say that I take back everything I ever said about her, and believe me it's been plenty."[18]

The hottest agenda item coming into the conference had been the continuing presence of French and British troops in Syria and Lebanon. The matter was referred to the Security Council, where, to Vandenberg's gratification, the two fragile Levantine states took temporary seats alongside the powers whose occupation they were protesting. "The difference in relative power and authority could scarcely approach greater extremes," Vandenberg wrote. "There they sat, with the mightiest of the earth, to have their untrammeled day in the court of world opinion."

Ernest Bevin, Britain's foreign minister, announced that his country would withdraw its troops. Moments later, Georges Bidault of France followed suit.[19] Accord was in the air as the United States offered a resolution expressing general opposition to the presence of unwanted occupying troops in peacetime. But harmony evaporated when the Soviet deputy foreign minister Vyshinsky tried to amend the American resolution by adding denunciations of the British and French: "The dove of peace flew in the window, but unfortunately, quickly it flew out again," wrote Vandenberg. This was not, he said, merely oil on troubled waters; "it was salt in reopened wounds." Vyshinsky further demanded that Bevin and Bidault abstain from voting, which in the spirit of peace, they did. But the Soviets still vetoed the resolution, leaving Lebanon and Syria back where they started—until Bevin and Bidault said their nations would abide by the terms of the resolution anyway. This graciousness was nevertheless eclipsed by the display of Soviet truculence, which seemed to be a harbinger of a new era.[20]

How to deal with Russia? Vandenberg did not find Secretary Byrnes to be a reliable colleague in this regard. In the Senate, the Carolinian with the sloping brows and long nose had been a gifted compromiser—but compromise had an entirely different feel when the party across the table was the Soviet Union. The line between give-and-take and appeasement was a fine one. Unlike Bevin, who addressed Soviet thuggery in Poland with bluntness and vigor, Byrnes, to Vandenberg's dismay, gave the Russians the limpest of warnings.[21] Vandenberg worried, wrote the Alsop brothers in their syndicated column, that Byrnes had been "loitering round Munich."[22]

The senator could have been anticipating George Kennan's legendary "Long Telegram" when he said the new order would require the United States to exercise unceasing pressure on Russia to comply with the Yalta and Potsdam pledges. It meant, he continued, "that we shall lift the powerful voice of America in behalf of the inviolable sanctity of international agreements to which we are a party." The first step was to raise the level of the rhetoric; more than ever, the diplomatic challenge was to "say what we mean and mean what we say." If that was not enough, then "we shall scrupulously collect our facts; draw our relentless indictment if the facts so justify; and present it in the forum of the United Nations and demand judgment from the organized conscience of the world." Such a course was a means short of war to turn up the heat on a country that was quickly becoming an adversary.[23] It was increasingly clear that the future of the United Nations turned on Soviet-American relations.

Vandenberg hoped that an American commitment to justice might show the Russians that "it is not impossible for us to learn to live together in reasonable amity." Perhaps he was too optimistic. "I hope not," he confessed. "Perhaps my judgment is warped by my ever increasing belief that collective security is the only hope of the world."[24]

Back home, Vandenberg retreated to his typewriter, bending over the old Smith-Corona in a cloud of cigar smoke. It was time for another speech. He typed and retyped and read aloud, first to himself, then to Hazel.

The galleries were packed on February 27, 1946, when he asked for the floor to report on his trip. There was some good news. In thirty-seven days, he said, "the United Nations turned a blueprint into a going concern." The machinery was in place.

But the overwhelming question was "What is Russia up to now?" Vandenberg leaned over his desk, grasping it in both big hands, shaking his head as though a heavy weight pressed down on his chest and shoulders. "What is Russia up to now?" he repeated. It could be asked in Manchuria, he said. "We ask it in Eastern Europe and the Dardanelles. We ask it in Italy. . . . We ask it in Iran. . . . We ask it in the Baltic and the Balkans. We ask it in Poland. We ask it in the capital of Canada," he continued, citing revelations of a Soviet spy ring in Ottawa. "We ask it in Japan. We ask it sometimes even in connection with events in our own United States." Again the question: "It is little wonder that we asked it at London. It is less wonder that the answer—at London and everywhere else—has a vital bearing on the destiny of the United Nations. . . . It is a question that must be met and answered before it is too late."

There stood "two great rival ideologies" with a "desperate need for mutual understanding." This required plain speaking that Stalin could understand. The United States had to "abandon the miserable fiction, often encouraged by our own fellow travelers, that we somehow jeopardize the peace if our candor is as firm as Russia's always is; and if we assume a moral leadership which we have too frequently allowed to lapse. The situation calls for patience and good will; it does not call for vacillation."

Americans should expect their leaders to be as frank as Bevin and Vyshinsky, Vandenberg said, in a slap at Byrnes. Moreover, he asserted, "There is a fine line beyond which compromises cannot go. Even if we have previously crossed that line under the pressures of . . . war, we cannot cross it again."

The United States "has no ulterior designs against any of its neighbors anywhere on earth," he concluded. "We can speak with the extraordinary power inherent in this unselfishness. We need but one rule. What is right? What is justice? There let America take her stand."[25]

It had been barely a year since his big speech calling for a postwar alliance. The world was much changed, but the response to Vandenberg's words was much the same. The Senate rose to its feet. A *Detroit Free Press* reporter wrote that the address "left you with a sense of history going on right now." Vandenberg was becoming something like the voice of America. "There have been few occasions on which a single Senator has so dramatically and so decisively dominated Senate opinion on world-wide issues," wrote James Wechsler of the liberal newspaper *PM*.[26] Arthur Krock of the *Times* found Vandenberg's text "much milder than its implications" but still a veiled attack on policy drift. *Time* called it "a clear challenge to the Secretary of State."

As Vandenberg's remarks resonated through Washington, so did the longest and most articulate cable in the annals of the State Department. From Moscow, George Kennan's Long Telegram laid out the strategic argument for pushing back against Soviet posturing. The American diplomat warned that the road to peace would be long and hard, and that Russian leaders were impervious to reason but sensitive to force.[27] Vandenberg and Kennan were singing from the same hymnal.[28]

Secretary Byrnes, obviously put out, accused the senator of "gun-jumping" by ignoring diplomatic protocol that would have had him speak first upon their return from London. The following night, Byrnes appeared to have torn a page from Vandenberg's typewriter. "If we are to be a great power we must act as a great power," he said in a scheduled speech. He attacked the Soviet Union for imposing troops upon "small and impoverished states." Arthur Krock suggested that whole sections of Byrnes's speech had been written in reaction to Vandenberg's, and pundits dubbed it the "Second Vandenberg Concerto."

The senator was relieved to have Byrnes back in his corner. Byrnes had shown "courageous candor," Vandenberg said. "I hope it is not too late."[29] Vandenberg saw himself as America's backbone. He applauded Byrnes for subscribing to his attitude of "no more appeasement." He was certain that this was the only hope of reaching "common ground" with the Soviets. There were to be "no more Munichs!" If that strategy would not work, it was best to know quickly. "America must behave like the *Number One World Power* which she is," he insisted. "Ours must be the world's moral leadership—or the world won't have any."[30]

· · · · · · · · · · · ·

CHAPTER 23

MUNICH IN REVERSE

· · · · · · · · · · · ·

The rapprochement with Byrnes came none too soon. Truman asked Vandenberg and Connally to extend their diplomatic service and join the secretary of state in Paris, at an April 1946 meeting of the Big Four foreign ministers.

The goal of the conference was to write peace treaties for the countries that had been Germany's allies: Hungary, Romania, Bulgaria, Finland, and, most prominently, Italy. Vandenberg joined Byrnes for coffee in a suite at La Meurice hotel that had formerly been occupied by a German general. The secretary said he also wanted to propose a four-power treaty akin to that which Vandenberg had suggested the year before, under which Germany would be permanently disarmed.

That afternoon police lined the streets as black sedans approached the Luxembourg Palace. "The French are making a super spectacle of it," Vandenberg wrote in his diary. Inside the palace, soldiers of the Garde Republicaine stood shoulder to shoulder on the grand staircase and along the echoing corridor, plumed helmets gleaming, sabers raised in salute as the delegates passed.

All the players were there: Bidault presided, with Bevin, Byrnes, and both Molotov and Vyshinsky in attendance. The presence of both Russians might give the meeting "an importance yet to be disclosed," Vandenberg noted.

Even agreeing to an agenda for treaty negotiations was a challenge—which country would they start with? And when would they tackle Germany itself? After an hour's wrangling, the powers agreed to take up Italy the next morning. Bidault invited his guests into the next room for champagne. "Everybody came except the Russkies," Vandenberg reported.[1]

But Molotov was ready the next day, demanding $300 million in reparations for the destruction caused by Italian troops on the Russian front. The Americans insisted that reparations depended on a country's capacity to pay, a logic that prevailed when Truman, Stalin, and Attlee met at Potsdam. Moreover, since the United States had recently pumped half a billion dollars into the Italian economy, any reparations would effectively be coming from America. Molotov professed that he had no wish to hurt the Italian economy, even as he held out for $100 million and more. Vandenberg told Byrnes to remind the Soviets that Italy was "where Shylock demanded his 'pound of flesh'— and was then confounded when he was required to take it without drawing a drop of blood."[2]

As conflicts arose, they were referred to successive panels of experts. "The amazing thing about this phase of the business is the way in which the Western democracies look out for a 'square deal' for defeated Italy," Vandenberg wrote. "It is all so *different* from the Soviet attitude wherever they see something they want."[3] The Russians coveted ships of the Italian navy, for example, but Byrnes forced Molotov to admit that the vessels were war booty and belonged to the British and Americans who had captured them. The United States, for its part, was asking for neither territory nor reparations. ("Our conquests are commercial," Vandenberg had written at the end of World War I.)

The lack of trust at the peace table was palpable. When Byrnes put forth his proposal for a treaty within the framework of the UN Charter that guaranteed German demilitarization for twenty-five years, Molotov was "maddeningly obdurate, and refused even to understand the proposition," Vandenberg wrote. "This treaty would be the fundamental answer to all the Russian 'security' pleas. It should have been pressed by F.D.R. at Yalta fifteen months ago. It would have robbed the Soviets of every excuse for seeking territorial expansion, and satellites, in the name of 'security.' "[4]

Even mundane matters could bring the conference to a halt. "We spend an entire afternoon throwing commas and colons at each other," Vandenberg complained, after hours of wrangling over the

Italian borders with Yugoslavia and Austria. The Russians, demanding more territory for the Yugoslavs, "had no intention of permitting any decisions at the moment. Apparently they want to keep everything liquid pending a 'grand deal' at the finish."[5]

After a frustrating week, the Americans sensed a showdown looming. "The shadow boxing is about over," Vandenberg reported. "There is no sense carrying on this Punch-and-Judy business." It was beneath the dignity of the United States "to be shoved around like a fourth-rate power by stubborn, contemptuous, irrational dictators from the Kremlin."

Twenty delegates circled the conference table. Vandenberg assumed the Russians regarded him—and Connally ("in a lesser degree," to the Democrat's chagrin)—as an obstacle.[6] Indeed, the communist press saw Vandenberg that way. He was accused in *L'Humanité*, the French newspaper, of plotting to sabotage the conference.

His aim was not sabotage, but justice. When Molotov repeated his demand for $100 million in Italian reparations "or there will not be a treaty," Byrnes turned to the senators. In a whisper he asked if they would support an ultimatum. They both nodded. The secretary of state looked at his Soviet counterpart. "If those are the alternatives," he said, "we might just as well sign up a new Italian armistice tomorrow and go home." The Russian was caught short. He "*immediately* denied that he had said *what he did say*," Vandenberg reported. "In other words, when his bluff was called . . ."

"There is no dove in sight tonight," Vandenberg wrote at the end of one long day. "This can't go on much longer." Or could it? "I confess that I admire the way Molotov argues tenaciously for his positions . . . the trouble is that they have had so much from us so long that they have not yet sensed the fact that our 'surrender days' are over."[7]

Molotov hinted that a favorable resolution of the border between Italy and Yugoslavia—giving the Yugoslavs control of Trieste—might soften his demand for reparations. Molotov's indifference to ethnic preferences reeked to Vandenberg of "old-fashioned 'power politics.' " Chip Bohlen whispered in the senator's ear, "This is a perfect example of the Soviet mind: if the facts bother you, just ignore the facts."[8] When

Byrnes passed a note asking if Vandenberg would consider trading off Trieste, the answer was a swift no.[9]

Vandenberg was protecting his country's interests as few other men could. But full-time diplomacy was not among his customary duties. Too often, he felt like a participant in a "pole-sitting contest." He told Byrnes that he had to return to Washington soon. "I sometimes think I am entirely too *impatient* for this sort of business," he mused. Over and over the parties postured on the same issues, "quite as if we were inmates of an Old Ladies' Home where there is nothing to do every afternoon except to chat over tea: I urged Byrnes yesterday to force a show-down." When Vandenberg wrote out a statement calling for a recess, Byrnes called Truman and secured a plane to fetch the delegates. Wrote Vandenberg: "Glory be!"[10]

On the last day the talk turned to Germany, and the same dynamics prevailed. Molotov cast doubt on Vandenberg's plan for a twenty-five-year alliance—only to be reminded by Byrnes that Stalin had approved the proposal in principle at their Moscow meeting. The French wanted details about control of the Rhineland and the Ruhr, one the historical invasion route to France, the other the heart of German industry. The Russians attacked the British over their occupation of the Ruhr. Bevin lashed back at Molotov over sharing of information among the allies. "And so," wrote Vandenberg, "to lunch."[11]

When the entourage returned to Washington, the senator received a note from the publisher of *Time*. Henry Luce quoted a French accusation that the Americans and British were ignoring Soviet hints at compromise while blaming the Russians for a deadlock. Vandenberg's frank response went to the heart of the Cold War. He argued that it had been essential in Paris to convince the Soviets that the time for "appeasement" was over. Confrontations at San Francisco had delivered "a slight but successful jolt." The Russians had received another in London, but "Byrnes gave away more than he should" when he met with Stalin in Moscow. "Appeasement simply feeds the hazard from which it seeks to escape," Vandenberg told Luce. "We now know that Munich was a ghastly mistake. This at least suggests that 'Munich in reverse' was wise at Paris."[12]

If Molotov *were* ready to negotiate, Vandenberg wondered how the United States would respond. "We can still bargain away the rights and lives and destinies of many helpless people," he huffed. Nothing could be more dangerous than to accept the notion that Soviet expansion was irresistible.[13]

Vandenberg intended to focus on his reelection bid in the fall, although he insisted, unconvincingly, "I can honestly say that (barring what would be a brief shock of injured vanity) I care very little about the outcome." But neither duty nor ego would have it. Byrnes and Truman wanted him, along with Connally, back at the peace table when treaties were ready for ratification.[14]

Thus, Truman soon bade them Godspeed before the *Sacred Cow* lumbered down the runway at Andrews airfield for another flight to France. Hazel joined him again, carrying a bulky hatbox. "A hat, to Paris?" a reporter asked. "Oh no," she said. She had fried potato doughnuts last night, a favorite Michigan recipe "for those sweet boys who've been flying us across the ocean all year in the *Cow*."[15]

Northern France was unseasonably cool. Vandenberg brought only his summer linens and what he soon concluded was the only straw hat in Paris. The French communist newspaper lamented the senator's return to the conference table. His presence was said to imply an American hard line.[16]

Indeed, Vandenberg returned with two governing thoughts. First, "the time is gone by when the Soviets can do as they please with the expansionist program under the guise of peace and security." Second, "within this rule, we shall prove to Russia that we want to be scrupulously fair and just with her."[17]

But things weren't looking good. The Americans worried that all of the delays were suiting the Soviets' larger agenda in Europe. There were reports of Red Army units massing along Yugoslavia's border with Italy. In Western Europe, communist parties promised an end to chaos for the desperate and disaffected—the very chaos that Vandenberg accused Stalin of perpetuating.[18] At one point, Connally brought up an old Texas story, comparing Molotov to a drunk and stubborn lawyer heading home to dinner. "If it isn't ready," he said, "I'll just raise hell. If it is ready, I won't eat a damned bite."[19]

These meetings, like those in San Francisco, put Vandenberg through the twists and turns of an emotional roller coaster. After days of wrangling, clouds would part. The ministers might quickly agree on some minor item—one ship for the Bulgarian "navy," for example. Then Molotov would say, "We might as well clean up the Franco-Italian frontier," and they promptly would. Disputed Aegean islands? "Very well," sighed Molotov, they could move on to Greece. Suddenly the ministers had progressed further in an hour than in all preceding days. The Americans could only wonder if Molotov was swayed by their firmness—or giving ground on smaller items so that if the council broke up over a big one, it might appear to be the Americans' fault? "Whatever it is," Vandenberg wrote in his diary at the end of one difficult day, "only one who has been through this 'war of nerves' can understand our feeling of at least temporary relief tonight."[20]

Most days were bad days, however. Vandenberg called the session of June 23 "Blue Monday," after witnessing Molotov's continuing intransigence on Yugoslav sovereignty over Trieste. "This would be oleo-de-luxe," Vandenberg sputtered. "He could not possibly be expected to be taken seriously." It was plainly just a stalling tactic. But "the cards are dealt," the senator concluded. "Somebody's hand is about to be 'called.' "[21]

The French and the Russians suggested internationalizing the border city. Vandenberg thought such a compromise unfair to Italy and argued that the matter should go to the UN General Assembly. "We are not here merely to carve up Europe," he said. "We are not here to white-wash cancers. We are here to build a permanent peace."[22]

Still, the Americans agreed finally to a statement "in principle" on the internationalization of Trieste—unsavory in itself, but a means to move the issue to the United Nations. Vandenberg found a typewriter in a palace anteroom and tapped out the proposal. With minor changes his draft was a good start, Molotov declared. And yet this scheme, too, later collapsed.

Vandenberg returned home long enough speak on foreign policy at the state convention of the American Legion and at the University of Michigan. He made an appearance between harness races at the Ionia Free Fair. He reported back to the Senate with news of five treaties. None perfect, he noted, but "the measure of success is the preservation of essential principles in spite of compromise"—not a bad summary of his political philosophy. He sketched terms on Trieste, frontiers, territories, and reparations, as well as plans for the next conference. The Senate's tradition of unlimited debate was nothing, he told his colleagues, next to the interminable wrangling in three languages among the foreign ministers.

On the future of Germany, so central to European peace, there remained "appalling disagreement." He saw no alternative to maintaining zones of military occupation. He had promised Russia cooperation in curbing German aggression, with the caveat that Americans could not "be driven, coerced, or pressured into positions that we decline voluntarily to assume; and that we will not bargain in human rights and fundamental liberties anywhere on earth." There had been quite enough of that with Poland. The days of Yalta were over.[23]

Vandenberg hoped that two trips to Paris would suffice. But Byrnes wanted him back once more, for the twenty-one-nation conference at which formal treaties for Italy, Finland, Bulgaria, Hungary, and Romania were to be approved. Less than ten weeks before Election Day, Byrnes and the senators climbed back on the *Sacred Cow*.

Their travels ranged beyond Paris. In early September, Vandenberg, Connally, and Byrnes flew to Berlin, then boarded what had been Hitler's personal train for a journey to Stuttgart. (Byrnes and his wife occupied the car once reserved for Hitler and Eva Braun.) The elegant train drew stares as it rumbled along restored roadbed. At each stop crowds approached the windows. The senators and the secretary witnessed the devastation visited upon the Third Reich—damage and suffering "past comprehension," Vandenberg wrote: "There certainly won't be any 'German menace' again in my lifetime."[24]

In Stuttgart they drove to the state opera house, the only sizable building in the city unharmed by Allied bombing. An army band played "Stormy Weather," which the delegates found apt for their work in Paris.[25] The last stop on the journey was Hitler's alpine retreat at Berchtesgaden—"an appalling trip up the side of a mountain (the last 1,000 feet in an elevator going up a shaft hewn from solid rock) where Hitler had his 'eagle's nest!' Jeez!" Vandenberg reported, "No wonder he went crazy."[26]

The trip inspired sobering reflections as the Americans returned to Paris. They were ready to take up tough issues. Commerce on the Danube? Vandenberg staked a position that reflected a world of change from his early days in thrall to Alexander Hamilton and protective tariffs. Peace, he declared, "is substantially related to the avoidance of international trade barriers that invite discrimination and dangerous frictions."[27]

While the Americans had hoped to settle down to work, they became distracted by an embarrassing transatlantic shouting match—aimed at them. Secretary of Commerce Henry Wallace's frustration with American policy had been simmering for months when he scheduled a mid-September address at Madison Square Garden. Wallace shared a portion of his speech with Truman, who told reporters that he approved of the remarks.

Truman did not anticipate the passion of the vocally pro-Russian crowd—or the warm-up comments of Florida senator Claude Pepper, who accused "conservative Democrats" (that would be Byrnes and Connally) "and reactionary Republicans" (that would be Vandenberg) of "making our foreign policy." It was all the Left could do, he continued, "to keep foolish people from having us pull a Hitler blitzkrieg and drop our atomic bombs on the Russian people." His noisy attack ended with a question: "What do you expect in a foreign policy which really meets the approval of Senator Vandenberg and John Foster Dulles?"[28]

Then it was Wallace's turn. He claimed he had Truman's blessing in declaring American policy toward the Soviet Union insufficiently conciliatory. The British were imperialists, Wallace said. The Republicans were isolationists, protectionists—doomed to extinction. Before the GOP "dodo" disappeared, however, "it may enjoy a brief period of power," Wallace warned, "during which it can do irreparable damage in the United States and to the cause of world peace."

In Paris, Vandenberg, Connally, and Byrnes were incredulous as they read the wire-service dispatches. Other delegates asked whether American policy had changed. Whose interpretation could they trust, the delegates' or Wallace's?

Vandenberg fumed. "Rightly or wrongly," he told reporters, "Paris is doubtful of unity this morning." But successful policy depended on unity. He was convinced that the American people were overwhelmingly on his side. Most Republicans had been "glad" to join most Democrats, "thus presenting a united American front to the world," he wrote. "This is the only road to organized peace and collective security. Those who leave this road jeopardize the very objective they profess to embrace."[29] He could hardly keep Republicans in line if members of the administration repudiated his efforts. As essential as bipartisan unity was unity within the administration. Republicans, he warned, "can only cooperate with one Secretary of State at a time."[30]

The tempest grew with publication of a memo Wallace had sent Truman, faulting Democrats for yielding to "isolationism masquerading as tough realism" for the sake of bipartisanship. Domestic unity that stirred up conflict with the Soviets was not just unsound; it was dangerous. This looked like a direct attack on Vandenberg's high-profile role—indeed, Wallace was said to have told Democrats they had been "sucked in" by Vandenberg to a policy that was too hard on the Russians.

Vandenberg felt as though a rug had been pulled out from under him. Byrnes was unhappy, too. If Truman could not control Wallace, he informed the president, he was resigning immediately. After a conference by Teletype with Byrnes, Vandenberg, and Connally, Truman extracted a promise from Wallace to refrain from comment on foreign policy for the duration of the Paris meeting. That satisfied neither Byrnes nor the senators. With Vandenberg at his elbow, Byrnes told the president that "the world is today in doubt not only as to American foreign policy, but as to *your* foreign policy. . . . You and I spent fifteen months building a bipartisan policy. We did a fine job convincing the world that it was a permanent policy upon which the world could rely. Wallace destroyed that in a day."[31]

The next day Truman asked for Wallace's resignation. In Paris, the Americans turned back to the conference table, and in early October the talks concluded. Even so, additional weeks of wrangling with the Soviets ensued. Finally, in June 1947 Vandenberg and Connally jointly presented Congress with the Italian treaty, which was approved by a vote of 79–10. Other treaties passed by voice vote.

Something new in the annals of American policy had emerged in the year and a half between San Francisco and the last meeting in Paris: something like consensus, and a sense of American leadership sturdy enough to withstand the assaults of Molotov and Vyshinsky from one direction and Henry Wallace from another. It was a remarkably consistent approach at a dangerous time. It was bipartisan to a degree the republic had never seen.

Finally back from Paris, Vandenberg still had no time to go home, and his reelection campaign went ahead without him. Truth be told, this was the status to which he had long aspired—so deep into crucial service that personal fortunes demanded recognition of that fact by his constituents. He kissed no babies, made no speeches, shook few hands. "I am not going to get my work for peace bogged down into politics," he wrote to Arthur Junior, who was running the campaign.

He did worry that a new generation of voters had come of age since he entered the Senate in 1928. "I must be more or less of a legendary character to many of them," he told a friend. "Similar circumstances have been fatal to better men than I." Retirement crossed his mind. "Just why I am willing even to consider another campaign—knowing what I do about the progressive burdens of the job—is more than I can explain to Hazel." But duty—"a very silly notion," he said, quite unconvincingly—compelled him.[32]

His stature was such that no one opposed him in the Republican primary—why, he was practically drafted. Democrats nominated James H. Lee, a little-known Detroit utilities lawyer whose backers included the powerful Michigan Congress of Industrial Organizations, or CIO, which opposed Vandenberg for his support of anti-strike legislation. Supporters of Henry Wallace also encouraged a "beat Vandenberg" campaign.[33]

The Michigan press was mostly in Vandenberg's corner. He may have been absent from the state, but his high profile meant he was rarely absent from the nation's newspapers. *Collier's Weekly*, his employer briefly four decades before, presented him with its first $10,000 distinguished service award for the most valuable member of the Senate. (He donated the proceeds to the American Red Cross, to which Hazel had devoted years of service.) Billboards boasted, "The world listens to the man from Michigan."[34]

Indeed, people listened. But they did not always like what they heard. Vandenberg's speech on behalf of the emergency loan to Great Britain had been a hit with much of the press—and with the new Englishwoman encouraged by British intelligence to consort with the senator, Eveline Paterson. (Her daughter averred that Mrs. Paterson and "Uncle Arthur," unlike Mrs. Sims, may have been "just friends.") But the *Chicago Tribune*, which had wide circulation in western Michigan, denounced him. *Tribune* cartoons portrayed Vandenberg as Benedict Arnold, or as a hayseed outsmarted by crafty Continental diplomats. When a constituent sent Vandenberg a *Tribune* editorial with a complaint about the senator's diplomatic activities, he replied, "I could not blame you if you scratched me off your list if you rely upon information printed in the newspaper to which you refer. I can give you at least one specific instance (in the editorial which you mention) of such brazen falsehood that I think it approaches malicious libel." To another correspondent he described McCormick's assault as "the most totally vicious and deceptive thing I have ever seen in journalism."

Criticism by Wallace and Pepper only strengthened his hand with many voters. He hoped one or the other might campaign against him in Michigan. "I would want to make a direct reply," he wrote, "and I would enjoy making it hot. . . . I will be glad to 'hit the roof.' "[35] His toughness had held particular appeal in Michigan's substantial Polish community. "No matter how little I may deserve the reputation," the senator told the editor of Detroit's *Polish Daily News*, "I believe I am considered Poland's 'first friend' in this and every other capital on earth. . . . An eloquent and overwhelming rebuff to the Communist pledge to liquidate me next November would be the most powerful message that Polish-Americans could send to Moscow or to Warsaw."

If anything, he was criticized by Polish Americans for not being tough enough. To one such critic Vandenberg replied, "My offense seems to be that I have not broken up each international conference because of Russia's presence or that I have not advocated immediate war. . . . Yes, I'll admit that I could have split this country wide open by playing politics with our foreign policy. But by splitting our country wide open, I would have crucified the American unity which is indispensable to 'stopping Moscow' and I would have invited Stalin to 'divide and conquer.' "[36]

He relished the vituperation of the communist press and reminded voters that he had opposed diplomatic recognition of the Soviet Union. "I am flattered to find myself at the top of the Communist 'purge' list all around the world," he boasted. A vote for Vandenberg was like "dropping a letter to Stalin in the mailbox." The *Detroit News* echoed his argument. "The world will watch Vandenberg's vote," wrote Jay Hayden. Powerful radio station WJR broadcast a dramatization of the senator's career with "Battle Hymn of the Republic" playing in the background.

Poor Lee, the Democrat, got little help from Washington. The president had an important ally in the Michigan senator. By firing Wallace, Truman had declared his confidence in the American delegation. "That means," Vandenberg told his son, "he has declared his confidence in me. Therefore, Michigan Democrats have every reason to vote for me." When the president campaigned, party leaders wanted him "to light into Senator Vandenberg," Truman said later. "It made a lot of those birds in Michigan unhappy, but I wouldn't do it."[37]

Vandenberg shied away from attacks on the administration just as the administration shied away from attacks on him. He was finally, for what might be a golden moment, almost on the plane beyond party to which he had long aspired.

At one break between meetings during his time in Paris, he had sat down at a typewriter to write, "Politics are important, but *peace is indispensable.*" And that was all there was to it; nothing else mattered: "Fortunately, there is *nothing I personally want* in 1948. *This is my last run.*"[38]

Only on the morning of Election Day did he step off the train at the Union Depot in Grand Rapids. For most of the year he had been living out of a suitcase—213 days away from Washington and Grand Rapids, immersed in diplomacy. Photographers caught him with a jaunty grin, cigar in hand, big eyes sparkling. There was barely time to unpack and cast a ballot before the crowd began to gather in the Pantlind Hotel ballroom to await the returns. Early numbers augured well for the incumbent. A landslide was in the offing. Well before midnight, party workers stopped updating county tallies on the enormous blackboards. This was more homecoming than election. Flowers were everywhere. In came carts of roast turkey and ham, streams of friends. Arthur Junior sat down at a piano and launched into "Hail to the Victors," fight song of the University of Michigan.

The Vandenberg reserve fell away as he slipped off the jacket of his navy-blue suit. On his vest gleamed the cherished identification button from the United Nations. As his margin topped half a million votes, the senator scratched out a victory statement. His reelection was an endorsement of bipartisan foreign policy, he wrote—a concept that had barely existed even two years before. A new Republican majority in Congress promised yet greater influence. For himself and his party, he concluded, there would be a new "rendezvous with destiny."[39]

CHAPTER 24

· · · · · · · · · · · ·

THE TRUMAN DOCTRINE

· · · · · · · · · · · ·

Two days after the election, a reporter asked the senator a sobering question. He had been a strong voice for the Republican minority, Esther Tufty wrote, "But will you be as big (I almost said 'great' but you aren't there yet) when you are top dog?"[1]

Vandenberg devoted the last days of 1946 to organizing Congress under its first GOP majority since the Hoover administration. Senate power in the Eightieth Congress belonged to two men, Robert Taft and Arthur Vandenberg. The dogged and cerebral Taft ran the domestic agenda; Vandenberg led foreign policy. Their positions were not always congruent, but each took pains to minimize conflict.

This Congress signaled what *Life* called a "significant shift in the government's center of gravity." Franklin Roosevelt had generally had his way with the legislature or, when things did not work out his way, used it as a scapegoat. Now, for an effective foreign policy, the Senate had to be a partner.[2]

"There will be more Republican voices," Tufty continued, with a sense of drama that suited her subject. "You are essentially an egotist, and I am glad, to a degree, that you are, or you would not have dared to be so outspoken about the things that matter in this post-war world. This is the moment when you might fail." He must not, she said, not only because it would hurt him personally, but also because "the negotiations of the world are so delicate and important to the point of survival that whether you sneeze in the morning can have earth-shaking results."[3]

Because an upstart named Joseph McCarthy had edged Robert La Follette Jr. in Wisconsin's 1946 GOP primary, one of the two Republicans senior to Vandenberg on Foreign Relations was gone. The other, Arthur Capper of Kansas, chose to chair the Agriculture Committee, bequeathing to Arthur Vandenberg chairmanship of the Foreign Relations Committee. He was also elected president pro tempore of the Senate. As Truman had no vice president, Vandenberg presided over the upper chamber. His keen sense of parliamentary possibilities, of history and tradition, combined with his vanity to invest the role of president pro tempore with more than its customary token status. He treated parliamentary rulings with a seriousness unrivaled in the memory of observers.

Since before the end of the war, his counsel had been critical to the Democratic occupant of the White House. Now, responsibility was his for translating policy into law and making legislative machinery responsive to the nation's new global role. Big debates found him on the rostrum, but so did much mundane business. Here his cartoonist's touch served him well. He filled his Senate stationery with elaborate doodles. The patriotic motif was a favorite, the foremost image of a tidy mind. Sometimes the discarded doodles were retrieved by a colleague or staffer. (A young Lyndon Johnson saved one from a joint session.)

Vandenberg's scrapbook bulged with news accounts and press photos. One story detailed the White House dinner in honor of the Senate president. At the head table, amid enormous bouquets of blue iris, pink roses, and snapdragons, with the light of the chandeliers sparkling off presidential crystal, sat Arthur and Hazel, Harry and Bess. They listened to the red-coated Marine Corps band and a star of the Metropolitan Opera. The senator reveled in his new status.

Every day at 8:30 a.m. Vandenberg arrived at the side door of the Senate Office Building in the vice presidential Cadillac (minus its seal). He would have read the New York and Washington papers over breakfast. With a nod to the guard, the senator strode down the marble corridor and entered his office through a back door. On his desk waited a sheaf of correspondence. The staff might learn of his arrival only after he rang up to begin dictation. Ever obsessed with preparedness, he spent hours preparing legislation that the Foreign Relations Committee would bring to the floor.

The committee usually convened at 10 a.m., the Senate at noon. At 11:45 Vandenberg arrived at the Capitol by the Senate subway and rushed to the office of the vice president, an elegant gilt and walnut room just off the Senate floor. Under an enormous crystal chandelier, "Tommy," the tiny doorman who attended decades of vice presidents, might usher in a foreign dignitary or important official for a brief audience. But the ritual Vandenberg cherished most commenced with the arrival of the charismatic young chaplain, Peter Marshall. With the "Dominie"—Vandenberg's affectionate nickname for the Presbyterian cleric with a Scottish brogue—he looked over the day's agenda. They would find something to inspire the invocation, then enter the chamber together, where the senator waited for Marshall's prayer before dropping the gavel.[4]

When the session recessed for lunch, Vandenberg repaired to the Senate dining room. In defiance of A. B. Smith, his physician and best friend, he might indulge in a snack of milk and pie. After the afternoon session he often consulted with State Department officials. Before dinner came another round of dictation. Sometimes he prepared speeches, but, as his son said, he had developed almost a sixth sense in knowing when to speak out for maximum effect, or when to keep silent—something that might have surprised observers of his younger self.

The back door of the senator's office locked behind him each day around 7 p.m. After two decades of Washington society, the demands of protocol were all that could rouse Arthur and Hazel from a quiet night at home. Rare were his recreations. He swam, but not often enough to suit Dr. Smith. He might steal away on a warm afternoon to watch the Senators play baseball, although their performance was often an affront to the dignity of the name. (The same could not be said of the football teams of the University of Michigan. Vandenberg tried to schedule a trip through Ann Arbor on at least one Saturday each fall.)

Vandenberg may have enjoyed the best press of any senator of his generation—maybe the last generation in which members of the world's greatest deliberative body were often household names—but reporters were not universal in their praise. A rookie's first encounter could be an ordeal. "He could be curt, uneasy, and even testy," his son observed. Allen Drury found Vandenberg at their first interview "very jolly, very cordial, very unproductive." Over and over the senator just said no, with "the big cigar poised in mid-air and the curiously little-boy smile on the big round face."

With press veterans, however, he was among peers. He spoke off the record, unless specifying otherwise, and would answer almost any question. Reporters relied on him, and he on them. He tested ideas on a group that included James Reston, columnist Marquis Childs, Bert Andrews of the *Herald Tribune*, and Hayden and Moody of the *Detroit News*. On Saturdays at noon he sometimes convened a little seminar. "School's in session," he might announce to William S. White of the *Times* or John L. Steele of the United Press. And then the lesson would begin.[5]

As the Eightieth Congress convened, it was apparent that the "war of nerves" with the Soviets would not become any easier. Russian vetoes in the Security Council were almost chronic. Americans wondered how their wartime alliance had gone so wrong. Fewer than eighteen months after victory, the world was again divided into hostile camps. Vandenberg warned that America needed to realize that "this will be two worlds instead of one."[6]

Many Americans bristled at Russian vetoes in the United Nations. Was it already time to amend the charter? Vandenberg counseled caution. Raising the issue would only disrupt further the fledgling organization. The veto had value for Americans in some circumstances anyway, and "a better sense of mutual good faith and good will" needed to precede any changes. The challenge was to reconcile weaknesses in the charter with the overarching need for an international forum. Improvement was evolutionary: "We must feel our way." The charter still offered peacemakers "pregnant possibilities."[7]

Vandenberg did think that Security Council vetoes should not be allowed for matters under the charter's chapter 6, which dealt with the pacific settlement of disputes. At some point, over some issue— perhaps atomic energy—one major power might use its veto in an intractable fashion. That would be the point at which east and west collided, and it might result in a United Nations that no longer included the Soviet Union. If that happened, Vandenberg wanted it to be "the plain and obvious result of Soviet intransigence."[8]

While Vandenberg continued to weigh in on these critical issues, his new role left no time for international diplomacy, for the negotiations that had dominated his life for a year and a half as he worked "to put united American post-war foreign policy on firm foundations." One-time antagonist Eleanor Roosevelt wished he were with her again at the United Nations. He could not serve two masters, he told her. If he helped make a decision at the United Nations, he could hardly be a free agent when the matter came before the Senate. He suggested that service in the American delegation be a full-time duty, to allow for better preparation. In New York the previous autumn, he had been struck, he told Mrs. Roosevelt, by a lack of "moral leadership" from the American team: "Because our program was essentially one of negation (except in one or two prominent instances with which you were particularly associated)." Seldom had American diplomacy seen stranger bedfellows.[9]

On the Foreign Relations Committee, Vandenberg's like-minded colleagues included young Henry Cabot Lodge Jr., newly returned from army service, Alexander Smith of New Jersey, Bourke Hickenlooper of Iowa, Alexander Wiley of Wisconsin, the new majority leader Wallace White, and Capper. Vandenberg supported a young Oregonian, Wayne Morse, when he lobbied for a seat, but the rest of the leadership pushed Charles Tobey of New Hampshire on the basis of seniority. Joining Connally on the Democratic side were the formidable Walter George, Robert Wagner of New York, Barkley of Kentucky, Elbert Thomas of Utah, and Carl Hatch of New Mexico.

For his chief of staff, Vandenberg chose Francis O. Wilcox, a foreign affairs expert from the Library of Congress. Vandenberg told Wilcox, "Go out and get the best people you can find to do the job we have to do." There would be no partisan appointments, and Vandenberg would not interview candidates. "But don't forget," he told Wilcox with a twinkle in his eye, "I'll hold *you* responsible for everything."[10]

In January 1947, nearly two years to the day after the speech that set out a vision of international cooperation and marked his emergence as an advocate for global engagement, Vandenberg addressed the Cleveland Foreign Affairs Forum in a joint appearance with Byrnes. Although there were still parts of the world where bipartisanship was not evident—China foremost—the spirit characterized the American approach to Europe and the United Nations, the "heart and core" of U.S. policy.[11]

Vandenberg had access to insights unavailable to the wizards of the State Department. He knew his way through the minefield of Capitol Hill. He could anticipate where opposition would come from and what consensus and compromise required.

In January 1947 Truman appointed the revered general George Marshall to replace Byrnes as secretary of state. No one tipped off Vandenberg—a lapse on the part of the White House that struck the senator as a "sudden and unusual interruption" in executive communication—but he nevertheless called an immediate meeting of the Foreign Relations Committee. He won its unanimous approval of Marshall in the morning and that of the full Senate in the afternoon.[12]

On February 27, congressional leaders were summoned to the White House for a meeting with Truman, Marshall, and Undersecretary Dean Acheson. The British ambassador had informed the State Department that His Majesty's government could no longer afford to support the government of Greece. The Greek economy was near collapse. A communist insurgency had become a civil war.[13]

Marshall argued that the United States had no choice but to step in. From Yugoslavia, Marshal Tito and the Russians were arming Greek guerillas who threatened to bring the cradle of Western democracy into the Soviet orbit. Also threatened was Turkey, where the Soviets were angling for control of the Dardanelles. If Greece fell, Turkey would find itself nearly encircled by hostile states. If both nations came under Soviet domination, Russian sway could extend in short order through the Middle East to India. An independent Turkey was critical to the defense of the eastern Mediterranean and the Middle East.

No one could guarantee that American aid would save the Greeks, but without help their government was unlikely to stand. The choice, said Marshall, was "between acting with energy or losing by default." Earlier that month, George Kennan had sent his thoughts, as "The Sources of Soviet Conduct," to Navy Secretary Forrestal. The paper, later published anonymously in *Foreign Affairs*, elaborated on the strategy of containment of the Russian threat, and that way of thinking was becoming the order of the day.

Senators were skeptical. How frustrating it was to know nothing of such an emergency until a decision was upon them. This was late-in-the-game bipartisanship. "When things finally reach a point where a President asks us to 'declare war' there is usually nothing left except to 'declare war,'" Vandenberg lamented. In fact, the administration had also been caught off guard.[14]

Acheson asked the senators to consider the implications of inaction for Western Europe. If Greece fell, what might happen in Austria, Hungary (not yet consolidated in the Russian sphere), Italy, even France? Moscow-backed communists were exploiting economic hardship in each of these war-ravaged countries. Here was the first expression of the domino theory at the highest level of American policy making. When Acheson finished, an aide recalled, "a profound silence ensued that lasted perhaps ten seconds."[15]

That silence was broken by Vandenberg. He turned to Truman. "Mr. President," he declared solemnly, "if you will say that to the Congress and the country, I will support you and I believe most of its members will do the same."[16] At least that's what Acheson said he said. Vandenberg's precise words were not recorded. But few phrases in Cold War history have been repeated as often as the one that others alleged he uttered: a warning that to win support for aid to Greece and Turkey, Truman had to "scare the hell out of the American people."

No source for the comment has been found. While the exact quote is suspect, and taken out of context to suggest a bullying Vandenberg intent on waging cold war, it also expresses a sentiment he would have subscribed to. There could be no successful commitment of American resources on this scale without the support of the people. The president had to make the case. This, Vandenberg told his friend Harry, was the new leader's "date with destiny."

On March 12, 1947, Truman addressed a joint session of Congress. He asked for an appropriation of $400 million, but he went beyond the scope of the State Department request by not limiting it to aid for Greece and Turkey. Rather, he made a blanket vow to "support free peoples who are resisting subjugation." He more than lived up to Vandenberg's apocryphal injunction. As the senator noted afterward, a statement regarding "Communism on-the-march" was overdue.

Pressed for a reaction to Truman's speech, Vandenberg called for a policy that kept faith with the UN Charter even as it addressed a situation for which the United Nations had neither the authority nor the resources. "The plain truth is that Soviet-American relationships are at the core of this whole problem," he said. His challenge, as he saw it, lay in translating the emotional insecurity felt by Americans in the face of Soviet belligerence into a consensus of "intellectual conviction" and firm response. Facing what he described as "practical realities," he declared, "We must either take or surrender leadership."[17]

Crucial details of the aid package remained for State and Congress to sort out. Uppermost in Vandenberg's mind was a need for senatorial consensus and an understanding of implications for the United Nations—to which Truman paid little heed. On the first issue, Vandenberg invited colleagues to submit questions about the aid request. More than a hundred inquiries, with State's replies, were published. This was a model for the sort of background information Congress demanded. (When the chairman of the Democratic National Committee invoked Vandenberg's name in urging his GOP counterpart to endorse the "Truman Policy," the senator was furious: "Bipartisan foreign policy is not the result of political coercion but of non-political conviction." He told the Republican chairman to reject the overture.)

Regarding the United Nations, Vandenberg fretted that it had not been advised of the proposed American action. Nor did the administration bill provide for bringing the aid program under the UN Charter—"a colossal blunder," he noted privately. On the Senate floor he was not so blunt, but he insisted that the bill recognize a future role for the United Nations. In late April, after Vandenberg pressed the point, Warren Austin, by then ambassador to the United Nations, notified the Security Council of plans for economic aid "of an emergency and temporary nature." Austin told the council the United States was offering assistance that the world organization itself might someday provide.[18]

That did not go far enough for Vandenberg. He drafted a preamble for the bill stating that the objective of the aid was to foster the "freedom and independence of all members of the United Nations in conformity with the principles and purposes of the Charter." Delegates meeting at Lake Success, New York, were reassured by the language, but still more by Vandenberg's daring caveat: a provision granting the United Nations authority to end the American program whenever "action taken or assistance furnished by the United Nations makes the continuance of such assistance unnecessary or undesirable."[19]

In April he rose in the Senate to announce unanimous Foreign Relations Committee support. His sales pitch turned on two points closest to his heart. He suggested that the aid proposal could have been entitled "a bill to support the purposes of the United Nations to maintain international peace and security," or "a bill to serve America's self-interest in the maintenance of independent governments." Two sides of the same precious coin, perhaps.

There were no guarantees, he said, repeating Marshall's argument. But this was a far cry from the old isolationist impulse: "It is a plan to forestall aggression which, once rolling, could snowball into global danger of vast design. . . . We do not escape war by running away from it. . . . We avoid war by facing facts." The sense of confrontation was palpable. "We plot no offense against the Soviet Union," said the man who had faced down Molotov. "We are not hunting world domination. . . . But what we deny to ourselves as a matter of morality we also must deny to others as a matter of conquest."

To those who wondered whether the United Nations should have greater involvement, he noted that even if it had the funds and infrastructure for such a task, the decision would have to come from the Security Council, where a Russian veto was certain. There was no better way to destroy the United Nations than to give it a job for which it was unprepared or ill suited. Lippmann thought that Vandenberg's idea of allowing the United Nations to terminate the assistance package under certain conditions corrected the Truman plan's most troubling defect "exactly, completely and handsomely."

The implications of the "Truman Doctrine" were uncomfortably broad. They colored American thought and action for more than forty years, until the exhaustion of the domino theory in Vietnam and then to the very end of the Cold War. A constituent asked Vandenberg whether there were any precedents. Not really, the senator replied, but "we cannot rely upon 'precedents' in facing the utterly unprecedented condition in the world today. Certainly there is no precedent for today's worldwide cleavage between democracy and communism." He did find a parallel, however, between the present crisis and that which confronted the democracies at Munich in 1939. "I can only say," argued Vandenberg, "that I think the adventure is worth trying as an alternative to another 'Munich' and perhaps to another war."

There was another concern as well. If Congress rejected the administration's request, bipartisanship was dead and American policy in jeopardy. A rebuff "would stunt our moral authority and mute our voice," Vandenberg warned. He could hardly sound more anti-isolationist when he asked, "What would you think if you were a citizen of Athens? . . . Of Ankara? . . . What would you think if you were a citizen of any other of the weary, war-torn nations who are wondering this afternoon whether the torch still burns in the upraised hands of liberty . . . ? And what would you think," he concluded, "if you were the Politburo in Moscow's Kremlin?"

Self-interest should govern American actions. Equivocation would be read as timidity. Vandenberg had no benefit of foresight, but he found perspective in recent history. "In a sense we are a tragic generation, despite our blessings and our place in the sun," he told colleagues. "We have been drawn into two World Wars. We finally won them both, and yet we still confront a restless and precarious peace. Something has been wrong. It is our supreme task to face these present realities, no matter how we hate them, and to mend the broken pattern if such be within human power."[20]

Critics on the Right and on the Left attacked the scheme. To the latter, aid to Greeks and Turks meant American imperialism succeeding British imperialism to rescue an unpopular Greek monarchy propped up by a military cabal. Pepper of Florida and Glen Taylor of Idaho insisted that any aid come through the United Nations— knowing it would not. Wallace launched repeated salvos—attacks, Vandenberg sniffed, of an "itinerant saboteur."

Renascent isolationists on the Republican side were stretched to the limit of their tolerance by participation in the United Nations and by the emergency loan to Great Britain. They fretted not only over costly foreign aid but also over allowing the British Labour government to unload its responsibilities. Kenneth Wherry of Nebraska called the aid package a big step toward at least one of two unsavory prospects: war or bankruptcy.

And yet, the "partisan drumfire" subsided. Late April brought Senate and House approval by overwhelming majorities. The new Republican leadership, in the person of Arthur Vandenberg, had been tested and had delivered. Acheson remarked upon Vandenberg's "unswerving loyalty to the project" once he was convinced of its necessity. The State Department was confirmed in its evolving view: it had found a partner.[21]

"Many people seem to think that I act as sort of a co-secretary of state," Vandenberg wrote later in 1947. That made him uneasy. (Between Vandenberg and Acheson, the prima donnas at either end of Pennsylvania Avenue, Truman, to his credit, often acted more as referee than as chief executive.)[22] Over the following two years, however, the line between advice and consent and making policy grew blurred.[23]

World affairs had developed in ways that would have been impossible to envision when Arthur Vandenberg joined the Senate. For the first time, American power was committed to an open-ended effort not tied explicitly to American interests. As Vandenberg said, this commitment "may easily be the thing which requires us to make some very fateful and far-reaching decisions." Acheson, in a memoir so sweeping it helped define the era, slighted Vandenberg (and Marshall) in describing his own presence "at the creation" of a new American role.

. . . .

CHAPTER 25

CALCULATED RISK

. . . .

When the Pan-American Union convened in Petrópolis, above Rio de Janeiro, in August 1947, only the U.S. delegation required interpreters. Vandenberg had never acquired even a rudimentary grasp of Spanish, let alone Portuguese. He sat at the conference table with his ears encased in bulky black headphones as the chairman recognized first one delegate, then another.

The senator listened intently, black brows furrowed, as each speaker was greeted with "tiene la palabra." Suddenly the bespectacled eyes betrayed a flash of recognition. "Palabra!" he boomed, turning to an aide, in a voice even louder than usual because his headphones muffled the sound. "He's always saying 'palabra' and then someone starts to talk. Now I know where the word 'palaver' comes from!" Staffers studied their notepads.[1]

Friends found endearing that curious blend of smugness and good humor, an aging Midwesterner, a big man with a big ego in the company of the suave and sophisticated, at once a know-it-all and an inquiring mind, open and earnest. His ascent to leadership was a role hard-won. He had been on the outside for so long, an intermittent attack dog who longed to be let in, but had to treat with his conscience and wait on the world to get there.

The Rio Conference, as it came to be called, was a building block of hemispheric unity, but also the occasion for Arthur Vandenberg and George Marshall to become friends. The austere secretary of state rarely addressed even his closest colleagues other than by their surnames. Arthur was the exception. The general had few intimates, but there was "nothing stuffy at all about him," Hazel Vandenberg reported. At Petrópolis the Vandenbergs came upon the Marshalls

playing Chinese checkers on the porch of their villa, "completely congenial and a simply grand pair." A winning strategy for Chinese checkers usually meant keeping your pieces in the center—and together.
Vandenberg and Marshall recognized the need for a similar strategy in
the work they undertook. It was a friendship of no small consequence
for American policy.[2]

Britain was nearly broke. On the Continent, conditions were worse.
Freakish droughts and storms plagued farmers and even hampered
mining. There were too few jobs. The violence of war was in the past,
but famine was on the rise. Despair was overtaking gloom in ruined
towns whose streets were strewn with debris. Vandenberg had witnessed the devastation in Germany; Marshall had flown over it en
route from Moscow. His undersecretary for economic affairs, Will
Clayton, had made a closer inspection.

Emergency shipments of American medicine, fertilizer, and food
crossed the Atlantic. In May 1947 the Senate authorized $350 million
in aid for Austria, Hungary, Poland, Italy, and Greece, as well as China.
Vandenberg pushed the bill through his committee without dissent,
warning that without it, "famine, disease and disaster will stalk a desperate Europe."

Everyone knew this was not enough. John Foster Dulles had been
dispatched on a secret mission to France to analyze the situation
there. Communists seemed poised to seize power; civil war might
erupt between them and the followers of Charles de Gaulle. The
country reeled from strikes and sabotage. Dulles called Vandenberg,
then flew to London to meet with Marshall. Marshall asked Vandenberg if he could assure the French government that more help was
on its way.

France was not alone in seeking relief against "winter hunger and
winter cold and against the lurking tyranny which feeds upon such
disaster." The "lurking tyranny" was of course the rising strength of
communists, an "overriding factor which none of us dare overlook,"
Vandenberg told Robert Taft. "We now apparently confront the Moscow challenge on every front and on every issue."

It was clear to Vandenberg, as threats mounted along with pleas for aid, that the situation demanded "an integrated foreign policy which is just as comprehensive as that of the Soviets. I am sure that General Marshall is fully alive to this fact."[3] Support for Greece and Turkey had been a stopgap measure. So was interim aid to other European countries. The dollars involved were less significant than the implications for the exercise of American leadership. These were bipartisan warm-ups.

Two months before, on June 5, 1947, Marshall, just back from London, had spoken at Harvard University's commencement. He outlined a plan for the United States to help war-ravaged Europeans. Marshall's remarks elicited little more than polite applause, but they set wheels in motion. Acheson signaled a trio of British journalists that this was no ordinary address. They alerted Foreign Secretary Ernest Bevin, who heard the offer of aid and called for a meeting with his Continental counterparts. This grand proposal to rescue a continent depended on the Europeans to plan their own recovery. This posed a challenge to the Russians, who faced the choice of joining an American scheme to restore market economies or spurning badly needed assistance.

The new secretary of state's call for a sustained commitment of massive aid was no more than rhetoric without congressional support, however. For that, the administration turned to Vandenberg. The patience and judgment, endurance and timing, he had cultivated over a career were the qualities in greatest demand. Partisanship had scant role here—did he not thrill to these moments? This was troubleshooting at its loftiest, where smoothing rough edges and anticipating potential sources of conflict was a high-wire act with the future of the world in the balance. He had to bob and weave, use his instinct for compromise to find a solution that did not eat away at the essence of the thing.

Many of his Republican colleagues, relishing their new majority status, had other priorities. Vandenberg sympathized with their determination to cut taxes and slash spending. They had had enough of wartime crisis, and more than enough of the New Deal. While enduring nothing like conditions overseas, Americans had lived with a degree of scarcity during the war. They had no wish to see their return to prosperity held back by the misery of Europe. Foreign aid had never been popular, and this audacious proposal threatened to drain American resources with no promise of success. For that matter, what was success in these terms? The United States was the undisputed colossus of the world. European recovery might translate chiefly into greater competition for American business.

These considerations left Vandenberg at first perplexed and more than a little wary of Marshall's ambitious plan. It was fraught with hazard, and he was not one to jump at novelty. He needed to know more. Two enormous questions loomed. What were the needs? Was the United States capable of meeting them? He asked the president to appoint a commission—nonpartisan, of course—to analyze the projected cost and its effect on the American economy. This had to come first, before he dared take up the plan with Congress. He told Truman he wanted an "overall inventory of our own resources to determine the latitudes within which we may consider these foreign needs." He insisted on "a total balance sheet" regarding the requirements of recipient nations. The result was "the most concentrated, yet broad-scaled, stocktaking in the nation's history."[4]

Truman did Vandenberg two better by forming three committees. A nineteen-member panel chaired by Secretary of Commerce Averill Harriman was charged with analyzing the scope of potential aid. Others would study the condition of American resources and assess the effect of foreign aid on the American economy.

Across the Atlantic, Bevin and French foreign minister Robert Schuman invited other nations to join the new Committee of European Economic Co-operation. Soviet Union representatives attended but withdrew when their demands fell on deaf ears. Sixteen nations met through the summer, jointly arriving at commitments for industrial and agricultural production, monetary policies, and trade practices. When they toted up their hopes, the Europeans outlined a program over four years amounting to $29 billion in aid. This had a wishful quality to it, of course. The number was cut to $22.4 billion, and later to $17 billion.

At the same time, the American study groups churned out reports enough to bow a five-foot shelf. The stocktaking had to give Vandenberg the ammunition to ask Congress for emergency winter aid—and set the stage for a long-term program. In November congressional leaders were summoned to the White House. "The President is trying to discriminate between 'stop-gap' aid for France and Italy to keep them afloat until spring, on the one hand," Vandenberg wrote, "and a permanent 'Marshall Plan,' on the other." The needs of the Europeans could seem limitless. As Arthur put it to Hazel, "Where to draw the line!"

The leaders who gathered around the cabinet table took heart in the latest intelligence reports from Western Europe. Soviet-backed communist parties appeared to be losing momentum. "This seems to be the time for us to 'make hay,' " Vandenberg wrote. "But if our friends in Western Europe are allowed to starve and freeze to death this winter, the Commies will be completely back in the saddle."[5]

The senator found himself compelled by the logic. One way or the other, the United States had to rescue Western Europe. "I do not see how we can avoid the necessity of keeping ourselves insulated against world-wide Communism by maintaining these sixteen nations of the Western union," he told his wife. "There's no question we would do it if we were at war with Russia. I'd prefer to do five per cent that much to make it plain to Russia that war would be fatal to her."

He felt a growing confidence in his convictions. But within the party came rumblings of discontent, notably from Taft. When another Republican senator tried to slash an interim aid bill, Vandenberg protested the futility of "throwing a 15-foot rope to a man drowning 20 feet from shore."[6]

And bipartisanship? It was only as strong as the personalities involved. Connally's long-simmering jealousy of his colleague was an open secret. He was "damn tired," he complained, "of Vandenberg this and Vandenberg that."[7]

In November, Vandenberg sat down after a long day's session to write to Hazel back in Michigan. "Guess I must be getting old," he told her. His back hurt. The day before, presiding over a joint session of Congress, he had struggled to climb the dais. There was the challenge, too, when the president spoke to frequent applause, of rising and sitting, rising and sitting. But the day's long committee meeting had brought a different pain. Connally had been particularly irksome, again and again criticizing his proposals. "I almost blew my top," Vandenberg reported. "Sooner or later this feud will explode."[8] These tiffs with Taft and Connally were skirmishes over stopgap support for Europe. If they were harbingers, he noted, "our friend Marshall is certainly going to have a hell of a time down here on the Hill when he gets around to his long-range plan."

The State Department proved adept in its preparations for the long-range Marshall Plan. Vandenberg was as impressed as he was intimidated by the mass of documentation. In particular, the senator approved of the report of the Harriman Committee, whose existence he took credit for. Three inches thick, "a magnificent piece of work," he wrote to Hazel. "That'll keep me busy over the weekend."

In late November the interim aid bill came to a vote. Opposition had dwindled to barely a dozen recalcitrant colleagues. Even Taft gave it support. Vandenberg reported, with no little relish, that *Izvestia*, the party organ in Moscow, once again numbered him among its chief international villains.

He could relax just a little, take time for a "sweat, swim and rub." On a late afternoon he might buzz Hubert, his chauffeur, to drive him to the Mayflower Hotel for lobster Newburg, "and then back home and so to bed about 8 p.m."[9]

While quibbles over stopgap aid subsided, the real challenge was in winning approval of the Marshall Plan itself. Throughout the summer and fall of 1947, Vandenberg and Marshall had plotted strategy at Blair House, down the street from the White House, away from the gaze of the press corps. "We could not have gotten much closer," said Marshall, "unless I sat in Vandenberg's lap or he sat in mine!"[10]

Some critics worried about the cost; others feared undercutting the nascent United Nations. Vandenberg was sensitive to both concerns.

To an ardent UN advocate, he confessed uncertainty. "The evolution of this vague thing which we now conveniently call the 'Marshall Plan' inevitably involves much more than 'economics' and inevitably requires a basic meeting of minds between the four great powers," he observed. "It will be a miracle . . . if these four great powers can get together on this thing at all."[11] Vandenberg came to believe that nothing would strengthen the world body more than the revival of the democracies in Europe. "I am entirely willing to admit that America herself cannot prosper in a broken world," he told a constituent. He hoped even ardent isolationists might understand the economics of the situation. The Europeans had no foreign exchange. They could not afford American goods. If their economies revived, they would be customers again. This was pure self-interest, "entirely aside from considerations of 'charity' or 'communism.' "[12]

What was right? "We are dealing with a world in unpredictable flux," he wrote to *Detroit Free Press* columnist Malcolm Bingay. So much was unknown. Good policy meant balancing one "calculated risk" against another. To Bingay's fears of an "international WPA"—relief on a global scale—Vandenberg replied tartly, "Is somebody proposing one? I hadn't heard about it." Marshall Plan aid was contingent upon European commitment and European results.

He was looking at the threat of the Iron Curtain reaching the Atlantic, surely a greater menace to American security than anything since Pearl Harbor. Unless something was done, he declared, "independent governments, whatever their character otherwise, will disappear," and "aggressive communism will be spurred throughout the world." Here was real hazard: that "the greatest creditor and capitalist nation on earth should find itself substantially isolated in a communist world where the competition would force us into complete regimentation of ourselves beyond anything we have ever experienced."[13]

At the State Department, Marshall assigned Undersecretary Robert Lovett to work out details with Vandenberg, who then coached Lovett on how to take the administration's case to Capitol Hill. The senator suggested inviting business leaders to testify as "aggressive witnesses" on the plan's behalf. This had to be a business program.[14] In a November speech, he suggested that "if self-help and self-sufficiency can be made to work, this objective [the Marshall Plan] may well be a bargain."[15]

The best intentions of bipartisanship faced a new challenge in 1948, an election year with Vandenberg increasingly seen as a presidential prospect. He disavowed any interest, lest it pose a distraction to the Marshall Plan. When the Senate convened in January, Vandenberg assumed responsibility for the fate of the most important and expensive act of foreign aid ever conceived. "He was," said Marshall, "just the whole show."

Chaplain Peter Marshall opened the session with what is likely the shortest prayer ever uttered in the upper house. "Our Father," he began, "thou knowest the difficulties these men have to face and the grave decisions they must make. Have mercy upon them, for Jesus' sake. Amen." As the chaplain stepped away from the rostrum, Vandenberg whispered with a smile, "Now I know just how a condemned man feels."[16]

Two days later, klieg lights were switched on in the ornate Caucus Room. Over four weeks, more than ninety experts, advocates, and opponents appeared before the committee. These were the first Senate hearings broadcast via the new medium of television. Never before had so many Americans witnessed such a searching debate. Often the room was filled. At other times, as the testimony dragged on, Vandenberg was the only senator present, patient and courteous as an obscure economist took the oath. When the committee was finally ready to take its deliberations behind closed doors, one pundit noted that Vandenberg had killed the opposition with kindness.

Patience and courtesy were not characteristics of the Republican caucus generally. A score of GOP "revisionists" wished to water down the legislation, maybe gut it altogether. Vandenberg was careful to listen to their reservations, looking for alterations he could accept. He hoped to wear down opponents before bringing what was formally known as the European Recovery Plan to the Senate floor.

The State Department draft proposed aid of $17 billion over four years and three months. Vandenberg thought this was not a strategic way to frame the request. Why stick your neck out with such a staggering number? Instead, he proposed a general authorization for a sum the administration and Congress would work out together. He argued for a statement of intent, without the weight of specifics. This denied his opponents a big bone to chew on—or to hear about from their constituents. Besides, appropriations by the current Congress did not bind a future one. Instead, with a statement of intent secured, the administration would come back for an annual appropriation.

Accordingly, the administration sent the committee a request for $6.8 billion for the first fifteen months of the program. In response, Republican calls for economy filled the air. Vandenberg proposed a twelve-month authorization of $5.3 billion (more than $50 billion in 2018 dollars). The monthly allocation remained the same, but the figure was less daunting. Congress would get an earlier look at the progress of the program before authorizing its extension, and Vandenberg could say he had trimmed the State Department's ambitious request.

Mail flooded his office. He assured one constituent that Marshall's plan called for no new taxes. "This question of 'what the bill will cost' is a very interesting one," he wrote. What no one could say was "what the failure to pass the bill will cost." He was not above employing alarmist rhetoric. He noted the inevitable need, if the European democracies collapsed, to heavily increase American military spending. "It is infinitely cheaper to defend ourselves by economic means," he insisted. "Peace is cheaper than war. War has no bargains. Peace does."[17]

Critics persuaded him to insist on stronger language regarding European self-help. The plan's administrator would have authority to end aid to any nation that failed to adhere to its agreement; Vandenberg wanted the details of this spelled out, and he added a provision for congressional oversight. He then took a further step to protect the integrity of the program; rather than administer it through the State Department, he called for an independent agency under presidential control—something researchers at the Brookings Institution had suggested after he asked them to investigate the question. This allowed Vandenberg to frame the aid program as a business venture beyond the purview and politics of the State Department.

The senator was the first to admit that many of the compromises and accommodations were window dressing. One colleague complained that language in the bill referring to its "impact on our domestic economy" was too vague. "That's perfectly all right," Vandenberg replied. "Just leave those words in. I can tell nineteen different senators . . . who are worried about something—'your problem is taken care of by that clause in the bill.'"

In February 1948 the Foreign Relations Committee voted 13–0 in favor of the European aid package. Such unanimity assured passage by the full Senate. Marshall cheered Vandenberg "as a truly great statesman."[18] For Vandenberg, it was, yes, time for a speech. He pecked through seven drafts on that portable at the Wardman.

On March 1 the galleries were packed, with most of the Senate present, and House members lining the walls of the chamber. In the name of "intelligent American self-interest," Vandenberg told the assemblage, here was a "mighty undertaking worthy of our faith." Only days before, any vestige of democracy in Czechoslovakia had been "gutted"—its pro-Western foreign minister, Masaryk, dead after a mysterious fall. There were fears that "brave little Finland" might succumb to Soviet intimidation soon: "This very afternoon, while we debate an axiom, namely that aggressive communism threatens all freedom and all security, whether in the old world or in the new, when it puts free peoples anywhere in chains."

He gave full rein to fears of "lurking tyranny." This was a dark night in much of the world. The bill before the Senate could be "a welcome beacon"—and "if a beacon is to be lighted at all it had better be lighted before it is too late." He spoke to those who held the view he had once championed. Who would not wish that we might "retire within our bastions, and dream of an isolated and prosperous peace"? That was no longer possible—"that which was once our luxury would now become our folly." This was "a foreshortened, atomic world" in which isolation might be an ideal, but "we must take things as they are."

The imperative was clear: "The greatest nation on earth either jus-
tifies or surrenders its leadership. We must choose." Opponents who
thought they could find "safety" by rejecting or subverting the plan,
he said, "have simply fled to other risks, and I fear far greater ones.
For myself, I can only say that I prefer my choice of responsibilities."

This program would mean as much to Americans as to Europeans.
"It aims to preserve the victory against aggression and dictatorship
which we thought we won in World War II," he said. "It strives to help
stop World War III before it starts. It fights economic chaos which
would precipitate far-flung disintegration." Finally, he echoed Marshall: "It sustains western civilization." Indeed, "it can be the turning
point in history for 100 years to come." If this was a touch melodramatic, it also reflected a genuine fear that a little "scare-hell" rhetoric
helped drive home.[19]

Fear of World War III was hardly confined to Washington. In ruined
Berlin—a hundred miles inside Russian-occupied eastern Germany
and parceled into four control zones—conflict was about to erupt.
While a cooperative spirit had governed the sectors overseen by the
United States, Great Britain, and France, guns and checkpoints de-
marcated the boundaries of the fourth sector, controlled by the Soviet
Union. Those checkpoints became flash points on March 1, 1948. The
very day Vandenberg argued for passage of the Marshall Plan, the
western sectors of the city suddenly lost travel, communication, and
freight links with the outside world. Russian troops, aiming to push
out their former allies, had blocked the autobahn and cut telephone
lines to western Germany. The Soviet Union was moving decisively
to fill a vacuum of military power: the Nazis had been defeated, most
of the American forces had returned home, and Western European
militaries were threadbare.

This escalation only put more pressure on Congress to endorse
the Marshall Plan. American policy makers saw a direct link between
Europe's economic salvation and the preservation of its democratic
institutions. Indeed, it was becoming ever clearer to Vandenberg that
American security depended on both. He chafed at delay. Countering

a colleague who questioned his haste to approve the plan, Vandenberg referred to himself in the third person: "The senator from Michigan thinks the world is on fire," he said. The European Recovery bill was "one hopeful fire extinguisher."[20]

The Senate debated the plan for two weeks. With Connally, Henry Cabot Lodge Jr., and others, Vandenberg smoothed out details and fended off attacks. Taft tried to slash the first-year appropriation by $1.3 billion but was defeated, 56–31. On March 14, at five minutes past midnight, roll was called on the final version of the bill. By a vote of 69–17, the Senate approved it. Quibbles in the House were addressed in conference, and in April 1948 the president affixed his signature.

The next step? Finding someone to run the vast undertaking. When Marshall floated the appointment of his undersecretary, Will Clayton, Vandenberg balked. He liked Clayton, but if the program were to be bipartisan, the administration had to extract it from the embrace of the State Department. Days later came a summons to the White House. "Van," Truman said, "I've found just the man for the job and he's willing to take it at great personal sacrifice."

"Fine," said the senator, "who is it?"

"Dean Acheson." There is no record of Vandenberg's expression, but his face must have fallen. He had no doubt, he told Truman, that Acheson, formerly a high official at both State and Treasury, was capable, "but the Senate won't confirm him."[21]

Vandenberg championed Paul G. Hoffman, president of the Studebaker automobile company, who had testified convincingly on behalf of the plan. A Truman aide called Hoffman in Hawaii, where he was on temporary assignment for the army. Hoffman, caught off guard, was not inclined to accept the offer, but he agreed to discuss it with the president. Before Hoffman went to the White House, he called Vandenberg. "You've got to take it," the senator said.

Replied Hoffman, "I've hired thousands of men in my time, but not a single man by saying that 'you've got to take it.'" Vandenberg was relentless. "He knocked all my defenses down," Hoffman said later, "and by the time I spoke to the President I couldn't say no."

The senator saw in Hoffman a reflection of himself as a young entrepreneur. "I found him to be the common denominator of the thought of the nation," he told colleagues. Hoffman was quickly confirmed. His performance over the following three years validated Vandenberg's choice. Such an enormous undertaking was bound to attract controversy, but Hoffman's work and character were never faulted. The program steered clear of political meddling—no small achievement. It was, Vandenberg said, "the best non-political organization which has ever been put together on a government project."[22]

While the House joined the Senate in approving the European Recovery Program, its appropriations chairman, John Taber, and other Republicans on the committee opposed the proposed expenditures. They voted to cut the first-year appropriation by 26 percent. "I do not know how anything could be more shocking or more subversive of every Republican pretense toward international cooperation," an indignant Vandenberg wrote to Dulles.

Peter Marshall opened the next day's session with a nod to Vandenberg's frustration. "Our Father," he intoned, "sometimes we are discouraged and disappointed in the government of this Nation; and the common people of other lands . . . cannot understand the difference between what we say and what we do."[23]

CHAPTER 26

．．．．．．．．．．．．

5OOG

．．．．．．．．．．．．

The House's action did not go unnoticed. From London, Ambassador Lewis Douglas radioed that the Taber proposal fed doubts in Western Europe about the reliability of the United States. The French, in the delicate language of diplomacy, had "apprehensions."

Vandenberg was enraged. This was no time for traditional niceties. The Republican national convention was soon to convene in Philadelphia, but party unity was not his priority. He took his protest of what his House colleagues had done to the Senate Appropriations Committee. Would this split open the party's old fault line between isolationists and internationalists? It was a risk worth taking.

Newsreel cameras whirred, flashbulbs popped, and there was Vandenberg. The Taber group, he told his peers, had taken a "meat-axe approach" to a plan of global consequence. The proposed cut "guts the enterprise," he roared. It was, in effect, a "veto" of the will of the Congress, expressed in its approval of the program. Worse, it was showing America to the world as "capricious, unreliable and impotent."[1]

Taber's "cynical reversal of policy," which "keeps the word of the promise to the ear but breaks it to the hope," was cavalier and confusing to a world seeking "confidence and faith as the basis of security and peace." It meant transforming a chance for true recovery into yet another stopgap stab at relief, "plunging us back into the dreary, hopeless, sterile and utterly costly routines which we must escape." The plan had to be endorsed in full, as intended. Once it was under way, there would be ample opportunity to reassess it.[2]

The Senate stood with him. Most of the funds were restored in conference committee. Bipartisan policy as Vandenberg defined it had withstood a difficult test. In a desperate bid for global security, a divided government had agreed on one of the costliest government programs ever conceived.

The Marshall Plan need not have borne the weight of the world if the United Nations had been able to play a stronger role. But Soviet vetoes—twenty-three within three years—had paralyzed the Security Council. Vandenberg was determined to secure the peace through stronger global institutions. If, in the short term, the United Nations could not act, however, he could see but one alternative: regional, collective self-defense.

Collective self-defense as most Americans understood it meant the Monroe Doctrine, period. In the Western Hemisphere, an attack on one nation could be construed as an attack on all. Article 51 had enshrined in the United Nations Charter the right to make such arrangements. The recent Rio Pact was an affirmation of the Monroe model. Now the State Department turned to Vandenberg to see how it might apply to Europe.[3]

For several weeks in the spring of 1948, at Vandenberg's invitation, Robert Lovett enacted a nightly ritual. When he left work at the State Department's new headquarters in Foggy Bottom, he would drive out Connecticut Avenue to the Wardman Park, then ride the elevator to the fifth floor. In apartment 500G, with the little balcony overlooking Rock Creek Park, Vandenberg poured martinis. Then, the two men would spend the evening grappling in secret with the two core problems confronting the United States overseas. The first was the Soviet Union's reflexive veto of collective action at the United Nations. The second was the question of how the United States might support regional and collective security arrangements, such as Europe's new Western Union, which had sprung into existence with the beginning of the Berlin blockade.

Vandenberg was searching for language that would commit the U.S. Senate to the protection of Western Europe if the Russians attacked. With their scribbled notes, he and Lovett were laying the groundwork for the North Atlantic Treaty Organization (NATO).

Eventually, they widened the circle of discussion. The State Department, collaborating with Vandenberg's staff, produced one draft after another of its proposal. Finally, a four-page document emerged. Vandenberg wanted something more concise: "We can say all we want to say in one page." Just how became apparent when the verbose old editor drew from his typewriter the draft of a Senate resolution that would become the centerpiece of American leadership in the post-war era.

Of course, anyone could write a resolution. It would take a different sort of skill to ensure that Congress would not consign it to a "cold storage plant." Despite pressure from State and from events in Europe, Vandenberg proceeded deliberately. He knew that haste might doom their efforts.[4]

Marshall had invited Vandenberg back to Blair House, where Lovett, Dulles, and other leaders joined them around the big dining table. Dulles expressed skepticism—until Vandenberg reached into his breast pocket and with a flourish presented the single sheet of text he had typed himself. Without knowing the hours that had gone into this distillation, his colleague was struck by its simplicity. Every word carried weight. The moment marked a turning point. A century and a half of foreign policy tradition, the "trail of a tradition" that Vandenberg once celebrated as something sacred, was turned on its head.

It had come to this:

Resolved, that the Senate reaffirm the policy of the United States to achieve international peace and security through the United Nations so that armed force shall not be used except in the common interest, and that the President be advised of the sense of the Senate that this government, by constitutional process, should particularly pursue the following objectives within the United Nations Charter:

(1) Voluntary agreement to remove the veto from all questions involving pacific settlements of international disputes and situations, and from the admission of new members.

(2) Progressive development of regional and other collective

arrangements for individual and collective self-defense in accordance with the purposes, principles, and provisions of the Charter.

(3) Association of the United States by constitutional process, with such regional and other collective arrangements as are based on continuous and effective self-help and mutual aid, and as affect its national security.

(4) Contributing to the maintenance of peace by making clear its determination to exercise the right of individual or collective self-defense under Article 51 should any armed attack occur affecting its national security.

(5) Maximum efforts to obtain agreements to provide the United Nations with armed forces as provided by the Charter, and to obtain agreement among member nations upon universal regulation and reduction of armaments under adequate and dependable guaranty against violation.

(6) If necessary, after adequate effort toward strengthening the United Nations, review of the Charter at an appropriate time by a General Conference called under Article 109 or by the General Assembly.

Vandenberg's single page aimed to organize the world without the Russians, who with their satellites represented one-sixth of the planet—or one-fourth if China slid behind the Iron Curtain. The senator was willing to face that event, if it came, but he did not wish to precipitate it. "Except as a last resort I do not want deliberately and now to make this a two-world earth and perhaps to make inevitable final war between the two," he later declared. Indeed, he saw this as a step toward a stronger peace: "If worse comes to worst, we can organize the whole world of peace-loving nations on this basis. . . . If the Russkies wish to join—o.k. If not, they have outlawed themselves."[5]

In May 1948 Vandenberg was ready to submit his resolution to the Senate Foreign Relations Committee. It called for the United States to support arrangements for mutual defense as permitted by the UN Charter—beyond the veto of the Security Council. It bowed to the United Nations while giving the United States the flexibility to pursue its own security goals.

Other resolutions regarding the United Nations had been piling up before the committee, but Vandenberg cautioned colleagues that most of them were dangerous. One, for example, had "raised unshirted hell in France" because it implied a secondary role for the French in creating an international army. Only his own resolution, he insisted, actually strengthened the United Nations without going to extremes. More specifically, only his resolution cleared the way for the United States to join in collective security arrangements with other countries, most notably those of Western Europe. There was much here that paralleled the rationale behind the Marshall Plan, he observed. Each depended on European self-help and, as he endlessly insisted, American self-interest.

The committee went over the document word by word. The paragraphs about a mutual defense pact faced the strictest scrutiny. In three long, closed-door sessions, Vandenberg assured colleagues that American forces could never be committed without the approval of Congress. On May 19, 1948, the committee reported out Senate Resolution 239—the Vandenberg Resolution—by the familiar vote of 13–0.

The president pro tempore, one Arthur Vandenberg, called for a vote in the full Senate on June 11. He took a mere ten minutes to describe the resolution and note the "tremendous efforts" then under way through the Marshall Plan to rebuild Europe. But "pending this blessed outcome," he added, "it is inevitable that related questions of physical security should arise." He offered a plan for "practical American cooperation under specified circumstances, within the framework of the United Nations." The treaty never, Vandenberg concluded, "steps outside the United Nations Charter . . . the Constitution of the United States . . . [or] the final authority of the Congress."[6]

Pepper, Fulbright, and others had questions, but at the end of the day—the single day—of debate, the Senate voted 64–6 to make history. Vandenberg knew it was that important, yet his shrewdly general remarks seemed to have softened the hard edge of its implications. The United States could extend to the noncommunist nations of the world, starting with Europe, the possibility of military assistance—to avoid war, but also to make war if it came to that. American security would be entangled with the security of Western Europe and ultimately with much of the world.

As momentous as that seems in retrospect, Vandenberg professed it to be merely a temporary expediency—although it was sometimes hard to tell when he was exercising care and when salesmanship, even in the State Department. Whatever the case, the resolution spelled out clearly that any mutual security pact was necessary only "until the Security Council has taken the measures necessary to maintain international peace and security." As with support for Greece and Turkey, when the United Nations was ready, it could take over. "That single word 'until' is the key to everything," Vandenberg said. The thrust of the Resolution was "*not* a trend toward 'military assistance' (although I would be the last to ignore it) but a device to *unlock the United Nations.*" The treaty would enable joint planning and shared equipment, the essentials of "preparedness," but without the threatening overtones of a conventional military alliance—except, perhaps, in the eyes of the Soviet Union.[7]

No one, after all, wanted to threaten the Russians. George Kennan was afraid the alliance might create "a danger which did not actually exist." (The senator's resolution, he said, was "typical of that mixture of arid legalese and semantic pretension that so often passes, in the halls of our domestic-political life, for statesmanship." It was also typical of the messy ways of democracy that he sometimes disdained.) Vandenberg insisted that his aim had always been a " 'live and let live' world." But that did not mean kowtowing to the Soviets, either. It was a delicate balance. There was value in "just keeping the talking going, because when we are still talking things out we are not shooting them out."

By late 1948, there had been no shooting. The Marshall Plan was in place, the Berlin airlift thwarted the Soviet blockade, and NATO was taking shape. The tide of the Cold War appeared to be turning.

"I think we are winning it," Vandenberg confided.[8]

The Marshall Plan and the Vandenberg Resolution redefined America's role in the world. They might somehow have happened without Arthur Vandenberg, but he was the hero of the hour. In some quarters the logic of a presidential candidacy was overwhelming. So was the belief that the Republicans' nominee in 1948 would also be the next president.

The very idea of a new Vandenberg candidacy was fraught with irony. The senator was viable because he had become the darling of the internationalists. Eight years before, when Vandenberg really wanted the job, Willkie had rolled over him with support from the same people who were booming "Vandenberg!" in the pages of *Time* and the *New York Herald Tribune*.

Yet the drumbeat had begun before the dust of 1946 had settled. The senator, true to form, insisted he was not running. "As for 1948—forget it," he told a friend. "My name has been on a ballot for the last time." But he understood the logic, and his ego would not allow him to stand aside completely. So Vandenberg took one more wistful turn as the Hamlet of presidential politics.

Not running? No one believed him. "Perhaps," he wrote later in his diary, "it's because even your best friends feel about it as did the little boy when he saw his first giraffe and said—'there ain't no such animal.'"[9]

In a letter to *Life* magazine in 1947, Vandenberg wryly laid out the challenges of the "non-candidate." He also admitted that perhaps his earlier denials had been "pretty cryptic." He said facetiously that *not* running for president might actually be harder than mounting a campaign. He had tried both, he reported: "Down to date, neither enterprise has been a success."

How many times could he say it? He was not a candidate, did not expect to be a candidate, would neither seek delegates nor approve of others doing so. On New Year's Day of 1948, he wrote Michigan Republicans: "I urge that my name shall not be presented or supported."[10] But that was not enough to settle the matter, especially among his friends. One such was Sinclair Lewis. "Dear Arthur," he had written in the spring of 1948, "I think the next president of the United States is going to be Arthur Vandenberg, who doesn't want the job. I have a great idea for helping him during the first three terms of his presidency: stay to Hell out of Washington."[11]

Dear "Red," came a swift reply, "I have a better idea than yours— skip the first three terms entirely and talk about 1960!"

He had other influential admirers. Walter Lippmann preferred a Vandenberg-Dewey ticket. Justice William O. Douglas, a Roosevelt appointee, called Vandenberg "the most realistic of all senators when it came to world affairs."[12] But the senator himself thought there was a more electable prospect: General Dwight Eisenhower, an ostensibly nonpartisan figure whom he had met at a small dinner party for Republican leaders in December 1947.

As usual, the Republican Congress had been fighting the domestic proposals streaming from a Democratic White House. This climate of partisan division on the home front led Vandenberg to reflect on his own ideology. He recalled his "favorite bit of Holy Writ" from Isaiah: "Look ye to the rock whence ye are hewn." The Constitution was that rock, yet he also saw the need for "a proper degree of 'social responsibility' " in government. "But the mere statement of this fact," he wrote a friend, "unavoidably involves the need for the greatest prudence and caution lest this evolution shall destroy the 'fundamentals' from which I think it logically springs." He concluded, "The present Democratic party cannot be entrusted with any such responsibility."

With a future Republican administration in prospect, he envisioned a powerful role for himself in Congress. "Without strong leadership there, a Republican president might be no more than an impotent White House prisoner." He was suited for that role—"that's where my vanity comes in." He liked to think that on the Hill he was indispensable.

He saw his role as peacemaker. He meant that literally. "Another war," he said, "will come pretty close to being the end of everything."

Even as he worked closely with the State Department, he worried that the White House might use Berlin and the European crisis to keep power in the fall election. "I may be all wrong," he said, "but my theory is that I am making it impossible for the Administration to success-fully 'exploit' any such plea that it alone can be entrusted with foreign policy."

Yet he was quick to dismiss suggestions that his candidacy could unify Republicans. He had bitter opponents, particularly in Colo-nel McCormick and other erstwhile isolationists from the Taft wing of the party: "At least two hundred members of the House—mostly Republican—hate my guts."[13]

Those two hundred, if there were that many, were a minority, however. "Vandenberg Boom Just Won't Bust" was a headline in the *Washington Daily News*. Michigan's GOP committeeman canvassed the country and found broad support. Michigan's dapper governor, "Hollywood Kim" Sigler, presumed loudly that Vandenberg's "unself-ish devotion to his country makes him available." Henry Cabot Lodge Jr. worked behind the scenes with the same goal. Dewey, the early front-runner, had been the losing candidate four years before, and a "Stop Dewey" movement was building.

In May a story by Richard Rovere in *Harper's* profiled "the unas-sailable Vandenberg." No public man stood higher in the eyes of his fellows. "His prestige is global," Rovere wrote. "The press of the world, that of Russia excepted, hurries to report everything he says. Here at home he is beyond reproach from his friends and, by the magic of bipartisanship, beyond judgment by his enemies." His worst enemies were the communists, with the McCormick press a distant second. These were not bad enemies to have. "One wonders," Rovere observed, "why Republican leaders don't jump at the chance to draft Vanden-berg." Sure, the GOP had plenty of aspirants, "but it certainly puzzles a bystander to see them enduring strife and discord in their search for a good candidate when all they have to do is draft the perfect candidate, Vandenberg, and call it a day."[14]

Newsweek polled fifty pundits. Vandenberg was the choice of an overwhelming majority. In June 1948, on the eve of the convention, a *US News and World Report* poll of 815 newspaper editors favored Vandenberg by a margin of two to one over Taft, Dewey, or Stassen.

Yet Vandenberg's observations about the party's divisions were proving apt. Among the GOP faithful, he seemed to be everybody's second choice.

CHAPTER 27

THE LAST CAMPAIGN

When the Republican convention opened on June 21, Arthur and Hazel shared a box lunch on a park bench before a throng of photographers. Reporters had waited for hours outside the Warwick Hotel, where Arthur Junior had secured a suite. The Vandenbergs slipped over to a sixteenth-floor apartment on Rittenhouse Square. Hazel wore long sleeves to conceal her swollen left arm, a symptom of the cancer no one spoke of.

That night, Vandenberg entered the hall through a side door and sat on the platform reserved for senators. Reporters crowded around the portly figure in the white linen suit. The state delegation called out greetings. Governor Sigler grabbed the state standard and led a file of shouting delegates down the center aisle, hoping to ignite a spontaneous demonstration that never came.

But Clare Boothe Luce roused the crowd. The tiny blonde in black suede shoes denounced Democratic presidents as "troubadours of trouble, crooners of catastrophe." Truman's time was up, she declared: "His situation is hopeless. . . . He is a gone goose." While praising Dewey, she reserved her warmest words for Vandenberg.[1]

Later, back at Rittenhouse Square, the senator persisted in refusing to "connive" on his own behalf. He rejected the pleas of party leaders. He had not opened a headquarters at the convention. One governor was seen stomping off, grumbling, after Vandenberg refused to see him. He even declined to say whether he would accept a draft. He just stayed in the Rittenhouse penthouse, watching most of the first televised convention on a small set.[2]

As Taft's fortunes waned over the course of the convention, Clare Boothe Luce asked him to withdraw in favor of Vandenberg. "Mrs.

Luce," came the croaking reply, "there is no one who admires Arthur Vandenberg more than I do. Certainly I prefer him to Dewey, but once I release my delegates, I can't control them. They will go to Dewey." Taft sent her to Stassen. Stassen refused to yield unless Vandenberg expressed explicit interest.[3]

Finally, she went to Vandenberg's apartment and begged him to endorse an effort on his behalf. Acerbic columnist Westbrook Pegler chided Henry Luce for setting "a trap" for Vandenberg, who, if elected, would appoint him secretary of state. Luce courted Pennsylvania governor James Duff to back Vandenberg in exchange for the vice presidential nomination. In the apartment that night, Clare was in tears. Van was letting the country down, she lamented, leaving the field to "this little chap who looks like the bridegroom on a wedding cake."[4]

The only circumstance in which Vandenberg thought he might enter the race was if he had to fight for his foreign policy. His columnist friends the Alsops had issued a warning: "The stage is set in Philadelphia for the final struggle between isolationists and men of the Vandenberg school, between backward looking and modern-minded Republicans."[5]

But in Philadelphia, he found, "it was speedily evident that *nobody* was willing to do serious battle for the antediluvian McCormick, *Chicago Tribune* point of view." Lodge ("Bless Him!") had shrewdly thrown in a few more expansive statements of bipartisan cooperation "for the express purpose of giving the little coterie of isolationists on his Committee something to knock out." Vandenberg vowed "to protect the GOP against a reversion to 'isolationism' or against desertion of the peace plans." The plank was approved unanimously—"which means that the Chicago Colonel and many of my bitter Congressional foes . . . must have voted for it," he crowed. "Life *does* have its amusing consolations." He did not need the nomination to feel vindicated.[6]

All the same, Sigler was determined to place the senator's homburg in the ring—even after Vandenberg dispatched a note begging him not to, "lest it destroy the entire character of my long-sustained position." Sigler assured him that he would make plain Vandenberg's disinterest. Finally, at 3 a.m. on June 24, Vandenberg's nomination reached the floor. The Michigan delegation decided, with no hint of encouragement from the senator, to commit its votes to him. Vandenberg acknowledged that he was their "problem child" as well as their favorite son.

His vanity and his reflexive preparedness did lead him to write an acceptance speech. But it never left the breast pocket of his linen suit. On the first ballot, Michigan cast its forty-one votes for Vandenberg; twenty-one more came from other delegations. But there was no deadlock. (There was also last-minute talk of drafting Dwight Eisenhower. "I believe the General would have accepted *if* the track could have been cleared for him," Vandenberg later wrote.) On the second ballot Dewey passed 500 delegates, just shy of the required 548. On the third, Taft withdrew and Dewey went over the top.[7]

In hindsight, Vandenberg confided, he would not have left the door ajar. He remembered advice he had received as a young man when he asked his boss about accepting another job: "It is far better to be thought worthy of a job and not take it than to take it and be found out." Or, as he joked, "When I die, I want the minister to be able to look down on me and say, 'There would have been a great president.'"[8]

Afterward, Vandenberg insisted on his consistency. "It was impossible for me to speak with greater finality unless one said, as General Sherman did once upon a time, that he would not run if nominated or serve if elected," he said. "Any such statement, in my circumstances, was ruled out as a breach of duty." And yet, he insisted, "I was a noncandidate to the end." He cited three reasons. First, bipartisanship had become his mission. In Congress he had "demonstrated some degree of competence to serve this cause—perhaps even some degree of temporary indispensability." That fired his sense of duty.

Then there was the matter of his age, sixty-four. Roosevelt had died younger. A. B. Smith found him in good health, despite the heart condition, the headaches, and what had been described as intermittent cervical arthritis. "But my own conscience constantly told me that it was an unfair speculation for the country." Did he have intimations of something else? He wasn't letting on.

Finally, he knew how seldom the nation elevated someone from the Congress to the presidency. He thought he personified a reason why: "In the many legislative battles for the bi-partisan foreign policies . . . I have unavoidably attracted many bitter enemies. . . . Many of my colleagues, sharply differing with my views, are human enough to 'remember.' "

There were other factors, too. A gossip column hinted at an anonymous senator's new female friend. An editor said that Vandenberg had been seen in the company of a woman from the British Foreign Service. On a more mundane level, he had been so engrossed in foreign policy that he was out of touch with some of the pressing domestic issues. Twenty years had passed since he had exercised administrative responsibilities, and then those of a midsize newspaper. And after the last few "supremely strenuous" years, he was tired.

But the most compelling factor may have been Hazel's health. She had undergone a radical mastectomy to stop the spread of breast cancer. As a consequence, her left arm had swollen. Milk arm, some called it, or elephant arm. She was uncomfortable and self-conscious; carefully draped scarves only partially concealed the condition. For his part, Arthur was terrified, as he confessed to Peter Marshall, chaplain of the Senate. There was a tragic dimension to this, for she had all the enthusiasm and intelligence to be well qualified for the role of first lady. Her husband, too, thought her "supremely eligible," but "despite her bravery about it, she recoiled" at the thought.

So many reasons not to run. Yet in some ways it didn't even seem to matter. It was obvious that whomever Republicans chose would beat Truman. The GOP would control both ends of Pennsylvania Avenue. Vandenberg was sure to have a major role.

With the nomination secured, Dewey invited Vandenberg to his suite at the Bellevue-Stratford to help choose a vice president from among Stassen, California governor Earl Warren, Ohio governor John Bricker,

Indiana representative Charles Halleck, even Michigan's junior senator, Homer Ferguson. Vandenberg vetoed the Midwestern isolationists, Bricker and Halleck. He recommended Stassen or Warren. The group adjourned at 4 a.m., settling on Warren. A dream pairing—popular governors of the two most populous states, a balance of east and west—and a team in accord with the policies of Arthur Vandenberg.

A month later, Vandenberg returned to the acceptance speech he never gave, that result of his strange brew of ego and preparedness. He had preserved it, he wrote, "purely as a curiosity." But even in his diary he felt that an explanation was necessary: "Probably it will be misunderstood as being some sort of proof that I was not sincere, at rock bottom, in my refusal to be a candidate. But that just isn't so." Friends kept predicting that he stood a chance of being the nominee. "So I 'prepared,'" he said, "and here it is. Thank Heaven it was and is an *undelivered* speech. It is simply an amusing freak of minor history"—but it was *his* history, so his pride could not let it go.

His text made standard pleas: for party unity, against "meddling bureaucrats," for a foreign policy "which neither 'zigs' nor 'zags,'" for fidelity to the United Nations, against the "entrenched political dynasty of the New Deal." He ended, somewhat dramatically, with a pledge to be a one-term president. Minus the last promise, it could have been the speech delivered by Thomas Dewey.[9]

But Vandenberg had a darker reason for returning to the speech: he added a postscript that reads like a sort of interior dialogue, his place in history contesting with his practicality. "If anything serious should happen to my health in the next few months, I want the following information made public," he wrote. His last physical, in late 1947, had given him a clean bill of health. So did a checkup just before Philadelphia. In Grand Rapids soon after the convention, however, chest X-rays with Dr. Smith revealed a spot on his left lung. A Washington doctor reviewing the pictures "told me frankly that they disclosed a lung involvement which might be tuberculosis," Vandenberg wrote.

The test for tuberculosis proved negative. He wished the record to show that if he had had any hint of a serious ailment, he would have slammed the door harder in Philadelphia. "Perhaps I had a sub-conscious warning which moved me to go as far as I did," he specu-lated. "Perhaps it inspired my constant comments that *any* man at 64, no matter how well he seemed to be, was inevitably in too hazard-ous an age-zone to enter a White House career." Vandenberg meant to draw a contrast with the late president, who ran for a fourth term when his intimates knew he was unlikely to survive it. "The point I want to nail down is that my doctors never had an inkling of this threat," he wrote. "I never had the remotest thought of such a thing until this morning, but it is simply appalling to think of the tragedy . . . if I were the Republican nominee for president."[10]

But this was speculation. Truman adviser George E. Allen sent Vandenberg $100 to pay off his wager that Vandenberg would win the nomination. "After this I am calling off all bets with you," Allen wrote. "Never know another man who would rather win a hundred dollars than the presidency of the United States."[11]

The president, reeling from the midterm loss of Congress, floun-dering in the polls, was desperate to rouse his splintering base. On the right, Southern Democrats rebelled against efforts to promote civil rights, nominating South Carolina governor Strom Thurmond to lead their upstart Dixiecrat party. On the left, former vice president Henry Wallace, disenchanted with Truman's—and Vandenberg's—Cold War, accepted the nomination of the Progressive Party.

The incumbent's strategy in response was to throw bipartisanship to the winds, demonizing congressional Republicans who had bedev-iled him on domestic issues. He attacked the "do-nothing" Eightieth Congress as the "worst" in history. Vandenberg was, perhaps pre-dictably, incensed at this blatantly political gambit. The president's attacks were "ridiculous," he wrote. Indeed, when it came to foreign affairs, the Eightieth Congress offered "the most amazing record of constructive cooperation ever written in *any* Congress," a unity that could "spell the difference between peace and war."[12]

Vandenberg felt betrayed by his old friend Harry. "Not even Wal-lace is saying things better calculated to split the country into snarling vendettas at a moment when our destiny cannot afford these soap-box luxuries," he lamented to Dewey campaign manager Herbert Brownell. He puffed up with pride as he reflected on the Foreign Relations Committee's work in the Eightieth Congress. "It is simply staggering," he wrote Hazel. "When I look at it in total I don't see how it could have happened."[13]

Truman called for a special session of Congress, the first in nearly a century, which he opened in late July with demands for action on a variety of domestic spending and labor issues. The president's tactic was transparent, his agenda more punitive than substantial. Some Republicans threatened to adjourn immediately. Vandenberg insisted that the country was expecting them to do *something*, at least, in response. But Truman had sprung his trap well. Republicans did little more than sputter and grumble.[14] The senator was in some respects a prisoner of the bipartisanship that had become his trademark. Afraid that if he attacked the administration, he might reduce his own effectiveness and that of the surely imminent Republican presidency, he found that he had effectively neutralized himself.

His zeal for guarding his bipartisan preserve was sometimes at odds with Dewey's need to stand apart from Truman. Vandenberg was uncomfortable, for example, with a Dewey promise to let Italy administer the colonies it had lost during the war. But Dewey needed the Italian American vote. "I hope you will be tolerant of the exigencies of the campaign and of the political influence from which Mr. Truman does not divorce himself and from which the Governor cannot *wholly* divorce *himself*," Dulles implored him.[15]

Dulles was Dewey's presumptive secretary of state. Columnist Joseph Alsop told Vandenberg that Dewey would offer him the post, with the expectation that he would decline and Dulles get the job. He and Dulles both knew that most isolationists in Congress had not changed their stripes. "They will be 'back at the old stand' next January," he wrote Dulles. "It is peculiarly our job—yours and mine—to see that bipartisan liaison in the next Congress does not become impossible. Otherwise November will be a pyrrhic victory."[16]

Trying to stay above the fray, Vandenberg found himself without a clear role in the campaign. He suggested to Brownell that he might be of use to John Sherman Cooper in Kentucky, who had been a strong backer of bipartisan policy. In other races, he might be more liability than asset. Even in Kentucky he had misgivings, for that was the home state of his old friend, Democratic vice presidential candidate Alben Barkley, an ally on the Foreign Relations Committee. Instead of stumping for specific candidates, he thought it wiser to make a national address. In early October he sat down before a microphone in a Washington studio.

The diplomatic achievements of the Eightieth Congress bore "Republican as well as Democratic trade-marks," Vandenberg told listeners. The GOP imprint was "a clue to the kind of action which we shall continue to pursue."[17] Dewey called to congratulate him, although the senator was less than satisfied with his own performance. His doubts grew the next day. "Our Harry," he wrote Hazel, asked him to stop by that night for a chat. As heavy rain pelted the White House windows, Truman praised Vandenberg for a "grand" address. "If that isn't a strange reaction to a campaign speech, I never heard one," Vandenberg said. "It almost makes me wonder if it did the GOP any good."[18]

While the presidential campaign dominated the headlines, Vandenberg and Lovett were in constant contact over the Berlin blockade. In July came another round of meetings at apartment 500G as they labored over a warning to the Soviets. "After much consideration I drew the final form on my own Corona one midnight," Vandenberg wrote. State toned down the language—though Vandenberg insisted that his phrasing "disowned any trends toward war"—but the note was the sternest challenge to Soviet action in the fifteen years of diplomatic relations between the two powers. It served notice that discussions on the future of the divided city could only begin when the "intolerable" blockade ended.[19]

To yield in Berlin risked any chance of peace in Europe, Vandenberg told Lovett. "Our 'basic position' is that we cannot be *forced* out of Berlin by duress," he wrote. And if war came, "it must be plain to the world that it is Soviet Russia which has 'asked' for it." The United States could not "indulge the luxury of interminable 'notes' at a time when the rapidly complicating conditions in the Berlin air can precipitate a miscalculated accident almost any time."[20]

Fear of a showdown over Berlin weighed on him. In a long letter to the publisher of the *Detroit Free Press*, he reflected on World War II and acknowledged his "insulationist" role. He wondered whether an America that abstained from the last war—until Pearl Harbor made the point moot—might not have been in a position to force peace upon the combatants as a price of continued abstention. Then, he said, he had not been among those responsible for pushing the United States toward war.

In 1948 the situation was different. He was among those "unavoidably responsible" for decisions "fraught with harrowed days and sleepless nights. It is a tragic obligation, which sometimes makes life itself all but unbearable. The 'blood of our sons' has driven me to subordinate every other objective, in my public service, to the pursuit of honorable peace and to the organization of a global conscience." Nothing else mattered.

He wore his self-importance on his sleeve. Peace was elusive, and he fancied himself responsible for helping hold on to it. "But how? *How*? *How*?" he asked publisher John S. Knight. "Everything depends on our poor, fallible human judgments." If the last war taught him nothing else, he learned that "appeasement merely precipitates the jeopardy it seeks to avoid." In a world of calculated risk, were current policies too provocative—or too ineffectual? "If war comes," he said, "I suppose it will be said that the 'blood' will be on *my* head, in a small way, among others."[21]

Truman had a different agenda, fixed on winning an election. In October he floated, then killed, a scheme that left not just Vandenberg but his own State Department aghast. He proposed sending his old congressional crony, Chief Justice Fred Vinson of the Supreme Court, to Moscow to meet with Stalin as his personal emissary. Vandenberg saw it as political theater on the eve of the election, made all the more obvious by Truman's shifting explanations of the purpose of the trip. First he said Vinson would appeal to Stalin to resolve the Berlin impasse, a venture reminiscent of when he dispatched Harry Hopkins to Moscow in 1945 to break the deadlock over the United Nations Charter. (At the United Nations, French and British diplomats worried that the United States might act unilaterally on Berlin.) Later came a report that the United States was soliciting Soviet cooperation to control the use of atomic energy. This was also a sad excuse, Vandenberg wrote, since atomic energy was a multilateral issue then before the Security Council.[22]

On the morning of October 5, Truman called Marshall, who was vehemently opposed to the enterprise. That afternoon, Vandenberg was summoned to the White House. Minutes later, the White House called back and canceled. That night, the phone rang in 500G. Truman was on the line, asking Vandenberg and Connally to come round. Vandenberg hoped that Truman was going to explain the proposed Moscow trip, "but he never mentioned the Vinson Mission at all," wrote the senator, who later inferred that this meant that Truman had abandoned the idea after talking with Marshall. Instead, the president talked about how he, too, was committed to bipartisan foreign policy.

The president also floated the notion that he might call Stalin himself. "He was not announcing his purpose to do so," Vandenberg added. "He was quite casually exploring the idea. I made no comment except to say that I thought a bi-lingual phone conversation would be rather difficult." But it was evident that Truman was anxious for some gesture. After an hour, the senators left.[23]

Vandenberg was in Grand Rapids just two weeks before the election when James Reston called. His boss, Arthur Krock, had heard a rumor that Truman was contemplating a variation of the Vinson mission. Vandenberg wondered whether Truman thought he had acquiesced to the idea of the president phoning Stalin directly. He fired off a telegram to the president's secretary, Matt Connelly, cryptically repeating the Krock rumor and adding his own "urgent hope" that Truman not contemplate such an overture.[24]

The president had embarked on the last leg of his whistle-stop campaign and was not immediately reachable. But the next day he wired Vandenberg: "Nothing will be done without consultation with you." Here, on the eve of an election, at the height of a hotly partisan campaign, was a declaration of cooperation with the other party's leader on foreign policy. Vandenberg would not forget that.[25]

Nearly everyone thought the president was finished. But Vandenberg awoke at the Wardman Park the day after the election to learn that Truman had beaten Dewey. The surprise was general, though nowhere greater than among Washington's political class. When Vandenberg arrived at his office the next morning, he waved his cigar before his assembled staff. "You've got to give the little man credit," he said. "There he was, flat on his back. Everyone had counted him out but he came up fighting and won the battle. He did it all by himself. That's the kind of courage the American people admire."[26]

It was a brave sentiment. But he feared what might happen next.

CHAPTER 28

THE ALLIANCE

· · · · · · · · · · · · ·

Arthur Vandenberg had known reversals, but the 1948 election result really took him by surprise. Ever since his ringing speech of January 1945, the senator had enjoyed growing prestige as he yoked onetime isolationists and ardent interventionists into a consensus. For four years it had been a great run: for the Congress, for the country, for the free world—and especially for Arthur Vandenberg.

Now that was changing. Not only had Truman prevailed; Democrats had regained control of both houses of Congress. The Republicans' stunning defeat meant an end to Vandenberg's aura of indispensability. He had expected to play sage to a new president of his own party. Suddenly, he was neither chair of the Foreign Relations Committee nor president pro tempore of the Senate. He had to move out of the vice president's office with the crystal chandelier and relinquish the Cadillac.

Truman had won by bashing the GOP Congress. This was hardly conducive to bipartisanship. Republicans were restive and resentful. Amid their recriminations, some suggested they had cooperated too readily with the administration. And Truman himself? He replied cordially to Vandenberg's letter of congratulations but made no effort to reach out—even as newspaper reports circulated that he might ask Vandenberg to replace the retiring George Marshall as secretary of state. Was there anything to this rumor? The senator was inclined to dismiss it, but he knew Truman had an impetuous streak. Vandenberg summoned presidential confidant Leslie Biffle, the Senate secretary, who admitted he had been promoting the notion. "While the idea had much superficial charm and persuasion," Vandenberg noted in his diary, "it was not calculated to 'work'—particularly remembering the White House habit of going off 'half-cocked' as in the Wallace and Vinson incidents."[1]

If he accepted, it could mean the end of bipartisanship. The leader of the loyal opposition would have defected. To be offered the appointment publicly and decline publicly would not look good either. Bipartisanship defined him, but sometimes it left him few options.

As Senate Republicans regrouped, a leadership struggle broke out. A coterie of younger senators, including Vandenberg disciple Henry Cabot Lodge Jr., wanted the party to steer a more moderate course. They plotted to remove Robert Taft as chair of the Republican Policy Committee. In an article for the *Saturday Evening Post* titled "What's the Matter with the Republicans?" Lodge called for new leadership.[2]

Vandenberg was torn between the younger rebels, many of them his protégés, and his old cronies on the party's right. It was Taft allies who had bedeviled him over the Marshall Plan and NATO. But he cautioned against a fight. The GOP was hardly lost, he told Lodge: "I miss a basic note of testimony to the inherent power of Republicanism— even in the current debacle." If only forty thousand votes had changed in the right places, Dewey would be in the White House. This was hardly apocalyptic. (In Michigan, where Governor Sigler fell to the soap heir G. Mennen Williams, Gerald R. Ford, a young lawyer and an ardent admirer of Vandenberg's, was elected to represent the senator's congressional district after defeating an incumbent isolationist in the Republican primary.)

While Vandenberg declined to endorse the effort by Lodge and others to challenge Taft, he felt differently about Senator Kenneth "Lightning Ken" Wherry of Nebraska. The floor leader was the only Senate isolationist to survive the recent election. Wherry described his philosophy as "fundamentalist," rather than conservative, and he had routinely challenged the unanimous reports coming out of Vandenberg's Foreign Relations Committee. "While I would ask no Senator to yield up his independence of action to the judgment of others," Vandenberg declared, that was a price that had to be "partially" paid. Wherry, however, prevailed as minority leader.[3]

The bigger threat to bipartisanship came from the other side of the aisle. During Vandenberg's chairmanship of Foreign Relations, the GOP maintained a ratio of seven Republicans to six Democrats. With this composition came unanimous action on some forty-eight treaties and bills. At its heart was a strong chairman who respected the views of the other party as well as those of opponents within his own. Back in the majority—indeed, with a larger majority—Democrats saw no need for reciprocity. They took eight seats and left the GOP only five.

This was a slap in the face, giving Republicans all the more reason to grumble about the cost of cooperation. Vandenberg condemned the move on the floor as "the first partisan action" on the committee in four years. Democrats had managed overnight to imply that Republicans were somehow not entirely reliable partners in making foreign policy.

The question was whether Vandenberg could rise above the affront. As his friend Jay Hayden of the *Detroit News* wrote, "Behind the flouting of Vandenberg is very definite resentment of the prominence he has acquired in the public eye. President Truman has winced increasingly because of the popular assumption that someone beside himself was directing American foreign policy, whether this role was attributed to Vandenberg or to his own appointees."[4]

Truman nominated Dean Acheson as Marshall's successor, but informed Vandenberg, to the latter's chagrin, only an hour ahead of the announcement. The relationship between Vandenberg and Acheson was "one of mutual, but distantly chilly, respect."[5] Still, the grandiloquent senator and the patrician lawyer had worked well together in the UN Relief and Rehabilitation Administration fracas. Vandenberg dismissed critics who attacked Acheson's support for Alger Hiss. He shared a growing distrust of Hiss as the New Dealer faced perjury charges stemming from his denial of involvement with the Communist Party, but he could not condemn Acheson's refusal to turn his back on a friend. Hiss had been secretary of the U.S. delegation at the UN organizing conference in San Francisco. ("The well-nigh universal opinion five or six years ago," Vandenberg said, "was that Alger Hiss was an exceptionally competent and faithful public servant. I had many official contacts with him at the time. I doubt it occurred to *any* of us that he had any such communist relationships as he has subsequently confessed.") While Taft did question Acheson's anti-communist credentials, Vandenberg found him "one of the few possible Truman appointees who has first-hand knowledge of all the dreadful complexities in our foreign affairs." Besides, the Soviet press condemned the nominee in tones sometimes reserved for the senior senator from Michigan.

After the Foreign Relations Committee approved the nomination unanimously, Connally released a brief statement, purportedly an excerpt from Acheson's closed-door testimony, designed to reassure critics that the nominee was not soft on communism. "It is my view," the statement read, "that communism as a doctrine is economically fatal to a free society and to human rights and fundamental freedom. Communism as an aggressive factor in world conquest is fatal to independent governments and to free peoples." Acheson, ever a felicitous writer, subscribed to the message, but the words had been written by Arthur Vandenberg, who would maintain a vestige of bipartisan harmony no matter who had won the election.[6]

For five crucial years, through two presidents and five secretaries of state, Vandenberg had been the constant in American foreign policy. Wounded by his diminished role, lacking enthusiasm for Acheson's nomination, he nonetheless threw his prestige behind the appointment. Acheson was confirmed, 86–6. The new secretary sent a note of thanks but showed no haste to consult with the one Republican who had once been indispensable. As columnist Stewart Alsop noted, "The bipartisan basis of foreign policy has been most gravely weakened."[7]

Vandenberg sensed the new climate. "The form of things . . . has changed, and responsibilities and initiatives have shifted," he said in February. But the need for cooperation remained: "In my view nothing has happened to absolve either Democrats or Republicans from continuing to put their country first."[8]

With the North Atlantic community poised to add Norway and Denmark, the question of American military aid grew more pressing. The

French, Vandenberg learned, were judging the value of the alliance by the scope of American supplies they might expect. The senator worried, lest divvying up hardware take precedence over broader principles.

President Truman had called in his inaugural address for ratification of the NATO treaty. Coming so soon after the Marshall Plan, NATO represented a dramatic departure for American policy.

"The basic question we have to settle is whether 'economic stability' can precede the creation of a greater sense of physical security" for the European democracies, Vandenberg wrote to a constituent. Could the Marshall Plan restore prosperity in the shadow of the Red Army? "I am inclined," he continued, "to think that 'physical security' is a prerequisite to the kind of long-range economic planning which Western Europe requires." (The Soviet Union took a different view, condemning the plan as a further effort by the United States to encircle Russia and dominate the world.)[9]

Vandenberg and Connally were bothered by two points in the proposed treaty: a pledge by all parties to consider an attack against one as an attack against all, and the absence of a reference to constitutional process. Acheson revised the language to require each signatory, in the event of an attack on a member state, to act "as it deems necessary, including the use of armed force." Thus was military action not automatic. In addition, a new provision called for its terms to be "carried out by the parties in accordance with their respective constitutional processes." Vandenberg also added a pledge that member states would provide "continuous and effective self-help" as well as mutual aid.[10]

The Foreign Relations Committee conducted sixteen days of hearings. At every step, Vandenberg was careful to build support among skeptical GOP colleagues. Two Republican senators not on the committee were allowed to sit in on the hearings. When Democrats complained about allowing the guests to question some of the ninety-six witnesses at length, Vandenberg threatened to withdraw if they were not allowed to proceed.

The senator argued that a war between Russians and Western Europeans would inevitably involve the United States. So Americans must make their position clear. Their objective was defensive; the treaty was not intended as a provocation. In fact, it was designed "to notify Soviet Russia in advance that she cannot start any . . . 'armed aggression' with any hope that she can 'divide and conquer' western civilization one country at a time (as both the Kaiser and Hitler undertook to do)."[11]

Vandenberg said Hitler would never have embarked on his disastrous course "if he had had any serious reasons to believe that it might bring him into armed collision with the United States." (The irony was thick. Of course it had been American neutrality laws, championed so forcefully by Arthur Vandenberg, that had persuaded Hitler otherwise.) "If an appropriate North Atlantic pact is written," he continued, "I think it will exactly reverse this psychology so far as Mr. Stalin is concerned, as and when he contemplates World War Three. Under such circumstances, I very much doubt whether World War Three happens." These were the words of a changed man.

Vandenberg thought it was crucial to clarify the limits within which the treaty would operate before debate moved to the Senate floor. So a structured exchange between Vandenberg and Acheson was arranged. Vandenberg asked, What action would require a response from the treaty signatories? Acheson replied: An armed attack.

Would application of the treaty cease "the first moment that the Security Council has taken measures necessary to maintain international peace and security?" Yes, said Acheson. With that, Vandenberg had disposed of two chief objections.

To those who worried that a regional security treaty would subvert the United Nations, he offered reassurance: "If the general membership of the United Nations is faithful to its obligation to the Treaty of the United Nations, this treaty [NATO] never becomes operative at all."

Acheson concurred: "That is certainly true."

Foreign Relations voted out the resolution, 13–0. That was only the start of the debate. Vandenberg may have changed, but some of his colleagues had not.[12]

During the hearings and throughout the spring, Hazel remained in Michigan. Her cancer was worse. Vandenberg frequently ended his day at his desk at the Wardman Park, writing her a letter. In mid-May came a visit from President Dutra of Brazil, a friend from the Rio Pact days. Without Hazel's guidance, the lonely senator fretted over protocol. He informed the Brazilian foreign minister that Hazel was "out of circulation," but that he hoped to greet the president. "When I met the old gentleman at the airport," Vandenberg told his wife, "he seemed quite overcome."[13]

At about that time, the Dulleses and Acheson were bound for Paris aboard Truman's new plane, preparing to resume talks with Russian, British, and French foreign ministers. Vandenberg looked upon the expedition with longing. "I kinda wish I was going along (with you)," the senator confided to his wife.[14]

His own health was below par, although he told Hazel his chronic headaches were no worse. Some of his fingers were a little numb, but people kept saying "how well you look," so that he could assure her, "I suspect there's nothing to worry about except the inevitable disintegration of old age."[15] A recent poll of senators for *Look* recognized Lodge as "handsomest," but Vandenberg was named by his peers as "most statesmanlike."

Vandenberg wrote Hazel of others' deterioration, too. In May came the funeral for James Forrestal. The nation's first secretary of defense, suffering from delusions and paranoia, had leapt to his death at the Bethesda Naval Hospital. "This was poor, old Jimmy Forrestal's 'goodbye' day," Vandenberg wrote Hazel. "And it was one of those things which tore me into emotional bits (as it would have *you*). It was a beautiful, clear day—but sharp and cold (and I all but froze in the Memorial Amphitheatre at Arlington)."

He had sat with Truman for the full military funeral, which drew nearly six thousand mourners. "Of course Jimmy wasn't very big—but the casket looked so little," he commented. Vandenberg found himself reflecting upon his own impromptu service with a somber Jackie band in northern Michigan three decades before. He was reminded of the time they had clambered off a train in the middle of nowhere to stand before the crude cabin of a mother and father whose soldier son had died. At Arlington, the senator wept when the navy band played Handel's "Largo." As the army band struck up "Onward, Christian Soldiers," he wrote Hazel, "I thought I would expire." Forrestal had fought alongside him in the Cold War: "There was something about it all which was so intimately tragic and yet so spiritually exalted I am sure Jimmy did not die in vain."[16]

Late in June, Acheson returned from the Paris meeting of foreign ministers with heartening news. The "Russkies" were on the defensive, "undoubtedly under great pressure from their satellites to get East-West trade going again," Vandenberg reported. The Marshall Plan's Economic Cooperation Administration and the NATO treaty were paying dividends, as Western Europe's economies began to stir and its ragged armies began to regroup. "This is the time of all times to keep up our peace momentum in Western Europe and not let down for a single instant—which means ECA, Atlantic Pact [NATO] and arms implementation."[17]

Dulles told Vandenberg that "the Politburo knows that it has lost the cold war in Western Europe; that it's nervous about holding the European satellites; that it's preparing to concentrate largely on Asia; and that its interest in keeping up these four-power conferences is largely for face-saving purposes." Vandenberg was confirmed in his opinion that the danger of a shooting war—over Berlin or elsewhere—was waning.[18]

He relaxed enough to even have some fun at the expense of his colleague Connally. "You know how he is always trying to talk me out of making Senate speeches," Vandenberg told Hazel. "Well—a few days ago he told me he thought it would be smart (when we opened the [NATO] pact debate) if neither one of us had much to say until the opposition opens up." Connally said he would speak no more than ten minutes. "Oh, I can't do that," Vandenberg replied, feigning great seriousness. "This is too important and I personally intend to open up with the speech of my life." Within days a Washington paper reported that Connally had sequestered himself in his office, "sending out word that he couldn't be disturbed because he was writing 'the speech of his life.' " Vandenberg "got a great kick out of that."[19]

In late June, Senator James Kem of Missouri introduced an amendment to the European Recovery Program appropriations bill requiring that aid be cut off to any country that nationalized any basic industries. Vandenberg thought this was no way to fight the Soviets. "Most of the ECA countries in Western Europe have some degree of 'socialism' in their governments," he told one constituent. But between Western European socialism and Eastern European communism yawned "a vast and ugly gap." The former, Vandenberg said, was characterized by a belief in God and the freedom of worship, by democratic governments and by human rights. Western Europeans, he said, had demonstrated that "they believe in peace (American style) and are opposed to armed aggression (Soviet style)." Maintaining their independence was "the greatest practical protection which we in the United States can have."[20] There should be no political tests for economic purposes. "Any such efforts would probably generate *political* resentments which would drive the people of these countries still farther 'left,' " he wrote. "If our friends abroad refuse to go along and we withdraw our aid, there will be an early collapse which will be terribly costly to *us* not only in economics but in renewed (and perhaps fatal) encouragement to Communism's cold war."

From another angle, critics worried that recovering European nations might produce goods that would compete with American exports or even flood the American market—that is, they might become too strong as capitalists. Vandenberg acknowledged the irony inherent in helping potential competitors. "I sometimes wonder," he observed, "whether *this* particular conundrum can ever be resolved except on [European Cooperation administrator Paul] Hoffman's theory that world peace and stabilization can create new markets for *everybody* by creating higher standards of living at least in the civilized parts of the earth."

He recognized the paradox: if Hoffman was wrong, the United States might win the Cold War but lose its economic advantage. "We cannot afford to jeopardize the former trend nor to continue the latter," he said. "I sometimes wonder whether the wit of man is equal to the simultaneous solution of both questions."[21]

With the Senate chamber closed for remodeling, debate on the NATO treaty opened on July 5, 1949, in the old Senate and Supreme Court meeting room. There, history offered precedent, for in that intimate space the Monroe Doctrine had been debated. Vandenberg spoke on the second day. He was on his feet for nearly two hours. The arguments were familiar, but his words carried the conviction that what had begun in San Francisco in 1945 was culminating in Washington now. Make no mistake in assessing the threat of communism, he told his colleagues: "We are the final target, though other independent peoples are in nearer jeopardy." Americans could argue themselves out of ratifying the pact, "but we cannot thereby argue ourselves out of the jeopardy which the Pact seeks to minimize."

Isolation was a thing of the past. "Times have changed," he declared. "Once upon a time we were a comfortably isolated land. Now we are unavoidably the leader and the reliance of freemen throughout this free world. We cannot escape from our prestige nor from its hazard." He recalled what the hero of his adolescence, Theodore Roosevelt, had said—that the United States had no choice but to play a great part in the world. The only choice was whether to play it well or badly. "We cannot turn back the clock. We cannot sail by the old and easier charts. This has been determined for us by the march of events." The prose was clean, simple, direct. For once, the billowing adjectives fell away.

The United States had played its part well in winning two world wars, but not so well at Yalta and Potsdam. The nation had muffed the role in China—as if it could have done otherwise—but played it well in Latin America, San Francisco, and more recently Berlin. Finally, the senator said, "we have played it so well in the cooperative rejuvenation of Western Europe that the momentum of confidence and peace is in formidable stride." The next act in this performance must be Senate approval of the North Atlantic Treaty.

The treaty's strength lay in binding together for action. That, said

Vandenberg, was "as powerful as an atomic bomb . . . [a] conclusive warning that 300 million people, united in competent self-defense, will never allow an armed aggressor to divide and conquer them pursuant to the pattern of the rapes of yesterday."[22]

On his desk the following morning was a message left by a voice from the near past: "Mr. Cordell Hull called to give his warmest congratulations to the Senator on 'one of the greatest speeches ever made.' "[23]

But isolationist impulses died hard. Taft joined the fight against the treaty. "The Taft speech will lengthen the battle because it lends a certain respectability to the opposition," Vandenberg wrote Hazel, "and some of those who wouldn't have dared to stand up on their own will now join the anti-parade." He had wanted to believe that Taft would not oppose him, but confided that "my friend from Ohio has given me a first-class headache tonight."[24]

He predicted no more than sixteen no votes, especially after one freshman declared the Vandenberg Resolution the "Magna Carta of new hope for freedom in a Communist-assaulted world." The decision to bring the bill to a vote would require assembling a quorum—no easy task in midsummer. It took an hour, and then only forty-nine senators, a bare quorum, could be corralled. "The other half is out of town and of course, all the House is gone," he wrote Hazel. "Nice way to run the country! I have never seen such contagious irresponsibility!" He was himself in pain—though he wouldn't say so—but he was there.[25]

On July 21, when the rest of the senators returned, the treaty was approved by a vote of 82–13. Vandenberg was deeply relieved. This was the climax, "one of the big dates," of his career. As he boasted to Hazel, "It all stems from the Vandenberg Resolution which you saw a-borning in 500G with dear old Bob Lovett as the midwife."[26]

Republicans supported the treaty—supported Vandenberg—by a vote of 32–11.

A major hurdle still loomed. Funds had to be appropriated to give the new alliance military muscle: European armies had to be rebuilt. How much should the United States spend to equip the French? How many

American troops should be deployed in Western Europe? These were grounds for fresh controversy. Even Vandenberg had reservations about the haste with which the administration was bent on sending soldiers back across the Atlantic.

Vandenberg and Acheson, two egos jockeying for their place in history, would have to hash this out. "Dean called up this afternoon and asked if he could drop in at the flat for a drink on his way home," the senator wrote his wife, "and drop in he did. It was slightly reminiscent of the old Lovett days." Acheson spoke of his frustrations on several fronts: Korea, China, atomic weapons, rearming Europe. "I wouldn't take his job for a million a week," Vandenberg confided. Still, the senator was genial and helpful, and the secretary of state asked if he could come back soon. This was just the sort of contact Vandenberg had missed in the previous few months—contact that Acheson had withheld until that point. (He never did fully appreciate the sincerity of Vandenberg's passion for consensus.) "It would be funny," Vandenberg told Hazel, "if everything were not so desperately serious these days."

At the end of July the Senate took up renewal of appropriations for the Marshall Plan: "Just one more Pandora's box," Vandenberg wrote. He kept his impatience private, as he kept his illness, the headaches, the backaches that left him in more or less continuous pain. His optimism was guarded. Of the Marshall Plan he wrote, "I think we can save enough of the pieces to keep Hoffman going. But I get so damned sick of that little band of GOP isolationists who are always in the way that I could scream."[27]

CHAPTER 29

· · · · · · · · · · · ·

THINGS FALL APART

· · · · · · · · · · · ·

"I must confess I am very tired," Vandenberg wrote early in 1949. He was counting down the days until the end of his term, though it was nearly four years away. Limping off the Senate floor, he felt the weight of far more than the NATO deliberations. Hazel was battling cancer in Grand Rapids. Their younger daughter, Betsy, was there, too, in the wake of a bitter divorce. Arthur Junior—"Ash"—looking beyond his father's final term, had accepted a job with Nelson Rockefeller's sprawling enterprise in São Paulo. Barbara was drinking too much; possibly all three of the children were. At the end of another long day on Capitol Hill, Vandenberg longed for nothing so much as a rubdown in the Senate gym.[1]

When Arthur Junior departed for Brazil, he had served his father as "indispensable" chief aide and alter ego for nearly twenty years. "Our partnership has been a very precious thing in my life, dear boy," "Pops" wrote to him. "We haven't talked together about such things, but I think you *know*." It also appears that father and son never spoke about Arthur Junior's homosexuality. The senator shared his awareness with his closest friend, A. B. Smith. To his son he wrote, "Just be true to yourself. I can even shorten that up. BE YOURSELF!"[2]

The Wardman apartment had become a lonely place. All of Washington—increasingly partisan Washington—could seem that way. The days when Bob Lovett would stop by to plan the Atlantic alliance over a martini were gone. It felt as if world events were evolving without him. The Berlin airlift had relieved one crisis, but West Germans still worried about the Red Army rolling through to the Rhine. The European democracies had a fragile treaty, but their bedraggled armies had few men, fewer guns, and mounting fear. Vandenberg was more wistful than bitter about the way the world had changed. With the election of 1948, Truman achieved a legitimacy that his sudden ascent to the presidency had not bestowed. New Democratic majorities made it less critical for the White House to cultivate both sides of the congressional aisles. Acheson depended less on Vandenberg to get a bill passed than Marshall had. And theirs was nothing like Vandenberg's intimate work with Lovett and friendship with Marshall.

There was a clock running somewhere. Vandenberg had a sense that he was racing against time—against the new political realities, against his own health—to cement crucial blocks of postwar policy.

The latest crisis was in China, where developments all but begged for partisan recrimination in Congress. After World War II, the struggle between the nationalists of Chiang Kai-shek and the communists of Mao Zedong had become a full-blown civil war. Now, the Nationalists were losing popular support. As China slipped out of Chiang's grasp, the State Department had seen enough to be convinced that further support was futile—and that the Chinese communists, unlike their Moscow comrades, were said to be agrarians and not so bellicose. But congressional Republicans, who had long backed the Nationalists, were not ready to accept the administration's verdict.

Early in 1948 Vandenberg had presented a bill authorizing a third of a billion dollars in economic aid to the Nationalist Chinese, with another $100 million in military assistance. The situation was "touch and go," he told colleagues, although "China is a maze of imponderables." He hedged his pledge with warnings that the United States was in no position to underwrite a civil war. And in no way would he support sending American troops. While the importance of "saving" China could not be exaggerated, there were limits to American resources, "and boundaries to our miracles." The bill passed.[3]

By late 1948, everything had gone wrong. The Nationalists were on the run, and Republicans, reeling from their election losses, were pointing fingers. Alf Landon claimed that the congressional GOP, in thrall to bipartisan policy, had been "gulled" by the administration.

Vandenberg bristled, even as he was unsure what to do (as was the White House). "We have poured more than two billion dollars into China in the last few years," he wrote in December, "but pouring money is not enough—as we have learned to our sorrow."[4]

Early in 1949 the Nationalists surrendered Beijing. Vandenberg, Connally, Eaton, and Bloom were summoned to a meeting in the White House Cabinet Room with Truman, Barkley, and Acheson. Only half of the military aid granted Chiang had been delivered; much of the balance awaited shipment. The president's advisers argued for suspending export licenses because the collapse of the Nationalists appeared imminent. This would block the shipment of any more equipment, which otherwise seemed likely to fall into the hands of Mao Zedong.

Truman canvassed the room. "Two or three of the gentlemen immediately fell in with the idea of stopping all export licenses forthwith," Vandenberg wrote in his diary. Then the president turned to him. Chiang was finished, Vandenberg acknowledged, "but there is something here vastly more important than what happens to $60 million worth of supplies." Suspending shipments was tantamount to withdrawing recognition of the Nationalist government—telling Mao the war was over. "We seal China's doom," he declared. "If we take *this* step at *this* fatefully inept moment, we shall never be able to shake off the charge that *we* are the ones who gave poor China the final push into disaster."

Instead, Vandenberg counseled inaction. Within weeks, events would be sorted out anyway, "*by China* and *in China*. . . . This blood must not be on *our* hands." No one spoke. Then Truman said, "Of course." The conference was over. Aid was gradually cut off, quietly, without sudden impact.[5]

But the China question was far from settled. Indeed, "Who lost China?" became a rallying cry for Republicans. Finger-pointing followed in the summer of 1949, when the Truman administration asked the Senate to confirm the appointment of State Department China expert R. Walton Butterworth as assistant secretary of state for Far Eastern affairs. Several Republicans decided to block Butterworth because of his support of the failed policy toward China.

Vandenberg refused to join the chorus of critics, but neither could he absolve the nominee. "I presume you have been reading about the flare-up . . . over our China policy," he wrote Hazel. "I had to get into it—couldn't stave it off any longer. If we ever needed a 'fresh view,' it's in *that* spot."[6] He could not find a bipartisan solution, but he could avoid joining his party's hysteria. When the time came for the Butterworth vote, his voice, raspier, low and stern, said, "Present."

For three years the Foreign Relations Committee had approved policies of far-reaching significance, policies that helped rebuild a good piece of the planet and protect freedom for tens of millions of people. All this had come on 13–0 votes. It had been a bravura performance. For Vandenberg to vote merely "present" reflected a rupture in the solidarity that he, more than anyone, inspired and cherished.

The headaches returned. Friends remarked on his limp, on how he had to turn his body to look over his shoulder. A. B. Smith wanted to get Vandenberg to University of Michigan Hospital in Ann Arbor, where a lesion on the left lung could be examined for cancer. But the senator refused to leave the capital while Congress debated military appropriations for NATO.

In the summer of 1949, Senate reporters occupied a temporary press gallery in a corridor off the old Supreme Court chamber. Vandenberg liked to linger there, slumped in one of its big black leather chairs and holding forth for the press corps. He was among friends there. He did not want to lose this. The humor and sly talk, tactical chatter and fanciful speculations, were his oxygen. Dr. Smith was beside himself.

The essence of the NATO alliance lay in its commitment to cooperative action, not the size of arms shipments to its members or funding for uniforms and training. Accordingly, the senator had withheld judgment on the scope of the Military Assistance Program that backed up the NATO treaty. Then the president, in July 1949, submitted a request for $1.45 billion in arms—with no prior consultation with the ranking Republican. This sent Vandenberg back to his typewriter. "My first impression is that the program must be rewritten and curtailed to get action at this session," Vandenberg wrote. Truman was asking for too much, too soon.[7]

The NATO treaty had called for an advisory council and defense committee that would produce plans for "self-help and mutual aid." But before any such council or committee had acted, Vandenberg fumed, Truman was asking for presidential authority to "sell, loan or give away the entire national defense establishment to anybody at any time and on any terms whenever [the president] thinks it is 'important to the national interest of the United States.'"[8]

And in any case, the goal of the Military Assistance Program was not to build a massive force to match the Red Army. The goal was to be *ready* to build such a force. "I do not believe there is any middle ground between this concept which still depends chiefly upon potentials and the complete rearmament which would turn Western Europe and America into an armed camp. . . . It seems to me that we must choose between 'potentials' and 'forces-in-being.' I choose 'potentials.'"[9]

"I served blunt notice today that I simply would not support the present bill," the senator told Hazel. "It's almost unbelievable in its grant of unlimited power to the Chief Executive." This was the power of a "war lord." Foreign Relations colleagues of both parties agreed. Walter George, Cabot Lodge, William Fulbright, Alex Wiley—all of them "backed me up one hundred per cent."

The administration had to write a new bill. "The old bipartisan business is certainly 'out the window' on this one," Vandenberg continued. "Yet I don't want to be shoved over into a position of seeming hostility to the *objective* (in which I deeply believe). So it's a pretty tight 'poker game' between Acheson and me."[10]

Vandenberg had been here before, bristling at executive overreach, tempering expectations, finding a way to make things work. But this new tone in what had been such a carefully cultivated bipartisan atmosphere was not lost on the press. Joseph Alsop observed that between Truman's election and Connally's long-simmering resentment of Vandenberg's prestige, bipartisan policy had been "utterly abandoned."

On August 2 the Foreign Relations and Armed Services Committees met in joint session. Acheson testified, as did Secretary of Defense Louis Johnson. Vandenberg laid out the "facts of life." As he told Hazel, "I gave 'em an ultimatum—write a new and reasonable bill or you will get no bill at all and it will be your fault!"

Truman's men got the message.[11]

Three days later, Acheson was back. "They have totally surrendered on eighty per cent of my criticisms," Vandenberg crowed. The new bill was still a little generous for his liking—that was the nature of compromise—but it removed Truman's blank check and specified recipient countries. "We have killed the 'war lord' bill," he wrote Walter Lippmann. But it took "the most vigorously candid speech" of his life before the joint committee. He was amused, after the administration backed down, to have each of the emissaries confide that they too had opposed the original draft.[12]

Republican cooperation could not be granted on a "me too" basis. The truth of the matter, Vandenberg told Lippmann, "is that the Republican contribution to 'bipartisan foreign policy' has always been the exact reverse of 'me too.' The only difference is that heretofore the 'surrenders,' if you want to call them that, have occurred in private and in advance."

The Senate and the State Department turned to wrangling over specific language. Meanwhile, in a bipartisan rebuke to the administration's heavy-handed request, the House of Representatives, despite a Democratic majority, voted in mid-August to cut the proposed funds by half. "The House sure 'put the crimps' into the arms bill!" Vandenberg reported to Hazel. "And I don't blame 'em much—the thing has been so miserably handled. Now Acheson and company are yelling to high heaven to help." And now the alterations Vandenberg wanted looked altogether mild. "Foster [Dulles] and I can 'write our own ticket,'" he observed. "But I don't propose to let them belatedly dump their problem in my lap. We'll help 'em trim their bill . . . into possible shape. But it's not going to be *my* bill." Soon Vandenberg and Acheson were meeting again to see what could be salvaged. Temporarily, at least—and more by necessity than temperament—bipartisan cooperation was restored.[13]

Yet such cooperation stood on shaky ground. Vandenberg told Walter Lippmann that no one could count any longer on the big majorities he had obtained so recently to approve the United Nations or the Marshall Plan.

The administration had pared its military aid request by nearly $300 million, but Vandenberg and Dulles demanded that it come down to an even billion dollars—half to be spent immediately, half to contract for matériel for the following year. In mid-September the joint committee approved the revised draft by a vote of 30–3. On September 20, his every movement dogged by pain, Vandenberg reassured colleagues on the Senate floor that a divided committee had found common ground. The final version of the bill included initiatives from both sides of the aisle. It was, he told his wife, "a tough day for the 'old man.'"

His speech that day was not one of his carefully prepared orations. He had no manuscript: "I proposed to 'take it easy' and just chat for not more than forty-five minutes at the outside." But the usual happened. Isolationists, mainly, peppered him with questions. All told, he was on his feet for two and a half hours. "When it was over I went straight to my hideout and lay down for two hours." This, he said, was "the last of my really big efforts."[14]

Doctors were advising immediate surgery on his left lung—they had been pressuring him for months. Although there was much work left to do to reconcile the House and Senate versions of the arms bill, Vandenberg predicted that by the end of September he would be ready to leave for Ann Arbor—"and I *mean* that I shall be ready." On September 22 the Mutual Defense Assistance bill, as amended by Vandenberg, won Senate approval, 55–24. The prolonged negotiations had drained him. "How I wish I could resign this devastating job right now," he complained. "The whole country is in a state of nerves. Everybody is under tension. Nothing is right." It was as if he were transferring his own pain to the country at large, much as he had long identified his own security needs with those of the American people.

"Everybody is mad about *something*," he wrote. Some note of civility was missing. But the nation had survived worse. There was the consolation of the plaque on his desk with the phrase "This too shall pass."[15]

He did not want to face what was coming in Ann Arbor. He was practically looking for excuses. The Soviet Union nearly gave him one. On September 23 the Joint Committee on Atomic Energy was summoned to "a very solemn" secret meeting. The Russians, they were told, had exploded their first atomic bomb. The American monopoly was gone.

"This is now a different world," Vandenberg wrote.[16] "Some of the boys who voted to gut the arms program are pretty sick of what they did."[17] A new chapter in the Cold War had begun.

"The first result, in my personal life," Vandenberg wrote Hazel, "is several insistent demands that I do not leave Washington during the next few weeks." This was what he wanted to hear, that the country could not get along without him. It was wishful thinking. "I have no illusions that I am indispensable," he told Hazel, as he thought to stave off major surgery, "but you might read this to the good doctor and get his reaction." Their friend was adamant. "If A.B. thinks it's a cold hard fact of life that I have no further option, then let's go ahead as planned and as soon as possible."[18]

Days after Vandenberg limped from the Senate floor, lifted himself out of a black leather chair in the press gallery, absented himself from the ashtray-laden hearing rooms, he was flown to Ann Arbor. Just a week after the report of the Russian bomb, he was eased onto a gurney at the University of Michigan hospital.

The surgery, on October 3, took five hours. Doctors removed half of Vandenberg's cancerous left lung and declared the operation a success. They prescribed three months' rest. This was not a welcome order. How could bipartisanship survive without him?

When Winston Churchill telegraphed a get-well message, Vandenberg replied, "Our job is *not* finished until we have stabilized a *free world* of *free men*."[19]

THE UPSTAIRS ROOM

· · · · · · · · · · · ·

Vandenberg wasted no time in reassuring Washington of his imminent return. "My 'job' is far from finished—if we are to have a decent peace without World War Three," he wrote, five days after the surgery. He spoke of January, and the coming session of the Congress: "I hope to play my full part yet in making collective peace effective. That is what keeps me going."[1]

Doctors foresaw a lengthy convalescence but did nothing to dampen the senator's hopes of serving out his term. Later in October he was transported back to the house on Morris Avenue in Grand Rapids. He envisioned retirement there come 1952. He wanted to write more than an autobiography. He wanted not only to justify his approach to foreign policy, but also to define practical bipartisanship. So often had he felt misunderstood—on both sides of the aisle.

He was still resting in Grand Rapids in December 1949 when the *Washington Times* worried that Republicans might revolt "to the extent of junking bipartisan foreign policy." Missing, the editorial observed, was Vandenberg's gift for setting dangerously complex issues "in their proper perspective in language that everyone can understand."[2]

But the senator's recuperation was slow. His back pain persisted. Doctors and friends beseeched him to rest quietly in a warm climate— but he had other thoughts. It became apparent that his return to the arena might actually spur his recovery. The week before Christmas 1949, with Hazel's condition serious but stable and Arthur far from fit, they flew back to Washington. It was a dubious decision. Back at the Wardman that first night, Vandenberg was in too much pain to sleep. At midnight he called his doctor, who prescribed a sedative.

"I have a press conference scheduled for tomorrow," he explained. "I want to be ready for it." The doctor challenged him. Vandenberg was adamant. "Look here, doc," he said, "let's get this straight. I'm paying you to fix me up so I can get there—not to keep me away."[3]

And kept away he was not. His chauffeur Hubert helped him climb out of the car as he winced with pain. At the press conference, the sort of reunion with newspaper friends that felt like a homecoming, he spoke of his fixed faith in bipartisanship. He said he would be back on the Senate floor for the session that would open in January 1950. This struck some of the reporters as too optimistic.

As the days went by, he remained confined to the apartment. Then he was admitted to Georgetown University Hospital. Hazel went in as well, and they were assigned adjacent rooms. He missed the opening session and listened to Truman's State of the Union address on the radio.

He relinquished his seat on the Atomic Energy Committee, releasing a statement suggesting the United States offer to abandon work on a new hydrogen bomb if the Soviets agreed to effective international control of atomic energy.

In February 1950 he wrote in his diary of a Republican committee's effort to draft a statement of party principles. The project originated with colleagues wary of working with the Democratic president. They "were frankly aiming at so-called 'Bi-Partisan Foreign Policy' in general," Vandenberg wrote, "and, I suspect, at *me* in particular." They tiptoed around identifying the missing leader by name, but his absence only increased their restiveness.

In the end, while the committee was less than enthusiastic about his influence, he wrote with relief, "It *did* recognize and validate some of the *fundamentals* underlying it." Many of the words in the committee's report were Vandenberg's—international in tone, emphasizing the danger of communism. ("We support aid to those states resisting Communism but such aid should be given only if it is essential to our national security.") Isolationism had not reclaimed the party, and there would be no stalemate between Republican partisans and the Truman administration. "It is chiefly Senator Vandenberg that the country must thank for what success has been achieved so far in bi-partisanship," the *Washington Post* observed.[4]

Yet for all the praise, events would roll on with Vandenberg on the sidelines. In a recent speech Acheson had described an American security perimeter in the Far East that omitted the Korean Peninsula, split at war's end between a communist regime north of the thirty-eighth parallel and an autocratic republic allied with the United States in the south. The north's belligerent dictator, Kim Il Sung, saw an opportunity to unite the peninsula under his rule. He asked his Soviet patrons to support his strategy. Stalin acquiesced, and in January 1950 North Korean troops launched a surprise attack on the south. Seoul, so close to the border, was quickly overrun. South Korean forces and the American army division stationed in Korea fell back in retreat. In a matter of weeks they yielded most of the peninsula, withdrawing to a small enclave around the coastal city of Pusan.

South Korea appealed to the United Nations. The Security Council (with Russia conveniently absent) approved dispatching an international force, dominated by the United States, to push back the invaders in what President Truman described as a "police action."

Here was the United Nations in action. But Vandenberg was reduced to following the conflict on radio and in the newspapers. While in private he was caustic, telling a constituent, "the Administration virtually notified any communist aggressors that they could have the right of way," he nevertheless applauded Truman's response to North Korea's aggression. "You have done a courageous and forceful thing," he wrote the president.[5]

Vandenberg had suspected that conflict with a communist insurgency somewhere was bound to come sooner or later. For most of his Senate career he would have been in the thick of the crisis, breathless with exertion, issuing statements, huddling with colleagues, helping to find a way forward, and then making a big speech. Now he was a bystander.

Nor would he be front and center when Washington witnessed the rise of an acid-tongued demagogue from Wisconsin, freshman Republican senator Joseph McCarthy, who saw communists under every American bed. Both parties had used fear of communists to rebuild Europe and develop the NATO alliance. Vandenberg had even been said to advise Truman to "scare hell out of the American people." McCarthy was doing just that, but he trafficked in falsehood and innuendo, with no regard for the reputations of those he attacked.

As McCarthy lobbed accusations at the State Department, many Democrats began to pine for what the *New York Times* described as "the clear, authoritative voice that rises above the buzz of party politics to define American policy to the world." More than any other American, the *Times* continued, Vandenberg could line up "the massive popular support that has been our greatest asset in the post-war years." His legislative stamp drew on "vision, experience and good-tempered statesmanship."[6] What ironies abound in a democracy! Democrats controlled the White House and Congress, yet it was the Republican Vandenberg to whom leaders turned their thoughts.

In the spring of 1950, as Republican attacks on Acheson and the State Department gained momentum, Vandenberg wrote Paul Hoffman: "I have tried to be scrupulously careful not to 'lecture' my colleagues from behind the 'iron curtain' of my convalescence." But he could not resist observing that the Marshall Plan had originated in a spirit of bipartisan cooperation, which enabled "our greatest safety in the presence of external hazards." Further, the Economic Cooperation Administration was chiefly responsible "for reversing the corroding gloom which threatened Western Civilization two years ago, and which might have brought the 'iron curtain' to the very rims of the Atlantic." The value of that reversal, in lives and dollars, was incalculable.[7]

At Vandenberg's request, Hoffman released his letter to the public. Truman understood its import. Writing to Vandenberg, he recounted his own involvement, as a senator, in legislation for postwar planning. He, too, recognized what security bipartisanship had brought about. Indeed, "the breakup of the bipartisan foreign policy at this time would mean but one thing—victory for Russia in Europe," he continued, "and in all probability definite approach to a shooting war."[8]

A week later, Truman wrote again. "You just don't realize what a vacuum there has been in the Senate and in the operation of our foreign policy since you left." Younger senators—Lodge, Wayne Morse, John Sherman Cooper—were anxious to carry on the crusade but lacked Vandenberg's stature. "It is very seldom that men really become statesmen while they are still alive, in the minds of the people and their associates," Truman said. Such encomiums vaulted Vandenberg into a marble realm.[9]

But the cancer was taking its toll. Through the spring of 1950 he was in and out of Georgetown Hospital. In April he underwent surgery to remove a tumor near his spine. Once again, doctors termed the procedure successful, but he was recovering only slowly and remained hospitalized. In the next room, Hazel, losing her own battle with cancer, sank into a swamp of painkillers.

Leading Republicans paid visits. First and foremost was Taft, of all people. When Clare Boothe Luce came in, Vandenberg drew from his bedside table the acceptance speech he had never delivered in 1948.

He was back at the Wardman Park on May 19, when, with help from a nurse and a daughter, he put on a suit, rode down the elevator, and climbed into the car that Hubert drove to Capitol Hill. Southern Democrats were filibustering a bill to establish the Fair Employment Practices Commission. Some Republicans preferred not to take a stand on this early civil rights measure. As the minority, they depended upon a coalition with Southern Democrats for leverage on domestic legislation.

Pain coiled about the senator's spine. Each step was an effort as he limped through the echoing corridors for the first time in months. With a roll call in progress, his arrival came unannounced. For colleagues who had not seen him since the winter, the pale apparition shuffling toward his desk was a shocking sight. All through the chamber heads turned. Vice President Barkley, on the rostrum, was among the first to take notice. The roll call was halted, and Barkley welcomed his ailing colleague. Senators made their way to Vandenberg's seat. As they rose, so did the clerks and pages. Someone started to clap. The applause grew into an ovation.

When the roll call resumed, Arthur Vandenberg voted for cloture as he knew his grandfather, the abolitionist doctor from upstate New York, would have wished. When the ruckus died, the filibuster held. But the vote was important. The senator limped back out to the shaking of hands and farewells fraught with sentiment.

On June 10, 1950, Hazel died in Georgetown Hospital. Vandenberg was cut loose from a mooring of thirty years. Yet there was also relief, for her pain had been relentless. Hazel was buried, not in the family plot near Arthur's first wife in Grand Rapids, but in Fort Wayne with her mother. Perhaps she was reluctant to be interred near Elizabeth; perhaps, some suggested, she was still bitter over the Sims affair.

Vandenberg remained in Washington, largely bedridden, anticipating each day's mail with its newspapers and well wishes. He cherished correspondence from General Marshall, who reminisced about the momentous times he and Vandenberg had shared, from Brazil to Blair House. "It would have been a great relaxer to sit down and have a drink with you and Bob Lovett and decide just how we were going to manage the world and then have done it," Marshall wrote.

"Those were truly 'great days,'" Vandenberg replied. "My part in them will always be my proudest record. Looking backward, it is really quite amazing how well we and the world got along together."[10]

Churchill inquired about the senator's prognosis. The two men had not known each other well, but the once and future prime minister said he felt close to Vandenberg, for they saw the world in similar terms. He sensed between them a "community of soul."

The senator stayed in Washington through the summer. In September 1950, yielding to the supervision of his best friend, he returned home. His younger daughter, Elizabeth, took charge of what he described as his "stubborn convalescence."[11] The illusion of recovery was useful all round. It left him with a voice, however muted, to address foreign policy, and a prospect for future influence that otherwise could not be sustained.

The Senate passed a resolution wishing him a speedy recovery. The senator, once so critical of Franklin Roosevelt's doctors for their lack of candor, appears to have dismissed any thought of resigning. Politics and psychology both argued delay. Resignation meant acknowledging a fate he was unwilling to accept. Besides, his successor would be chosen by a Democratic governor.

When Truman appointed Lodge to the American delegation to the United Nations, Vandenberg was gratified. "You can take over the responsibilities which I had to initiate in the first two General Assemblies," he told his protégé. "If you ever face an 'imponderable' which needs the advice of 'the old man' I shall be delighted to hear from you."

To Lodge, as to others, he said he hoped to be back in the Senate when the next session convened.

He was painfully frail, his bones brittle. He broke a rib. He watched from his porch as children from nearby Lafayette School trooped past in their Halloween costumes. He listened to the radio as bandleader Fred Waring dedicated to him a performance of his beloved "Whiffenpoof Song." There is no press record, only student memories, of a quiet visit he paid in a wheelchair, in the company of young congressman Jerry Ford, to Lafayette School for a Christmas assembly.[12]

But he was at pains to keep up with the wider world. When the United Nations celebrated its fifth anniversary, Vandenberg felt, he said, "somewhat like an ancient mariner." Five years seemed more like fifty, so much had happened in the interval. The United Nations had faced its first dire crisis, the war in Korea, and survived. Now it stood, he thought, "an excellent chance of justifying the hopes and aspirations with which we wrote and signed the Charter."[13]

In late November came a letter from Edward R. Murrow, who was planning a CBS radio documentary on the first half decade of the Cold War. He proposed using the actual voices of Truman, Churchill, Stalin, and other principals, with the words and speeches of Vandenberg providing the narrative thread. It was his "words and spirit," Murrow wrote, that "made the bipartisan foreign policy a living, working thing." Perhaps Spencer Tracy could supply the senator's voice. Spencer Tracy! Certainly the project was appealing. How could he not endorse an enterprise so dear to his heart—and one that might bolster bipartisanship? To his regret, Vandenberg confided to Murrow, he was too sick to help.[14]

When Congress reconvened in January 1951, Vandenberg was still in Grand Rapids. The number of visitors declined along with his condition. On rare occasions a nurse or one of his daughters helped slide him gingerly from his sickbed and exchange pajamas for a suit and tie. He bucked himself up, began to imagine Washington in the spring, and came carefully down the stairs. He was gaunt, but still with a dignified bearing, restored, if only briefly, to his customary role.

"My 'internment' is a source of constant and keenest regret," he wrote George Marshall. "I want to be on the 'firing line' again. These times call for everything that any of us can do with an eye to the 'next generation' rather than the 'next election.'"[15] The need, he had told Murrow, "is to consult national rather than political destiny."

He spent much of January in the hospital, "fighting an immobility which attacked my right leg, and an angry chest which insisted upon reminding me of the Spanish Inquisition." By mid-February, he was missing "the great debate" over presidential authority to deploy troops to a NATO army under Dwight Eisenhower's command. He refused to lecture his colleagues "from the safe sanctuary of a sick room."[16] He then went on for pages laying out the constitutional and practical issues around congressional approval of military action. Truman claimed authority to bolster American forces through executive order. Senate minority leader Kenneth Wherry insisted no additional troops could be deployed without congressional approval.

This was the perennial question in a new form. Vandenberg had been skeptical initially of maintaining a standing American army in Europe. He hoped the potential for deterrence in the NATO framework would suffice. However, what happened in Korea changed his mind—the ability to do so being still one of his most endearing features. Vandenberg wrote Wherry that it was "dangerous and futile" for

Congress to place too many limitations on the president. He thought it better for the president and Congress to agree voluntarily on the general basis of NATO support without reference to the president's constitutional prerogative, which had been disputed since the founding of the republic and did not have to be resolved right then.

Truman was commander in chief, and his constitutional function should not be impaired. Further, he wrote, "to transfer any portion of this authority to Congress is to subordinate military decision to the political judgments of Congress. We partially tried that in the Civil War when the Committee on the Conduct of the War set a tragic precedent." Yet only Congress retained the authority to declare war—one constitutional question colliding with another. The force of circumstance had to carry the day, and it usually sustained presidential prerogative.

If the constitutional question could never be settled satisfactorily, perhaps the better approach was a rule of conduct. When there was time, in a crisis, there should be consultation. The eternal debate cried out for a sense of accommodation between the executive and the legislature. "We found it before," he wrote. "We must find it again."

In late February, still lucid between intervals of excruciating pain and morphine-induced sleep, Vandenberg longed for news. A year had passed since his brief return to Capitol Hill. Since then, McCarthy had made headlines with claims that dozens of State Department officials were communists. He attracted a national following, and fellow travelers among Senate Republicans. Some were drawn to his strategy; others were fearful of his power. Taft had no brief for McCarthy, but there was a sense in the party that he was holding his nose while the junior senator attacked the administration.

"The complaisance of the Senate is what cannot be explained," wrote journalist Herbert Agar later. With only a few exceptions, "the whole of this privileged body of powerful and experienced men seemed to be hypnotized by McCarthy's atrocious talk—or even worse, they seemed to be afraid." He noted the absence of "the great Vandenberg," who "did not scare easily." While Vandenberg could do little except plead for sanity, one of his acolytes, Senator Margaret Chase Smith of Maine, was the first to call for McCarthy's censure.

Vandenberg could only hope that Eisenhower might emerge to wrest the party from what Taft was tolerating. "The sane philosophy of the 'middle road' is indispensable to the preservation of our threatened American unity," Vandenberg wrote to Eisenhower after one of the general's speeches. "No one can lead this indispensable 'revival' quite so well as you. This means more than meets the eye. I am one of those who deeply believe in you." This was praise from a master, Eisenhower replied.

In February, after Vandenberg listened to an Eisenhower speech on the television in his bedroom, a reporter called for a comment. "I feel as though a great load has been lifted from my back," Vandenberg declared. He assumed that the general would be the next president: "Things will be all right with Ike at the helm." Eisenhower "will help to put us back on a main track of collective security in the Western world."[17]

Vandenberg could no longer type his own letters. He had nurses round the clock. "Forgive the pencil and paper," he wrote to Clare Boothe Luce. "I am sitting up about two hours a day but I have not yet reached the 'pen and ink' or the 'typewriter' stage of my stubborn recuperation." He had not replied to her Christmas greeting two months earlier. He admitted to having "an unusually rough time"—sixteen months of suffering by then. Yet he still talked about returning to Washington "this spring *sometime*."

At sixty-six years old, he had outlived two wives. Although his daughters could not fill the void left by a loss of intimacy with power and influence over great events, they were a partial antidote for the loneliness that threatened to envelop him. Too much time to think was troubling. For so many years, reflection had been forsaken in the busyness of career and the rush of history.

"Yet every cloud has a silver lining," he wrote Clare Luce, "and the spiritual values in life come surging to the fore. They are so much more important than anything else." To the devout Catholic convert he noted, "I have a little 'prayer meeting' all by myself each night."[18]

By late February, the agony was unremitting—the cancer had metastasized along his spine. Changing the sheets was torture. Yet it was not just senators and generals and the president for whom he summoned the will to communicate. In a reply to a Princeton student's questions, he seized a chance to summarize his career. World War II and the atom bomb had "rendered obsolete all of our prior thinking regarding our national security. In other words, I believe I have only been keeping abreast realistically with the progress of our times." He was a "nationalist" before Pearl Harbor, he continued, insisting that his willingness to join the League of Nations with reservations and his vote for adherence to the World Court showed his openness to international cooperation. "I suppose I am now called an 'internationalist,'" he acknowledged. "But I still think that our first American fidelity must be to our own American security." Security—the search was lifelong.[19]

As his condition deteriorated, doctors and family acknowledged the inevitable. That did not, however, keep A. B. Smith from trying an extraordinary new protocol—an illegal one that began with sending the nurse home when a doctor from Chicago flew in to administer an experimental drug called krebiozen, derived from horses' hooves. There were days of startling relief and recovery. Suddenly Vandenberg was sitting up in bed, coughing up plugs of cancerous tissue, even smoking a cigar on his sixty-seventh birthday.[20] For a brief time, the acrid smell of tobacco smoke replaced the medicinal odor of the sickroom. But it didn't last. For nearly six weeks in the spring of 1951 he slipped in and out of consciousness.

Daughter Betsy was home the day Mitzi Sims called from Florida. Mitzi was following the news and wanted to hear for herself. Betsy was candid, out of the senator's earshot. Years later, however, she remembered debating with herself over whether she should tell her father about the call. Would hearing of Mitzi stir good feelings or bad? She could remember mulling it over; she could not remember if she told him.

Betsy wished she could comfort him. She and her sister were again two little girls, "trying to bring a giggle out of papa," she wrote, but "he's always been such a lone, unconfiding person."

In his increasingly infrequent lucid spells he struggled to read. He might peruse a newspaper or the book at his bedside, *Nightrunners of Bengal.* The just released historical novel tells of a dashing officer in India who loses his young wife to cholera as native troops revolt against British rule. After he falls in love a second time, his new love becomes gravely ill as he makes his way to an embattled garrison. Did Vandenberg see himself in these pages, in a story of empire under siege? Is the reader, the big senator gone gaunt, his breathing labored under an oppression of pain, left to wonder whether the hero will be widowed for a second time?

In a climactic battle, Bengal mutineers attack the fort the hero is defending. He "felt his mind slipping away from him as the heat and noise and dust racketed him to the edge of insanity." In the furious struggle he puffs on a cigar as his outnumbered countrymen fall at their posts. "Surely to God," he wonders, "no one could stand this much longer—not very much longer?"

The battle was nearly over. On the evening of April 18, 1951, A. B. Smith, who had been tending the patient in his upstairs room, descended the stairs. Betsy rose from her chair. The doctor was crying. His friend was gone.

EPILOGUE

WHAT TOMORROW SPEAKS

On April 19, 1951, the American flag was lowered over the Capitol.

But the Senate's attention—and the country's—was on other business: General Douglas MacArthur, relieved by President Truman of his command in Korea, had arrived on Capitol Hill to address a joint meeting of Congress. He said something memorable, about how "old soldiers never die, they just fade away." A standing ovation echoed through the marble halls.

Columnist Drew Pearson had often sniped at Arthur Vandenberg, but death and coincidence led to this assessment in his diary: "Vandenberg, if he had arrived from a peace conference . . . would never have received the ovation that was given MacArthur today. . . . Yet in my opinion, Vandenberg's contribution to world peace was far, far greater than anything the glittering general has given the world. The trouble is that we get too close to our political heroes."

When applause in the House subsided, a young Foreign Relations Committee staffer named Nancy Dickerson repaired to the Senate gallery. The upper chamber was empty save for a few returning senators and Foreign Relations staffers. As sirens wailed with the departure of the general, Dickerson listened to eulogies from Vandenberg's colleagues. "His integrity and personal charm gave him a unique power and standing in the Senate," she observed. "He imbued committee members with the thought that partisanship had no place in foreign affairs—that while dissent was permissible and welcomed at home, when we presented ourselves to other nations we should appear as a unified whole."[1]

Walter Lippmann spoke of "the influence of a conspicuous personal example" in Vandenberg's evolution. When, he said, "a sudden and tremendous change of outlook has become imperative in a crisis, it makes all the difference in the world to most of us to see a man whom we have known and trusted, and who has thought and felt as we did, going through the experience of changing his mind, doing it with style and dash, and in a mood to shame the devils of his own weakness."

Vandenberg was, John Foster Dulles recalled, a controversial figure, "but all great Americans have been controversial." A *New Yorker* writer noted that Vandenberg's memory was shrouded in contradictory myths: was he a statesman endowed "with superior gifts of prophecy" or "a stooge, a captive Republican who did what he was told" by the Cold War architects of the Truman administration?

He was neither, of course.

The funeral at Park Congregational Church was Grand Rapids' largest between those of middleweight champion Stanley Ketchel in 1910 and Vandenberg protégé Gerald Ford in 2007. He was buried in Oak Hill Cemetery. Vice President Barkley stood in for President Truman. A host of Washington friends paid homage—Taft, Acheson, Dulles, senators, diplomats, reporters. A. B. Smith collapsed with a heart attack. (He survived.)

That week, Edward R. Murrow closed his radio broadcast with a tribute to a man who "was a little more than life-sized in the field of foreign policy." Like war hero George Patton, Murrow said, Vandenberg in his later years "never bothered about his flanks, drove straight ahead. Those on his right and left are now in confusion and contention and he is silent."

"We are now divided—bitterly, hysterically." Alluding to the climate of fear fostered by McCarthy, Murrow said of Vandenberg, "Had he lived, he would have gloried in this conflict—and steadied it. And he would have been confident that at the end of the day little men of loud voice and small faith . . . will yield to the collective judgment of the American people."

Murrow read from the last letter he had received from the senator, who wrote of "the grave need . . . to find a meeting of the minds which will assure our own country and the world that our democracy can function in time of crisis."[2]

Vandenberg did not live to see Dwight Eisenhower elected president, but he took comfort in the prospect. The Midwestern voice he heard on his bedside radio had a timbre not unlike his own. In both style and substance it offered a sort of afterlife for the dying senator. Eisenhower was once asked to name the great men he had known. He started with Churchill, added Marshall, and then noted two senators: Walter George and Vandenberg.[3]

Long after his last cigar, Arthur Vandenberg lingers vaguely in civic memory. His name offers an iconic shorthand for cooperation between the political parties. Particularly in foreign affairs, and particularly when there is divided government.

A decade after Vandenberg's death, then-congressman Gerald Ford recalled his mentor's book, *If Hamilton Were Here Today*. "We may well wonder," said the future president, "as to how the responsibilities of future issues would be met if Vandenberg were here today."[4]

When the executive branch reaches out to Congress, the cry goes up, "Where is there a Vandenberg now?" From time to time someone rises to that occasion. But the bitter divisions recur. The value of the post-war world order Vandenberg fought so hard to create has been called into question: The UN? Trading alliances? NATO? The new fortress of collective security in which he sought refuge is now under siege.

Americans wonder and debate: What role does the United States play on the world stage? That question has vexed the republic from its founding. From the allure of self-sufficiency, with the safeguards, real or imagined, of ocean moats (or border walls) to an expectation of leadership among nation-states jostling for advantage and increasingly interconnected, the alternatives have been argued since Washington's Farewell Address.

Arthur Vandenberg was a student of self-help. "Enlightened self-interest" was his mantra. The words of Emerson in his essay "Self-

Reliance" were familiar: "Speak what you think now in hard words and tomorrow speak what tomorrow thinks in hard words again, though it contradict everything you said today." Be ready to change. The world requires this of its leaders, but seldom gets it.

For Vandenberg, "enlightened self-interest" was both personal and patriotic. When self-interest is too narrowly construed, the capacity to contend with uncertainty and chaos is diminished. Vandenberg longed for security, but *enlightened* is the crucial qualifier for American policy in what he called "this foreshortened world." His mastery of bipartisan collaboration at a time when his fellow citizens hungered for direction echoes down the years. To not note his relevance today feels almost irresponsible.

. . . .
ACKNOWLEDGMENTS
. . . .

This book began with a phone call. In 1989, at the invitation of the historian Gordon Olson, I had addressed a meeting of the Historical Society of Michigan. The subject: Senator Vandenberg and the neutrality debate of 1939. (Six people showed up, including the mayor of Grand Rapids.) Olson knew of my almost kindred interest in the senator, who, like me, was a native of the Furniture City. Vandenberg had also been a cross-country runner and student at the University of Michigan, a young editor with literary and maybe political aspirations.

Arthur Vandenberg was an enigmatic figure, nearly forgotten even in his hometown. His full story had never been told. In 1970 C. David Tompkins published *Arthur Vandenberg: The Evolution of a Modern Republican.* Though thorough, the book ends in 1945, on the cusp of the senator's most influential years.

What is published often defines the past. In his essay on missing history in the nation's capital, David McCullough cited the need for further study of Arthur Vandenberg.

When Tompkins died in 1990, his adult daughter was charged with settling his estate. He had been teaching in Chicago, and his basement office held scores of files for an unwritten second volume. Joan Tompkins Alderton was loath to dispose of her father's extensive research. She called the Historical Society of Michigan. Did they know of anyone with an interest in Senator Vandenberg? Just weeks earlier, I had spoken at their conference. They gave her my number. From her call came a truckload of books and papers. And with those papers came a mission a biographer could hardly resist.

With a jump start on the research, I sought out people who knew Arthur Vandenberg. Most were elderly, of course. Some shared a passion to finally give the senator his due. The novelist Allen Drury had covered the Senate as a young reporter in the 1940s. He offered a blurb when my first draft was still a dream. Others wondered at the folly—that would include Gore Vidal, who agreed to two interviews. A teenager when he met the man he called "the Great Van," he was more intrigued by the search than by the subject. Vidal warmed to the project, however, and Vandenberg figured prominently in his final novel of twentieth-century America, *The Golden Age.*

Vandenberg's younger daughter, Elizabeth Vandenberg Sands, shared perceptive memories over the course of several years, as did grandson John Knight, granddaughter Barbara Pfeiffer, and other family members.

My research began at the University of Michigan's Bentley Historical Library, home to Vandenberg's papers, as well as in the Michigan Room of the Grand Rapids Public Library, where the *Grand Rapids Herald* is on microfilm.

The Bentley came to feel like home away from home. Its archivists define the best of their profession. Both of the directors during my work there have provided invaluable counsel. (Their predecessor, Robert Warner, was archivist of the United States and my entrée to the National Archives.) Francis Blouin, who guided the Bentley so well for a quarter century, introduced me to James Tobin, noted biographer of Ernie Pyle, the Wright brothers, and Franklin Roosevelt. Jim's editorial guidance was crucial in shaping this book. Fran's successor, historian Terrence McDonald, not only critiqued the manuscript but also introduced Rob Havey, a writer and Bentley researcher whose assistance in organizing sources from my decades of much-riffled files has been indispensable. So many of their colleagues have also been helpful, including Nancy Bartlett, Bill Wallich, and Tom Powers.

The U.S. Senate Historical Office in Washington, DC, is a welcoming haven for a senatorial biographer. Richard Baker and Don Ritchie encouraged this work from the start.

Throughout its odyssey, the manuscript benefited from critical readers and editors. First came Larry ten Harmsel of Western Michigan University and Leslie Stainton of the University of Michigan. Leslie and I traded draft chapters as she wrote the definitive life of Federico

García Lorca. D. M. Thomas offered the first formal critique of an early version.

Invaluable in later drafts were the evaluations of Walter LaFeber, legendary diplomatic historian at Cornell University, and Richard Baker, historian emeritus of the United States Senate. Insightful editorial advice came from legal scholar and biographer Jeff Rosen, president of the National Constitution Center, and from Amity Shlaes, historian, journalist, and the guiding spirit of the Calvin Coolidge Foundation.

Tobin, McDonald, Rosen, and the incomparable Richard Norton Smith, who opened so many doors, helped me navigate the publishing waters until, through the good offices of agent Rafe Sagelyn and assistant Jake de Bacher, the manuscript was accepted by the University of Chicago Press.

In the course of this undertaking, filmmaker Michael Grass and Gleaves Whitney, director of the Hauenstein Center for Presidential Studies at Grand Valley State University, collaborated with me on *America's Senator*, a documentary on the life of Arthur Vandenberg that enhanced and energized research for this book.

At Meijer, Mark Murray critiqued the manuscript and Pam Kleibusch provided valuable administrative support. Janet Kelly, Frank Guglielmi, Stacy Behler, Michelle Vancalbergh, and others lent their assistance.

The manuscript was also read all or in part by Martin Allen, Mark Barger-Elliott, Frank Boles, Kevin Boyle, H. W. Brands, James R. Brown, Robert Ferrell, Mike Grass, Nigel Hamilton, Ray Hill, William Isaac, Charles Jennings, Henry Kissinger, Liesel Meijer, Peter Meijer, Gordon Olson, Catherine Redlich, Don Ritchie, David Roll, Liz Shrayer, Bill Smith, Richard Norton Smith, Bob VanderMolen, John Ward, Gleaves Whitney, and others to whom I am grateful. The habitués of the Cottage Bar salon have been unflagging in their encouragement.

At the University of Chicago Press, executive editor Tim Mennel combined his discerning editorial judgment and enthusiastic support with the distinguished work of a team that included Rachel Kelly, Erin

DeWitt, Carrie Adams, Levi Stahl, and ace copy editor Katherine Faydash. Publicist Angela Baggetta found ways to reach more readers.

With so much help, any oversights or errors are mine alone.

Finally, there is family at the heart of this decades-long endeavor. Brothers, parents, and in-laws, along with Haley, Peter, Hanna, Cali, and Hardy, have borne witness to stories of senatorial intrigue and American leadership. Above all, Liesel Litzenburger Meijer, the writer in our household, offered generous advice, continuing inspiration, and the love upon which I rely.

A NOTE ON SOURCES

Arthur Vandenberg did not live to write the memoir he had envisioned, something that would be not only an autobiography but also an argument for bipartisanship, particularly in foreign policy. A year after his death, in 1951, Arthur Vandenberg Jr. published an elegant sampling of his father's later career as *The Private Papers of Senator Vandenberg*. The *Private Papers* complements chronologically David Tompkins's *Arthur Vandenberg: The Evolution of a Modern Republican*, as the latter ends in 1945. Together they constitute the chief secondary sources.

There is no other comprehensive biography of the senator. Two recent volumes—Lawrence Kaplan's *The Conversion of Senator Arthur H. Vandenberg* and Lawrence J. Haas's *Harry and Arthur: Truman, Vandenberg, and the Partnership That Created the Free World*—offer fresh perspectives on Vandenberg's influence.

Primary materials are concentrated in the Arthur H. Vandenberg Papers (AHV) at the University of Michigan's Bentley Historical Library (BHL). These include letters and scrapbooks, as well as the diaries and other writings of Hazel Vandenberg. Also at the Bentley are the Ralph L. Smith Papers (RLS), a comprehensive series of scrapbooks by a Grand Rapids newspaperman and Vandenberg contemporary who, like Tompkins, did not live to write a planned biography of the senator. The Bentley also houses the papers of Michigan political figures who were Vandenberg's confidants and contemporaries.

Voluminous research files gathered by David Tompkins, as well as papers from the senator's younger daughter, Elizabeth Vandenberg Sands, are in the possession of the author.

The *Grand Rapids Herald* and *Grand Rapids Press* are available on microfilm in the Michigan Room at the Grand Rapids Public Library.

Some of Vandenberg's short stories can be found in the periodical collection at Calvin College.

Other institutions important for research on Vandenberg include the U.S. Senate Historical Office, the Harry S Truman Presidential Library, the Franklin D. Roosevelt Presidential Library, and the Herbert Hoover Presidential Library. The Seeley G. Mudd Library at Princeton University holds the papers of John Foster Dulles and H. Alexander Smith. The papers of Francis Wilcox are at the University of Iowa.

At the Library of Congress, the extensive diaries of Courtney Letts de Espil, wife of Argentina's ambassador to the United States in the 1930s and 1940s, are a hidden treasure of Washington diplomatic and political life in that era. The newsreel collections at the National Archives offer scenes of the walking, talking Vandenberg.

People who had known or worked with the senator, as well as scholars who have studied the era, shared valuable perspectives with the author. First among many was Elizabeth Vandenberg Sands. Also interviewed were Carol Smith Ankerson, John Bailey, Richard Baker, Lucius Battle, Betty Beale, Lawson Becker, Virginia Becker, Richard Bissell, Chet Bock, Herbert Brownell, Horace Busby, Marie Cady, Liz Carpenter, Marshall Carter, Dudley Clendinen, Clark Clifford, Louise Corl, Geraldyne Creagan, Richard Deem, Marguerite Doyle, Albert Engel, Gerald Ford, William Fulbright, Nathan French, David Ginsburg, Lincoln Gordon, Yvonne Griggs, Louis Hankey, Joseph C. Harsch, Ralph Hauenstein, Ken Heckler, Stuart Hoffius, Margaret Jack, Charles Jennings, William Johnston, Mary Kindel, Charles Kindleberger, John Knight, William Leece, John Logie, Neil MacNeil, Murray Marder, Nell McCracken, George Meader, Leonard Meeker, Hope Ridings Miller, Mrs. William D. Pawley, Barbara Pfeiffer, Forrest Pogue, Lee Potter, Mike Radigan, George Reedy, Don Ritchie, Chalmers Roberts, George Romney, Dean Rusk, Walter Russell, Arthur Schlesinger Jr., Fred Schwengel, A. B. Smith Jr., Barbara Smith, Lawrence Spivak, Harold Stassen, John L. Steele, Robert Stuart, Paul R. Sweet, Helen Thomas, Mary Thoits, Stanton Todd, Andrew Transue, Walter Trohan, Harold G. Tufty, Hoyt Vandenberg Jr., Helen VanderVelde, Werner Veit, William Vermeulen, Gore Vidal, and Frank Waldrop.

Among those interviewed for *America's Senator: The Odyssey of Arthur Vandenberg* were Jonathan Alter, Greg Behrman, H. W. Brands, Liz Carpenter, Jennet Conant, John Dingell, Lawrence Finklestein, John Steele Gordon, Ralph Hauenstein, David Kennedy, Walter LaFeber, Carl Levin, George McGovern, Don Ritchie, Stephen Schlesinger, Ellen Schrecker, Amity Shlaes, Kiron Skinner, Richard Norton Smith, Gore Vidal, and Daniel Yergin.

Earlier versions of chapters 12 and 16 of this book appeared in *Michigan Historical Review* 16, no. 2 (1990) and 19, no. 2 (1993).

NOTES

PROLOGUE

1. Courtney Letts de Espil Diaries, 1934–1945, 119–20, box 2, Courtney Letts de Espil Papers, Library of Congress, Washington, DC.

2. Ibid.

3. "Arbiters of Foreign Policy," Editorial, *The Economist* 153 (1948): 184.

4. Arthur Vandenberg, "The Mackinac Charter," radio address, September 22, 1943, Bentley Historical Library (BHL), University of Michigan.

5. Frank McNaughton Papers, *Time*, March 17, 1948, folder March 16–31, 1948, box 15, Harry S. Truman Library, Independence, MO.

6. Richard Rovere, "The Unassailable Vandenberg," *Harper's*, May 1948, 396; Murrow to Vandenberg, November 21, 1950, microfilm roll 4, Vandenberg Papers, BHL.

CHAPTER ONE

1. Bill Davidson, "Two Mr. Vandenbergs," *Collier's*, June 1948, 80; C. David Tompkins, *Senator Arthur H. Vandenberg: The Evolution of a Modern Republican, 1884–1945* (East Lansing: Michigan State University Press, 1970), 2.

2. John Barry, "Newton Man's Kid Brother May Be Next President," *Boston Sunday Globe*, October 20, 1935; "Vandenberg," *Current Biography, 1948* (New York, 1949), 637; Tompkins, *Senator Arthur H. Vandenberg*, 1.

3. Frank Cobb, "Learned Newspaper Work 'under Dire Compulsion,'" in *Incidents in the Lives of Editors*, ed. Arthur Scott White (Grand Rapids, MI: White Publishing, 1920), 43.

4. Bureau of Labor and Industrial Statistics, *Annual Report of Inspection of Factories in Michigan*, 1894–1896, 1898–1902, Bentley Historical Library (hereafter BHL), Ann Arbor, MI; Jonathan Mitchell, "Vandenberg: Heroes' Child," *New Republic*, April 8, 1940, 461–62; "Will Make Harness," *Grand Rapids Press*, September 25, 1903, 2.

5. James B. Reston, "Case for Vandenberg," *Life*, May 24, 1948; William A. McGarry, "Go into Politics: To Give—Not to Get," *Association Men*, 1928, 398.

6. *Mantion*, Grand Rapids Central High School annual, 1900.

7. "Grand Rapids High School Oratorical Contest," April 1900, microfilm roll 6, BHL.

8. *Mantion*, Grand Rapids Central High School annual, 1900.

9. George R. Cullen, "When the Big Chance Came," *Success*, May 1922.

10. *Herald*, November 18, 1900.

11. Ralph L. Smith was a journalist from Michigan who collected newspaper clippings of Vandenberg's career in hopes of writing a biography. He never did, but

Smith's scrapbooks are an invaluable amalgamation of articles by and about Vandenberg. Ralph L. Smith Scrapbook (hereafter RLS Scrapbook), February 17, 1934, 357, Ralph Laws Smith Papers, BHL; Barry, "Newton Man's Kid Brother," *Boston Sunday Globe*, October 20, 1935.

12. Genevieve Forbes Herrick, "Women in the News," *Country Gentleman*, Hazel diary, March 1936, Hazel Vandenberg Papers, BHL.

13. Tompkins, *Senator Arthur H. Vandenberg*, 5; Arthur Hendrick Vandenberg, "The Shrewdness of Hawkins," *Lippincott's Monthly*, February 1905, 203–11.

14. "Romantic Rise of Young Solon," *Boston Post*, April 2, 1928.

15. *Herald*, June 7, 1914; Vandenberg to Elizabeth Watson, November 4, 1903, Arthur Vandenberg Papers, BHL.

16. "The Story of $100,000,000," *Herald*, January 17, 1906.

17. "Who's Who in Grand Rapids—XI," *Grand Rapids Spectator*, March 24, 1928, 5–6.

18. Cullen, *Success*, 38.

19. Beverly Smith, "Grand Rapids Boy Makes Good," *American Magazine*, January 1938, 122.

20. *Saturday Evening Post*, 1902, oversize vol. 23, Vandenberg Scrapbooks, BHL.

CHAPTER TWO

1. Tompkins, *Senator Arthur H. Vandenberg*, 7–8. Aurie Nichols Dunlap, "The Political Career of Arthur H. Vandenberg" (PhD diss., University of Michigan, 1955), 10.

2. *Herald*, May 10, 1908; *Herald*, May 12, 1908.

3. *Herald*, May 6, 1908; *Herald*, April 3, 1910; *Herald*, January 13, 1908; *Herald*, June 10, 1906; *Herald*, January 18, 1915.

4. Arthur H. Vandenberg, "Revolt of the Puppets," *Popular Magazine*, November 1906, 60–67.

5. *Herald*, February 12, 1908.

6. *Herald*, June 14, 1908.

7. Ibid.; *Herald*, June 17, 1908.

8. *Herald*, June 18, 1908.

9. *Herald*, November 1, 1908; *Herald*, November 2, 1908.

10. *Herald*, November 3, 1908; *Herald*, November 4, 1908.

11. *Herald*, December 10, 1914; *Herald*, February 8, 1914; *Herald*, April 21, 1914; Vandenberg Scrapbook I, insert, April 2, 1929, BHL. (Hereafter all Vandenberg scrapbooks are referred to by the abbreviation VS and a roman numeral indicating sequence in the collection.)

12. *Herald*, June 17, 1911.

13. *Herald*, July 25, 1909; *Herald*, November 20, 1910.

14. *Herald*, February 15, 1910; Dunlap, "Political Career," 17.

15. *Herald*, February 13, 1911; *Herald*, June 7, 1912.

16. *Herald*, June 18, 1912; *Herald*, June 17, 1912; *Herald*, June 12, 1912.

17. *Herald*, June 21, 1912; *Herald*, June 22, 1912.

18. *Herald*, June 20, 1912; Barry, "Newton Man's Kid Brother," *Boston Sunday Globe*, October 20, 1935; *Herald*, October 11, 1912; *Herald*, October 28, 1912.

19. *Herald*, November 6, 1912; *Herald*, November 7, 1912, *Herald*, November 13, 1913; *Herald*, November 13, 1912.

CHAPTER THREE

1. *Herald*, November 22, 1908.

2. Carl M. Saunders, *I Was There*, unpublished autobiography, Carl M. Saunders Papers, BHL, 15; Gertrude Franklin Atherton, *The Conqueror: Being the True and Romantic Story of Alexander Hamilton* (New York: Frederick A. Stokes Company, 1902), 124.

3. *Herald*, January 17, 1917; "If Hamilton Were Here," *Herald*, September 26, 1914; "If Jefferson Were Here," *Herald*, September 29, 1914.

4. *Herald*, August 11, 1915; *Herald*, July 1, 1914; *Herald*, September 9, 1915; *Herald*, March 26, 1916.

5. *Herald*, November 27–30, 1916; *Herald*, December 1, 2, and 4–7, 1916.

6. *Detroit Free Press*, November 30, 1937.

7. *Herald*, August 6, 1914; *Herald*, August 16, 1914; *Herald*, July 27, 1914.

8. *Herald*, August 20, 1914.

9. *Herald*, December 15, 1914.

10. *Herald*, August 24, 1914.

11. *Herald*, September 7, 1915; *Herald*, September 8, 1915.

12. *Herald*, November 15, 1914; *Herald*, January 5, 1915; *Herald*, May 2, 1914; *Herald*, April 7, 1915; *Herald*, December 19, 1916.

13. *Herald*, March 31, 1915; *Herald*, May 8, 1915; *Herald*, May 9, 1915.

14. *Herald*, May 18, 1915; *Herald*, May 24, 1915.

15. *Herald*, June 10, 1915; *Herald*, July 16, 1915.

16. *Herald*, April 25, 1915; *Herald*, March 18, 1916.

17. *Herald*, December 16, 1916; *Herald*, December 17, 1916; *Herald*, May 1, 1916.

18. Bill Davidson, "Two Vandenbergs," 80.

19. *Herald*, April 20, 1916.

20. *Herald*, May 4, 1916.

21. *Herald*, August 8, 1916; *Herald*, September 13, 1916; *Herald*, September 14, 1916; *Herald*, October 5, 1916.

22. *Herald*, December 22, 1916.

23. *Herald*, February 2, 1917; *Herald*, February 5, 1917; *Herald*, February 8, 1917.

24. *Herald*, February 27, 1917; *Herald*, March 3, 1917; *Herald*, March 8, 1917; *Herald*, March 17, 1917.

25. *Herald*, March 19, 1917; *Herald*, March 24, 1917; *Herald*, March 30, 1917.

26. *Herald*, April 3, 1917; *Herald*, April 4, 1917.

27. *Herald*, April 9, 1917; *Herald*, April 5, 1917; *Herald*, March 5, 1917; *Herald*, March 7, 1917; *Herald*, April 11, 1917.

28. Eulogy booklet, April 1917, microfilm roll 10, BHL.

29. *Herald*, June 7, 1917; *Herald*, June 13, 1917; *Herald*, June 6, 1917; *Herald*, June 7, 1917; *Herald*, June 8, 1917.

30. *Herald*, December 8, 1917.

31. "Annual Meeting to Be Out of Ordinary," *Commerce Club News*, August 15, 1917; "Big Crowd Attends Club's Annual Meet," *Commerce Club News*, August 22, 1917.

32. Rex P. Dryer, "Arthur the Freshman," speech given at Delta Upsilon's eleventh annual convention, September 6, 1951, Rex P. Dryer collection, BHL.

33. *Toledo (OH) Blade*, September 19, 1917.

34. *Herald*, April 2, 1918; *Herald*, April 22, 1918.

35. Vandenberg to Hazel, and Hazel to Vandenberg, April to May 1918, "AHV letters to Hazel Whitaker 1918" folder, microfilm roll 5, Arthur Vandenberg Papers, BHL.

36. Enriqueta David, "Only the Wife," May 20, 1933, Hazel diary, BHL.

37. Vandenberg to Hazel, June 10, 1918, microfilm roll 5, Arthur Vandenberg Papers, BHL.

38. Ibid.

39. Ibid.

40. *Herald*, November 6, 1918; *Herald*, November 8, 1918.

41. *Herald*, November 18, 1918.

42. *Herald*, November 3, 1918; *Herald*, December 1, 1918; *Herald*, May 28, 1919; *Herald*, December 22, 1918; *Herald*, June 25, 1919.

43. *Herald*, November 20, 1918; *Herald*, December 1, 1918.

44. *Herald*, December 3, 1918.

45. William C. Widenor, *Henry Cabot Lodge and the Search for an American Foreign Policy* (Berkeley: University of California Press, 1980), 35, 39.

46. Ibid., xiv, vii, x, xii.

47. *Herald*, June 1, 1920.

48. Letter and survey both on microfilm roll 2, Arthur Vandenberg Papers, BHL.

49. *Herald*, May 28, 1920; Vandenberg to Frank Knox, August 18, 1919.

50. Henry Cabot Lodge to Arthur Vandenberg, July 15, 1919; Herbert F. Margulies, "The Moderates in the League of Nations Battle: An Overlooked Faction," *Historian* (Winter 1998): 273–88.

51. Vandenberg to Frank Knox, August 18, 1919.

52. Vandenberg to Earl Kettle, October 1, 1919.

53. Spencer Ervin, *Henry Ford vs. Truman H. Newberry: The Famous Senate Election Contest; a Study in American Politics, Legislation and Justice* (New York: R. R. Smith 1935), 18–21, 305–8; *Herald*, May 21, 1920.

CHAPTER FOUR

1. *Herald*, June 6, 1920; *Herald*, June 10, 1920; *Herald*, June 7, 1920; *Herald*, June 8, 1920.

2. *Herald*, June 12, 1920; *Herald*, June 13, 1920.

3. *Herald*, June 14, 1920; "A Statesman's First Steps," RLS Scrapbook, 4.

4. Richard H. Rovere, "The Unassailable Vandenberg, *Harper's*, May 1948, 400.

5. Albert Nelson Marquis, ed., *Who's Who in America* (Chicago: A. N. Marquis & Company), 2895; Cullen, *Success*, 38.

6. *Herald*, June 30, 1920.

7. Discussion of survey results in Vandenberg, *If Hamilton Were Here Today: American Fundamentals Applied to Modern Problems* (New York: G. P. Putnam's Sons, 1923), 11–64.

8. Ibid., 64, 347.

9. Wayne E. Stevens, "Minor Notices," *American Historical Review*, January 1922, 364.

10. Arthur Hendrick Vandenberg, *If Hamilton Were Here Today*, vii, 65, 144, 201.

11. Ibid., 25, 219–25.

12. Maurice Francis Egan, "Hamilton's Ghost Walking the Stage of Politics," *New York Times Book Review*, June 10, 1923, VS I, BHL.

13. Arthur Hendrick Vandenberg, *The Trail of a Tradition* (New York: G. P. Putnam's Sons, 1926), v.

14. Ibid., v–vi.

15. Vandenberg, "Internationalism—Good and Bad," speech, April 16, 1925, BHL; William Borah to Arthur Vandenberg, April 20, 1925.

16. Sinclair Lewis, "Self-Conscious America," *American Mercury*, October 1925, 139.

17. Arthur O'Dane, "Hymn to an Oasis," *American Mercury*, October 1925, 194.

18. *Grand Rapids Press*, April 2, 1928.

19. John Kelly "The Day the KKK Was Here," n.d., VS, 23.

20. Ibid.

CHAPTER FIVE

1. Frank B. Woodford, *Alex J. Groesbeck Portrait of a Public Man* (Detroit: Wayne State University Press, 1962), 153, 187–88.

2. Woodford, *Alex J. Groesbeck*, 250; Tompkins, *Senator Arthur H. Vandenberg*, 38.

3. M. E. Linch, "Romantic Rise of a Young Salon," *Boston Post*, April 2, 1928, VS I, BHL; Vandenberg to James Couzens, December 3, 1926, box 45, James Couzens Papers, Library of Congress, Washington, DC.

4. Vandenberg to Chase S. Osborn, April 2, 1927, microfilm roll 1, BHL.

5. Sparks to Chase S. Osborn, December 23, 1926, microfilm roll 1, BHL.

6. RLS Scrapbook, September 3, 1935, 512.

7. Tompkins, *Senator Arthur H. Vandenberg*, 42; *Grand Rapids Press*, RLS Scrapbook, February 18, 1928.

8. Tompkins, *Senator Arthur H. Vandenberg*, 43–44.

9. Chase S. Osborn to C. David Tompkins, October 23, 1962, letter in possession of the author.

10. Saunders, *I Was There*, 24; *Detroit News*, March 29, 1928.

11. *Grand Rapids Press*, March 31, 1928, VS I, 1.

12. Vandenberg to Carl Saunders, April 2,1928.

13. Hazel diary, "the big week of april [*sic*] 1 1928," BHL.

14. Elizabeth Vandenberg Sands personal interview, Bantam, CT, September 25, 1991.

15. Hazel diary, April 21, 1928, BHL; Vandenberg speech to the Society of American Newspaper Editors, April 24, 1928, BHL.

16. *Herald*, April 18, 1928.

17. Newspaper clippings, May 13, 22, 25–27, 1928, VS I, 12–20; Hazel diary, May 1, 1928, BHL.

18. *Brooklyn Eagle*, June 29, 1934, RLS Scrapbook, 385.

19. Rex P. Dryer, "Arthur the Freshman," speech at Delta Upsilon's eleventh annual convention, September 6, 1951, Rex P. Dryer collection, BHL.

20. "Vice President Lauds Vandenberg," 1928, RLS Scrapbook, 20; Joseph R. Hayden to Arthur Vandenberg, April 2, 1928, box 2, Joseph R. Hayden Papers, BHL.

21. "'Rainy Day' Work Plan Is Given Senate," May 14 and 17, 1928, RLS Scrapbook, 34.

22. VS I, September 19, 1928.

23. VS I, "The Big Week of April 1, 1928," 7.

24. Frank Knox to Arthur Vandenberg, December 1, 1928.

CHAPTER SIX

1. Vandenberg diary, December 13, 1928, VS I, 38, BHL; Fred Rodell, "Vandenberg of Michigan," *American Mercury*, January 1947, 6; Note from Bob F., December 20, 1928, RLS Scrapbook, 12.

2. *Herald*, January 13, 1929; *Herald*, March 23, 1929.

3. *Washington Post*, January 1929, VS I, 51.

4. Mark Sullivan, "A City Victory over Country," *New York Tribune*, March 23, 1929, VS I, 79.

5. Tompkins, *Senator Arthur H. Vandenberg*, 49.

6. *Herald*, April 19, 1929; Hazel Vandenberg diary, February 25, 1929; Tompkins, *Senator Arthur H. Vandenberg*, 48.

7. Hazel diary, March 4, 1929; VS I, April 14, 1929, 82; VS I, May 29, 1929, 118; Hazel diary, May 29, 1929; VS I, June 10, 1929, 124.

8. Vandenberg diary, December 13, 1928; Rodell, "Vandenberg," 6; VS I, April 22, 1929, 84.

9. *Herald*, January 24, 1929; VS I, December 14, 1929, 43; "Rookies of the Senate," *New York Herald Tribune*, VS I, February 3, 1929, 55.

10. Hazel diary, May 19, 1929; Stella M. Champney, *Detroit News*, May 12, 1929; Hazel diary, November 23, 1929.

11. *Congressional Record*, 71st Cong., 2nd sess. 1, 1929; VS II, January 10–30, 1930, 59–64.

12. H. L. Mencken, "Two Views of Justice," *Baltimore Sun*, October 21, 1929; VS II, October 8, 1929, 19.

13. *New York Times*, July 1, 1930 1, 2; *New Republic*, December 1929, RLS Scrapbook.

14. Elliot Thurston, "Politics from the Sidelines," VS II, July 21, 1930, 132.

15. November 21, 1929, RLS Scrapbook, 119.

16. "Chronology of 'Young Turk' Movement," Vandenberg Diary, VS II, November 22, 1929, 49.

17. VS I, May 31, 1928, 26; "He's New and Has Very Odd Ideas for Senator," *San Francisco Chronicle*, March 26, 1930, VS II, 84; "Offers Compromise on Flexible Tariff," *New York Times*, March 26, 1930, VS II, 89.

18. Tompkins, *Senator Arthur H. Vandenberg*, 55; Hoover to Arthur Vandenberg, April 19, 1930, microfilm roll 1, Vandenberg Papers, BHL.

19. "The Parker Vote," Vandenberg diary, May 7, 1930, VS II, 104–5.

20. "A Postscript to the Parker Vote," Vandenberg diary, VS VI, 55.

21. *Herald*, May 8, 1930; Vandenberg diary, May 7, 1930, VS II.

22. "Conversation with Senator Borah in Senate Cloak Room," Vandenberg diary, February 17, 1930, VS II, 70–71; RLS Scrapbook, December, 1929, 160.

23. *Grand Rapids Press*, June 10, 1930, VS II, 117; "London Naval Treaty," Vandenberg diary, June 4, 1930, VS II, 115.

24. "Vandenberg Gives Four Major Issues of Peace," VS III, December 1930, 4.

25. Vandenberg profile by Herbert Plummer, *Associated Press*, 1930, VS III, 108.

26. VS III, 50.

27. *Grand Rapids Press*, December 5, 1930, VS III, 6.

28. Tompkins, *Senator Arthur H. Vandenberg*, 61; "Just one more of those little Hoover mistakes," Vandenberg diary, VS III, 5.

29. "Another Needless War," Vandenberg typescript, February 1930, VS III, 15.

30. VS II, September 28, 1929, 16.

31. "The Advice Squad," *Collier's*, January 30, 1931, VS III, 14; *Collier's*, January 9, 1931, RLS Scrapbook, 210; RLS Scrapbook, August 25, 1932, 265.

32. VS IV, 64; "Senator Increases Store of New Words Added to Politics," *Washington News*, VS IV, 86; RLS Scrapbook, March 28, 1932, 253; RLS Scrapbook, September 15, 1932, 273.

33. VS III, June 20, 1931, 49–50; VS IV, January 8, 1932, 14.

34. "[Bonus] Expedition Force, 1932, Vandenberg diary, VS IV, June 17, 1932, 75.

35. RLS Scrapbook, October 12, 1932, 275.

CHAPTER SEVEN

1. Jay G. Hayden, "Farmer's $1,410 Burned but U.S. Makes It Good," *Detroit News*, January 7, 1933, VS V, 19.

2. Tompkins, *Senator Arthur H. Vandenberg*, 76; John T. Flynn, "Michigan Magic," *Harper's*, December 1933, 5, 8–9.

3. Harry Barnard, *Independent Man* (New York: Charles Scribner's Sons, 1958), 222–49.

4. Ibid., 227–29.

5. Ibid., 233–34; "Michigan's 'Bank Holiday,'" February 9, 1933, Vandenberg Diary, VS V, 34–35.

6. "Michigan's 'Bank Holiday,'" February 9, 1933, Vandenberg Diary, VS V, 34; Barnard, *Independent Man*, 237–39; Tompkins, *Senator Arthur H. Vandenberg*, 79; RLS Scrapbook, 299.

7. Barnard, *Independent Man*, 240, Tompkins, *Senator Arthur H. Vandenberg*, 80.

8. Barnard, *Independent Man*, 242–44, 249; Tompkins, *Senator Arthur H. Vandenberg*, 80–82; Vandenberg to Ernest Kanzler (president of Guardian Detroit Union Group), March 7, 1933, microfilm roll 1, Arthur Vandenberg Papers, BHL.

9. Tompkins, *Senator Arthur H. Vandenberg*, 82.

10. Ibid., 83–84.

11. Ibid., 85.

12. Ibid., 87; Jones, "Fifty Billion Dollars," 45.

13. "Insure Deposits of Banks at Once, Vandenberg Plea," VS V, May 19, 1933, 72; Tompkins, *Senator Arthur H. Vandenberg*, 88–89; Jones, "Fifty Billion Dollars," 45.

14. Bascom Timmons, *Garner of Texas: A Personal History* (New York: Harper & Brothers, 1948), 194–95.

15. Dunlap, "Political Career," 135; Tompkins, *Senator Arthur H. Vandenberg*, 90.

16. *Detroit Free Press*, June 5, 8, 1933, RLS Scrapbook, 307–8.

17. *Detroit Free Press*, June 9, 1933, RLS Scrapbook, 309; Tompkins, *Senator Arthur H. Vandenberg*, 93.

18. Tompkins, *Senator Arthur H. Vandenberg*.

19. Typed note, February 15, 1934, VS VI, 30; *Associated Press*, September 9, 1933, VS VI, 104.

20. Tompkins, *Senator Arthur H. Vandenberg*, 258.

21. Raymond Moley, *The First New Deal* (New York: Harcourt, Brace & World 1966), 208.

22. William Edward Leuchtenburg, *Franklin D. Roosevelt and the New Deal, 1932–1940* (New York: Harper and Row, 1963).

23. Tompkins, *Senator Arthur H. Vandenberg*, 98.

24. "Memo to Senator Couzens from Senator Vandenberg," in VS VI, March 4, 1934, 36.

25. RLS Scrapbook, 356; *Herald*, June 23, 1934, RLS Scrapbook, 380; Tompkins, *Senator Arthur H. Vandenberg*, 101.

26. *Grand Rapids Press*, October 26, 1933, RLS Scrapbook, 335.

27. Hazel diary, April 10, 1934, BHL.

28. Tompkins, *Senator Arthur H. Vandenberg*, 101–2.

29. Vandenberg speech to the Gridiron Club, December 9, 1933, microfilm roll 6, Arthur Vandenberg Papers, BHL.

30. RLS Scrapbook, February 19, 1934, 356; RLS Scrapbook, January 6, 1934, 344;

Herald, February 13, April 4, 1934, Tompkins, *Senator Arthur H. Vandenberg*, 103; *Herald*, February 17, 1934, RLS Scrapbook, 357.

31. *Detroit News*, June 23, 1934, VS VI.

32. Tompkins, *Senator Arthur H. Vandenberg*, 108–9; *New York Post*, November 9, 1934, RLS Scrapbook, 428; VS VI, April 15, 1934, 47.

33. Tompkins, *Senator Arthur H. Vandenberg*, 107; *Detroit News*, June 23, 1934, VS VI, 82.

34. Ray Tucker, "Marked Man," *Collier's*, March 9, 1935, 26.

35. RLS Scrapbook, 378; *Herald*, November 4, 1934, RLS Scrapbook, 422.

36. Tompkins, *Senator Arthur H. Vandenberg*, 108–9; *Herald*, January 3, 1935, RLS Scrapbook, 452.

37. VS VI, June 17, 1934, 83; *New York Times*, September 30 and October 16, 25, 1934; Tompkins, *Senator Arthur H. Vandenberg*, 109.

38. Tompkins, *Senator Arthur H. Vandenberg*, 110; *Grand Rapids Chronicle*, November 17, 1934, RLS Scrapbook, 432.

39. *New York Post*, November 9, 1934, RLS Scrapbook, 428.

CHAPTER EIGHT

1. "Arms and the Men," *Fortune*, March 1934, 53–57, 113–26; H. C. Engelbrecht and F. C. Hanighen, *The Merchants of Death* (New York: Dodd, Mead & Company, 1934); Johannes Steel, "World's Greatest Racket," *Nation*, June 6, 1934, 646–48; "Murder Incorporated," *New Republic*, April 25, 1934, 298.

2. John E. Wiltz, *In Search of Peace* (Baton Rouge: Louisiana State University Press, 1963), 25–36; Tompkins, *Senator Arthur H. Vandenberg*, 125.

3. Vandenberg, "How Can We Bankrupt the God of War," *Liberty*, VS VI, September 1, 1934, 86.

4. Wiltz, *In Search of Peace*, 42.

5. Ibid., 51.

6. The *Chicago Tribune* despised Roosevelt but declared Raushenbush a Marxist, Nye a collectivist, and half the staff socialist.

7. RLS Scrapbook, December 17, 1934, 451; Wiltz, *In Search of Peace*, 44.

8. Wiltz, *In Search of Peace*, 120.

9. Mark Foote, *Grand Rapids Press*, September 6, 1935, RLS Scrapbook, 502.

10. Wiltz, *In Search of Peace*, 175.

11. Ibid., 139–40.

12. Vandenberg to Cordell Hull, October 29, 1935, cited in Tomkins, *Vandenberg*, 126.

13. Vandenberg speech to the Michigan Press Club, "Can America Stay out of the Next War?," November 14, 1935, microfilm roll 6, Arthur Vandenberg Papers, BHL; Tompkins, *Senator Arthur H. Vandenberg*, 127.

14. *Grand Rapids Press*, October 16, 1935, RLS Scrapbook, 521.

15. Wiltz, *In Search of Peace*, 205–7.

16. VS VIII, June 8, 1936.

CHAPTER NINE

1. *Herald,* May 5, 1935, RLS Scrapbook, 369; *Grand Rapids Press,* September 10, 1935, RLS Scrapbook, 515.

2. *Herald,* May 5, 1935, RLS Scrapbook, 369; VS VI, March 9, 13, 1934, 37–38.

3. *Herald,* September 6, 1935, RLS Scrapbook, 513; Tompkins, *Senator Arthur H. Vandenberg,* 118.

4. Associated Press, March 6, 1935, RLS Scrapbook, 468; *Grand Rapids Press,* April 21 and 22, 1935, RLS Scrapbook, 478.

5. *New York Times,* April 28, 1935, RLS Scrapbook, 479; Tucker, "Marked Man," 26.

6. Tompkins, *Senator Arthur H. Vandenberg,* 121.

7. Vandenberg to Fred Green, February 7, 1935, microfilm roll 1, Arthur Vandenberg Papers, BHL.

8. *Herald,* August 8, 12–13, 1935, RLS Scrapbook, 503–7.

9. Tompkins, *Senator Arthur H. Vandenberg,* 121.

10. Ibid., 122–23.

11. *Herald,* January 2, 1935, RLS Scrapbook, 451; *Detroit Free Press,* June 15, 1935, RLS Scrapbook, 489.

12. Vandenberg to Hazel, May 1937, microfilm roll 2, Arthur Vandenberg Papers, BHL.

13. *Herald,* January 8, 1936; *Literary Digest,* May 23, 1936, RLS Scrapbook, 650.

14. Hazel Vandenberg diary, March 14 and May 4, 1935.

15. Hazel Vandenberg diary, May 13, 1935.

16. Associated Press, April 1, 1936, RLS Scrapbook, 600.

17. *Grand Rapids Press,* September 9, 1935, RLS Scrapbook, 513; *Grand Rapids Press,* August 20, 1935, RLS Scrapbook, 507.

18. Trip recounted in Hazel Vandenberg diary, October 1935, Hazel Vandenberg Papers, BHL.

19. *Herald,* October 1929.

20. Mark Schorer, *Sinclair Lewis: An American Life* (New York: McGraw-Hill, 1961), 608.

21. Hazel diary, October 11, 1935; *Grand Rapids Press,* October 16, 1935, RLS Scrapbook, 521.

22. *Baltimore Sun,* January 22, 1936, RLS Scrapbook, 553.

23. *New York Herald Tribune,* February 6, 1936, RLS Scrapbook, 571.

24. *Lawrence (MI) Press,* March 18, 1936, RLS Scrapbook, 585; *New York Tribune,* March 24, 1936, RLS Scrapbook, 587; *Detroit News,* March 25, 1936, RLS Scrapbook, 588; *Herald,* May 16, 1936, RLS Scrapbook, 637.

25. *Washington Herald,* April 7, 1936, RLS Scrapbook, 601.

26. Vandenberg Diary, VS VIII, 7.

27. Hazel diary, January 1, 1936.

28. Hazel diary, April 8, 18, 1936.

29. VS VIII, January 4, 1936, 23; Tompkins, *Senator Arthur H. Vandenberg,* 123.

30. *Washington Post,* April 26, 1936, RLS Scrapbook, 624.

31. "Credit Is Given Vandenberg for Saving Two-Party System," *Christian Science Monitor*, March 24, 1936, 4.

32. *Barron's Weekly*, May 11, 1936.

33. "Light for a Dark Horse," *Literary Digest*, May 23, 1936.

34. Tucker "Marked Man," 26.

35. Tompkins, *Senator Arthur H. Vandenberg*, 131.

36. *Detroit Free Press*, February 5, 1936, RLS Scrapbook, 537; *Washingtonian*, February 21, 1936, RLS Scrapbook, 582.

37. Jonathan Mitchell, *New Republic* profile of Vandenberg, April 15, 1936, RLS Scrapbook, 613.

38. *Detroit News*, May 28, 1936, RLS Scrapbook, 656.

39. Tompkins, *Senator Arthur H. Vandenberg*, 132.

40. Ward Morehouse, *Forty-Five Minutes Past Eight* (New York: Dial Press, 1939), 212; Tompkins, *Vandenberg*, 134; *New York Herald Tribune*, June 6, 1936, RLS Scrapbook, 674.

41. Tompkins, *Senator Arthur H. Vandenberg*, 134.

42. Ibid., 136

43. Hazel diary, June 1936, BHL.

44. Tompkins, *Senator Arthur H. Vandenberg*, 137–38.

45. VS VIII, October 19, 1936.

46. Tompkins, *Senator Arthur H. Vandenberg*, 139.

47. Morehouse, *Forty-Five Minutes*, 212.

CHAPTER TEN

1. Tompkins, *Senator Arthur H. Vandenberg*, 141.

2. Vandenberg diary, January 19 and 20, 1937, BHL.

3. Tompkins, *Senator Arthur H. Vandenberg*, 157.

4. Ibid., 141–44; Vandenberg to Lawrence, December 28, 1936, microfilm roll 2, Arthur Vandenberg Papers, BHL.

5. Tompkins, *Senator Arthur H. Vandenberg*, 146; Vandenberg diary, May 9–19, 1937, BHL.

6. Bascom Timmons, *Garner of Texas: A Personal History* (New York: Harper & Brothers, 1948), 216; Vandenberg diary, May 13, 1937, BHL.

7. Vandenberg diary, February 6, 1937, VS IX, 7.

8. Ibid., May 19, 1937.

9. David Brinkley, *Washington Goes to War* (New York: Alfred A. Knopf, 1988).

10. Vandenberg diary, July 1937, VS IX.

11. Hazel diary, November 21, 1937, BHL.

12. Tompkins, *Senator Arthur H. Vandenberg*, 149.

13. Ibid., 153; Walter Lippmann, *The Good Society* (New Brunswick, NJ: Transaction Publishers, 1938), 35, 53.

14. Vandenberg, "Where Do We Go from Here?" radio address, November 22, 1937, microfilm roll 6, Arthur Vandenberg Papers, BHL.

15. Vandenberg to Landon, October 1937, quoted in Tompkins, *Senator Arthur H. Vandenberg*, 152.

16. Tompkins, *Senator Arthur H. Vandenberg*, 153–58.

CHAPTER ELEVEN

1. Hazel diary, May 1937, pages in possession of author.

2. Ibid.

3. Hazel diary, February 2, 7, 1938.

4. Hazel diary, February 19, 1938.

5. Arthur Krock, *The Consent of the Governed, and Other Deceits* (Boston: Little, Brown and Co., 1971), 164.

6. Hazel diary, March 9, 1938.

7. Hazel diary, March 22–30 and June 11, 1938.

8. Tompkins, *Senator Arthur H. Vandenberg*, 158.

9. Smith, "Grand Rapids Boy," 23; Tompkins, *Senator Arthur H. Vandenberg*, 167.

10. Personal interview with Ralph Hauenstein, Grand Rapids, MI, June 10, 1991.

11. Vandenberg to Lawrence, August 19, 1937, box 3, Howard C. Lawrence Papers, BHL.

12. VS IX, May 1937.

13. Vandenberg diary, February 1939, VS VI.

14. Courtney Letts de Espil diary, February 29, 1939, Diaries, 1934–1945, box 2, 119–220, Courtney Letts de Espil Papers, Library of Congress, Washington, DC.

15. Walter Trohan, *Political Animals: Memoirs of a Sentimental Critic* (New York: Doubleday, 1975), 142.

16. Tompkins, *Senator Arthur H. Vandenberg*, 168; VS XI, November 27, 1938.

17. Arthur Vandenberg Jr. to Howard Lawrence, June 8, 1939, box 3, Howard C. Lawrence Papers, BHL.

18. Tompkins, *Senator Arthur H. Vandenberg*, 169–70.

19. Vandenberg to Lawrence, June 8, 1939, Howard C. Lawrence Papers; Tompkins, *Senator Arthur H. Vandenberg*, 169.

20. *Herald*, August 18, 1939.

CHAPTER TWELVE

1. Tompkins, *Senator Arthur H. Vandenberg*, 160.

2. James MacGregor Burns, *Roosevelt: The Lion and the Fox, 1882–1940* (New York: Harcourt, Brace & World, 1956), 38.

3. Tompkins, *Senator Arthur H. Vandenberg*, 161.

4. Ester Van Wagoner, "Michigan in Washington," *Holland (Michigan) Evening Sentinel*, July 11, 1939.

5. Ester Van Wagoner, "Michigan in Washington," *Holland (Michigan) Evening Sentinel*, July 19, 1939; July 9, 1939. For a general account from Roosevelt's perspective, see Burns, *Roosevelt*, 387–97.

6. Tompkins, *Senator Arthur H. Vandenberg*, 161; 12 *Congressional Record*, 76th Cong., 1st sess., 1920–1924, 5098; Vandenberg to C. Morrill, January 29, 1940.

7. Tompkins, *Senator Arthur H. Vandenberg*, 162; Vandenberg to J. R. Hayden, March 11, 1932, box 3, Hayden Papers, BHL.

8. Tompkins, *Senator Arthur H. Vandenberg*, 162–63.

9. Joseph C. Grew, *Turbulent Era: A Diplomatic Record of Forty Years, 1904–1945* (New York: Books for Libraries Press 1952), 2:1211–12.

10. Julius Pratt, *Cordell Hull, 1933–1944* (New York: Cooper Square Publishers, 1964), 1:635–40.

11. Tompkins, *Senator Arthur H. Vandenberg*, 177.

12. Hazel diary, May 1939.

13. Vandenberg diary, June 8, 1939.

14. Hazel diary, June 8, 1939.

15. *Herald*, August 8, 1939.

16. Manfred Jonas, *Isolationism in America, 1935–1941* (Ithaca, NY: Cornell University Press, 1966), 10.

17. *Herald*, August 8, 1939.

18. *Herald*, August 17, 1939.

19. Ibid.

20. Ibid.

21. *Herald*, September 2, 1939.

22. *Herald*, August 29, 1939.

23. *Herald*, September 4, 1939.

24. Ronald Steel, *Walter Lippmann and the American Century* (Boston: Atlantic Monthly Press, 1980), 380.

25. Richard Moe, *Roosevelt's Second Act: The Election of 1940 and the Politics of War* (New York: Oxford University Press, 2013), 148.

26. Vandenberg speech, "Homecoming Day," September, 6, 1939, microfilm roll 6, Arthur Vandenberg Papers, BHL.

27. *Herald*, September 13, 1939.

28. *Herald*, September 17, 1939.

29. Ibid.

30. Vandenberg to Randolph G. Adams, September 27, 1939, Vandenberg Papers, BHL.

31. *Herald*, September 15, 1939.

32. Vandenberg diary, September 15, 1939, Vandenberg Scrapbook XII.

33. Frank Sparks, *Herald*, September 16, 1939.

34. VS XII, September 1939.

35. *Herald*, September 15, 1939.

36. Vandenberg to John W. Blodgett, October 28, 1939, microfilm roll 2, Arthur Vandenberg Papers, BHL.

37. *Herald*, September 20, 1939.

38. Tompkins, *Senator Arthur H. Vandenberg*, 173.

39. *Time*, October 2, 1939, 15.

40. *Herald*, September 2, 1939.

41. *Herald*, October 13, 1939.

42. *Herald*, September 16, 1939.

43. *Time*, October 2, 1939.

44. *Herald*, September 22, 1939.

45. Ibid.

46. William M. Pinkerton, *Herald*, October 8, 1939.

47. Vandenberg to Newbold Noyes (correspondent for the *Washington Evening Star*), October 10, 1939, microfilm roll 2, Arthur Vandenberg Papers, BHL.

48. *Time*, October 2, 1939.

49. *Herald*, October 5, 1939.

50. *Herald*, October 2, 1939.

51. *Herald*, October 5, 1939.

52. "Big Michigander," *Time*, October 2, 1939, 13.

53. VS XII.

54. Vandenberg to Howard Lawrence, October 16, 1939, microfilm roll 2, Arthur Vandenberg Papers, BHL.

55. Vandenberg to John W. Blodgett, October 28, 1939, microfilm roll 2, Arthur Vandenberg Papers, BHL.

56. *Liberty*, January 6, 1940, VS XII.

57. Vandenberg to John W. Blodgett, October 28, 1939, microfilm roll 2, Arthur Vandenberg Papers, BHL.

58. Herman Page to Vandenberg, September 11, 1939, microfilm roll 2, Arthur Vandenberg Papers, BHL.

59. "The Battle over the Arms Embargo," Vandenberg diary, September 15, 1939, VS XII, 2.

CHAPTER THIRTEEN

1. Vandenberg, "The New Deal Must Be Salvaged," *American Mercury*, January 1940, 2.

2. Vandenberg to Lawrence, November 29, 1939, microfilm roll 2, Arthur Vandenberg Papers, BHL.

3. Memorial address on William Borah, January 20, 1940, microfilm roll 6, Arthur Vandenberg Papers, BHL.

4. Courtney Letts de Espil diary, February 29, 1939, Diaries, 1934–1945, box 2, 119–220, Courtney Letts de Espil Papers, Library of Congress, Washington, DC.

5. Moe, *Roosevelt's Second Act*, 151.

6. Richard Norton Smith, *Thomas E. Dewey and His Times* (New York: Simon and Schuster, 1982), 298.

7. Vandenberg speech to the Gridiron Club, April 13, 1940, microfilm roll 6, Arthur Vandenberg Papers, BHL; Vandenberg diary, April, 1940.

8. Moe, *Roosevelt's Second Act*, 147.

9. Tompkins, *Senator Arthur H. Vandenberg*, 183; Vandenberg to R. T. Hart, May 31, 1940, microfilm roll 3, Arthur Vandenberg Papers, BHL.

10. Tompkins, *Senator Arthur H. Vandenberg*, 178–79; Vandenberg to Roosevelt, May 24, 1940, copy in VS XII, 118; Vandenberg to Davies, April 16, 1940, microfilm roll 3, Arthur Vandenberg Papers, BHL.

11. Hazel diary, June, 1940.

12. Vandenberg diary, "Inside Stuff—Real History," Arthur H. Vandenberg Jr., *The Private Papers of Senator Vandenberg* (Boston: Houghton Mifflin, 1952), 5–6. Before Vandenberg's papers were donated to the University of Michigan William Clements Library (later transferred to BHL), Arthur Vandenberg Jr.'s edited selection of his father's papers was the only access researchers had to diaries, scrapbooks, and letters. Where possible, both the diary citation and the *Private Papers* citation are provided in notes to later chapters for ease of research.

13. Howard Lawrence campaign scrapbook, Howard C. Lawrence Papers, BHL.

14. *Jackson (MI) Citizen-Patriot*, September 14, 2013, 4.

15. Vandenberg diary, "Inside Stuff—Real History," *Private Papers*, 77.

16. Ibid.

17. Espil diary, July 1, 1940, 1189–91, Espil Papers.

18. Ellsworth Barnard, *Wendell Willkie: Fighter for Freedom* (Marquette: Northern Michigan University Press, 1966), 258.

19. Moe, *Roosevelt's Second Act*, 268.

20. Trohan, *Political Animals*, 142–43.

CHAPTER FOURTEEN

1. Vandenberg diary, March 8, 1941, *Private Papers*, 10.

2. Vandenberg diary, January 7, 1941, *Private Papers*, 8.

3. Vandenberg Jr., *Private Papers*, 9.

4. Tompkins, *Senator Arthur H. Vandenberg*, 188.

5. Ibid., 188–89; Vandenberg diary, March 8, 1941, *Private Papers*, 10.

6. Vandenberg diary, March 8, 1941, *Private Papers*, 10.

7. Henry Kissinger, *Diplomacy* (New York: Simon and Schuster, 2011), 389.

8. Vandenberg diary, March 8, 1941, *Private Papers*, 11.

9. Vandenberg Jr., *Private Papers*, 12.

10. Vandenberg diary, undated, *Private Papers*, 13–15.

11. Vandenberg diary, undated, *Private Papers*, 12–13.

12. Vandenberg diary, undated, *Private Papers*, 15.

13. Vandenberg diary, December 8, 1941, *Private Papers*, 16–17.

14. Vandenberg diary, December 11, 1941, *Private Papers*, 19–20.

15. Vandenberg diary, December 8, 1941, *Private Papers*, 16–17.

16. Vandenberg Jr., *Private Papers*, 1.

17. Hazel diary, April 16, 1942.

18. Ibid.

19. Hazel Vandenberg, "Will Michigan Go Republican?," October 1942, Hazel scrapbook.

20. Hazel diary, April 21, 1942.

21. Vandenberg diary, January 27, 1942, *Private Papers*, 27–28.

22. Vandenberg diary, February 16, 1942, *Private Papers*, 28–29.

23. Trohan to McCormick, May 14, 1942, box 10, Herbert Hoover Presidential Library, West Branch, IA.

24. Robert Alphonso Taft and Clarence E. Wunderlin, *The Papers of Robert A. Taft* (Kent, OH: Kent State University Press, 2003), 3:400.

25. Wendell Wilkie, *One World* (Champaign: University of Illinois Press, 1966), xxiii.

26. Vandenberg to Major George Fielding Eliot, February 10, 1942, *Private Papers*, 33.

27. Vandenberg to Mark Sullivan, December 29, 1942, VS XV, 10.

28. Vandenberg diary, April 21, 1942, *Private Papers*, 30.

29. Hazel diary, January 1943.

30. Vandenberg diary, February 1942, *Private Papers*, 76.

CHAPTER FIFTEEN

1. Vandenberg diary, March 26, 1943, *Private Papers*, 35.

2. Tompkins, *Senator Arthur H. Vandenberg*, 199–200.

3. Vandenberg diary, March 24, 1943, *Private Papers*, 42.

4. Vandenberg diary, April 15, 1943, *Private Papers*, 44–45.

5. Vandenberg diary, March 31, 1943, *Private Papers*, 42–43.

6. Vandenberg diary, April 7, 1943, *Private Papers*, 43–44.

7. Vandenberg diary, April 21, 1943, *Private Papers*, 46–47.

8. Vandenberg diary, May 1, 1943, *Private Papers*, 48.

9. Vandenberg diary, May 10, 1943, *Private Papers*, 49.

10. Vandenberg diary, May 19, 1943, *Private Papers*, 50.

11. Vandenberg diary, May 22, 1943, *Private Papers*, 50–51.

12. Piers Brendon, *The Decline and Fall of the British Empire, 1781–1997* (New York: Vintage Books, 2010), 546.

13. Tompkins, *Senator Arthur H. Vandenberg*, 214–15.

14. Vandenberg diary, July 3, 1943, *Private Papers*, 55.

15. Dean Acheson, *Sketches from Life: Of Men I Have Known* (New York: H. Hamilton, 1962), 124–25.

16. Tompkins, *Senator Arthur H. Vandenberg*, 205.

17. Vandenberg Jr., *Private Papers*, 68–69; Acheson, *Sketches*, 125.

18. Vandenberg to John T. Flynn, August 24, 1943, *Private Papers*, 72.

19. Tompkins, *Senator Arthur H. Vandenberg*, 210–11.

20. Vandenberg to Joseph P. Savage, July 2, 1943, *Private Papers*, 79.

21. Robert A. Divine, *Second Chance: The Triumph of Internationalism in America*

during World War II (Garden City, NY: Doubleday, 1967), 130. Divine offers the best analysis of the Mackinac Conference in its historical context. Other studies of foreign policy in the period tend to give it scant mention.

CHAPTER SIXTEEN

1. "History of the First Attempt to Commit Our Post-War Objectives," Vandenberg diary, VS XV.

2. Esther Van Wagoner Tufty, *Holland (Michigan) Evening Sentinel*, July 29, 1943; VS XV, 60.

3. *Chicago Times*, August 1943, RLS Scrapbooks, 14.

4. *Herald*, September 11, 1943.

5. Vandenberg to Lamont, August 4, 1943, Vandenberg Papers, BHL.

6. Vandenberg to Thomas W. Lamont, August 4, 1943, *Private Papers*, 55–56; Vandenberg to Samuel B. Pettengill, August 24, 1943, *Private Papers*, 56.

7. Vandenberg to Dewey, August 13, 1943, VS XV.

8. Telephone interview with Liz Carpenter, Austin, TX, September 13, 1993.

9. News media quotes from RLS Scrapbook, September 1943; *Time*, September 20, 1943; *New York Herald Tribune*, September 12, 1943.

10. Walter Lippmann, *U.S. Foreign Policy: Shield of the Republic* (Boston: Little Brown and Company, 1943), 126.

11. Smith, *Thomas E. Dewey*, 171.

12. *Time*, September 13, 1943.

13. *Herald*, September 7, 1942, 12.

14. Ibid.

15. *New York Herald Tribune*, September 7, 1943, RLS Scrapbook, 14.

16. Sheldon A, Silverman, "At the Water's Edge: Arthur Vandenberg and the Foundation of American Bipartisan Foreign Policy" (PhD diss., UCLA, 1967), 301.

17. *New York Herald Tribune*, September 7, 1943, RLS Scrapbook, 14.

18. *Herald*, September 8, 1943, 1.

19. *Herald*, September 11, 1943, 1.

20. *Time*, September 20, 1943.

21. Divine, *Second Chance*, 131.

22. *Washington Herald*, September 7, 1943, RLS Scrapbooks, 14.

23. Vandenberg, "The Mackinac Charter," radio address, September 22, 1943, microfilm roll 7, Arthur Vandenberg Papers, BHL.

24. Vandenberg to Henry R. Luce, September 24, 1943, BHL.

25. *Private Papers*, 74.

26. Vandenberg diary, September 30, 1943, *Private Papers*, 61.

27. Tompkins, *Senator Arthur H. Vandenberg*, 215.

28. Allen Drury, *Senate Journal, 1943–1945* (New York: Da Capo Press, 1972), 78, 80; Vandenberg to Acheson, September 25, 1943, VS XVI, BHL.

CHAPTER SEVENTEEN

1. Drury, *Senate Journal*, 86; Tompkins, *Senator Arthur H. Vandenberg*, 221.
2. Vandenberg diary, May 11, 1944, *Private Papers*, 95.
3. Ibid., 96.
4. Ibid., 98.
5. Vandenberg diary, May 19, 1944, *Private Papers*, 99–100.
6. Vandenberg diary, May 26, 1944, *Private Papers*, 102.
7. Vandenberg diary, May 23, 1944, VS XVI.
8. Vandenberg diary, May 26, 1944, *Private Papers*, 103.
9. Acheson, *Sketches*, 123.
10. Vandenberg diary, May 29, 1944, *Private Papers*, 107.

CHAPTER EIGHTEEN

1. Vandenberg diary, February 1942, *Private Papers*, 76.
2. MacArthur to Vandenberg, April 12, 1943; Vandenberg diary, April 19, 1943; *Private Papers*, 77–78.
3. Sylvia Jukes Morris, *Rage for Fame: The Ascent of Clare Boothe Luce* (New York: Random House, 2014), 36; Vandenberg diary, July 2, 1943, *Private Papers*, 79.
4. Vandenberg diary, September 30, 1943; *Private Papers*, 82.
5. *Private Papers*, 82–83.
6. Ibid., 83–84.
7. Vandenberg diary, April 30, 1944, *Private Papers*, 85–86; Smith, *Thomas E. Dewey*, 385.
8. *Washington Star*, July 5, 1943, VS XV.
9. Vandenberg diary, June 26–29, 1944, *Private Papers*, 87.
10. *Private Papers*, 88–89.
11. Ibid., 112.
12. *Private Papers*, 113, 123.
13. Vandenberg to Dulles, November 11, 1944, *Private Papers*, 124.

CHAPTER NINETEEN

1. Vandenberg to Hull, August 29, 1944, *Private Papers*, 117.
2. Vandenberg diary, August 25, 1944, *Private Papers*, 116; Vandenberg to Hull, August 29, 1944, *Private Papers*, 118.
3. Vandenberg to Lippmann, September 14, 1944, *Private Papers*, 118–19.
4. Vandenberg diary, November 24, 1944, *Private Papers*, 121–22.
5. Drury, *Senate Journal*, 260; *Private Papers*, 124.
6. Vandenberg diary, November 24, 1944, *Private Papers*, 122.
7. Frank McNaughton Papers, box 8, Harry S. Truman Library, Independence, MO; Drury, *Senate Journal*, 250.
8. Drury, *Senate Journal*, 332.
9. McNaughton Papers, box 8.

10. Richard R. Gregg, "A Rhetorical Re-examination of Arthur Vandenberg's Dramatic Conversion, January 10, 1945," *Quarterly Journal of Speech* (April 1975): 156.

11. Vandenberg diary, July 8, 1848, *Private Papers*, 20.

12. Tompkins, *Senator Arthur H. Vandenberg*, 238.

13. McNaughton Papers, box 8.

14. Vandenberg speech, January 10, 1945, *Private Papers*, 132–38; John Lewis Gaddis, *The United States and the Origins of the Cold War* (New York: Columbia University Press, 1972), 167.

15. McNaughton Papers, box 8.

16. Vandenberg speech, January 10, 1945, *Private Papers*, 135–38.

17. McNaughton Papers, box 8.

18. Vandenberg speech, January 10, 1945, *Private Papers*.

19. Tompkins, *Senator Arthur H. Vandenberg*, 238–39; *Private Papers*, 138–39.

20. Drury, *Senate Journal*, 343.

21. *Private Papers*, 139.

22. Richard R. Gregg, "A Rhetorical Re-examination of Arthur Vandenberg's Dramatic Conversion, January 10, 1945," *Quarterly Journal of Speech* (April 1975): 165.

23. Drury, *Senate Journal*, 335.

24. *Private Papers*, 138–39.

25. Lester Pearson to N. A. Robertson, L. MacKenzie King Papers, correspondence, primary series, O'Boyle-Pick, 1945 (M.G. 26, J 1, vol. 389, pp. 349004–35017), Library and Archives Canada, Ottawa.

26. *Private Papers*, 141.

27. Ibid.

28. *Private Papers*, 142–43.

29. Ibid., 144.

30. Gaddis, *Cold War*, 169.

CHAPTER TWENTY

1. James MacGregor Burns, *Roosevelt: The Soldier of Freedom* (New York: Harcourt Brace Jovanovich, 1970), 360–61.

2. *Private Papers*, 146; Vandenberg to Roosevelt, February 15, 1945, *Private Papers*, 149; Vandenberg to Joseph Grew, February 19, 1945, *Private Papers*, 150.

3. *Private Papers*, 150; Drury, *Senate Journal*, 367.

4. Vandenberg to Roosevelt, March 1, 1945, *Private Papers*, 153.

5. Roosevelt to Vandenberg, March 3, 1945, *Private Papers*, 153.

6. McNaughton Papers.

7. *Private Papers*, 147.

8. McNaughton Papers.

9. Gaddis, *Cold War*, 167.

10. McNaughton Papers; Vandenberg to Frank Januszewski, March 7, 1945, *Private Papers*, 155.

11. *Private Papers*, 154–55.

12. Vandenberg to Leo Pasvolsky, March 20, 1945, *Private Papers*, 158.

13. Vandenberg diary, March 23, 1945, VS XVII.

14. Vandenberg diary, March 27, 1945, *Private Papers*, 159–60.

15. McNaughton Papers, March 30, 1945.

16. Vandenberg diary, April 2, 1945, *Private Papers*, 161.

17. McNaughton Papers, box 8.

18. Vandenberg diary, April 3, 1945, *Private Papers*, 161–63.

19. Vandenberg diary, April 9, 1945, *Private Papers*, 163.

20. Vandenberg diary, April 12, 1945, *Private Papers*, 165.

21. *Private Papers*, 166.

CHAPTER TWENTY-ONE

1. Vandenberg diary, April 13, 1945, *Private Papers*, 167–68.

2. Vandenberg diary, April 13 and April 17, 1945, *Private Papers*, 167–69.

3. Hazel diary, April 1945, BHL.

4. Vandenberg diary, April 24, 1945, *Private Papers*, 175–76.

5. Vandenberg diary, April 25, 1945, *Private Papers*, 176.

6. Vandenberg diary, April 26, 1945, *Private Papers*, 179.

7. Ibid., 179–80.

8. Vandenberg diary, April 30, 1945, *Private Papers*, 182.

9. Vandenberg diary, May 2, 1945, *Private Papers*, 183–84.

10. Vandenberg diary, May 9, 1945, *Private Papers*, 190; *Private Papers*, 184.

11. Vandenberg to Sparks, April 17, 1945, *Private Papers*, 172.

12. Vandenberg diary, May 4, 1945, *Private Papers*, 184–86.

13. Vandenberg diary, May 5, 1945, *Private Papers*, 186–88.

14. Vandenberg diary, May 7, 1945, *Private Papers*, 188–89.

15. Vandenberg diary, May 13, 1945, *Private Papers*, 191–92.

16. Vandenberg diary, May 15, 1945, *Private Papers*, 192–93.

17. Vandenberg diary, May 23, 1945, *Private Papers*, 197–98.

18. Vandenberg diary, June 9, 1945, *Private Papers*, 210.

19. Vandenberg diary, May 16, 1945, *Private Papers*, 194.

20. Vandenberg diary, May 19, 1945, *Private Papers*, 194–95.

21. Vandenberg diary, May 26, 1945, *Private Papers*, 199–200.

22. Vandenberg diary, June 2, 1945, *Private Papers*, 201.

23. *Private Papers*, 205–6.

24. Vandenberg diary, June 3, 1945, *Private Papers*, 201–2.

25. Vandenberg diary, June 5, 1945, *Private Papers*, 203–4.

26. Vandenberg diary, June 8, 1945, *Private Papers*, 209.

27. Vandenberg diary, June 7, 1945, *Private Papers*, 207.

28. Vandenberg diary, June 7 and June 8, 1945, *Private Papers*, 208.

29. Vandenberg diary, June 17, 1945, *Private Papers*, 212–13.

30. Ibid.

31. Vandenberg diary, June 20, 1945, *Private Papers*, 213–14.

32. Vandenberg diary, June 23, 1945, *Private Papers*, 214–15.

33. Ibid., 216.

34. McNaughton Papers, Vandenberg diary, undated, *Private Papers*, 217.

35. McNaughton Papers, June 29, 1945.

36. *Private Papers*, 218.

37. Vandenberg to Hazel, undated, *Private Papers*, 218–19.

CHAPTER TWENTY-TWO

1. *Private Papers*, 220.

2. Ibid., 221.

3. McNaughton Papers.

4. Vandenberg to L. F. Beckwith, November 13, 1945, *Private Papers*, 224.

5. Vandenberg to Reverend Edward A. Thompson, October 26, 1945, *Private Papers*, 223.

6. McNaughton Papers, October 6, 1945; *Private Papers*, 226–27.

7. Philip White, *Our Supreme Task: How Winston Churchill's Iron Curtain Speech Defined the Cold War Alliance* (New York: Public Affairs, 2012), 20, 30; *Private Papers*, 227.

8. Dulles to Vandenberg, November 20, 1945, box 27, John Foster Dulles Papers, Seeley G. Mudd Manuscript Library, Princeton, NJ.

9. *Private Papers*, 230.

10. Vandenberg diary, December 10, 1945, *Private Papers*, 228.

11. Vandenberg diary, December 11, 1945, *Private Papers*, 229.

12. Vandenberg to B. E. Hutchinson, December 29, 1945, *Private Papers*, 232–33.

13. Vandenberg diary, December 19, 1945, *Private Papers*, 231.

14. Vandenberg diary, February 12, 1945, *Private Papers*, 231.

15. Vandenberg to Dulles, December 19, 1945, *Private Papers*, 230.

16. *Private Papers*, 237–38.

17. Ibid., 239–40.

18. Robin Gerber, *Leadership the Eleanor Roosevelt Way* (New York: Penguin Group, 2002), 234.

19. "Report on the United Nations Meeting in London," Vandenberg, Senate speech, February 27, 1946, *Private Papers*, 241–42.

20. *Private Papers*, 243.

21. Ibid., 244.

22. *Private Papers*, 246.

23. March 23, 1946, *Private Papers*, 244–45.

24. Vandenberg to H. F. Armstrong, April 2, 1946, *Private Papers*, 245.

25. "Report on the United Nations Meeting in London," Vandenberg, Senate speech, February 27, 1946, *Private Papers*, 247–49.

26. *Private Papers*, 250.

27. George Frost Kennan, *Memoirs, 1950–1963* (New York: Pantheon Books, 1983), 310.

28. *Private Papers*, 250.

29. Vandenberg to Armstrong, April 2, 1946, microfilm roll 4, BHL.

30. Vandenberg diary, April 28, 1946, *Private Papers*, 266–67.

CHAPTER TWENTY-THREE

1. Vandenberg diary, April 25, 1946, *Private Papers*, 262–64.

2. Vandenberg diary, April 26, 1946, *Private Papers*, 264–65.

3. Vandenberg diary, April 27, 1946, *Private Papers*, 265–66.

4. Vandenberg diary, April 29, 1946, *Private Papers*, 267–68.

5. Vandenberg diary, April 30, 1946, *Private Papers*, 268–69.

6. Vandenberg diary, May 1, 1946, *Private Papers*, 269–71.

7. Vandenberg diary, May 2, 1946, *Private Papers*, 271–73.

8. Vandenberg diary, May 4, 1946, *Private Papers*, 273–74.

9. Vandenberg diary, May 6, 1946, *Private Papers*, 276.

10. Vandenberg diary, May 13, 1946, *Private Papers*, 279.

11. Vandenberg diary, May 15, 1946, *Private Papers*, 283.

12. Vandenberg to Henry R. Luce, May 28, 1946, *Private Papers*, 285–86.

13. Ibid.

14. Vandenberg to Byrnes, May 21, 1946, *Private Papers*, 287–88.

15. Ibid., 288.

16. Vandenberg diary, June 15, 1946, *Private Papers*, 289–90.

17. Vandenberg diary, June 21, 1946, *Private Papers*, 291–92.

18. Vandenberg diary, June 22, 1946, *Private Papers*, 292.

19. *Private Papers*, 296

20. Vandenberg diary, June 27, 1946, *Private Papers*, 292–93.

21. Vandenberg diary, June 23, 1946, *Private Papers*, 292.

22. Vandenberg diary, July 1, 1946, *Private Papers*, 293–94.

23. Vandenberg, Senate speech, July 12, 1946, *Private Papers*, 297–98.

24. *Private Papers*, 299.

25. James Francis Byrnes, *All in One Lifetime* (New York: Harper & Brothers, 1958), 369.

26. *Private Papers*, 300.

27. Ibid., 299.

28. David Pietrusza, *1948, Harry Truman's Improbable Victory and the Year That Transformed America's Role in the World* (New York: Union Square Press, 2011), 24.

29. *Private Papers*, 300–301.

30. Herbert Agar, *The Unquiet Years, U.S.A., 1945–1955* (London: Hart-Davis, 1957), 64.

31. Ibid.

32. Vandenberg to John Blodgett, December 24, 1945, *Private Papers*, 304.

33. *Private Papers*, 395.

34. Ibid., 307–8, 311.

35. Vandenberg to Arthur Vandenberg Jr., September 21, 1946, *Private Papers*, 312.

36. Vandenberg to Frank Januszewski, June 27, 1946, *Private Papers*, 314.

37. Merle Miller, *Plain Speaking: An Oral Biography of Harry S. Truman* (New York: Black Dog & Leventhal, 2005), 280.

38. Vandenberg to Arthur Vandenberg Jr., September 21, 1946, *Private Papers*, 312.

39. *Private Papers*, 315-17.

CHAPTER TWENTY-FOUR

1. Vandenberg to Esther Tufty, November 7, 1946, *Private Papers*, 324.

2. *Private Papers*, 322.

3. Vandenberg to Esther Tufty, November 7, 1946, *Private Papers*, 324.

4. *Private Papers*, 326.

5. Ibid., 329.

6. Vandenberg diary, June 19, 1946, *Private Papers*, 291.

7. Vandenberg to T. Roberts, December 20, 1946 *Private Papers*, 320-21.

8. Vandenberg to Roberts, March 15, 1947, *Private Papers*, 322-23.

9. Vandenberg to Eleanor Roosevelt, January 9, 1947, *Private Papers*, 330-31.

10. *Private Papers*, 334.

11. Vandenberg speech in Cleveland, January 11, 1947, *Private Papers*, 334-36.

12. *Private Papers*, 338.

13. Kennan, *Memoirs*.

14. Vandenberg to Bruce Barton, March 24, 1947, *Private Papers*, 342.

15. Lloyd C. Gardner, *Architects of an Illusion: Men and Ideas in American Foreign Policy, 1941-1949* (Chicago: Quadrangle Books, 1970), 218.

16. Dean Acheson, *Present at Creation, My Years in the State Department* (New York: W. W. Norton, 1987), 219.

17. Vandenberg diary, March 13, 1947, *Private Papers*, 343-44.

18. Gardner, *Architects*, 225.

19. *Private Papers*, 346.

20. "The Whole Greek Loan Story," Vandenberg, Senate speech, April 8, 1947, *Private Papers*, 346-50.

21. *Private Papers*, 351.

22. Vandenberg to John B. Bennett, March 5, 1947, *Private Papers*, 340; interview with Clifford, June 3, 1992, Washington, DC.

23. Vandenberg diary, June 6, 1947, *Private Papers*, 339.

CHAPTER TWENTY-FIVE

1. *Private Papers*, 369.

2. Ibid., 372.

3. *Private Papers*, 374.

4. Vandenberg diary, June 13, 1947, *Private Papers*, 376; *Private Papers*, 377.

5. Vandenberg to Hazel, November 1947, *Private Papers*, 378.

6. McNaughton, *Time*, November 28, 1947.

7. Ritchie, *Congress*, xx.

8. Vandenberg to Hazel, November 18, 1947, *Private Papers*, 379–80.

9. Ibid.

10. Walter Isaacson and Evan Thomas, *The Wise Men: Six Friends and the World They Made* (New York: Simon & Schuster, 1997).

11. Vandenberg to Clark M. Eichelberger, June 25, 1947, *Private Papers*, 381.

12. Vandenberg to R. C. Schmitt, undated, *Private Papers*, 381–82.

13. Vandenberg to Malcolm W. Bingay, December 29, 1947, *Private Papers*, 382–83.

14. Vandenberg to Robert A. Lovett, November 10, 1947, *Private Papers*, 383.

15. *Private Papers*, 383.

16. Peter Marshall, *Prayers of Peter Marshall* (New York: McGraw Hill, 1949), 196.

17. Vandenberg to Herman E. Chamberlain, March 13, 1948, *Private Papers*, 386.

18. *Private Papers*, 389.

19. Vandenberg speech, March 1, 1948, *Private Papers*, 389–92.

20. McNaughton, *Time*, March 13, 1948.

21. McNaughton Papers, March 13, 1948.

22. *Private Papers*, 393–95.

23. Marshall, *Prayers*, 227.

CHAPTER TWENTY-SIX

1. *Private Papers*, 396.

2. Vandenberg speech, June 9, 1948.

3. Vandenberg to Nelson Rockefeller, April 28, 1949, *Private Papers*, 403.

4. *Private Papers*, 405–6.

5. Vandenberg to Lodge, December 11, 1948, *Private Papers*, 415–17.

6. Vandenberg, Senate speech, June 11, 1948, *Private Papers*, 408–11.

7. Vandenberg to Harry M. Robbins, December 9, 1948, *Private Papers*, 418–19.

8. Vandenberg to Ralph E. Flanders, December 6, 1948, *Private Papers*, 414.

9. Vandenberg diary, undated, *Private Papers*, 421.

10. *Private Papers*, 423–24.

11. Ibid., 421–22.

12. Pietrusza, *1948*, 88–89.

13. Ibid., 89.

14. *Private Papers*, 426–27.

CHAPTER TWENTY-SEVEN

1. W. A. Swanberg, *Luce and His Empire* (New York: Scribner, 1972), 269.

2. Vandenberg diary, June 20–25, 1948, *Private Papers*, 437–38.

3. Stephen C. Chadegg, *Clare Boothe Luce* (New York: Simon & Schuster, 1970), 221–22.

4. Swanberg, *Luce*, 269, 271, 276; Smith, *Dewey*, 496.

5. Pietrusza, *1948*, 188.

6. Vandenberg diary, June 20–25, 1948, *Private Papers*, 428–29.

7. Vandenberg diary, June 20–25, 1948, *Private Papers*, 437–38; Smith, *Dewey*, 498–99.

8. Vandenberg diary, "Philadelphia—1948," *Private Papers*, 431–37.

9. Vandenberg diary, undated, *Private Papers*, 442–43.

10. Vandenberg diary, July 31, 1948, *Private Papers*, 444–45.

11. *Private Papers*, 441.

12. Susan Hartman, *Truman and the 80th Congress* (Columbia: University of Missouri Press, 1971), 194.

13. Vandenberg to Hazel, July 26, 1948, *Private Papers*, 447–49.

14. Pietrusza, *1948*, 283.

15. *Private Papers*, 447.

16. Vandenberg to Dulles, July 2, 1948, *Private Papers*, 447.

17. Vandenberg speech, October 4, 1948, *Private Papers*, 450–52.

18. Vandenberg to Hazel, October 6, 1948, *Private Papers*, 452.

19. Vandenberg diary, July 1948, *Private Papers*, 453.

20. Vandenberg diary, July 19, 1948, *Private Papers*, 452–54.

21. Vandenberg to John S. Knight, August 1948, *Private Papers*, 454–55.

22. Vandenberg diary, undated, *Private Papers*, 457.

23. Vandenberg diary, October 5, 1948, *Private Papers*, 457–58.

24. Vandenberg diary, Friday, October 22, 1948, *Private Papers*, 459.

25. Vandenberg diary, October 23, 1948, *Private Papers*, 459–60.

26. *Private Papers*, 460.

CHAPTER TWENTY-EIGHT

1. Vandenberg diary, November 5, 1948, *Private Papers*, 463.

2. *Private Papers*, 464.

3. Eric Frederick Goldman, *Rendezvous with Destiny* (New York: Ivan R. Dee, 2001), 300; Vandenberg diary, January 1, 1949, *Private Papers*, 466–67.

4. *Private Papers*, 468–69.

5. VS, January 10, 1949.

6. Ibid., 470.

7. Clifford interview.

8. Vandenberg, Lincoln Day speech, February 10, 1949, *Private Papers*, 472–73.

9. Vandenberg to James H. Sheppard, January 27, 1949, *Private Papers*, 475.

10. *Private Papers*, 476.

11. Vandenberg to Benjamin G. Pinx, April 8, 1949, *Private Papers*, 478; Vandenberg to Henry Hazlitt, April 15, 1949, *Private Papers*, 479.

12. *Private Papers*, 481–82.

13. Vandenberg to Hazel, May 18, 1949, *Private Papers*, 484–85.

14. Vandenberg to Hazel, May 19, 1949, *Private Papers*, 485.

15. Vandenberg to Hazel, May 25, 1949, *Private Papers*, 486–87.

16. Ibid.

17. Vandenberg to Hazel, June 1949, *Private Papers*, 487.

18. Vandenberg to Hazel, June 1949, *Private Papers*, 487–88.

19. Vandenberg to Hazel, June 1949, *Private Papers*, 489.

20. Vandenberg to Boyce K. Muir, June 27, 1949, *Private Papers*, 489–90.

21. Vandenberg to John Francis Neyland, July 16, 1949, BHL.

22. Vandenberg speech, July 6, 1949, *Private Papers*, 493–98.

23. *Private Papers*, 498.

24. Vandenberg to Hazel, July 11, 1949, *Private Papers*, 498.

25. Vandenberg to Hazel, July 1949, *Private Papers*, 499.

26. Vandenberg to Hazel, July 21, 1949, *Private Papers*, 499–500.

27. Vandenberg to Hazel, July 1949, *Private Papers*, 500–501.

CHAPTER TWENTY-NINE

1. RLS Scrapbook, 1949.

2. Vandenberg to Arthur Vandenberg Jr., 1949, BHL.

3. *Private Papers*, 523–25.

4. Vandenberg to William Knowland, December 11, 1948, *Private Papers*, 527–28; Vandenberg to Rev. Allen J. Lewis, December 14, 1948, *Private Papers*, 529.

5. Vandenberg diary, February 5, 1949, *Private Papers*, 530–31.

6. Vandenberg to Hazel, June 1949, *Private Papers*, 534.

7. *Private Papers*, 503.

8. Vandenberg to Carl W. Saunders, August 1, 1949, *Private Papers*, 506–8.

9. Vandenberg to John Scott Everton, August 25, 1949, *Private Papers*, 511.

10. Vandenberg to Hazel, July 25, 1949, *Private Papers*, 503–4.

11. Vandenberg to Hazel, August 2, 1949, BHL.

12. Vandenberg to Hazel, August 5, 1949, *Private Papers*, 508; Vandenberg to Lippmann, August 9, 1949, *Private Papers*, 508–9.

13. Vandenberg to Hazel, mid-August 1949, *Private Papers*, 513.

14. Vandenberg to Hazel, September 20, 1949, *Private Papers*, 515–16.

15. Vandenberg to Hazel, September 1949, *Private Papers*, 515–16.

16. Vandenberg to Hazel, September 23, 1949, *Private Papers*, 519.

17. Vandenberg to Hazel, September 24, 1949, *Private Papers*, 518.

18. Vandenberg to Hazel, September 23, 1949, *Private Papers*, 519.

19. *Private Papers*, 546.

CHAPTER THIRTY

1. Vandenberg to Albert L. Miller, October 28, 1949.

2. *Private Papers*, 551.

3. Ibid., 552.

4. "New Statement of Republican Principles," Vandenberg diary, *Private Papers*, 553–56.

5. Vandenberg to Truman, July 3, 1950, *Private Papers*, 543; Vandenberg to H. Tom Collord, August 5, 1950, *Private Papers*, 543–44.

6. *Private Papers*, 556–57.

7. Vandenberg to Hoffman, March 24, 1950, *Private Papers*, 557–58.

8. Truman to Vandenberg, March 27, 1950, *Private Papers*, 559.

9. Truman to Vandenberg, March 31, 1950, *Private Papers*, 560.

10. Vandenberg Correspondence, BHL.

11. Vandenberg to James H. Duff, February 17, 1951, *Private Papers*, 568.

12. *Private Papers*, 324.

13. Vandenberg to Michael A. Gorman, October 24, 1950, *Private Papers*, 564–65.

14. Vandenberg to Edward R. Murrow, November 24, 1950, *Private Papers*, 565–66.

15. Vandenberg to Marshall, January 2, 1951, BHL.

16. Vandenberg to Duff, February 17, 1951, *Private Papers*, 568.

17. *Herald*, August 20, 1952.

18. Unfinished letter from Vandenberg to Clare Boothe Luce, February 10, 1951, *Private Papers*, 575–76.

19. Vandenberg to John L. Bell, February 26, 1951, *Private Papers*, 577–78.

20. Interview with Dr. Johnston.

EPILOGUE

1. Nancy Dickerson, *Among Those Present* (New York: Ballantine Books, 1977), 10–11.

2. Edward R. Murrow broadcast, April 1951.

3. Jim Newton, *Eisenhower: The White House Years* (New York: Anchor Books, 2012); William Fulbright interview, January 7, 1992.

4. Gerald R. Ford, remarks to the U.S. House of Representatives, April 18, 1961.

SELECTED BIBLIOGRAPHY

Abramson, Rudy. *Spanning the Century: The Life of W. Averill Harriman, 1891–1986*. New York: William Morrow and Co., 1992.

Acheson, Dean. *Present at the Creation: My Years in the State Department*. New York: W. W. Norton, 1987.

———. *Sketches from Life of Men I Have Known*. New York: Frank P. Lualdi, 1962.

Adler, Selig. *The Isolationist Impulse: Its Twentieth Century Reaction*. New York: Collier Books, 1961.

Agar, Herbert. *The Price of Power*. Chicago: University of Chicago Press, 1965.

———. *The Unquiet Years: USA 1945–1955*. London: Rubert Hart-Davis, 1957.

Alsop, Joseph W. *I've Seen the Best of It: Memoirs with Adam Plat*. New York: W. W. Norton, 1992.

Ambrose, Stephen E. *Rise to Globalism*. New York: Penguin Books, 1980.

Angle, Paul M. *The Uneasy World*. Greenwich, CT: Fawcett Publications, 1964.

Bacon, Donald C., Roger H. Davidson, and Morton Keller, eds. *The Encyclopedia of the United States Congress*. New York: Simon & Schuster, 1995.

Baker, Richard Allan. *The Senate of the United States: A Bicentennial History*. Malabar, FL: Robert E. Kreiger Publishers, 1988.

Barber, James David. *The Presidential Character: Predicting Performance in the White House. Upper Saddle River, NJ*: Prentice-Hall, 1985.

Barnard, Ellsworth. *Wendell Willkie: Fighter for Freedom*. Marquette: Northern Michigan University Press, 1966.

Barnard, Harry. *Independent Man: The Life of Senator James Couzens*. New York: Charles Scribner's Sons, 1958.

Barnet, Richard J. *The Rockets' Red Glare: When America Goes to War*. New York: Simon & Schuster, 1990.

Beale, Betty. *Power at Play*. Washington, DC: Regnery Gateway, 1993.

Behrman, Greg. *The Most Noble Adventure*. New York: Free Press, 2007.

Beisner, Robert L. *Dean Acheson: A Life in the Cold War*. New York: Oxford University Press, 2006.

Berle, Adolf A., Jr. *A Primer of Foreign Relations: Tides of Crisis*. New York: Reynal & Co., 1957.

Bernstein, Barton J., ed. *Politics and Policies of the Truman Administration*. Chicago: Quadrangle Books, 1970.

Bevin, Ernest. *Foreign Secretary, 1945–1951*. New York: W. W. Norton, 1983.

Binkley, Wilfred E. *American Political Parties: Their Natural History*. New York: Alfred A. Knopf, 1948.

{ 405 }

Bishop, Jim. *FDR's Last Year*. New York: Pocket Books, 1975.

Bohlen, Charles E. *Witness to History*. New York: W. W. Norton, 1973.

Bowen, Elizabeth, and Charles Ritchie. *Love's Civil War*. Toronto: McClelland & Stewart, 2008.

Blum, John Morton. *Cold War and Détente: The American Foreign Policy Process since 1945*. New York: Harcourt Brace Jovanovich, 1975.

———. *The Price of Vision: The Diary of Henry A. Wallace, 1942–1946*. Boston: Houghton Mifflin, 1973.

———, ed. *Public Philosopher: Selected Letters of Walter Lippmann*. New York: Ticknor & Fields, 1985.

———. *V Was for Victory*. New York: Harcourt, Brace Jovanovich, 1976.

Brendon, Piers. *The Decline and Fall of the British Empire, 1781–1997*. New York: Vintage Books, 2010.

Brinkley, David. *Washington Goes to War*. New York: Alfred A. Knopf, 1988.

Brinkley, Douglas, ed. *Dean Acheson and the Making of U.S. Foreign Policy*. New York: Palgrave Macmillan, 1993.

Burns, James MacGregor. *Roosevelt: The Lion and the Fox*. New York: Harcourt, Brace & World, 1956.

———. *Roosevelt: The Soldier of Freedom*. New York: Harcourt Brace Jovanovich, 1970.

Byrnes, James F. *All in One Lifetime. New York:* Harper & Brothers, 1958.

Campbell, Thomas M. *Masquerade Peace: America's UM Policy, 1944–1945*. Tallahassee: Florida State University Press, 1973.

Campbell, Thomas M., and George C. Herring, eds. *The Diaries of Edward R. Stettinius, Jr., 1943–1946*. New York: New Viewpoints, 1975.

Cannon, James. *Time and Chance: Gerald R. Ford's Appointment with History*. Ann Arbor: University of Michigan Press, 1994.

Carleton, William G. *The Revolution in American Foreign Policy: Its Global Range*. New York: Random House, 1963.

Caro, Robert. *The Years of Lyndon Johnson: Master of the Senate*. New York: Vintage Books, 2002.

Childs, Marquis. *Eisenhower: Captive Hero*. New York: Harcourt, Brace and Co., 1958.

Charmley, John. *Churchill's Grand Alliance*. New York: Harcourt Brace and Company, 1995.

Childs, Marquis. *Eisenhower: Captive Hero*. New York: Harcourt Brace and Company. 1958.

Churchill, Winston. *The Great Republic: A History of America*. New York: Modern Library, 2001.

Cole, Wayne S. *Roosevelt & the Isolationists, 1932–45*. Lincoln: University of Nebraska Press, 1983.

———. *Senator Gerald P. Nye and American Foreign Relations*. Minneapolis: University of Minnesota Press, 1962.

Cooke, Alistair. *The American Home Front, 1941–1942*. New York: Atlantic Monthly Press, 2006.

———. *Memories of the Great and the Good*. New York: Arcade, 1999.

Costigliola, Frank. *Roosevelt's Lost Alliances*. Princeton, NJ: Princeton University Press, 2012.

Crowder, Richard. *Aftermath: The Makers of the Post War World*. New York: I. B. Tauris & Co., 2015.

Dahl, Robert A. *Congress and Foreign Policy*. New York: W. W. Norton, 1964.

Dallek, Robert. *Harry S. Truman*. New York: Times Books, 2008.

———. *The Lost Peace: Leadership in a Time of Horror and Hope, 1945–1953*. New York: HarperCollins Publishers, 2010.

Daniels, Roger. *Franklin D. Roosevelt: The War Years, 1939–1945*. Urbana: University of Illinois Press, 2016.

Davidson, Bill. "The Two Mr. Vandenbergs." *Collier's*, June 19, 1948.

Davis, Kenneth S. *FDR: The New Deal Years*. New York: Random House, 1986.

Dawes, Charles G. *Notes as Vice President, 1928–1929*. Boston: Little, Brown and Co., 1935.

Department of State, *Postwar Foreign Policy Preparation, 1939–1945, 1949*. Washington, DC: US Department of State.

Detzer, Dorothy. *Appointment on the Hill*. New York: Henry Holt and Co., 1948.

Dickerson, Nancy. *Among Those Present*. New York: Ballantine Books, 1977.

Diggins, John Patrick. *The Proud Decades: America in War and in Peace, 1941–1960*. New York: W. W. Norton, 1988.

Dirksen, Louella, and Norma Lee Browning. *The Honorable Mr. Marigold: My Life with Evert Dirksen*. Garden City, NY: Doubleday & Co., 1972.

Divine, Robert, A. *American Foreign Policy*. New York: World Publishing Company, 1965.

———. *The Reluctant Belligerent: American Entry into World War II*. 2nd ed. New York: John Wiley & Sons, 1979.

———. *Second Chance: The Triumph of Internationalism in America during World War II*. New York: Atheneum, 1971.

Dobbs, Michael. *Six Months in 1945: FDR, Stalin, Churchill and Truman—From World War to Cold War*. New York: Alfred A. Knopf, 2012.

Donald, Aida D. *Citizen Soldier: A Life of Harry S. Truman*. New York: Basic Books, 2012.

Donaldson, Gary A. *Truman Defeats Dewey*. Lexington: University Press of Kentucky, 1999.

Donovan, Robert J. *Tumultuous Years: The Presidency of Harry S. Truman, 1949–1953*. New York: W. W. Norton, 1982.

Dorril, Stephen. *MI6: Inside the Covert World of Her Majesty's Secret Intelligence Service*. New York: Simon & Schuster, 2000.

Drummond, Donald F. *The Passing of American Neutrality, 1937–1941*. New York: Greenwood Press, 1968.

Drury, Allen. *Advise and Consent*. New York: Pocket Books, 1961.

———. *A Senate Journal, 1943–1945*. New York: McGraw Hill, 1963.

Dulles, Foster Rhea. *America's Rise to World Power, 1898–1954*. New York: Harper & Row, 1963.

Dunlap, Aurie Nichols. "The Political Career of Arthur H. Vandenberg." PhD diss., University of Michigan, 1955.

Dunn, Susan. *1940: FDR, Willkie, Lindbergh, Hitler—The Election amid the Storm*. New Haven, CT: Yale University Press, 2013.

Earl of Halifax. *Fulness of Days*. London: Collins, 1957.

Engelbrecht, H. C., and F. C. Hanighen. *The Merchants of Death*. New York: Dodd, Mead & Company, 1934.

Ervin, Spencer. *Henry Ford vs. Truman H. Newberry: The Famous Senate Election Contest; a Study in American Politics, Legislation and Justice*. New York: R. R. Smith, 1935.

Farley, James A. *Jim Farley's Story: The Roosevelt Years*. New York: McGraw-Hill, 1948.

Farnsworth, David N. *The Senate Committee on Foreign Relations*. Urbana: University of Illinois Press, 1961.

Fecher, Charles A. ed. *The Diary of H. L. Mencken*. New York: Vintage Books, 1991.

Ferrell, Robert, H. *American Diplomacy: A History*. New York: W. W. Norton, 1959.

———, ed. *Truman in the White House: The Diary of Eben A. Ayers*. Columbia: University of Missouri Press, 1991.

Fleming, Thomas. *The New Dealers' War*. New York: Basic Books, 2001.

"Foreign Relations: To the World." *Time Magazine*, April 30, 1945.

Freeland, Richard M. *The Truman Doctrine and the Origins of McCarthyism*. New York: New York University Press, 1985.

Fromkin, David. *In the Time of the Americans*. New York: Alfred A. Knopf, 1995.

Furman, Bess. *Washington By-Line*. New York: Alfred A. Knopf, 1949.

Gaddis, John Lewis. *George F. Keenan: An American Life*. New York: Penguin Press, 2011.

———. *The Long Peace: Inquiries into the History of the Cold War*. New York: Oxford University Press, 1987.

———. *The United States and the Origins of the Cold War, 1941–1947*. New York: Columbia University Press, 1973.

Gardner, Lloyd C. *Architects of Illusion: Men and Ideas in American Foreign Policy, 1941–1949*. Chicago: Quadrangle Books, 1970.

———. *Spheres of Influence: The Great Powers Partition Europe, from Munich to Yalta*. Chicago: Ivan R. Dee, 1993.

Gellman, Irwin F. *Secret Affairs: Franklin Roosevelt, Cordell Hull, and Sumner Welles*. Baltimore: Johns Hopkins University Press, 1995.

Gerber, Robin. *Leadership the Eleanor Roosevelt Way*. New York: Portfolio, 2003.

Gilbert, James. *Another Chance: Postwar America, 1945–1985.* Chicago: Dorsey Press, 1986.

Gillon, Steven M. *Pearl Harbor: FDR Leads the Nation into War.* New York: Basic Books, Perseus Group, 2011.

Goldman, Eric F. *The Crucial Decade—And After: America, 1945–1960.* New York: Vintage Books, 1956.

———. *Rendezvous with Destiny: A History of Modern American Reform.* New York: Vintage Books, 1956.

Gordon, John Steele. *An Empire of Wealth: The Epic History of American Economic Power.* New York: Harper Perennial, 2005.

Goulden, Joseph C. *The Best Years, 1945–1950.* New York: Atheneum, 1976.

Graebner, Norman A. *Cold War Diplomacy: American Foreign Policy, 1945–1960.* Princeton, NJ: D. Van Nostrand Co., 1962.

Graham, Katharine. *Washington.* New York: Alfred A. Knopf, 2002.

Grantham, Dewey W. *The United States since 1945: The Ordeal of Power.* New York: McGraw-Hill, 1976.

Grew, Joseph C. *Turbulent Era, a Diplomatic Record of Forty-Years, 1904–1945.* New York: Books for Libraries Press, 1952.

Griffith, Robert. *The Politics of Fear: Joseph McCarthy and the Senate.* Amherst: University of Massachusetts Press, 1970.

Gunther, John. *Inside U.S.A.: 50th Anniversary.* New York: Book of the Month Club, 1997.

Haas, Lawrence J. *Harry and Arthur: Truman and Vandenberg, and the Partnership That Created the Free World.* Lincoln, NE: Potomac Books, 2016.

Hachey, Thomas E., ed. *Confidential Dispatches.* Evanston, IL: New University Press, 1974.

Halle, Louis J. *The Cold War as History.* New York: Harper Perennial, 1991.

Hamby, Alonzo L. *The Imperial Years: The United States since 1939.* New York: Weybright and Talley, 1976.

Harper, John Lamberton. *American Visions of Europe.* New York: Cambridge University Press, 1994.

Hartman, Susan. *Truman and the 80th Congress.* Columbia: University of Missouri Press, 1971.

Hiltzik, Michael. *The New Deal: A Modern History.* New York: Free Press, 2011.

Hiss, Alger. *Recollections of a Life.* New York: Little, Brown and Co., 1988.

Hodgson, Godfrey. *The Colonel: The Life and Wars of Henry Stimson, 1867–1950.* New York: Alfred A. Knopf, 1980.

Hoopes, Townsend. *The Devil and John Foster Dulles: The Diplomacy of the Eisenhower Era.* Boston: Little, Brown and Co., 1973.

Hoopes, Townsend, and Douglas Brinkley. *Driven Patriot: The Life and Times of James Forrestal.* New York: Alfred A. Knopf, 1992.

Hoover, Herbert. *The Memoirs of Herbert Hoover: The Cabinet and the Presidency.* New York: Macmillan, 1952.

Hurd, Charles. *Washington Cavalcade.* New York: E. P. Dutton & Co., 1948.

Isaacson, Walter, and Evan Thomas. *The Wise Men.* New York: Simon & Schuster, 1986.

Isherwood, Christopher. *Diaries: Volume One, 1939–1960.* New York: HarperCollins, 1996.

Jensen, Kenneth, ed. *Origins of the Cold War: The Novikov, Kennan and Roberts "Long Telegrams" of 1946.* Washington, DC: United States Institute of Peace Press, 1993.

Jessup, John K., ed. *The Ideas of Henry Luce.* New York: Atheneum, 1969.

Johnson, Donald Bruce. *The Republican Party and Wendell Willkie.* Urbana: University of Illinois Press, 1980.

Johnson, Robert David. *Congress and the Cold War.* New York: Cambridge University Press, 2006.

Johnson, Walter. *1600 Pennsylvania Avenue: Presidents and the People since 1929.* Boston: Little, Brown and Co., 1960.

Jones, Jesse H. *Fifty Billion Dollars: My Thirteen Years with the RFC, 1932–1945.* London: Macmillan, 1951.

Jones, Joseph Marion. *The Fifteen Weeks: February 21–June 5, 1947.* New York: Harcourt, 1964.

Kaplan, Lawrence S. *The Conversion of Senator Arthur H. Vandenberg: From Isolation to International Engagement.* Lexington: University Press of Kentucky, 2015.

———. *NATO and the United States: Updated Edition.* New York: Twayne Publishers, 1994.

Karabell, Zachary. *The Last Campaign: How Harry Truman Won the 1948 Election.* New York: Alfred A. Knopf, 2000.

Kee, Robert. *The World We Fought For—1945.* Boston: Little, Brown and Co., 1985.

Keech, William R., and Donald R. Matthews. *The Party's Choice.* Washington, DC: Brookings Institution, 1976.

Kemler, Edgar. *The Irreverent Mr. Mencken.* Boston: Little, Brown and Co., 1950.

Kennan, George Frost. *Memoirs, 1950–1963.* New York: Pantheon Books, 1983.

Kennedy, David M. *Freedom from Fear: The American People in Depression and War, 1929–1945.* New York: Oxford University Press, 1999.

Kennedy, Susan E. *The Banking Crisis of 1933.* Lexington: University Press of Kentucky, 1973.

Ketchum, Richard M. *The Borrowed Years, 1938–1941: America on the Way to War.* New York: Doubleday, 1991.

Kissinger, Henry. *Diplomacy.* New York: Simon & Schuster, 1994.

Krock, Arthur. *The Consent of the Governed, and Other Deceits.* Boston: Little, Brown and Co., 1971.

———. *Memoirs: Sixty Years on the Firing Line.* New York: Funk & Wagnalls, 1968.

Kurth, Peter. *American Cassandra: The Life of Dorothy Thompson.* Boston: Little, Brown and Co., 1990.

LaFeber, Walter. *America, Russia, and the Cold War, 1945–2006*. New York: McGraw-Hill, 2008.

Langer, William I., and S. Everett Gleason. *The World Crisis and American Foreign Policy: The Challenge to Isolation, 1937–1940*. New York: Harper and Brothers, 1952.

Latham, Robert. *The Liberal Moment*. New York: Columbia University Press, 1997.

Leuchtenburg, William E. *Franklin D. Roosevelt and the New Deal, 1932–1940*. New York: Harper & Row, 1963.

Lewis, Sinclair. *Babbitt*. New York: Harcourt Brace Jovanovich, 1922.

———. *It Can't Happen Here*. New York: Doubleday, 1935.

Lilienthal, David E. *The Atomic Energy Years, 1945–1950*. New York: Harper & Row, 1964.

Lingeman, Richard. *The Noir Forties: The American People from Victory to Cold War*. New York: Nation Books, 2012.

Lippmann, Walter. *An Inquiry into the Principles of the Good Society*. Boston: Little, Brown and Co., 1937.

———. *U.S. Foreign Policy: Shield of the Republic*. Boston: Little, Brown and Co., 1943.

Lubell, Samuel. *The Future of American Politics*. New York: Doubleday, 1956.

Lydens, Z. Z., ed. *The Story of Grand Rapids*. Grand Rapids, MI: Kregel Publications, 1966.

MacNeil, Neil, and Richard A. Baker. *The American Senate: An Insider's History*. New York: Oxford University Press, 2013.

Mahl, Thomas E. D*esperate Deception: British Covert Operations in the United States, 1939–44*. Washington, DC: Brassey's, 1998.

Marshall, Catherine, ed. *The Prayers of Peter Marshall*. New York: McGraw Hill, 1949.

Matthews, Donald R. *U.S. Senators and Their World*. New York: Vintage Books, 1960.

May, Ernest R. *"Lessons" of the Past: The Use and Misuse of History in American Foreign Policy*. London: Oxford University Press, 1973.

Mayer, George H. *The Republican Party, 1854–1964*. London: Oxford University Press, 1967.

McCullough, David. *Truman*. New York: Simon Schuster, 1994.

McDougall, Walter A. *Promised Land, Crusader State*. Boston: Houghton Mifflin, 1997.

McFarland, Keith D., and David L. Roll. *Louis Johnson and the Arming of America*. Bloomington: Indiana University Press, 2005.

McLellan, David S., and David C. Acheson. *Among Friends: Personal Letters of Dean Acheson*. New York: Dodd, Mead and Co., 1980.

Mee, Charles L., Jr. *The Marshall Plan*. New York: Simon and Schuster, 1984.

Meijer, Hank. "Arthur Vandenberg and the Fight for Neutrality, 1939." *Michigan Historical Review* 16 (Fall 1990): 1–21.

———. "Depression, Detroit and the New Deal of Senator Arthur Vandenberg." *Historical Society of Michigan: Chronicle & Newsletter*, Fall 2003.

———. "Hunting the Middle Ground: Arthur Vandenberg and the Mackinac Charter, 1943." *Michigan Historical Review* 19 (Fall 1993): 1–21.

Meilinger, Phillip S., and Hoyt S. Vandenberg: *The Life of a General*. Bloomington: Indiana University Press, 1989.

Mencken, H. L., ed. *The American Mercury: A Monthly Review*. New York: Alfred A. Knopf, 1925.

Merry, Robert W. *Taking on the World: Joseph and Stewart Alsop—Guardians of the American Century*. New York: Penguin, 1997.

Messer, Robert L. *The End of the Alliance*. Chapel Hill: University of North Carolina Press, 1992.

Miller, Merle. *Plain Speaking: An Oral Biography of Harry S. Truman*. New York: Berkley Publishing, 1974.

Millis, Walter. *The Forrestal Diaries*. New York: Viking Press, 1951.

Miscamble, Wilson D. *George F. Kennan and the Making of American Foreign Policy*. Princeton, NJ: Princeton University Press, 1992.

Mitchell, Jonathan. "Vandenberg: Heroes' Child." *New Republic*, April 8, 1940.

Moe, Richard. *Roosevelt's Second Act: The Election of 1940 and the Politics of War*. New York: Oxford University Press, 2013.

Moley, Raymond. *The First New Deal*. New York: Harcourt, Brace & World, 1966.

Morehouse, Ward. *Forty-Five Minutes Past Eight*. New York: Dial Press, 1939.

Morris, Sylvia Jukes. *Rage for Fame: The Ascent of Clare Boothe Luce*. New York: Random House, 2014.

Morrison, Samuel Elliot. *The Oxford History of the American People*. Vol. 3. New York: New American Library, 1972.

Mosley, Leonard. *Marshall: Hero for Our Times*: New York: Hearst Books, 1982.

Neal, Steve. *Dark Horse: A Biography of Wendell Willkie*. New York: Doubleday, 1934.

———. *Harry and Ike: The Partnership That Remade the Postwar World*. New York: Scribner, 2001.

Neal, Steve. *McNary of Oregon*. Portland, OR: Western Imprints, 1985.

Newton, Verne W. *The Cambridge Spies: The Untold Story of McLean, Philby and Burgess in America*. Lanham, MD: Madison Books, 1991.

Nicolson, Nigel, ed. *Harold Nicolson: Diaries and Letters*. London: Phoenix, 2004.

Niebuhr, Reinhold. *Leaves from the Notebook of a Tamed Cynic*. San Francisco: Harper & Row, 1980.

O'Dane, Arthur. "Hymn to an Oasis." *American Mercury: A Monthly Review*, October 1925, 190–196.

Offner, Arnold A. *Another Such Victory: President Truman and the Cold War, 1945–1953*. Stanford, CA: Stanford University Press, 2002.

Parrish, Thomas. *Roosevelt and Marshall: Partners in Politics and War*. New York: William Morrow and Co., 1989.

Paterson, Thomas G. *Meeting the Communist Threat*. New York: Oxford University Press, 1988.

———. *Soviet-American Confrontation*. Baltimore: John Hopkins University Press, 1973.

Patterson, James T. *Mr. Republican a Biography of Robert A. Taft*. Boston: Houghton Mifflin, 1972.

Patterson, J. W. "Arthur Vandenberg's Rhetorical Strategy in Advancing Bipartisan Foreign Policy." *Quarterly Journal of Speech* 56 (October 1970): 284–95.

Pearson, Drew. *Diaries: 1949–1959*. New York: Holt, Rinehart and Winston, 1974.

Peters, Charles. *Five Days in Philadelphia*. New York: Public Affairs, 2005.

Phillips, Cabell. *The Truman Presidency*. New York: Macmillan, 1966.

Pietrusza, David. *1948: Harry Truman's Improbable Victory and the Year That Transformed America's Role in the World*. New York: Union Square Press, 2011.

Pisani, Sallie. *The CIA and the Marshall Plan*. Lawrence: University Press of Kansas, 1991.

Plokhy, S. M. *Yalta: The Price of Peace*. New York: Viking, 2010.

Pogue, Forrest C. *George C. Marshall: Statesman*. New York: Viking, 1987.

Pratt, Julius. *Cordell Hull, 1933–1944*. New York: Cooper Square, 1964.

Reich, Cary. *The Life of Nelson A. Rockefeller*. New York: Doubleday, 1996.

Reichard, Gary W. *Politics as Usual: The Age of Truman and Eisenhower*. Arlington Heights, IL: Harlan Davidson, 1988.

Reston, James. "Arthur Vandenberg: American Foreign Policy and the Accident of Greatness." *Michigan Quarterly Review*, Spring 1969.

———. "The Case for Vandenberg." *Life Magazine*, May 24, 1948.

Richie, Charles. *The Siren Years: A Canadian Diplomat Abroad, 1937–1945*. Toronto: Macmillan of Canada, 1987.

Richie, Donald A., ed. *Congress, and Harry Truman: A Conflicted Legacy*. Kirksville, MO: Truman State University Press, 2011.

Rodell, Fred. "Vandenberg of Michigan." *American Mercury*, January 1947.

Roosevelt, Eleanor. *The Autobiography of Eleanor Roosevelt*. New York: Da Capo Press, 1992.

Roosevelt, Elliott. *As He Saw It*. New York: Duell, Sloan and Pearce, 1946.

Rose, Lisle A. *The Cold War Comes to Main Street*. Lawrence: University Press of Kansas, 1999.

Rovere, Richard M. *The American Establishment and Other Reports, Opinions, and Speculations*. New York: Harcourt, 1962.

Rusk, Dean. *As I Saw It: By Dean Rusk as Told to Richard Rusk*. New York: Penguin Books, 1990.

Salter, J. T. *The American Politician*. Westport, CT: Greenwood Press, 1975.

Schlesinger, Arthur M., Jr. *The Coming of the New Deal*. Boston: Houghton Mifflin, 1959.

———. *The Crisis of the Old Order*. Boston: Houghton Mifflin, 1957.

———. *The Imperial Presidency*. 1973. Boston: Houghton Mifflin, 1989.

———. *A Life in the 20th Century*. Boston: Houghton Mifflin, 2002.

———. *The Politics of Upheaval*. Boston: Houghton Mifflin, 1966.

Schlesinger, Stephen C. *Act of Creation: The Founding of the United Nations*. Boulder, CO: Westview, 2003.

Shadegg, Stephen. *Clare Boothe Luce: A Biography*. New York: Simon & Schuster, 1970.

Sherwood, Robert. *Roosevelt and Hopkins*. New York: Harper and Brothers, 1948.

Shlaes, Amity. *Coolidge*. New York: HarperCollins, 2014.

———. *The Forgotten Man: A New History of the Depression*. New York: HarperCollins, 2007.

Silverman, S. A. *At the Water's Edge: Arthur Vandenberg and the Foundation of American Bipartisan Foreign Policy*. Los Angeles: University of California, 1967.

Smith, Beverly. "Russia's Pet Whipping Boy." *Saturday Evening Post*, April 5, 1947.

Smith, Gaddis. *The Last Years of the Monroe Doctrine*. New York: Hill and Wang, 1994.

Smith, Merriman. *The Good New Days*. Indianapolis: Bobbs-Merrill, 1963.

Smith, Richard Norton. *On His Own Terms: A Life of Nelson Rockefeller*. New York: Random House, 2014.

———. *Thomas E. Dewey and His Times*. New York: Simon & Schuster, 1982.

———. *An Uncommon Man: The Triumph of Herbert Hoover*. Worland, NY: High Plains Publishing, 1984.

Stacks, John F. *Scotty: James B. Reston and the Rise and Fall of American Journalism*. Boston: Little, Brown and Co., 2003.

Steel, Ronald. *Walter Lippmann and the American Century*. Boston: Little, Brown and Co., 1980.

Stoler, Mark A. *George C. Marshall: Soldier-Statesman of the American Century*. Boston: Twayne Publishers, 1989.

Swanberg, W. A. *Luce and His Empire*. New York: Scribner, 1972.

Taft, Robert Alphonso, and Clarence E. Wunderlin. *The Papers of Robert A. Taft*. Vol. 3. Kent, OH: Kent State University Press, 2013.

terHorst, Jerald F. *Gerald Ford and the Future of the Presidency*. New York: Joseph Okpaku, 1974.

Timmons, Bascom N. *Garner of Texas: A Personal History*. New York: Harper & Bros., 1948.

Tompkins, David C. *Senator Arthur H. Vandenberg: The Evolution of a Modern Republican, 1884–1945*. East Lansing: Michigan State University Press, 1970.

Trohan, Walter. *Political Animals: Memoirs of a Sentimental Critic*. New York: Doubleday, 1975.

Truman, Harry S. *Memoirs: Year of Decisions*. New York: Signet, 1955.

Truman, Margaret. *Harry S. Truman*. New York: Avon Books, 1993.

Unger, Debi, with Stanley Hirshson. *George Marshall: A Biography*. New York: HarperCollins, 2014.

United States. *Foreign Relief Assistance Act of 1948: Hearings before the Senate*

Committee on Foreign Relations. 80th Cong., 2nd sess. on aid. Historical Series. Printed for the use of the Committee on Foreign Relations, 1973.

———. *Legislative Origins of the Truman Doctrine: Hearings before the Senate Committee on Foreign Relations.* 80th Cong., 1st sess. on S. Res. 938. Historical Series. Printed for the use of the Committee on Foreign Relations, 1973.

———. *Military Assistance Program: 1949—Joint Hearings before the Senate Committee on Foreign Relations and the Committee on Armed Services.* 81st Cong., 1st. sess. on S. Res. 2388. Historical Series. Printed for the use of the Committee on Foreign Relations, 1974.

———. *The Vandenberg Resolution and the North Atlantic Treaty: Hearings before the Senate Committee on Foreign Relations.* 80th Cong., 2nd sess. on S. Res. 239. Historical Series. Printed for the use of the Committee on Foreign Relations, 1973.

"U.S. at War." *Time Magazine*, April 30, 1945.

Vandenberg, Arthur Hendrick. *If Hamilton Were Here Today.* New York: Knickerbocker Press, 1923.

———. "Let's Try to Prevent World War III." *Saturday Evening Post*, March 17, 1945.

———. "The New Deal Must Be Salvaged." *American Mercury*, January 1940, 1–10.

———. *The Trail of a Tradition.* New York: Knickerbocker Press, 1926.

Vandenberg, Arthur H., Jr., and Joe Alex Morris, eds. *The Private Papers of Senator Vandenberg.* Boston: Houghton Mifflin, Riverside Press, 1952.

Vandenberg, Arthur H., Mrs. "This Is the Life: Of a Senator's Wife." *Republican*, 1940.

Vidal, Gore. *The Golden Age.* New York: Random House, 2000.

———. *Palimpsest.* New York: Random House, 1995.

———. *United States: Essays, 1952–1992.* New York: Random House, 1993.

Wapshott, Nicholas. *The Sphinx: Franklin Roosevelt, the Isolationists, and the Road to World War II.* New York: W. W. Norton, 2015.

Ward, Barbara. *The West at Bay.* New York: W. W. Norton, 1948.

Watson, Robert P., Michael J. Devine, and Robert J. Wolz, eds. *The Natural Security Legacy of Harry S. Truman.* Kirksville, MO: Truman State University Press, 2005.

Weiss, Stuart L. *The President's Man: Leo Crowley and Franklin Roosevelt in Peace and War.* Carbondale: Southern Illinois University Press, 1996.

White, Philip. *Our Supreme Task: How Winston Churchill's Iron Curtain Speech Defined the Cold War Alliance.* New York: BBS Public Affairs, 2012.

White, William S. *Citadel: The Story of the U.S. Senate.* New York: Harper & Brothers, 1956.

———. *Majesty and Mischief: A Mixed Tribute to F.D.R.* New York: Macfadden, 1963.

———. *The Taft Story.* New York: Harper & Brothers, 1954.

Widenor, William C. *Henry Cabot Lodge and the Search for an American Foreign Policy.* Berkeley: University of California Press, 1980.

Wilkie, Wendell. *One World*. Champaign: University of Illinois Press, 1966.

Wilson, Richard. "Vandenberg: Man in the Middle." *Look Magazine*, May 10, 1946.

Wiltz, John E. *In Search of Peace*. Baton Rouge: Louisiana State University Press, 1963.

Wolff, Wendy, and Donald A. Ritchie. *Minutes of the Senate Republican Conference:* Washington: U.S. Government Printing Office, 1999.

Woodford, Arthur M. *Detroit and Its Banks*. Detroit: Wayne State University Press, 1974.

Woods, Randall B., and Howard Jones. *Dawning of the Cold War: The United States' Quest for Order*. Chicago: Ivan R. Dee, 1994.

Yergin, Daniel. *Shattered Peace: The Origins of the Cold War and the National Security State*. Boston: Houghton Mifflin, 1977.

Zelizer, Julian E. *The American Congress*. New York: Houghton Mifflin, 2004.

———. *Arsenal of Democracy*. New York: Basic Books, Perseus Group, 2010.

INDEX

Note: Initials "AV" refer to Arthur Vandenberg in this index.